Teaching and Studying Social Issues

Major Programs and Approaches

Teaching and Studying Social Issues

Major Programs and Approaches

Edited by

Samuel Totten and Jon E. Pedersen

INFORMATION AGE PUBLISHING, INC.
Charlotte, NC • www.infoagepub.com

Library of Congress Cataloging-in-Publication Data

Teaching and studying social issues : major programs and approaches / edited by Samuel Totten and Jon E. Pedersen.
  p. cm.
  Includes bibliographical references.
  ISBN 978-1-61735-044-3 (pbk.) – ISBN 978-1-61735-045-0 (hardcover) – ISBN 978-1-61735-046-7 (e-book)
1. Social sciences–Study and teaching. 2. Education–Social aspects. I. Totten, Samuel. II. Pedersen, Jon E., 1960-
  H62.T275 2011
  300.71–dc22

                                    2010012642

Printed in the United States of America

CONTENTS

INTRODUCTION

TEACHING AND STUDYING SOCIAL ISSUES

Major Programs and Approaches

Samuel Totten and Jon E. Pedersen

Teaching and Studying Social Issues: Major Programs and Approaches focuses on many of the major innovations developed over the past 90 years by noted educators to assist students in the study and analysis of key social issues that impact their lives and society. This book complements earlier books that we have produced that address other aspects of studying and addressing social issues in the secondary classroom: *Researching and Teaching Social Issues: The Personal Stories and Pedagogical Efforts of Professors of Education* (Lexington, Books, 2006); *Addressing Social Issues in the Classroom and Beyond: The Pedagogical Efforts of Pioneers in the Field* (Information Age Publishing, 2007); and *Social Issues and Service at the Middle Level* (Information Age Publishers, 2009).

The current book ranges in scope from Harold Rugg's pioneering effort to develop textbooks that purposely addressed key social issues (and thus provided teachers and students with a major tool with which to examine social issues in the classroom) to the relatively new efforts over the last 20 to 30 years, including global education, environmental education, Science/

Teaching and Studying Social Issues: Major Programs and Approaches, pages vii–ix
Copyright © 2011 by Information Age Publishing
vii

Technology/Society (STS), and genocide education. We believe that it behooves educators to be cognizant of and conversant with those innovators and innovations that have preceded them so that they can:

1. learn from past efforts, particularly in regard to what worked and didn't work and why;
2. glean new ideas, methods and approaches for use in their own classrooms; and
3. craft new methods and approaches based on the strengths of past innovations.

By their very nature, books are limited to how much they can include between their covers. That is simply the world of publishing. Be that as it may, we have tried our best to include a broad array and a solid representation of the most notable and powerful models, programs and approaches to teaching and learning about social issues that have been developed over the past 90 years in U.S. schools. Be that as it may, space constraints preclude us from including at least a half dozen other models, programs, approaches, that definitely merit inclusion herein. Among them are the following: *Models* (Cooperative Learning models, including Jigsaw and Jurisprudential Inquiry; Structured Inquiry; Role-Playing; Case-Based Teaching, and Gaming and Simulations); *Programs* (Educators for Social Responsibility; National Issues Forums; Centre for Social Action and the National Writing Project); and *Approaches* (special internet approaches designed to teach about social issues; addressing social issues in the English classroom; and interdisciplinary approaches).

A notable set of scholars/authors, many of whom have made important contributions to the field of social issues education, have contributed chapters to this book. In alphabetical order, they are as follows: Allan R. Brandhorst (Valparaiso University); Ronald Evans (San Diego State University); Thomas Fallace (Mary Washington University); William Fernekes (Hunterdon Central Regional High, Flemington, New Jersey); Sherry L. Field (University of Texas, Austin); Christopher McGrew (a doctoral student in Curriculum and Instruction at Purdue University); Merry Merryfield (The Ohio State University); Jeff Passe (Towson State University); Jon Pedersen (University of Nebraska, Lincoln); Mark Previte (University of Pittsburgh, Johnstown); Karen Riley (Auburn University); Barbara Spector (University of South Florida); Barbara Stern Slater (James Madison University); Mindy Spearman (Clemson University); Felisa Tibbits (Co-founder and Director of Human Rights Education Associates); Samuel Totten (University of Arkansas, Fayetteville); Philip J. VanFossen (Purdue University); Bob Yager (University of Iowa); Elizabeth Yeager Washington (University of Florida); and Jack Zevin (Queens College).

In writing their chapters, authors were asked to follow, as closely as possible, a template provided by the editors. The purpose of providing such a template and making such a request was an attempt to provide consistency throughout the chapters and book. The template consisted of the following: Introduction; I. Overview (a. Description/Focus/Purpose; b. Goals); II. Research Base (a. Strengths; b. Weaknesses or Limitations); III. Implementation (a. Strengths; b. Weaknesses or Limitations; c. Barriers—Confronted/overcame/defeated by); IV. Impact of When Initially Implemented; V. Impact Over the Long Term; and VI. Conclusion.

By producing this book, we hope to provide secondary level educators, students in teacher education programs, professors of teacher education, and those new to the field of teaching about social issues, with a broad overview of many of the most significant approaches, methods, programs, and, in some cases, personages and topics, that have been prevalent in the field over the past 90 years or so. It is our hope in doing so that educators will revisit such programs, learn from them, perhaps implement them, and/or use them as a foundation for further study and the development of new approaches, programs, and methods. At the least, the book provides educators with a sense of the history of the field of teaching about social issues (including its genesis and evolution), and major foundational efforts.

In closing, we wish to thank O. L. Davis, Emeritus Professor of Curriculum and Teaching at the University of Texas, Austin, and Series Editor, for his wonderful and ongoing encouragement and support to develop and publish books on the teaching of social issues, George Johnson, Founder and Publisher of IAP, for his strong support as we go about developing a series of interconnected volumes on the teaching of social issues; and to all of the fine contributors who took the time, thought, and energy to write chapters for inclusion in this book.

CHAPTER 1

FROM VISION TO VILIFICATION TO REHABILITATION

Harold Rugg, A Journey

Karen L. Riley and Barbara Slater Stern

Within the last four decades of the twentieth century, perhaps only a handful of teacher educators or educational historians might be able to recall the name Harold Rugg. If remembered at all, Rugg likely conjures up faint memories of a distant unpleasantness, and thus, some might think, the memory is best left forgotten. From his somewhat rapid ascent up the curricular ladder, to his painful fall from grace, Rugg's story stands as an example of what happens to educators who challenge the fundamental element of education—"purpose." According to distinguished educational historian Gerald Gutek, since the dawn of the Enlightenment in the western world, one cannot separate schools from the government in power. Hence, the aims of government become the aims of schools. Many believe that the textbooks Rugg developed, which became widely disseminated and used in public schools across the nation, were attacked because they were unpatriotic and therefore dangerous. *They weren't and he wasn't—unpatriotic.* Yet, the accusations took on a life of their own.

Teaching and Studying Social Issues: Major Programs and Approaches, pages 1–30
Copyright © 2011 by Information Age Publishing
All rights of reproduction in any form reserved.

1

Rugg's work, if implemented, and implemented properly, promised to fundamentally change the purpose of education, which had been, at least since the common school movement, to educate for citizenship. In that regard, one could argue that Rugg's vision of social reconstruction (reconstructing society in order to bring about equality through education) was the ultimate form of citizenship education.

The form of citizenship education experienced by American public school students for more than 100 years—or up to the point that Rugg and other social Reconstructionists articulated their progressive vision of education—took the form of national celebration, memorization of presidential terms of office, naming of important military commanders, and listing the laws and policies of the land. Inspired by an unprecedented economic collapse in 1929, which exposed the "tooth and claw" nature of capitalism, and by colleagues who shared his vision, Rugg began converting his series of social studies pamphlets into textbooks aimed at teaching students how to identify social ills and inequities and then how to solve the problems they had found. Rugg's approach to social studies methods—problem solving—while vilified in the late 1930s, 1940s, and even 1950s, by any number of ultra-patriotic groups, was later vindicated and even celebrated in the 1960s with the then popularization of the *New Social Studies* movement, *sans* credit to Rugg.

In the 1930s, the American Legion and other ultra-patriotic groups (Daughters of the American Revolution, etc.), as well as the manufacturing sector, set about bringing down Harold Rugg by exposing him as a closet communist. In its attempt to tarnish the reputation and work of one of the Progressive Era's most prominent progressive educationists, the American Legion did so out of a long-standing conviction that any form of anti-Americanism must be met head on and extinguished in the most expedient manner. Legion members, ever alert to anti-American rhetoric (or what it perceived as such), believed that they had discovered a genuine threat disguised as an educator in Rugg, one whose goal was to turn red-blooded American children away from democratic principles and towards a malevolent political and economic system (communism) that could bring America to her knees. Rugg, they believed, would accomplish this task through his textbook series aimed at public school children.

The heightened patriotism of World War II was the historical context for the American Legion's attack on progressive education in general and Rugg in particular. In 1941, as the United States prepared for war, the Legion was busy writing and distributing pamphlets titled *The Complete Rugg Philosophy*, which outlined, Legion officials believed, Rugg's plan to indoctrinate students away from what it termed "Americanism" and toward Socialism or even Communism (*The Rugg Philosophy Analyzed*, 1941). These pamphlets were not the only vehicles for Legion writers. *The American Legion Magazine* was also a forum for the ultra conservative ideas of Rugg's detractors.

Rugg, who was attacked by the American Legion for spreading un-American ideas through schoolbooks, has yet to be completely understood in terms of his philosophy and where it figures into his textbook writings. His materials were condemned, yet the un-American rhetoric in Rugg's materials is lacking.

A few decades after his books vanished from school library shelves, pamphlets developed under the auspices of the New Social Studies began to appear. Their content and inquiry method of learning was eerily familiar, yet the strident voices of the 1940s were no longer raised in opposition. When looking for answers to this conundrum, one might reasonably ask the following questions: Why then was Rugg and his inquiry method to teaching and learning social studies lambasted and decried in such a strident manner? Where did the American Legion get the idea in the first place that Rugg's philosophy tilted in the direction of Stalin's Soviet Union? Were these textbook threats real or imagined? Where are the clues that will help us to understand under what circumstances the Rugg philosophy developed or emerged? Additionally, should Rugg be singled out in history as a sort of lone wolf of social reconstruction or were his ideas within the mainstream vis-à-vis the framework of social reconstruction (as an arm of progressive education)? That said, the goals of this chapter are as follows:

1. To share with the reader Rugg's vision for the social studies, which included an examination by individual students into the problems of American society, its government and economic system, and subsequently a "collective" effort to come up with answers to problems such as inequality, poverty, or injustice;
2. To examine the nature of opposition to Rugg's ideas and social studies materials; and
3. To discuss how Rugg has been treated in academic and popular literature.

VISION, VILIFICATION, REHABILITATION

Harold Rugg's article, "Curriculum Design in the Social Sciences: What I Believe . . . After Twenty Years, 1919–1939," probably best represents his vision and his Social Reconstructionist philosophical approach to K–12 education in general and social studies in particular. Rugg sets this article against the background of three major problems: the declaration of war against Germany by the western democracies (the U.S. excluded in 1939), the Great Depression (Rugg in Mitchner, 1939, p. 140), and the Progressive movement of the 1920s with its potential to use science and technology to solve the nation's problems. Ultimately, Rugg's approach to Social Reconstructionism can be seen as an offshoot of the Progressive movement that expands Progressivism to include a mission to solve the problems of society through school curriculum. Rugg explains this belief in "Young Americans Working to Solve the American Problem," the subtitle of the second section of this social studies curriculum discussion.

Rugg defined the American Problem as follows: "To bring forth on this continent—in some form of co-operative commonwealth—a civilization of abundance, democratic behavior, and the integrity of expression and of appreciation which is now potentially available" (Rugg in Mitchner, 1939, p. 141). He did not believe that schools could accomplish such a task alone but rather that the "new school" should be committed, as a leader in society, to the graduation of "youth who do understand American life as it is actually lived, who are deeply concerned to help build a decent civilization on our continent and are convinced it can be done" (Rugg in Mitchner, 1939, p. 141). In terms of curriculum design, this goal was to be accomplished via fifteen social science factors that students had to master in order to understand the American Problem. "Why these fifteen factors?" is the question that immediately comes to mind?

According to Nelson (1978), the Rugg curriculum writing team identified 888 social studies generalizations that were then broken into 69 groups to be utilized in preparing the Rugg materials (p. 129). The process started by the writing of letters to individuals that Rugg and his team identified as being the leading experts in their fields (in general, the Frontier Thinkers Rugg so admired). The letters solicited the names of the most important books in each field. The books were then collected and read to distill the most frequently appearing concepts and generalizations. A Rugg student and colleague, Neal Billings, compiled the information in *A Determination of the Generalizations Basic to the Social Studies Curriculum* (Billings, 1929, p. 289). These generalizations were sorted under the fifteen factors for a social studies curriculum.

In keeping with the Progressive faith in scientific method and his engineering background, Rugg asserted that this constituted a scientific approach to analyzing what content should comprise a student's knowledge base. He, however, never accounted for his bias in selecting the experts nor did he use the advice of people outside of his team in crosschecking the text analyses, etc. Therefore, the Rugg social studies program reflected a social reconstructionist view of what is important to know and understand despite Rugg's claim that the approach was to be a completely scientific, and, therefore, unbiased, approach to the issue of deciding curriculum content.

Included among the aforementioned fifteen factors were the following:

1. Economic factors related to the ability to produce, distribute and consume goods and services;
2. Unregulated power over communication, government and wealth by a minority unwilling to make changes in the social system in order to establish a modicum of equity;
3. The failure of schools to teach people literacy and democracy [including the pretense that social classes do not exist in America];
4. The apathy of the populace to suffering, coupled with the tendency of politicians and leaders to make only superficial changes in the system;
5. The influence and power of interest groups;
6. The dangers of propaganda and of demagogues using mass media to convince people into following them in an unthinking manner;
7. The failure to understand the interdependence of society and to seek solutions that take that complexity into account; and
8. The "menace of lack of time" (Rugg in Mitchner, 1939, p. 142).

Rugg advised curriculum designers to place these factors in the forefront of their minds as they designed their program of study.

These principles began with the concept that an overall program must contain something we now refer to as "scope and sequence." Second, Rugg stated that this design must arise from the current culture of the people as opposed to "some other classic entrenched curriculum" (Rugg in Mitchner, 1939, p. 148). Third, each unit of study was to be centered on a human "problem," institution or social system that was complex and interdependent rather than based on a single subject. Fourth, the curriculum had to challenge students' maximum growth in their knowledge, encouraging both interest and self-discipline or hard work (a call for rigor). Fifth, the program had to balance current interests of children with what was necessary to be studied later on in school and in adult life. Sixth, which was based on the above, resulted in the creation of "Schools of Living," concepts borrowed from Dewey. Seventh, which focuses on depth, was the "mastery of essentials rather than superficial acquaintance with it all" (Rugg in Mitchner, 1939, p. 148). This necessitated [eighth] a flexible grade placement in terms of cognitive developmental maturity rather than by age placement (multi-age grades). Ninth, the focus of curriculum on problem solving was to make use of dramatic episodes to set the problem aiming for generalizations with repeated occurrence to reinforce concepts and patterns. Lastly, number ten, which made use of much more historical data than generally found in traditional history courses, stated that the concentration of the study would be on the facts and concepts that produced contemporary conditions and problems (again depth over breadth).

The rest of the article concentrated on the "why" and the "how" of his curriculum design. In an idea surely springing from the Progressive approach to education, Rugg explains what he calls the "organic" (interdisciplinary) approach to learning as being more valid than the "mechanistic" or single subject approach. In this sense, one can understand why his entire course of study is entitled "Man and His Changing Society" (Rugg in Mitchner, 1939, p. 149). Rugg states that the approach he suggests differs from traditional studies in three ways:

> They [integrated social sciences] build a vast body of concepts and attitudes that formal courses ignore; they start from the social and personal needs and experiences of the students; because young people must assemble the data to answer their own questions, the study cuts ruthlessly across conventional subject boundaries . . . to make available all meanings essential for understanding. . ." (Rugg in Mitchner, 1939, p. 15)

Differentiating between the typical progressive approach and the reconstructionist, Rugg notes that in the latter approach curriculum-design is a product of the balancing of "doing what I need to do today (Progressive) with getting ready to do things I shall have to do tomorrow" (Social Reconstructionist) (Rugg in Mitchner, 1939, p. 152). He follows with a discussion of the school as an instrument of the study of society and his belief in active learning for societal reconstruction. Students must not only learn about government, but also must take part in governing for the study to be effective (Rugg in Mitchner, 1939, p. 152). Ultimately, Rugg goes on to discuss the role of controversial issues and history, specifically, in the social studies curriculum.

As already mentioned, Rugg was heavily influenced by the "Frontier Thinkers" and used economic interpretations of history and geography in his program rather than the traditional political approach to these subjects. A review of the curriculum outlined in the aforementioned article includes an emphasis on world history and world problems at a time when the United States was in a neo-isolationist period as demonstrated by its failure to join the League of Nations following World War I. Additionally, Rugg focuses on groups in America traditionally ignored in social studies textbooks of the time period: immigrants, minorities, and women.

Rugg and his colleagues designed and marketed a series of social studies textbooks that purported to implement the philosophy described above. The "First Course" (elementary school level) was comprised of eight volumes: I. *The Book of the Earth*; II. *Nature Peoples*; III, *Communities of Men*; IV. *Peoples and Countries*; V. *The Building of America*; VI. *Man at Work: His Industries*; VII. *Man at Work: His Arts and Crafts*; and VIII. *Mankind Throughout the Ages*. The six volumes in the "Second Course" (junior high and secondary school level) were later revised into two groups. The first group was comprised of the following: I. *Our Country and Our People*, II. *Changing Countries and Changing Peoples*, III. *The Conquest of America*; and IV. *America's March Toward Democracy*, while the second group, *Community and National Life*, included volume V. *Citizenship and Civic Affairs* (Book One) and volume VI. *America Rebuilds* (Book Two.) At the height of the series' popularity, more than five million students were using the Rugg social studies materials. For all intents and purposes, the latter basically constituted an attempt at forging a new, national social studies curriculum.

This chapter undertakes an analysis of one Rugg textbook from the second group of the second course, Community and National Life, Book One, Volume V. *Citizenship and Civic Affairs* (Rugg, 1940), as well as multiple writings by and about Rugg's social studies materials, in order to determine whether Rugg was actually able to design and implement the curricular change he called for in his 1939 article. The methodology consisted of designing two instruments for the text analysis. One chart (Appendix 2) is based on the fifteen social studies factors students need (according to Rugg) to master, and the second chart (Appendix 1) is based on the ten principles of curriculum design called for in the article. The selected material was analyzed using these instruments.

Volume 5 was selected for several reasons. First, the text was designed for a civics/government course, a course of study that has become increasingly fact-laden, boring and meaningless to many secondary students who do not understand the role the government plays in their lives after they complete the course. Second, government can be seen as a course that focuses inherently on controversial issues and problems. Considering the criticism of the Rugg textbooks series in the late 1930s and 1940s (Riley & Stern, 2002), this volume seemed particularly pertinent to the charges leveled against Rugg. Given the conservative nature of schools then and now, and the Progressive/Reconstructionist changes called for in Rugg's article, the question under consideration is: Was Rugg actually able to do as he said? In other words, is there consistency between what Rugg said was ideal and the materials created to implement this ideal? Third, especially in light of the fact that the books became a commercial venture for Rugg and Ginn and Company as they moved from their original pamphlet form to hardcover textbooks designed for wide distribution, were the revised editions faithful to the Rugg vision?

Several authors have analyzed the Rugg textbooks over the years in terms of content (Bosenberg & Poland, 2001, pp. 640–71; Muchinske, 1974, pp. 246–49; Nelson, 1977, pp. 64–83; Nelson, 1982, pp. 69–82; Nelson & Singleton, 1978; Riley & Stern, 2002; Sabine, et al., 1942, p. 28), with most primarily interested in the political attacks against the Rugg textbooks. The latter generally examined the textbooks removal from the schools and/or the unfairness of the charges leveled against Rugg and his writing team. The aforementioned authors generally begin by explicating Rugg's philosophy on curriculum design. Nelson (1978) cites the process by which Rugg approaches curriculum design as stemming from his background as an engineer. Rugg believed in approaching a problem scientifically, in planning and executing the solutions in an organized fashion based on the gathering of evidence and the testing of that evidence. Nelson (1978) notes that the Rugg textbook series represents the earliest comprehensive curriculum design "developed and utilized on a nationwide basis in social studies" (p. 124). This fact alone makes the study of the Rugg materials important for curriculum theorists and social studies specialists.

Following a review of the literature, we found that Rugg actually put his curriculum design plan into effect, and our analysis thus concurs with earlier scholars who believe Rugg was successful in achieving his ten principles of design (See Appendix 1). The success of his effort in regard to those social studies factors that students needed to master was more problematic (See Appendix 2). The latter relates to the difficulty of defining what is meant by real knowledge in any given discipline grouped under the umbrella of the social sciences.

Rugg was educated as an engineer, not as a social scientist, and certainly neither as an historian, a geographer, an economist nor a political scientist. Neither was he a specialist in any of the academic disciplines he was trying to merge. This may have been less problematic at the elementary school and at the junior high school levels (where, due to the newness of junior high schools, there was a dearth of materials available and therefore a ready-made market to develop), but as the materials moved to the high school level and to wide commercial acceptance they became more open to academic challenge from experts in the subject fields who believed their individual disciplines were being slighted.

How much of the battle over the actual disciplinary content of the Rugg materials would have played out if his approach had been less incendiary is hard to know but the chart focused on social studies (Appendix 2) reveals less content knowledge, especially in history, than Rugg believed was contained in these books. And, not only is there less historical knowledge, but also different knowledge than was generally included in the time period and for a good while thereafter. In other words, Rugg's choice of historical materials was less traditional and more in keeping with the Frontier Thinkers' approach (economic and social history) versus the more typical/traditional approach (political, diplomatic, and military history) usually found in public schools during that period of time. That made the work more controversial than it would be today.

In exploring Rugg's charts in depth, one finds the following: the chart analyzing the Ten Principles of Design (Appendix 1) focuses on the preface to the book as that is where Rugg explains his concept of how the text fits into the fully implemented social science program, as well as how this particular textbook was created. By using quotations from the preface addressing the design concerns and then looking for evidence to back up these claims in the execution of the chapters, it is clear that Rugg was successful in most of his design claims. For example, the program was clearly designed as an integrated social science entity, and the titles of the books in the series—along with Rugg's explanation of their scope and sequence (preface vi–vii)—attest to that fact. They also attest to the fact that the theme for design was to explain how America and the larger world it was a part of came to be as they are. Finally, they attest to the fact that the program addresses the type of problems that need to be examined and solved in order to ensure a better future.

. While a few of the sections in the book left something to be desired in regard to the amount of content included, what was clearly covered in the design of the text were as follows:

1. The focus on social problems and the push in each chapter for substantive discussions where students would need to form opinions about these problems and their possible solutions points towards both "doing now" and getting ready for tomorrow;
2. During a period when recitation of facts was the *modus operandi*, this textbook with its emphasis on the multiple perspectives of differing opinions [generally by social class] on problems and discussion was really revolutionary; and
3. In terms of "rigorous principle of selection," Rugg's choice of topics was extraordinary for a high school textbook. For example, Rugg focused on gangs, the influence of political bosses, changing roles of women in society, increases in divorce rates, and the history of education.

The reader comes away from the text with a conceptual understanding of how government was generally expected to operate. The information is useful in seeing how the system really works, as opposed to its structure on paper, enabling a student to understand how to become an active citizen and where problems, e.g. political corruption, need solving.

Principle nine—dealing with controversial topics—is fully realized in the text. There are vignettes [dramatic episodes] that center on controversial issues or social problems at the start of most chapters. Further, the recurrence of concepts, especially the focus on different aspects of economic problems and their impact on different social groups and segments of society, are repeated throughout the book.

The most questionable of the Rugg design principles is his claim, in principle ten, that there is more historical data, rather than less, in his approach. While there is statistical data that was rarely seen in earlier textbooks due to the fact that earlier texts take a political rather than economic or social approach to history, there is clearly a surfeit of historical factual material in this text. As this was a government and not a history book, the lack of historical data may not be a major criticism, but the mention of historical importance without the facts to back up the claim is dismaying. In many cases, the reader is left wondering about omissions, e.g. the discussion of the addition of the Bill of Rights to the U.S. Constitution is particularly poorly done without any mention of the *Federalist Papers* or the refusal of some states to ratify without promises of the addition of the Bill of Rights. The discussion of the failures and success of the Articles of Confederation is similarly glib and lacking in enough factual material to promote true understanding of the issues. The resources consulted by the authors (Riley & Stern) regarding the rest of the textbook series reveal a similar concern with a paucity of history in a subject area where the consensus, then and now, is that history is the centerpiece of any social studies curriculum.

Ultimately, though, whether one appreciates (or agrees with) Rugg's curriculum design approach or not, what is clear about his work is that it was not filled with sinister methods or ideas hostile to "Americanism," which would undermine the loyalty of American students in favor of foreign governments or economic systems (communism) as feared by his most ardent critics. As for his critics, rather than "rid the schools" of Rugg's influence, they unwittingly gave him the notoriety that he might have otherwise lacked through the simple publication of a series of social studies textbooks, his penchant for flamboyancy notwithstanding.

RUGG'S REPORT TO THE
NATIONAL EDUCATION ASSOCIATION

As chair of one of the powerful National Education Association (NEA) committees charged with identifying problems within the United States and then designing an educational plan that would reverse what NEA leaders believed were dangerous governmental policies, practices, and precedents, which led to the economic collapse during the Hoover administration, Rugg presented a report to the 1934 mid-annual NEA meeting.

Rugg's mission was to deliver a committee report on the economic and social conditions of the United States and offer recommendations for solutions. The contents of the Rugg report outlined what NEA educators had been discussing for over three years—disillusionment with federal policies that bred inequality and an economic system that only served the wealthy.

A quick perusal of the 1934 NEA proceedings discovers the degree to which educators concerned themselves with the then current crisis of the Depression. Some spoke to the issue of economic inequality, while others addressed the type of "new social order" Americans should create and how could it be realized. John K. Norton, Professor of Education, Teachers College, Columbia University, and Chairman of the Joint Commission on the Emergency in Education, spoke to those assembled on the work of the commission and its plans for 1935. Norton included in his remarks research findings by the Brookings Institute on the economy. What he said was that rather than view the Depression as a four-year punishment for the "gay joyride of the twenties, during which we spent money, and wickedly burned up capital…," especially in the area of extravagant expenditures for education, an excuse leveled by government officials, "We" need only look at the economic facts of 1929: "In 1929 our income was fifteen billion dollars less than it could have been if we had used the labor force and the capital goods already in our possession…" (Norton, 1934, pp. 33–34).

Norton went on to say that if the United States had used its economic power, it could have raised the income level of more than sixteen million families by some $2000, who, according to Norton, actually received less than this amount. By his account, if the U.S. economic productivity had not been wasted, it would have supported public education from kindergarten through college, five times over (Norton, 1934, p. 34). Norton's address, like those who followed, focused on implications for schools in light of America's economic crisis: school closings and the threat of federal control over the nation's schools. He outlined three areas concerning "educational recovery and reconstruction" (Norton, 1934, p. 36). They were:

1. Activities—Norton failed to elaborate on this issue—designed to revise how schools are funded;
2. Collaboration between educational professionals and public-spirited citizens for the purpose of defining the role of education in solving the country's economic and social problems illuminated by recent events; and
3. The need for long-term programs aimed at improving educational procedures and results—again.

Norton leaves the reader to interpret what he means (p. 36). However, his concluding remarks were clear:

> [W]e are urging that teachers dream great dreams and see great visions as to what education may mean to every state, and to the nation as a whole. The road which lies ahead is no easy one. Every step of educational advance in the twentieth century will be contested as it was in the nineteenth century, by the forces of ignorance, prejudice, greed, and narrow vision. But those forces can be defeated. They break and run in the face of intelligence, open-mindedness, courage, and social vision. Intelligent and courageous teachers and parents can supply these indispensable ingredients of educational and social advance (Norton, 1934, p. 37).

Despite Norton's high sense of purpose and flattering words used to describe the role of teachers and parents in thwarting prejudice and ignorance, we are reminded that in only a few years following the 1934 NEA meeting, some of the groups that his words described—American Legion and Daughters of the American Revolution—joined together in their collective narrow vision and attacked the NEA and some of its most influential members for spreading un-American ideas disguised as problem-solving learning. Two of the Legion's favorite targets in the late 1930s and 1940s were John Dewey and Harold Rugg.

While most of the speakers at the 1934 meeting were educators, a few from "affiliated" groups were invited to speak. One such affiliate was the American Legion. Its National Director of the Americanism Commission, Russell Cook, reminded listeners that "proper education," which the Legion supported, demanded adherence to the American way and that "the teaching of strange tenets in government has no place in the schoolroom" (The National Education Association, 1934, p. 113). Like any good watchdog agency, the Legion was only too aware of what kind of teaching was being conducted in the nation's schools. Cook alerted the audience to the fact that it was known to the Legion that "in the last few years there has grown up a movement in which too many of our teachers are creating ideas in the schoolroom for what is called a new social order" (The National Education Association, 1934, p. 113). The Legion, he stated, "is opposed to that movement" (The National Education Association, 1934, p. 113). Although Cook did not point his finger at any one individual, what can be deduced from his remarks is that six months prior to the July 1934 meeting in Washington D.C., Rugg and his committee had outlined, in crystal clear fashion, at the February meeting of the Department of Superintendence of the NEA in Cleveland, exactly what the new social order would look like and how it could be achieved. Little wonder that Legion attacks on Rugg and his textbook series throughout the 1940s and 1950s always pointed to the Cleveland meeting as the tell-tale smoking gun. Yet, throughout its 900 plus pages of the addresses and proceedings of the 1934 NEA meeting, the streams of thought ran clear. One speaker after another addressed the then current economic disaster brought about by the stock market crash, sought financial aid for the immediate school crises, and offered a vision for the future, which rested upon a "different" social order. A social order that was planned, streamlined, and whose aim was to be fair to one and all.

John Dewey, who spoke on the issue of teacher education, argued for an education that introduced students to the "realities of the present order— or disorder, order being a courtesy name for the present chaos" (The National Education Association, 1934, p. 744). He vigorously warned against "the idolizing of correct knowledge..." (The National Education Association, 1934, p. 745). Young people, said Dewey, leave school expecting to be told what to do rather than to inquire and examine. Dewey and other speakers at the 1934 meeting capitalized on the effects of the Depression to advance their fundamental belief in problem-based education. As Dewey saw it, a change in teacher education was the key to a more humane and just social order. Well-prepared teachers would, in turn, better prepare students to play out their roles as active citizens. After all, students were the nation's future judges, lawyers, doctors, teachers, business and government leaders, and collectively, problem solvers. Hence, he outlined a three-pronged plan aimed at restructuring teacher education:

1. The material at hand for reorganization could be found in the work of committees such as the Commission on Social Trends, the Commission on Social Studies, and the Neal's Committee on Social and Economic Goals—will also contribute their findings;
2. There was a need for new approaches to teaching that reject indoctrination in favor of critical inquiry; and
3. There was a critical need for a socially centered curriculum directed at restructuring society for social purposes.

We must, argued Dewey, educate a generation of children who can "deal intelligently with our social troubles..." (The National Education Association, 1934, p. 752).

And so, the parade of speakers who advocated for education to take the lead in casting out the old dysfunctional order, steeped as it was in tooth-and-claw competition, in favor of a new social order based upon social cohesion, justness, and fairness, seemed endless. Speakers filled with visions of an emerging great society were breathless in their condemnation of past sins committed by ruthless businessmen and government officials who not only turned a blind eye, but actually encouraged such a raw contest. The problem, as they saw it, was clear: decades of schoolhouse indoctrination had disposed students to uncritically accept the status quo. The folly of laissez faire brought the whole house down, and now, thought these educators, it was time for "schoolmen" to step in and change the economic, political, and social landscape through a newly invigorated plan for education. This plan called for scientific fact-finding and scientific problem solving. Hence, committees such as the one on social trends would examine trends and offer solutions. American youth could be taught to become problem solvers and free themselves from the yoke of unbridled capitalism. But, as previously mentioned, there was one big problem afloat, and that was the fact that at this very same meeting, representatives from conservative groups such as the American Legion and the Daughters of the American Revolution were in attendance and when they spoke they made it abundantly clear that what they expected of the schools was transmission, not critical inquiry.

Unknown to those who attended the 1934 meeting, the battle lines were drawn. The future would determine the victor.

In his seminal work on Progressive education, Lawrence Cremin (1961) had the following to say about Rugg, "Certainly if any single career symbolizes the constantly changing image of progressive education during the decades after World War I, it was Harold Rugg's" (p. 181). One writer, H. W. Odum (1934), characterized Rugg's passion for progressivism in this way:

> There were many who saw new and unprecedented opportunities in the rise of new governments which would reach such composite power as had not hitherto been recorded. Thus, "there lies within our grasp the most humane, the most beautiful, the most majestic civilization ever fashioned by any people." (p. 604)

That Rugg's work came to be associated by the Legion with the rise of one of the new governments of which Odum spoke is all too obvious. Yet, Rugg consistently included democracy in nearly all of his discussions in his plan for a "New Education." Rugg may have entertained a certain intellectual curiosity when it came to the fundamentals or theory of Communism, but his textbook writings indicate a dedication to a democratic way of life with citizens freed from burdens imposed on them by the whims and fancies of unfettered capitalism. Only when the federal government assumed control of the forces of production and engineered a planned economy could citizens release their creative energies in order to engage in problem solving on a large scale, so thought Rugg.

At the time that Rugg wrote a number of his social science textbooks, in the early 1930s, the world had yet to witness with complete clarity the abuses of the Communist state. It was too early to count the millions lost to starvation or brutalized by a draconian secret service. Communism in its infancy likely looked as though it might be the great social and economic equalizer. What's more, the American public at this time had not "digested" the Orwellian version of the totalitarian communist state in *Animal Farm.* Yet the mere thought of a new social order caused many to have nightmares in which social upheaval and displacement were center stage. That was enough to convince any stouthearted loyal American to resist in any form the slightest talk of a radical change. Hence, when Rugg's textbook series first appeared and his star began to rise, the opposition to his work took on a fierce and strident tone. As Apple and Christian-Smith (1991) have aptly observed in *Politics of the Textbook*, the real battle over textbooks and official knowledge generally "signifie[s] more profound political, economic, and cultural relations and histories. Conflicts over texts are often proxies for wider questions of power relations. They involve what people hold most dear" (p. 3). This was certainly true as to how conservatives in the 1930s and 1940s viewed educational liberalism. Thus, the American Legion, only one organization out of a pantheon of many, took up its figurative sword and prepared to do battle.

THE BATTLE BETWEEN THE
CONSERVATIVES AND THE PROGRESSIVES

As world leaders mobilized for the real war in 1941, American Legion writers began to defame Rugg by characterizing him as an academic dictator, bent on destroying the American way of life and supplanting it with foreign ideas of socialism, or worse, communism. Rugg was not in any way whatsoever acting in isolation. In fact, the Progressive Education Association (PEA), the National Education Association (NEA), and a host of other organizations worldwide embraced by both academic and political leaders, had been meeting throughout the 1930s and into the 1940s on the topic of "schools for the world of tomorrow" (Letter from the Legation of the U.S., 1933). The substance of these meetings could be viewed even today as revolutionary. In fact, the utopian visionaries attending these international conferences, when one looks at their proposed agendas, seem decidedly disconnected from political realities. It was no surprise that they ended up fanning Legion fires.

Throughout the 1930s, the World Conference of New Education Fellowship held meetings at various places around the globe. In 1934, for example, the meeting was held in Johannesburg, South Africa, and the focus of the meeting was "social regeneration through education reconstruction." In attendance were an array of who's who of 20th Century education professors and practitioners at the time, including John Dewey and Harold Rugg.

Throughout the years, the agenda and program of the conferences were greatly influenced by American educators. For example, the theme of the 1940 conference program—"Human and Material Resources for the World of Tomorrow"—was reminiscent of statements crafted in a 1934 NEA committee report credited to Harold Rugg. The rationale for the program began as follows: "Mankind stands at the threshold of a great adventure. He has at his command the material resources to make the good life...He stands at the threshold of plenty and he looks to education to furnish the means for ushering in an age that is nearer mankind's hearts desires" (Letter from Frederick L. Redefer, 1939). Tellingly, Rugg's committee wrote similar words some five to six years earlier when it delivered its final report on current social problems and their possible solutions (Committee Report of the NEA, Our Social-economic Situation and the New Education, 1934).

Fueled by the excitement of a worldwide effort on the part of educators and political leaders to change the future of the economically disenfranchised, Rugg, as only one of any number of educators worldwide, contributed to the goals of the "New Education" movement through the publication of secondary social science textbooks. With the success of the Rugg materials also came the critics. To ultra conservative groups such as the American Legion, Harold Rugg embodied all that was wrong with the New Education efforts of educationists and politicians across the globe: internationalism, which, to them, meant un-Americanism. With their founding mission in mind, Legion writers pointed out to readers the real motives of Rugg and his followers—to turn American schoolchildren away from America's traditional stories of its past and transmission of American cultural values toward a future filled with problems and how the nation itself helped to create them.

The man who the Legion hired as an expert in the field of education to help rid public school classrooms of "the Rugg philosophy" was R. Worth Shumaker, a graduate of West Virginia Wesleyan University and a former county superintendent from 1935 until his acceptance as chief education analyst for the American Legion (Jones, unpublished dissertation, 1957). In "No 'New Order' for Our Schools," Shumaker opened with equal amounts of scare tactics and platitudes. For example, he paints a picture for the reader of Hitler and Mussolini meeting in 1940 in the Austrian Alps for the purpose of forging an alliance to "blackout" democracy throughout the world (Shumaker, 1941, p. 5). He did so in order to attempt to contrast the actions and motives of these two dictators to life in the United States by picturing America as a land where all can come to the figurative floor to be heard and where everyone's voice counts, while asserting that the citizens of the Soviet Union or Nazi Germany were subject to the whims of despots (Shumaker, 1941, p. 5). While Legion members may have believed these two views themselves—bad guys versus good guys—countless educators, social workers, and intellectuals knew better. They knew that the voices of immigrants and minorities went largely ignored in conservative political circles with in the U.S. And, in fact, this was one of the aspects of American life progressive reformers had hoped to change.

Shumaker's (1941) article, hardly an unbiased view of progressive education, heaped praise upon America's educators, pointing out that "[i]n general, the builders of curricula, the writers of textbooks, and the classroom teachers, have performed their tasks most creditably" (p. 5). The author went on to call the National Education Association (NEA) an organization that was part of a collaboration responsible for ... "building a great educational system which is the pride of the nation" (p. 5). Interestingly, the NEA, some seven years before, sponsored the Rugg committee report that stood as a blueprint for progressive educational reform, calling for such things as "A New Education," one that would vividly present pressing social and economic issues. It was that very committee, Rugg's committee, that insisted that through every avenue of information and education social issues must be presented, including such concerns as a..." *poverty economy* (italics not added) resulting from an out-moded laissez-faire economic system on the one hand and on the other a *plenty economy* (italics not added) which could result from a designed social system..." (Committee Report of the NEA, 1934, p. 540). Amusingly, Shumaker seemed unaware that the NEA had actually sponsored this "detestable" document authored, in large part, by the Legion's arch enemy, Harold Rugg.

In attempting to convey the Legion's message in a certain homespun fashion, Shumaker capitalized on the use of clichés throughout. In one such attempt, the author likened the United States to an old ship: "'The old ship of State may have sprung a few leaks but there has been no scuttling of any part of our great heritage—the leaks have always been closed up and the ship continues seaworthy'" (Shumaker, 1941, p. 6). In other words, yes, the United States has problems, but it has always been able to fix them without getting rid of its form of government. Shumaker's purpose was clear: to convey the idea that what Rugg and other Frontier thinkers were calling for was an overthrow of the existing system as a way to fix any number of social and political problems. He went on to disparage the field of social studies by revealing its integrated nature as though an integrated treatment of social, political, historical, economic, and geographic issues and content were something unthinkable. The Legion favored the traditional treatment of social science subjects as isolated subject areas—history, geography, economics, etc.

Shumaker leaves the reader with little doubt that he and other Legion officials believed that Rugg and other Frontier thinkers were behind a plan to transplant the Soviet Union's model of collectivism to the United States through the agency of the school. In keeping with the Legion's original 1919 mission of rooting out un-American activity, the publicity division of the American Legion issued a special news bulletin on April 5, 1941, which stated, in part:

> ...Specific information to aid American Legion Posts everywhere in their discussion of textbooks used in the public schools everywhere is to be supplied by the National Americanism Commission of the American Legion.
>
> Following up his article NO NEW ORDER FOR OUR SCHOOLS, Assistant National Americanism director R. Worth Shumaker is preparing a series of pamphlets to discuss the textbooks that The Legion considers subversive in text and philosophy. These will be distributed in the near future.
>
> Legion organizations in the field interested in the battle to eliminate subversive teachings in the textbooks supplied for classroom work will have new background material for their studies... (American Legion, *NewsBulletin*, 1940).

A cover message from the publishers cautions Americans to:

Examine your child's textbooks. Demand to see the teacher's guides. Find out
if "social science" textbooks have replaced courses in civics, history and geography. Look for subversive material, protest at once to school officials, the
board of education, and school associations. Remember most of your teachers are loyal. Support them. (American Legion, *NewsBulletin*, 1940)[1]

Other charges brought about by Shumaker (1941) against Rugg included
Rugg's:

lack of emphasis on true American life and too great an emphasis on the
unfavorable aspects, failure to give due acknowledgment to the deeds of our
great American heroes, questioning private ownership, too favorable emphasis on what has been done in the Soviet Union, the creation of doubt in the
minds of pupils and teachers as to the ability of our democracy to function
successfully, the dissemination of alien propaganda, statements that the United States Supreme Court favors vested interests. (p. 7)

To bolster the Legion's position on Rugg, Shumaker quoted extensively
from Rugg's work, most notably his *Great Technology*, which was not a book
designed for secondary school consumption. At the same time, Shumaker
offered little criticism of Rugg's actual textbook content for secondary students.

RUGG'S *PROBLEMS OF AMERICAN CULTURE*

An examination of Rugg's textbook entitled *Problems of American Culture* reveals that far from being a vehicle of propaganda, it took a rather straight-
forward approach in dealing with pressing social, political, and economic
issues of the day. For example, at one point Rugg posed this question: "Is
there a place for better planning in the development of the press?" Basically, he was asking students to analyze for themselves the role of the press.
He added that since the advent of universal elementary education more
and more individuals were reading newspapers, magazines, and books. To
Rugg, the greater the ability to reach individuals through the written word,
the greater the responsibility for accuracy in reporting. Although not alone
when it came to exposing the problems of the press, he was, nevertheless,
a prime target of the Hearst papers, itself allied with the American Legion
for the purpose of disposing with Rugg and his ideas (Gellerman, 1938, pp.
763–764). But what had he actually told students or young people about the

---

[1]On one level, the sort of political activity is surprising if one takes into account that the American
Legion's constitution reads that the organization "'shall be absolutely non-political and shall not be
used for the dissemination of partisan principles'" (Fish, Jr. in Gellerman, 1931, p. 42).

press and its problems in his textbook? In *Problems of American Culture*, Rugg (1931) simply posed the question of whether or not there was room for better planning in the development of the press. He challenged youngsters to consider that:

> [w]e have noted the important role of advertising and business in determining the content of newspapers and magazines. We have seen the widespread tendency for tabloid picture newspapers and other sensational periodicals to print "news" without too great regard for accuracy. Hence, although reputable publishers are already doing much to improve the character of the press, insistent problems present themselves. Underlying them are difficult questions of propaganda and censorship. Similarly, there emerge the equally important problems of the more fundamental education of our people, of the cultivation of a taste for better literature and of a demand for a more scientific attitude in the press (p. 604).

Rugg was certainly not the first to speak of things like sensationalism in the press. All one had to do was, for example, recall the allegations leveled at press organs that sensationalized the "Sinking of the Maine" in the Havana harbor some 30 years earlier. Why were Rugg's proposals on journalistic practice treated as something new?

THE BATTLE AGAINST RUGG CONTINUES

There is no doubt about it, Rugg advocated change. In fact, the type of change that he and others, many others, sought to effect might even be considered radical or drastic. However, such radical changes could be viewed as proportional to the problems that progressive reformers perceived and sought to ameliorate. Be that as it may, as Oliver succinctly reminds us in her discussion of how the "right" functions, "[t]hroughout the United States, national organizations have been formed by conservatives to fight against what counts as 'official knowledge' in schools (Oliver in Apple, 1996, pp. 42–43). This was certainly true of the battles that took place from the 1930s to the 1950s during which ultra conservatives attempted to destroy the progressive message of Rugg and his followers.

A second article on Rugg appeared in the next issue of the *American Legion Magazine*, May 1941. In "Ours to Reason Why," the author, H. Hicks, opened with a more scholarly, but no less damning, account than Shumaker of Rugg and his proposal for a New Education. However, when one reads past the first several pages, the article begins to break down into a confusion of surreal images of youngsters tricking their parents by leading them into the chaos of a totalitarian state after years of subtle Rugg propaganda in their schools. Hicks actually went further in condemning Rugg than did

Shumaker when he likened the Frontier thinker to Adolf Hitler. In fact, Hicks (1952) absurdly claimed "*The Great Technology* is Rugg's *Mein Kampf*" (p. 57). As proof of Rugg's malevolent methods and motives, Hicks pointed out that a Legion post held an essay contest for high-schoolers in which students were given a plan to stabilize the world of business based upon both a Soviet and Nazi government model. Students were asked to write an essay without benefit of consulting any texts, dictionaries, or other printed materials. The results of the essay startled Legion members. The students, all of whom had attended a school which utilized the Rugg materials, responded as follows: three recognized the plan as either communist or Nazi inspired; three others pointed out the pros and cons; and three thought the plan to be excellent. These outcomes likely confirmed what Legion rank and file believed all along, as long as Rugg and his sort were allowed to influence American youth, America was doomed.

Like Legion articles published in the early 1940s, those produced in the 1950s linked Rugg to the most perverse type of subversive activity—teaching the youth of America to find fault with its government. Also like the articles of the early 40s, the authors likened Rugg to Hitler, Stalin and Mussolini, although Hitler remained the favorite. Unlike the 1941 Shumaker article, in which the author heaped praise upon the NEA, another article "Your Child is their Target," by I. C. Kuhn, alerted the reading public to a different NEA. In doing so, she asserted that

> [o]ne of the strongest forces today in propagandizing for a socialistic America is the hierarchy of the National Education Association. They have had things pretty much their own way for a long time, too, but the public opposition and nation-wide parents' rebellion which have sprung up in the past two years may force the NEA into a re-examination of itself. It is too soon, though, to say how the organization will eventually react. Some of its performances have been more typical of the tactics of a captured labor union complete with goon squads, than of a respectable national organization of more than a half million teachers. The NEA has no reason to be proud of those goon squads which have turned up to do a discrediting job on citizens whenever there has been an uprising in a community against "progressive" education (Kuhn, 1952, p. 52).

The mistrust of organizations such as the Legionnaires and other ultra-conservative groups of their schools, teachers, administrators, along with professional teaching organizations, is palpable in this 1952 article. Nearly 20 years after the 1934 Cleveland meeting of the NEA, when Rugg and his committee took up the challenge of articulating a philosophy of social reconstruction presented as a committee report on America's social and economic problems and their implications, the Legion continued to beat the same drum in its organization's publications. Kuhn, like Shumaker some 20 years before, trotted out all of the data on that decades-old meeting as if it were a new red flag.

While the *American Legion Magazine* published other articles excoriating Rugg and his contemporaries, the few presented here suffice as examples of the type of message and method of delivery employed by one of the largest ex-servicemen's and patriotic organizations in the U.S. Perhaps far more than magazine articles, the Legion's three-volume series on the philosophy of Harold Rugg was the most damaging of its efforts. In *The Complete Rugg Philosophy*, the Legion laid at the doorstep of one educator the entire blame for what its members collectively believed was a communist plot to subvert the minds of American children. This step-by-step analysis of the "Rugg program" relied on excerpts from Rugg's work juxtaposed with original interpretations by Legion-employed experts of his work. In volume two, the writers assert that

> [t]he Legion recognizes the right of freedom of speech. This is a precious heritage which must be preserved. The Legion is firm in its position, however, that this right ceases to be a privilege when controversial issues are presented to children through textbooks which serve as an instrument of propaganda to promote the personal ideas and program of the author (The American Legion, 1941, Vol. II, p. 2).

While Rugg clearly held ideas that America could and should be a better place to live for all of her citizens, he never advocated the kind of collectivism as practiced in Stalin's Soviet Union. Perhaps he used the wrong language—democratic collectivism—to introduce his ideas, or perhaps his terminology was correct and the terms were simply perverted by the totalitarian-minded. Whatever the case, Rugg was only one of hundreds, if not thousands, of educators in the United States, and worldwide, who eagerly sought the promise of progressivism and the hope for mankind ushered in by a "New Education."

RUGG'S IMPACT ON THE SOCIAL STUDIES

While the promise of progressivism may have faded from view, once an idea enters the river of thought its essence flows along with the current. Time always announces its re-appearance. What then can be said of Rugg's long-term impact on the social studies? For one, the very concepts and methods that Rugg advocated throughout the 1930s until into the 1950s re-surfaced in the 1960s in the form of sociology projects as part of the New Social Studies (and that is despite the fact that most historians of education consider the New Social Studies to have been a curricular reform movement of great promise that, unfortunately, met with disappointing results). The Sociology Resources for the Social Studies or SRSS was the centrepiece of the sociology project. The over-arching objective of the SRSS project was for students to engage in a sort of detached inquiry thereby mimicking the type of research and study conducted in the real world by practicing sociologists. On the surface, one might ask, "How could something so seemingly promising fail so miserably?" After all, what could be wrong with teaching students how to examine the problems of their world and then find solutions to fix them? (Riley, 2009)—a question that Rugg and other social reconstructionists would have understood only too well. The New Social Studies movement, it seems, faded from educational view perhaps as quickly as did social reconstruction methods, materials, and the name of Harold Rugg, albeit without the spotlight of unwanted publicity.

However, the notion that students should be something more than simply passive learners remained. The idea that students should actually engage in extended study and use the tools of the discipline in order to construct meaning, drew thousands of teachers and other educators to the latest (1990s–2000s) educational approach—authentic learning. Fred Newmann's work in the area of authentic learning quickly brings to mind one of the Rugg methods and materials. Newmann advocates deep study and problem solving as a goal of learning, while Rugg advocated the same thing, but as a goal of change. Rugg saw students as agents of change. Newmann's work is distinctly void of the political dimensions found in social reconstruction, yet similar to Rugg's work in its approach to learning. And of course, we must not forget that the fear which gripped the men and women of those ultra-patriotic groups more than a half a century ago no longer exists. Gone is the Red Scare of the 1930s, 40s, 50s, and 60s. Thus, and examination of American history with a "fine tooth comb" no longer scares patriotic watchdog groups as it once did. As a result, scores of authentic learning admirers blissfully carry out their teaching assignments using authentic learning principles without fear of reprisal or without fear that their school librarian had wiped the shelves clean of "controversial" resources (as was done some sixty years ago when Rugg's books were removed) that showed their students—to borrow the title of a well-known book by Jacob Riis—"how the other half lives."

CONCLUSION

If the story of Harold Rugg were cast as a Greek play, his tragic flaw might surface in the form of arrogance. He enjoyed the attention of his notoriety until it took him down, both financially and in terms of his educational legacy. Yet, within the past decade teacher educators and educational historians have witnessed a renewed interest in Harold Rugg. Why, one might ask, is Rugg's story so appealing, when in the late 1930s and throughout the 1940s he was an "untouchable," condemned by ultra-patriotic and conservative groups across the land? One answer is that the distance of time has likely made it possible to examine Rugg without the emotional dimension present at the mid-century mark. We must not forget that the word "communism" raised eyebrows and caused incredible angst inside and outside of Washington.

Rugg was attacked in the press for peddling communist ideas to innocent school children vis-à-vis his social studies textbooks. Yet, at the height of his popularity more than 5 million school children engaged in social studies activities through his textbooks using inquiry methods. But the story of Harold Rugg, in many ways, is the story of a noble experiment. It is really the story of a collective group of individuals who believed that America should fulfill her promise to all of her people. However, Rugg, rather than being a sinister foe, in one sense, was the King's messenger. Not through his textbooks, because they are devoid of anti-American rhetoric, but through the social reconstructionist philosophy outlined in the NEA's 1934 mid-year report. While it is true that Rugg delivered the report as chair of the committee, it is also true that he was merely the spokesperson for a committee comprised of influential educators from across the country. Moreover, the ideas set down in the committee's report echoed those of leading educators, philosophers, and others, across the globe, all of whom anticipated an interdependent world. Rugg and other social reconstructionists around the world laid the groundwork decades ago for today's focus in schools on inquiry, collaboration, and cooperation. More importantly, Rugg's methods are evident today in the growing body of work on historical thinking and historical empathy, as well as the ever-popular authentic learning approach articulated by Fred Newmann and others.

Certainly, what may have accounted for Rugg's downfall, other than his legendary arrogance, is timing. The timing was all wrong. Like in comedy, timing is everything when it comes to the introduction of new ideas. Rugg's ideas (and those of others on his 1934 committee) came at a moment in time when the words he used in his writings such as "collective democracy" and "collective creativity" were lost in a sea of fear and angst. The surviving—red flag—word was "collective," and while Rugg simply meant that ten minds were better than one in terms of problem solving, what others heard was collective as in terms of a re-distribution of wealth—take from the rich and give to the poor. In a land that was weaned on "pull yourself up by your own bootstraps" as a daily staple, the take from the rich and give to the poor approach held little to no appeal to the powers that be. But good ideas rarely die; they are in that great river of thought that flows from one generation to the next. Social reconstruction as a concept will always hold appeal to those who believe that schools should be places where future adults learn how to identify problems that their generation will face. And, while the anti-social reconstructionist forces succeeded in silencing Rugg all of those decades ago, the noble experiment still flows.

APPENDIX 1: TEN PRINCIPLES OF DESIGN

Design Principles	Evidence from Rugg Textbooks
1. The program is designed	Preface viii: A Unified Course in Social Science
2. It is designed directly from the culture of the people	Preface vi: explanation that the First and Second Course are an integrated study of civilization.
3. Each unit of study is centered on a human "problem," institution, social system	Preface vii: "It [the text] serves the special purpose of introducing the economic, political and social problems of American culture"
4. It is designed on rapidly rising growth curves to bring about maximum development each year	Preface vi: "a carefully graduated and steadily maturing plan" Topics discussed throughout the book certainly push students to deal with issues on a mature level. Some topics may not contain needed background to enable full comprehension.
5. The design balances "doing now" with getting ready for tomorrow.	Preface ix: "The chief goal of the social studies is active and intelligent participation in American civilization . . . *Young people grow in understanding only by participating actively in the study of society around them*" [italics original]. There is less actual doing than Rugg appears to believe there is but there is considerable discussion as opposed to recitation.
6. It makes school the chief instrument for social study	Preface v: "It is of the utmost importance that schools bend every effort to introduce our young people to the chief conditions and problems which will confront them as citizens of the world." The book does center all chapters on these problems, particularly economic and social stratification in America; the preference for democracy over dictatorship as a form of government.
7. It is designed on a rigorous principle of selection	Preface vii: Topics were chosen by "specialists on the frontier of thought who see society from a height, who detect its trends and the long-time movement of its affairs." Clearly, emphases throughout the text was on the topics that created the problems Rugg believes America needs to solve.

Design Principles	Evidence from Rugg Textbooks
8. It is designed on a flexible program of grade-placement . . . in terms of maturity of meanings, concepts generalizations and attitudes	The preface suggests grade level for students in the series by both the order of the books and the separation into First and Second Courses. This volume would fall around 9th or 10th grade but the issues involved and their presentation are generally taught in the old "PAD" course or in 12th grade government today. The book really combines civics (generally 8th or 8th grade) and government (generally 12th grade).
9. To guarantee maximum understanding it builds around problems and controversial issues, training in problem solving and generalization . . .It employs dramatic episode and generalization alternately and develops understanding by the designed recurrence of concepts.	Many chapters open with a "scenario" to engage students. These scenarios often involve controversial issues such as illegal immigration and its effect on wages. A recurring theme is the difference in lifestyle among social classes in America. This is illustrated in various chapters by vignettes describing the homes (physical), interests, activities, jobs, educational levels, etc. of different social classes throughout the book. And this is done in easily understandable terms, e.g. the number of bedrooms and bathrooms in dwellings occupied by each social class.
10. While employing more historical data . . rather than less, it concentrates study upon the identical factors and trends that produced contemporary conditions and problems.	Preface viii: "This has not caused a reduction in the amount of history or of geography included in the course. Rather it has produced a sharp increase in the amount of these subjects in the curriculum and, in addition, has added to the curriculum a wealth of new material." There is a significantly lower amount of history in the book for two reasons: one is the glossing over of facts to concentrate on concepts, the other is the increase in other social science information, particularly integrated sociology and economics in the text. Nonetheless, while the conceptual framework is quite strong, the factual underpinnings are somewhat glossed over except where graphic data (tables and photos) are presented for analysis..

APPENDIX 2: FIFTEEN SOCIAL STUDIES FACTORS NECESSARY FOR STUDENTS TO UNDERSTAND

Social Studies Knowledge	Evidence from the Textbook
1. The giant capacity of the American economic system to produce goods and services	The first chapter focuses on how a new Industrial Revolution has been changing American ways of living since 1890. Sections focus on mass production and robots to increase production.
2. The lag of the ability to distribute goods and services behind the capacity to produce them	The text discusses the distribution of electric power and the time it took to electrify most of the country. The distribution difficulties in this text are focused on the inherent inequities in unrestrained capitalism and a lack of governmental planning.
3. The undue control over wealth, communication and government by a minority who believe in relatively uncontrolled individualism and who oppose social change.	The book is concerned about special interests, lobbyists and influence of the elite over the mass of American working people. It is clear that Rugg believes that entrenched power and, in many cases, political corruption have led to opposition to social change that would lessen the gap between the rich and the poor. Discussion of the Hearst newspapers spreading control of the media through mergers and Rugg's attack on yellow journalism exemplifies this (as well as explaining Hearst's role in the campaign against Rugg).
4. The nationwide commitment to democracy as maximum individual development leading to a belief that society is devoid of social classes.	The Rugg belief in democracy as the best form of government is patently clear throughout the text even as the text consistently points to gaps among the lifestyles and beliefs of the different social classes. Thus, the book focuses on social class to disabuse students of the belief that social class does not exist in America. The sections on the growth of education, private and public, do point to maximizing individual development as a means to reduce class difference but Rugg does point our the difficulty poor people have in attaining higher education.
5. The nationwide conviction that free play of intelligence among people should determine social policy.	Rugg believes that people are basically good and the reader picks this up in repeated discussions on the desire of the people to force Congress to pass the Income Tax law. Additionally Rugg discusses the American Spirit and the influence of the muckrakers as illustrations of the goodness of American intention once citizens have the facts.
6. The achievement of a structure of universal elementary education and making people literate	Rugg cites the founders of the country and traces the history of education in America in more depth than one would find in most Foundations of American Education classes at the university level. Clearly he believes in education as vital in a free society and he illustrates this by pointing to the difference in school curriculum in Nazi Germany and Fascist Italy from that of the United States.

Social Studies Knowledge	**Evidence from the Textbook**
7. The failure of mass education to practise (sic) democratic method by building a program of study and discussion of the conditions and problems of life as it is actually lived today	Here is where Rugg's spiral discussions of social class really come to light. He focuses on neighborhoods and prejudice based on income; he describes the numbers of bedrooms and bathrooms in dwellings based on income. These discussions would still not be found at this depth (if at all) in current American civics/government textbooks.
8. The lack of real understanding of the American Problem by the people, and their corresponding susceptibility to the propaganda of demagogues	Rugg spends a considerable amount of time describing the roles of participants in city governance. He explains how local party bosses come to power and influence in ways that demonstrate that Rugg believes people award this power to corrupt influence because they do not know or understand how to deal with these issues. By focusing on local politics, describing alternatives like city commissions, city planning and city managers, Rugg is attempting to change the lack of understanding and control citizens exhibit.
9. The widespread apathy of the people to matters of public concern and the inertial of potential leaders of an informed thinking citizenry.	Although alluded to in several parts of the book, the target? starting on p. 416 is a section titled "One of the Greatest Difficulties: The Indifference of Most People." Rugg then uses the example of jury-dodging (getting out of jury duty) to illustrate his point. At other earlier points in the text he also speaks of apathy in voting, lack of attention to the poor or to national issues, etc.
10. The powerful appeal of symptoms of mass suffering (caused by unemployment, poverty, disease) and the tendency of political leaders to be content with treating them superficially instead of eliminating the causes.	The descriptions of housing and education, the plight of illegal immigrants and the reality of the Great Depression are highlighted repeatedly in the book. Rugg clearly believes that passing laws, such as graduated income tax which he lauds as a reform of the people for the people, is an exception. Overall, Rugg believes that planning (his engineering background shining through here) and city management will be the solution but that political leaders are preventing this from occurring. The discussions of crime in America (pp. 394–400) exemplify this concept.
11. The fact that government in our democracy is carried on by the interplay of "interest groups." Policy making in the long run will represent the will of the people	Rugg does believe in democracy and he does discuss interest groups and lobbying in the sections on how laws are made by Congress. He illustrates for students a basic understanding of the committee system and the jockeying of interests in adding amendments and riders to bills. These discussions are much less detailed than the average American government textbook would contain today.

Social Studies Knowledge	Evidence from the Textbook
12. The success of creative minds in inventing and building powerful and world-side systems of instantaneous communication of ideas and moods among the people.	On p. 47, Rugg focuses on immigrants who became scientists and created alternating current, improved long distance telephone calls. He mentions General Electric and the spread of power and communications as well as discussing the impact of these changes in modern society. One can only imagine what this book would contain if it were being written in today's age of telecommunications and computers.
13. The danger that people will believe the propaganda of the demagogues of the press, radio and platform who offer the easy way of unthinkingly following rather than endure the hard, democratic way of study, thought, discussion, group decision and action.	Rugg is concerned with the power of advertising and the business of the media (press and radio). He is concerned with bias in the news due to influences that inhibit Americans from making good choices. Thus the book emphasizes reading multiple sources, and discussing and listening to multiple perspectives to improve democracy. The media and modern life are corrupting to the extent that neighbors see each other less and the town meeting is not attended as frequently as the size of a town increases— this leads to less hard, democratic decision making and more impersonal, boss run politics which Rugg sees as dangerous to democracy.
14. The complex interdependence of society.	A constant theme throughout the text is the danger posed by the modernization and urbanization of America. The sections on problems of cities and the changing American family illustrate this point. Rugg compares the original New England town with the modern city and seeks to have students wrestle with how to solve the problems wrought by industrialization.
15. The menace of a lack of time.	This problem is discussed only tangentially in the early part of the book when Rugg questions how Americans will use the leisure time created by labor saving devices created by industrialization. He also bemoans the lack of reading by most American and attributes this, on p. 494, to a lack of time. This point is not clearly made in the text although given today's modernization, students would have no trouble relating to this concept.

REFERENCES

The American Legion. (1941). *Rugg Philosophy Analyzed* (Vol. II). Indianapolis, IN: National Americanism Commission, The American Legion.

Apple, M. W., & Christian-Smith, L. K. (1991). The politics of the textbook. In M. W. Apple & L. K. Christian-Smith (Eds.), *The politics of the textbook* (pp. 1–21). New York: Routledge.

Billings, N. (1929). *A determination of the generalizations basic to the social studies curriculum.* York, PA: Maple Press.

Boesenberg, E., & Poland, K. S. (2001). Struggle at the frontier of curriculum: The Rugg textbook controversy in Binghamton, NY. *Theory and Research in Social Education, 29*(4), 640–671.

Committee Report of the NEA. (1934). Our social-economic situation and the new education. *Journal of Educational Sociology, 7*(9), 533–534.

Cremin, L. (1961). *The transformation of the school.* New York: Vintage Books.

Gellerman, W. (1938). The American Legion as educator. *American Sociological Review, 82*(5), 763–764.

Fish, Jr., H. (1931, July). *The Forum, 29*, 42.

Hicks, H. (1941). Ours is to reason why. *The American Legion Magazine,* (May), 50, 54.

Hicks, H., (1952). Ours to reason why. *The American Legion Magazine, 1952*(6), 10.

Jones, O. E. (1957). *Activities of the american legion in textbook analysis and criticism, 1938–1951.* Doctoral Dissertation, University of Oklahoma.

Kuhn, I. C. (1952). Your child is their target. *The American Legion Magazine, 52* (18/19), 54–60.

Legation of the United States of America, Pretoria, Union of South Africa (1933). Letter to the Secretary of State, Washington D.C., 28 August, National Archives, Box 14, 542.AP, 1/1.

Muschinske, D. (1974). American life, the social studies and Harold Rugg. *Social Studies, 65*(6), 246–249.

Nelson, M. R. (1977). The development of the Rugg social studies materials. *Theory and Research in Social Education, 5*(3), 64–83.

Nelson, M. R. (1978). Rugg on Rugg: His theories and his curriculum. *Curriculum Inquiry, 8*(2), 119–132.

Nelson, M. R., & Singleton, H. W. (1978). Governmental surveillance of three progressive educators. Paper presented at the annual meeting of the American Educational Research Association (Toronto, ON, March 27–31).

Nelson, M. R. (1982). The Rugg Brothers in social education. *Journal of Thought, 17*(3), 69–82.

NewsBulletin. (1940, 16 December). National Publicity Division, The American Legion, Indianapolis, Indiana. Cited in Jones (1957) *Activities of the American Legion in Textbooks.* Doctoral Dissertation, University of Oklahoma.

Norton, J. K. (1934). Proceedings of the National Education Association Annual Meeting. pp. 33–34.

Odum, H. W. (1934). A New Deal popular bookshelf: How much social realism, how much social science, how much grinding grist? *Social Forces, 12*(4), 604.

Oliver, A. (1996). Becoming right: Education and the formation of conservative movements. In Michael A. Apple (Ed.) *Cultural politics and education* (pp. 42–67). New York: Teachers College Press.

Proceedings of the National Education Association. (1934). Washington, DC: The National Education Association.

Redefer, F. L. (1939). Letter from Frederick L. Redefer, Executive Secretary of the Progressive Education Association to Ben Cherrington, United States Department of State, Washington, D.C., Division of Cultural Relations, 24 October 1939. In *Program of the New Education Fellowship Meeting* files, National Archives, 811.427 10, Washington–Education/605.

Riley, K. L., & Stern, B. S. (2002). "A bootlegged curriculum": The American Legion versus Harold Rugg," *International Journal of Social Education, 17*(2),62–72.

Rugg, H. O. (1931). *Problems of American culture.* Boston, MA: Ginn and Company.

Rugg, H. O. (1939). Curriculum-design in the social sciences: What I believe . . . . In James A. Michner (Ed.). *The Future of the Social Studies* (pp. 140–158). Cambridge, MA: National Council for the Social Studies.

Rugg, H. O. (1940). *Citizenship and civic affairs.* Boston, MA: Ginn and Co.

Sabine, G. H., Mitchell, W. C., & the American Committee for Democracy and Intellectual Freedom. Committee on Textbooks (1942). *The text books of Harold Rugg, an analysis.* New York: American Committee for Democracy and Intellectual Freedom.

Shumaker, R. W. (1941). No "New Order" for our schools. *The American Legion Magazine, 1941*(6), 5.

CHAPTER 2

MAURICE P. HUNT AND LAWRENCE E. METCALF

Teaching High School Social Studies— Reflective Thinking, Closed Areas of Culture, Problem Solving Models, and Values in Social Studies

Sherry L. Field, Jeff Passe, Mary Lee Webeck, and Michelle Bauml

In the field of social studies, Hunt and Metcalf[1] are best known for their scholarship in secondary social studies methods. They co-authored two editions of *Teaching High School Social Studies* (1955, 1968), both of which continue to be influential in contemporary social studies educational thought. In their work together, singly, and with other co-authors, they advocated for deep and reflective thinking about solving real problems in American society and recognized the key role that teachers play in that endeavor.

---

[1] Maurice P. Hunt and Lawrence E. Metcalf bonded while they were doctoral students together at The Ohio State University in the 1940s. As graduate students, they had the opportunity to work with Boyd Bode, Alan Griffin, and H. Gordon Hullfish, who were decided influences upon both Hunt's and Metcalf's scholarship, their stances toward active learning in the secondary school classrooms, and their respective research agendas. Each began and continued academic careers throughout their lives, Hunt at Fresno State University and Metcalf at the University of Illinois.

Teaching and Studying Social Issues: Major Programs and Approaches, pages 31–42

Four memorable concepts emerged from *Teaching High School Social Studies*: reflective thinking, closed areas of culture, problem solving models, and values in social studies, all of which will be discussed in this chapter. The chapter concludes with thoughts from contemporary scholars on the influence of Hunt and Metcalf's work.

REFLECTIVE THINKING

Hunt and Metcalf's ideas about reflective theory, and, later, reflective thinking, were heavily influenced by the philosophy and educational thought of numerous scholars and seminal figures in the field of education: John Dewey (Field, Webeck, & Robertson, 2007; Passe, 2007); H. Gordon Hullfish, Hunt's mentor at The Ohio State University (Webeck, Robertson, & Field, 2007); and Alan Griffin, Metcalf's mentor at the same university (Metcalf, 1963). In 1963 Metcalf stated that "although the fact has not been generally recognized, Griffin stands almost alone in his attempt to elaborate in practical and theoretical terms what reflective theory means for teaching history and for the subject-matter preparation of high school history teacher" (p. 934). Metcalf (1963) went on to say that Griffin's (1942) dissertation "ranks as a major intellectual achievement in social studies education within the past two decades" (p. 934). And both Hunt and Metcalf (1968) commented that within their own work, "the imprint of H. Gordon Hullfish's thinking will... be visible, particularly in the ...interpretation of moral conflicts in representing choice between competing goods" (acknowledgements page, n.p.). Hullfish, coauthor of *Reflective Thinking: The Method of Education* (Hullfish & Smith, 1961), advocated reflective thinking as a method of learning and a means for attaining freedom. In fact, for Hullfish and Smith, developing reflective, independent thinkers was an important endeavor for the teacher.

TEACHING HIGH SCHOOL SOCIAL STUDIES

Upon its publication, and thereafter, *Teaching High School Social Studies* (Hunt & Metcalf, 1955) was widely considered to be both innovative and creative. Fully half of the textbook was devoted to the *theory* upon which the practice of social studies teaching should be built. This stands in stark contrast to contemporary social studies methods textbooks, which generally refer to theory but its prominence is typically slight.

Hunt and Metcalf felt compelled to address theory in a good amount of detail for three major reasons. First, their theoretical stance was radically different from other social studies educators, and they wanted to make the whys and hows of that explicit. Second, the field of teacher education had a very different set of circumstances than it does today in that the largest teacher education institutions in the country had laboratory schools connected to their programs. Because the express intent of laboratory schools was to connect theory to practice, it seemed logical to Hunt and Metcalf that an emphasis on theory would be among the foremost criteria when professors from such institutions selected a methods textbook. Third, in an emerging field of study, theoretical discussion was seen as a priority.

Hunt and Metcalf's elaboration of theoretical underpinnings did not last over time, however. By the time the second edition of *Teaching High School Social Studies* was published over a decade later (1968), they had revised the text substantially, and the role of theory was vastly reduced. In the Preface to their second edition they stated that they felt compelled to simplify and concretize their approach due to the fact that some readers of the first edition complained about its difficulty for the beginning student. Readers also asserted that "insufficient attention had been given to the how-to-do-it aspects" (Hunt & Metcalf, 1968, p. vii).

Tellingly, Cox and Massialas (1967) opened their book, *Social Studies in the United States: A Critical Approach,* with a tribute to the prescience of Hunt and Metcalf in predicting the future of social studies. In doing so, they stated that

> [i]t is increasingly clear that there are changes afoot in social studies. Not the least of these was heralded...by Hunt and Metcalf's *Teaching High School Social Studies.* Perhaps more than any other single publication, this text in social studies education clearly predicted future trends in the field. Hunt and Metcalf asserted in 1955 that social education in a democracy demands a "much greater emphasis on developing higher thought processes, with all that this implies for reflective examination of critical social issues." They predicted that the social studies curriculum would "eventually rely heavily on data supplied by social scientists, particularly in the fields of sociology, anthropology, psychology, and psychiatry." The demand, they hypothesized, was for a more systematic means of social judgment in a democracy; the curriculum trend would necessarily be toward a wider spectrum of social knowledge, emphasizing the disciplines of social analysis. (Cox & Massialas, 1967, p. 1)

CLOSED AREAS OF CULTURE

During their collaboration, Hunt and Metcalf were aligned with sociological and anthropological contemporary thought. They believed that through the intensive study of culture, democracy in the United States would not only be analyzed, discussed, and debated but also preserved. Their understanding of appropriate pedagogy for accomplishing this daunting task were teaching strategies that utilized discussion, problem solving, and reflection. Hunt and Metcalf (1968) challenged teachers to embrace reflective teaching through discussion of what they called "closed areas" of a culture—or, certain areas of conflicting belief and behavior...[in which people] usually react to problems blindly and emotionally" (p. 26). Hunt and Metcalf urged teachers to move beyond traditional problems, such as war or balance of power between the legislative, executive, and judicial branches, in their problem-solving lessons. Instead, they urged teachers to engage students in thoughtful discussions about deep and troubling societal problems. These closed areas of culture, they argued, were most likely ignored in secondary social studies classroom discussions of the day. Furthermore, if the closed areas did receive attention in schools, Hunt and Metcalf believed, it was attention of an uncritical nature.

The use of the term "closed" was interesting. It indicated that the problems were not discussed rationally, if they were discussed at all. Thus, important issues that would enhance both student interest in and understanding of secondary social studies, and more importantly, the society in which they lived, were essentially locked out. Examples of closed areas provided by Hunt and Metcalf (1968) included:

1. Power and the law;
2. Religion and morality;
3. Race and minority group relations;
4. Social class;
5. Sex, courtship and marriage;
6. Nationalism and patriotism; and
7. Economics (p. 27).

Hunt and Metcalf believed that by keeping closed areas inaccessible, students lose any long-term interest in social science content. By 1968, Hunt and Metcalf changed the category of "closed areas" to "problematic areas of culture" because the society had begun to address them to some degree.[2]

Aligning the future of social studies research with that of Hunt and Metcalf and their predecessors, Edgar B. Wesley (1950) proposed five objectives for studying world history that undergird the purposes of advocating open and free discussions of the closed topics advocated by Hunt and Met-

---

[2]Still, the authors of this chapter contend that many of the social categories that were closed in 1955 and that were considered problematic in 1968 might unfortunately still be considered problematic by some in schools today. We do recognize, however, that attention emanating from exciting research in social justice (Brown & Brown, in press; Wade, 2007), multicultural citizenship education (Dilworth, 2004; Marri, 2008; Mathews & Dilworth, 2008), multicultural democratic education (Marri, 2005), and critical multicultural citizenship (Castro, 2009) and ensuing conversations in the field hold great promise for the future.

calf. More specifically, Wesley (1950) suggested that the study of world history provides for:

1. An overview of the contemporary world;
2. An introduction to world problems;
3. The recognition that culture is international;
4. The derivation and application of generalizations; and
5. The understanding of the world of tomorrow.

In gauging the impact of the introduction of the concept of "closed aspects" of society to the American school curriculum by Hunt and Metcalf, we know that many of their colleagues referred to closed areas in their work (Passe, 2007; Webeck, Robertson, & Field, 2007). For example, Massialas, Sprague, and Hurst (1975) turned to Hunt and Metcalf's ideas about studying interpersonal and intrapersonal social conflicts and paying special attention to the closed areas in our culture: power and the law, nationalism and patriotism, religion and morality, economics and business, race and minority-group relations, social class and customs, and sex, courtship, and marriage.

PROBLEM SOLVING MODEL

In addition to proposing that closed areas of society be opened for discussion, Hunt and Metcalf maintained that if a teacher were to do this, the use of a "problem solving model" was essential. This assertion reveals Dewey's influence on Hunt and Metcalf's ideas about problem solving as a reflective process. In their discussion of contemporary social studies models which included that of Hunt and Metcalf, Nelson and Michaelis (1980) point to Dewey's (1933) influence on reflective thinking and reflective decision-making that included phases such as:

1. Perplexity, confusion, doubt, due to the fact that one is implicated in an incomplete situation whose full character is not yet determined;
2. A conjectural anticipation—a tentative interpretation of the given elements attributing to them a tendency to affect certain consequences;
3. A careful survey (examination, inspection, exploration, analysis) of all attainable consideration which will define and clarify the problem at hand;
4. A consequent elaboration of the tentative hypothesis to make it more precise and more consistent…;

5. Taking one stand upon the projected hypothesis as a plan of action which is applied to the existing state of affairs: doing something overtly to bring about the anticipated result, and thereby testing the hypothesis (cited in Nelson & Michaelis, 1980, p. 91).

Like other models of thinking and problem solving in the social studies (see Nelson & Michaelis, 1980), Hunt and Metcalf's model extended Dewey's ideas and applied them directly to social studies instruction.

The Hunt and Metcalf Problem Solving Model (Hunt & Metcalf, 1968) continues to be used by contemporary social studies educators such as Nelson and Michaelis (1980, p. 151) and Evans and Saxe (1996). This Problem Solving Model, developed by Hunt and Metcalf for their first edition of *Teaching High School Social Studies* (1955), was also an important centerpiece of the second edition in 1968.

Nelson and Michaelis (1980) reference Hunt and Metcalf's (1955, 1968) Reflective Thought Model as one of the earliest models conceptualized for the social studies, preceding Nelson's Model of Inquiry, Fenton's Mode of Inquiry, and Cassidy and Kurfman's Decision-Making Process. The Hunt and Metcalf Reflective Thought Model included a series of steps including the following: defining a problem, formulating hypotheses and considering their logical implications, testing hypotheses, and articulating a conclusion.

Across the nation, social studies teachers seeking instructional approaches to promote classroom discussion and open dialogue adopted The Problem Solving Model and found it both useful and practical for clarifying values about controversial topics (Field, Webeck, & Robertson, 2007). Oliver and Shaver (1966) proposed that Hunt and Metcalf's work was also instrumental in clarifying values conflicts: "These authors suggest that conflict between two values may be resolved by referring to a more basic third value upon which there is agreement" (p. 34). Similarly, Charles S. Hyneman (1965) suggested that teachers, while employing pedagogical methods found in the problem-solving and values-clarification models, ensure that the learning experience of students:

...should be one of examining positions; of making an inventory of value holdings; of confirming, reshaping, and rejecting premises; of enlarging vision and sharpening focus, of throwing off old habits and fixing new habits of working and thinking; of developing know-how for getting evidence, evaluating evidence, and extending evidence by reasoning. (pp. 218–219)

Problem solving discussions advocated by Hunt and Metcalf were amplified by other social studies researchers. For example, Nelson and Michaelis (1980) suggested that teachers use an inquiry or reflective thinking model by first:

drawing attention to the purpose of the model, then defin[ing] the problem, stat[ing] a hypothesis, refin[ing] it, collect[ing] evidence and draw[ing] a conclusion," with additional time spent for "discussing rules…defining terms and giving examples, learning to be critical by discussing the topic and not making personal remarks, and exploring how mutual respect helps to create an atmosphere that encourages all students to participate. (p. 150)

VALUES AND SOCIAL STUDIES

Bringing values and moral conflict to the forefront of social studies education also gained Maurice Hunt and Lawrence Metcalf attention during the era of the New Social Studies and into the 1970s. Values clarification, values awareness, and other forms of values education gained attention at the same time. According to Hunt and Metcalf (1955), "social studies teachers must focus on 'questions of policy at the level of moral conflict' if they want moral education to be something more than indoctrination in the right virtues" (p. 90). These authors drew a sharp distinction between methods of instruction that emphasize the importance of choice in the face of two conflicting goods and those methods that merely differentiate good from evil. It is the former approach to instruction in values that represents the crux of moral education. More specifically, as Lange (1975) states:

> If the difficult decisions of life involved only choices between good and evil, where would be the problem? Who would deliberately choose evil? Unfortunately, moral choice is not this simple. It never involves merely distinguishing between right and wrong. For a person making a choice, moral decision requires distinguishing between two or more good things. It is when at least two desired courses of action come into conflict that moral choice becomes necessary (p. 279).

Hunt and Metcalf provided teachers with an outline of the teaching procedures for dealing with both conceptual and empirical aspects of valuation. According to the outline, teachers should first engage students in defining the nature of the object, event, or policy being evaluated. This would include student analysis and deliberation to specify criteria for defining the issue. Next, anticipated consequences of the issue or problem should be explored with special attention given to the use of evidence to support valuation. Throughout the process, disagreements among students are to be treated as enriching grounds for deeper discussions. In the final stage, after possible consequences of the issue have been explored, students identify criteria for evaluating the desirability of those consequences. Hunt and Metcalf believed that this type of model could help teachers solicit "intentional definitions of value concepts" (Hunt & Metcalf, 1968, p. 139) among students and thus instill habits of reflective thought upon values. Therefore, the question of what to do with students' divergent views on controversial topics, for Hunt and Metcalf, was to bring them to the surface for closer examination, reflection and discussion. Likewise, the question of a teacher sharing personal positions on topics with students was an important one, and one that was later deliberated by Banks and Clegg (1973), who believed that a teacher:

> …cannot and should not be asked to assume a neutral position when discussing such explosive topics as racism, legalized abortion, artificial contraceptives, and women's liberation. To demand that a teacher be neutral on such issues is, as Hunt and Metcalf cogently argue, "to deny him the freedom and right to voice his opinion openly in a public forum. (p. 333)

They suggest that the teacher should express opinions at an appropriate time but after the students have had ample time to arrive at their own positions and …deal with social issues honestly and openly.

Massialas, Sprague, and Hurst (1975) also drew upon the work of Hunt and Metcalf in their book, *Social Issues Through Inquiry*, as did Jack Fraenkel (1980) in his *Helping Students Think and Value: Strategies for Teaching the Social Studies* by noting the pedagogical significance of the study of and discussion of controversial issues. Fraenkel (1980) applied Hunt and Metcalf's ideas for teaching about controversial issues in a vignette that continues to be relevant today: the intervention of the United States in the affairs of other nations. This vignette, in a chapter entitled "Teaching Strategies for Developing Valuing," was meant to prompt discussion during a class setting using Hunt and Metcalf's model:

> The value term involved in the statement must be clearly defined, and the consequences of following this particular policy assessed. Accordingly, one of your first tasks is to help students analyze and arrive at a clear definition of the term….(Fraenkel, 1980, p. 256)

Elsewhere in his book, Fraenkel (1980) provided a series of questions from Hunt and Metcalf as an effective strategy to elicit responses from students after viewing a movie:

1. Some incidents in the movie are more important than others. Which incidents or scenes seem to you to be the most important?
2. Why do you think these incidents are important? What makes them significant as far as you are concerned?
3. How could each situation be improved so as to contribute to the growth of everyone in the situation? (Hunt & Metcalf, 1968, p. 257 as cited in Fraenkel, 1980, p. 338).

The last question in particular signifies Hunt and Metcalf's concern for moving students beyond thinking about the self to considering a solution for the betterment of all.

A LASTING PRESENCE

A scholar's longevity and lasting influence can be partially measured by a continued presence in contemporary academic literature, which could be considered especially true if the academic literature is devoted to one of the scholar's key area of interest. For example, in 1996, *NCSS* [National Council for the Social Studies] *Bulletin 93* was devoted to teaching social issues. Within the pages of the latter, which was officially entitled *Handbook on Teaching Social Issues* and edited by Ronald Evans and David Saxe, many of its 44 chapters, either directly or indirectly, built on Hunt and Metcalf's secondary social studies education scholarship which was conducted some forty and fifty years earlier.

A series of interviews[3] with leading scholars in the field of social studies education indicated that their own study of Hunt and Metcalf came well into their educational careers, usually at the graduate level. Upon exposure to the topic of reflective teaching, one scholar, Linda Levstik, now a Professor of Social Studies Education at the University of Kentucky, said, "it struck a chord." Another, Carole L. Hahn, Charles Howard Candler Professor of Comparative Education and Social Studies Education at Emory University, said that the Metcalf volume on values "confirmed my belief." A third respondent, William Stanley, was using a problem-solving approach that was "not as sophisticated" as the Hunt-Metcalf approach, and was able to adapt various aspects.

The delay in learning about Hunt and Metcalf can be attributed to the authors' writing style. It was often described by the respondents as "dense" and "difficult." To address that obstacle, almost all of the scholars now use Hunt and Metcalf in very specific ways:

1. Always with advanced masters or doctoral students;
2. Usually with excerpts or abridgements; and
3. Frequently tied in with other approaches (e.g., Engle and Ochoa).

---

[3]Interviews were conducted by Jeff Passe in September, 2008, with Michael Berson (University of South Florida), Ronald Evans (San Diego State University), Carole Hahn (Emory University), Diana Hess (University of Wisconsin), John Hoge (University of Georgia), Linda Levstik (University of Kentucky), Murry Nelson (Pennsylvania State University), Walter Parker (University of Washington), Nancy Patterson (Bowling Green State University), Mark Previte (Penn State—Altoona), and William Stanley (Monmouth University).

As a result of these adaptations, the Hunt and Metcalf methods textbook is not used to teach methods today. Instead, it is typically used to promote curricular goals (e.g., problem-solving, controversial issues, values education) or to provide insight into the theoretical foundations that undergird modern social studies instructional techniques. Thus, although Hunt and Metcalf wrote their textbook for use by pre-service educators, it has evolved into an advanced graduate-level reference.

Part of the explanation for Hunt and Metcalf's indirect impact has to do with the times in which their textbook was written. The 1955 edition, which was truly seminal, was out of print by the time most of today's scholars were studying to become teachers. The 1968 edition, which may have been more contemporary, appeared during a time of great social unrest, when radical ideas (in education and elsewhere) were fairly common. Furthermore, their book was simply one of many at the time that addressed values, problem solving, and reflection. Be that as it may, now some 50 years later, the revolutionary ideas that Hunt and Metcalf advocated have become standard elements in social studies methods texts. That pattern, moving from new ideas to one among many, gradually becoming standard, is a basic model for intellectual impact.

The most-referenced aspect of Hunt and Metcalf's work appears to be the concept of closed areas of culture. The idea of closed areas of culture truly began with Hunt and Metcalf. It continues to resonate today among scholars old and young. One veteran professor and a leader in the movement for issues-centered education, Ronald Evans, a Professor of Social Studies at San Diego State University, described himself as "stunned" when he first read about closed areas. Several new faculty members, including Nancy Patterson, have expressed how impressed they were to learn that those ideas were introduced so long ago.

Yet, as noted earlier, some closed areas remain unopened. For all of their substantial impact on the writing and teaching on almost all of today's scholars, their influence on the teaching of social studies may be less apparent. It appears that Hunt and Metcalf have made a major contribution to the thinking of social studies scholars, but that influence does not necessarily extend inside the classroom door to areas of contemporary curriculum and pedagogy. That said, we can and should be heartened by the work of teachers and scholars who continue to be committed to social justice and in bringing about change in curriculum and schooling.

CONCLUSION

Maurice P. Hunt and Lawrence E. Metcalf, whose work in social studies was most influential from 1950 through 1996 (Hunt & Metcalf, 1996) would most likely want to be remembered for the stance they took toward social studies curriculum and pedagogy. They would want to be remembered for expanding Dewey's notions of learning. They would want to be remembered for introducing and passionately promoting the inclusion of closed areas of society into the curriculum. They would want to be remembered for the values that they introduced pedagogically and embraced personally. They would want to be remembered for creating a prominent model for reflective thinking, problem solving, and discussion. But most of all, they would want to be remembered as social studies researchers and practitioners who revealed problems in society, in the social studies curriculum and in classroom practice, and sought to solve them.

REFERENCES

Banks, J. A., & Clegg, Jr., A. A. (1973). *Teaching strategies for the social studies: Inquiry, valuing, and decision-making.* Reading, MA: Addison-Wesley Publishing Company.

Brown, A. L., & Brown, K. (2010). Strange fruit indeed: Interrogating contemporary textbook representations of racial violence towards African Americans. *Teachers College Record.*

Castro, A. J. (2009). *Promoting critical multicultural citizenship: A case study of preparing social studies teachers.* The University of Texas at Austin: Unpublished doctoral dissertation.

Cox, C. B., & Massialas, B. G. (1967). *Social studies in the United States: A critical approach.* New York: Harcourt, Brace, & World, Inc.

Dewey, J. (1933). *How we think.* Boston, MA: Heath.

Dilworth, P. P. (2004). Multicultural citizenship education: Case studies from social studies classrooms. *Theory and Research in Social Education, 33*(2), 153–186.

Evans, R. W., & Saxe, D.W. (1996). *Handbook on teaching social issues: NCSS Bulletin 93.* Washington, D.C.: National Council for the Social Studies.

Field, S. L., Webeck, M. L., & Robertson, S. (2007). Maurice P. Hunt: Activist teacher, scholar, collaborator. In S. Totten & J. E. Pedersen (Eds.), *Addressing social issues in the classroom and beyond: The pedagogical efforts of pioneers in the field* (pp. 187–200). Charlotte, NC: Information Age Publishing.

Fraenkel, J. R. (1980). *Helping students think and value: Strategies for teaching the social studies* (2nd ed.). Englewood Cliffs, NJ: Prentice-Hall, Inc.

Griffin, A. F. (1942). *A philosophical approach to the subject matter preparation of history.* Unpublished dissertation, Ohio State University.

Hullfish, H. G., & Smith, P. G. (1961). *Reflective thinking: The method of education.* New York: Dodd, Mead.

Hunt, M. P., & Metcalf, L. E. (1955, 1968). *Teaching high school social studies.* New York: Harper and Row.

Hunt, M. P., & Metcalf, L. E. (1996). Rational inquiry on society's closed areas. In Walter C. Parker (Ed.) *Educating the democratic mind* (pp. 97–116). Albany, NY: State University of New York Press.

Hyneman, C. S. (1965). Some crucial learning experiences: A personal view. In R. H. Connery (Ed.), *Teaching political science* (pp. 217–237). Durham, NC: Duke University Press.

Lange, D. (1975). Moral education and the social studies. *Theory into Practice, 14*(4), 279–285.

Marri, A. R. (2005). Building a framework for classroom-based multicultural democratic education: Learning from three skilled teachers. *Teachers College Record, 107*(5), 1036–1059.

Marri, A. R. (2008). Connecting diversity, justice, and democratic citizenship: Lessons from an alternative U.S. History class. In J. S. Bixby & J. L. Pace (Eds.), *Educating democratic citizens in troubled times: Qualitative studies of current efforts* (pp. 58–80). Albany, New York: State University of New York Press.

Massialas, B. G., Sprague, N. F., & Hurst, J. B. (1975). *Social issues through inquiry: Coping in an age of crises.* Englewood Cliffs, NJ: Prentice-Hall, Inc.

Mathews, S. A., & Dilworth, P. P. (2008). Case studies of preservice teachers' ideas about the role of multicultural citizenship education in social studies. *Theory and Research in Social Education, 36*(4), 356–390.

Metcalf, L. E. (1963). Research on teaching the social studies. In N. L. Gage (Ed.) *Handbook of research on teaching* (pp. 929–966). Chicago, IL: Rand McNally.

Nelson, J. L., & Michaelis, J. U. (1980). *Secondary social studies: Instruction, curriculum, evaluation.* Englewood Cliffs, NJ: Prentice-Hall, Inc.

Oliver, D. P., & Shaver, J. P. (1966). *Teaching public issues in the high school.* Boston, MA: Houghton Mifflin Company.

Passe, J. (2007). Lawrence E. Metcalf: In the right place at the right time. In S. Totten & J. E. Pedersen (Eds.), *Addressing social issues in the classroom and beyond: The pedagogical efforts of pioneers in the field* (pp. 235–252). Charlotte, NC: Information Age Publishing.

Wade, R. (2007). *Teaching social studies for social justice.* New York: Teachers College Press.

Webeck, M. L., Robertson, S., & Field, S. L. (2007). H. Gordon Hullfish: Teacher, reflective thinker, democratic defender, . In Samuel Totten and Jon E. Pedersen (Eds.) *Addressing social issues in the classroom and beyond: The pedagogical efforts of pioneers in the field* (pp. 71–80). Charlotte, NC: Information Age Publishing.

Wesley, E. B. (1950). *Teaching social studies in high schools* (3rd ed.). Boston, MA: Heath.

CHAPTER 3

CITIZENSHIP EDUCATION USING RATIONAL DECISION MAKING

Donald Oliver, James Shaver, and Fred Newmann's Public Issues Model

Barbara Slater Stern

In a republican nation whose citizens are to be led by reason and persuasion and not by force, the art of reasoning becomes of first importance.—Thomas Jefferson to David Harding, 1824.

Teaching young people the specifics of civic engagement is, arguably, the crucial component of creating a democratic self and society. "In creating a democratic self, young people need to learn how to bring their fellow citizens together around common concerns; how to give a (loud but articulate) voice to their ideas, support, and objections; how to persevere when faced with disagreement or opposition; and how to not lose heart when they have lost a battle.—Education Commission of the States, 2000

Teaching and Studying Social Issues: Major Programs and Approaches, pages 43–65
Copyright © 2011 by Information Age Publishing

43

INTRODUCTION

From the Founding Fathers to current times, preparing students for democratic citizenship has been at the forefront of American aims regarding education. Yet by all accounts traditional approaches to citizenship education have not achieved their desired effect (Griffin, 1942; National Center for Learning and Citizenship, 2004). Civic engagement as measured by knowledge, beliefs, skills, and active participation of Americans is widely reported to be less than desirable on measures such as knowledge of United States history, tolerance and willingness to compromise, civil disputation, and voting in local, state and national elections (National Council for the Social Studies, 1992). While social studies/history teachers are not the only educators charged with promoting citizenship, a job so important that *all* educators need to be concerned with this aspect of their profession, it is certainly true that the bulk of citizenship preparation falls within the parameters of the social studies curriculum in our schools. Thus the question arises: How can social studies teachers be more effective in the preparation of their students for their responsibilities as citizens in our democracy?

This chapter explores that question by focusing on the work of Donald W. Oliver, James P. Shaver, and Fred M. Newmann and the Harvard Social Studies Project (HSSP). The HSSP was developed in the late 1960s and early 1970s as part of the educational reform movement known as the New Social Studies. One spin-off project, also known as the *Public Issues Series*, offered teachers an interdisciplinary curriculum approach coupled with instructional strategies that focused on cultivating rational decision-making as a basis for examining controversies that occur when conflicts arise over traditional American values.

The intention of the project was to improve the teaching of history/social studies with the goal of helping students analyze and discuss persisting human dilemmas related to public issues in a democratic setting (Oliver & Newmann, 1967a). Despite a seemingly inherent interest on the part of students to the pressing issues of the day, teachers (both then and now) were reluctant to broach controversial issues in class due to being fearful of the emotions aroused in students and concerns expressed by some administrators and parents. Thus, the materials were never widely adopted. Although some social studies teachers today continue to implement specific strategies suggested by Oliver and his associates (e.g. Socratic discussion or the jurisprudential instructional model), teaching controversial issues in the secondary classroom is possibly rarer now than it was in the turbulent era of the 1960s when the materials were developed.

Although some of the Public Issues Series materials have been updated and released for purchase from the Social Science Education Consortium, most of the Public Issues Series is currently out of print. The instructional methods suggested are still widely promulgated by social studies teacher educators but are shied away from by classroom teachers who are under significant pressure from No Child Left Behind (NCLB) legislation. That is due to the fact that NCLB requires states to undertake standardized testing that, in general, is incompatible with the pace and type of learning required when studying social issues (including student research and open discussions and debate, which are time-consuming). Furthermore, the study of social issues readily lends itself to evaluative instruments such as research papers and essays versus the closed end, short answer format found on most standardized tests.

That said, herein an argument is made as to why the teaching model and materials of the *Harvard Social Studies Project/Public Issues Series* are still relevant and deserve careful consideration by classroom teachers as a way both to revitalize the teaching of history/social studies and to focus on the mission of preparing citizens for our democratic society.

BACKGROUND AND RESEARCH BASE

As early as 1957, Donald Oliver was struggling with the issue regarding the type of content that was most apropos for social studies courses offered in public schools in the United States ("Selection of Content in the Social Studies" (Oliver, 1966a). In his introduction to "Selection of Content in the Social Studies," Oliver (1966a) contends that "defining adequate criteria for the content to be taught has to be rethought due to two changes: the knowledge accrued from the relatively new behavioral sciences and the concurrent belief that humans can control their own destinies if only they could learn to cooperate with one another" (p. 17). Speaking more specifically of the expansion of subject matter in the social studies, Oliver (1966a) asserts that "[o]nce the social science curriculum is consciously molded by the belief that direct morality should be taught via social science content—rather than the use of such content only to clarify moral issues—the door is open to an inevitable expansion of the social studies into ethical areas which have to be thought through clearly" (p. 17).

Continuing, Oliver (1966a) makes a distinction between the social sciences as separate academic disciplines and as general education marking the difference as the fact that the social sciences as subject matter "presumably, will contribute to the general intellectual competence of all citizenry" (p. 7). Oliver illustrates this point by using an example from the study of history, specifically the Jacksonian Age of United States history, stating that a teacher, proceeding from an academic discipline point of view, might select particular content from this Age because of personal interest or in a hope of sparking student interest for the simple sake of knowing. Thus, from a disciplinary standpoint, the justification of any content in a given academic subject is quite simple—it is whatever the teacher decides he or she wishes to teach which will increase student knowledge of that content.

When addressing the general education position, Oliver (1966a) confronts the question "How does one justify choosing particular content areas and giving them priority over others?" (p. 18). As Oliver (1966a) noted, the trend, largely put in place by curriculum developers and textbook companies, was to continually increase the scope of the survey courses in order to include an ever-widening range of what is taught. ". . . e.g., the yearly extension of 'United States History' courses to include contemporary events; and the current popularity of the courses commonly called 'World Civilization,' which literally cover recorded history from the first caveman to the last atom" (p. 18). To even attempt to teach such a course was, according to Oliver (1966a), "absurd" (p. 18). It is, of course, no less absurd today, although teachers are still charged with trying to accomplish this impossible feat. Oliver (1966a) went on to posit a question along the following lines: If teachers cannot teach in their entirety the methodology and/or substantive content found in the social sciences, and assuming that some knowledge is more valuable in citizenship education than other information, how does the teacher (or, today, the state in developing standards) select and justify the content to be taught?

At this point, Oliver reviews four scholarly organizations that had, over the years, tackled this very problem; and in doing so, he traces the trajectory of history/social studies curriculum development from the Report on the Committee of Seven of the American Historical Association published in 1899 through the Preliminary Report of the Committee on Concepts and Values of the National Council for the Social Studies in 1956. Ultimately, it became apparent to him that no matter whether teachers were urged to implement a subject matter approach or a thematic approach, the actual content (be it geography, economics, cultural sociology, political science or history), "ironically remain the same" (p. 21).

Oliver (1966a) also notes the difficulties presented by the thematic approach recommended in the 1956 report by the Committee on Concepts and Values of the National Council for the Social Studies for he argues that it "indiscriminately mix[ed] moral dicta with social science directives" (p. 24): "If the Themes are interpreted as values or moral directives, they leave little choice but to seek social science data that might bear out the 'fact' that the values actually do imply 'correct' conduct, e.g. if war is 'bad,' we demonstrate that war has never paid off" (p. 24). Of course, historically such claims could not be substantiated.

Oliver continues with his discussion of the 1956 report by condemning the failure of the Themes to deal with the relationship between knowledge and values and their confounding of various types of knowledge. The latter is related to "an implicit but important set of assumptions endorsing the ultimate goodness of man and the perfect ability of human societies. They [the Themes] fail to consider the possibility that the fundamental problems which face man may be unending because of the nature of man himself" (p. 25). Here Oliver adds that the notion of perfectibility has deep roots in American society. The problem, though, as Oliver notes, is that people may be not be perfectible. He further argues that if all people are perfect then society should be perfect and vice versa. Oliver argues that no one can agree on what constitutes "perfect," and that results in a host of conflicting ideologies amongst and between various stakeholders—the state and its citizens, parents and teachers, the school system and teachers, et. al. Oliver sees the inevitable result as a conflict of deeply held, and generally legitimate, value claims.[1] Given that reality, he posits the significant question: How do we decide what to teach and how to teach it?

At this point Oliver is clearly searching for a basic value in American society around which to organize a social science curriculum. He decides, *a priori*, that the basic value is the "dignity and worth of the individual" often known as the Judeo-Christian ethic. Oliver (1966a) states that as education functions as a bulwark of our society, the fundamental value judgment must be "a citizen should have maximum freedom of individual choice in shaping his own destiny, in pursuing his own personal fulfillment" (p. 28). He stresses that this is, in U.S. society, an almost sacred value. It is important to note that he does not justify the latter but rather simply accepts it as a starting point for social studies education. Ultimately, his position was corroborated and reinforced by two of his former doctoral students and co-authors, James Shaver and Fred Newmann (personal communication, March 7, 2005) as a given.

That said, it stands to reason in a diverse, or "multi-value," society like the United States that conflict will arise. As Oliver (1966a) states: "We[2] have made the assumption that a free society will tend inevitably to have severe conflicts over the definition of public policy because of the variety of choices made by individuals and groups about the conditions they perceive as leading to personal fulfillment as well as the variety of definitions of what type of fulfillment are desirable" (p. 29).

---

[1]Many today may reject Oliver's assertion cum assumption that different value claims are legitimate. Be that as it may, what many teachers try to do today is teach that individuals should show tolerance for different viewpoints. Oliver, however, is saying that what is needed is much more than tolerance. The crux of his argument is that teachers must teach the skills of rational decision-making, and only in that way will students be able to make sound choices and decisions in regard to the different viewpoints they are confronted with in life. Via his argument, Oliver is basically asking: How do we decide which viewpoint to teach in a democracy? Ultimately, he answers that you can't. It is up to the individual to make rational decisions.

[2]The "we" here refers to the "royal we."

At this point in his seminal article, Oliver (1968) refers to "the American Dilemma." According to Oliver, Gunnar Myrdal sees the American Dilemma as the "difference between what men say is right and what men actually do" (p. 32). Oliver (1968) then suggests reinterpreting the dilemma in terms of ". . . two sets of moral standards: one which applies to the conduct of a particular group at a particular time; and one which applies to men in society at any time" (p. 32). Oliver asserts that the inconsistency stems from two sets of beliefs learned at different points in the education of the individual: one public and one private—that is, between what people say and what they actually do. The solutions, he argues, are found in Constitutional guarantees of our liberal democratic tradition, e.g. rule of law, trial by jury, separation of powers, and checks and balances. The understanding of, respect for, and exercise of these guarantees—with their concurrent rights and responsibilities—for the purpose of resolving the inconsistencies should become the centerpiece of social studies education (Oliver, 1966a, p. 33). Oliver believed that the basic processes of socialization had already taken place through their traditional coursework in history and other social studies classes by the time students reach high school. That means that the student will "already [have] a descriptive knowledge of his culture and has internalized the specific beliefs of his family or clan as well as some of the more general beliefs and values of the total society, e.g. liberty, equality, love of country" (Oliver, 1966a, p. 34).

The genesis of the public issues series can probably be traced to the following statement:

> When the student has reached this stage of development, we[3] propose that the relationship between personal values, the general canons of tolerance of our society, and the determination of public policy for the regulation of human affairs be made the center of the social studies curriculum in the public school. The basic core of content would consist of the study of existing and predicted conflicts caused by differing definitions and interpretations of the meaning of liberty, security, and public welfare (Oliver, 1966a, pp. 34–35).

Ultimately, Oliver (1966a) was searching for instruction that would allow the student to develop a method of approaching conflicts and controversy in a rational manner rather "than a blind adherence to some ideology learned during early socialization" (p. 37) According to Oliver (1966a) this would require a dramatic shift in the type of content taught in secondary schools. The focus would be on exploring major areas of conflict and the content studied would be interdisciplinary in nature with a de-emphasis on traditional historical literature (Oliver, 1966a, p. 37). In fact, according

---

[3]Again, the "we" constitutes the "royal we."

to Oliver, the approach would necessitate omission of large areas of traditional American history.

It is important to note that Oliver believes that traditional United States history will continue to be taught unabated in earlier schooling—presumably elementary and, to some extent, middle school. Of the history taught in schools, he asserts that "we would not call either the combined fact-myth-legend representation of history taught in most public schools or a purely descriptive account of immediate and distant cultural settings 'social studies'" (Oliver, 1966a, p. 37). Despite this seeming excoriation of traditional history courses, Oliver (1966a) goes on to state "that without the tempering influence of history to give a broader perspective to the present, there is a great danger of distortion in a picture of current social reality" (p. 39). The key distinction he seems to be making is that when history is taught well, it does not consist of popular simple memorization of historical data but rather the problematizing of history requiring research and problem solving. Additionally, studying history, according to Oliver, calls for depth over mere coverage.

In the conclusion to this important early article, Oliver comments that he expects severe criticism regarding his suggested approach. He comments that those who are wedded to traditional history as *the one and only approach* to social studies as well as those who have problems with teaching conflict and controversy versus, as he puts it not a little sardonically, love and harmony are the two factions who are most likely to be the loudest and most vociferous critics. He calls for such critics to philosophically defend their criticisms by building a case for why they believe their approaches are more educationally sound than his approach (Oliver, 1966a, pp. 41–42).

Oliver and his students all found history as traditionally taught to be problematic, including the facts that course materials seemed unconnected to student's lives, uninteresting, if not outright boring, and that the instructional strategies used to teach it resulted in student passivity. Such a stance resulted in an in-depth examination by Oliver and his team of graduate students into such questions as: What should be taught? How do we know the facts being taught are correct? How many perspectives are we viewing? (Oliver, Shaver, Berlak, Van Seasholes, 1962). Harkening back to Dewey, Oliver and his students demonstrated their belief in an inquiry approach, along with the development of specific instructional strategies that valued intellectual discussion by the teachers and students engaged in the study.

During the 1960s Oliver had a "burning faith in Jeffersonian enlightenment" (Oliver, 1978, p. 595), and translating this faith into materials, issues and procedures to be developed and used in schools became his goal. Those Jeffersonian beliefs are the fundamental American values and processes on which the United States bases its government and which are found in the *Declaration of Independence*, and the *U.S. Constitution*—including, of course, the *U.S. Bill of Rights* and such supporting documents as *The Federalist Papers.* In his work, Myrdal refers to the ideals and normative concepts inherent in these documents as the American Creed (see Oliver and Shaver with Berlak and VanSeasholes, 1962).

Oliver and Shaver adapted the American Creed for use by high school students and teachers by listing the values clearly—via major concepts and related terms—in their 1966 book, *Teaching Public Issues in the High School.* More specifically, they began with a section entitled "Ethical Principles Underlying the Analysis of Controversy in a Democratic Society: A Summary," which defines the values of human dignity and rational consent as the foundation upon which American government rests. They then make the case for the use of law to restrain federal and state governments thereby insuring the protection of individual rights.

Newmann and Oliver (1970) define the Creed as a set of values which most Americans accept, including the preeminent worth and dignity of the individual; equality; inalienable rights to life, liberty, property and the pursuit of happiness; consent of the governed; majority rule; due process of law; community and national welfare; and rights to freedom of speech, press, religion, assembly, and private association. These fundamental values are described as comprising America's constitutional morality. In addition, these values are underscored by fewer enumerated constitutional values but just as basic American beliefs including brotherhood, charity, mercy, nonviolence, perseverance or hard work, efficiency, competence and expertise, competition and rugged individualism, compromise, cooperation, honesty, loyalty and integrity of personal conscience (Oliver and Shaver, 1966, pp. 11–19). Newmann and Oliver describe these values as having historic roots in Western society, including the Judeo-Christian tradition, the Enlightenment, English Common Law, Puritanism, the frontier and American capitalism.

In a footnote, Newmann and Oliver comment on the obvious, reminding readers that the Creed is an ideal and one that is rarely followed in its totality by most U.S. citizens. Harkening back to Oliver's concern with the difference between what men say and what men do, Newmann and Oliver (1970) remind us that the actual behavior of Americans might display a greater commitment to such values as "materialism, conformity, sensationalism, hedonism, aggression and violence, and hypocrisy" (1970, p. 12). Nevertheless, the authors believe that the virtues listed in the Creed are solid values and should serve as guidelines for public policy, implementation and enforcement rather than the negatives listed in the footnote. It follows that to educate students on public issues that illustrate and reinforce the values of the American Creed would be to educate students in how to become good citizens striving towards meeting the ideals that all Americans agree upon in general. Of course, as Oliver repeatedly pointed out in his writings, it is when these values become more concrete in terms of specific situations that conflicts inevitably arise. For example, in the introduction to a civil rights topic, the vignette describes a widow who owns a boarding house and wishes to bar a Negro from renting a room. There the right of equal access to fair housing clashes with the widow's right to use her property as she sees fit. The conflict arises because both claims are legitimate American values. Which one should take precedence?

Significantly, Oliver's, Newmann's, and Shaver's program was entitled the *Public Issues Series not* the social issues series. The authors did not see these terms as synonymous—some issues they defined as private (e.g. abortion) and these were understood to be social, not public issues. Furthermore, public issues were not simply "current events." From their perspective, "public issues" are those problems or value dilemmas *persisting* throughout history and across cultures (italics in the original) (Oliver & Newmann, 1967a, p. 3). To clarify further, at no time did the Harvard Public Issues Series curriculum call for social action beyond understanding the issues in class—teaching about such issues was *not* an agenda of social action.

The reality is that public issues are quite complex and often the generality and abstraction of the values involved leads to a clash between/among values and a need to prioritize them. In the scenario mentioned above regarding the woman with the room for rent and the Negro who wished to rent a room, students would need to prioritize the conflicting values of the sanctity of private property versus the value of equal treatment under the law. Which claim is most just? The goal of the *Public Issues Series* was to help students clarify positions, and then learn to rationally discuss issues where there were two or more legitimate positions or where two or more American values clashed. Ultimately, teaching materials and instructional strategies were developed (and/or suggested) for the express purpose of enabling teachers and their students to undertake these tasks in their social studies/history classrooms.

THE MATERIALS AND THEIR IMPLEMENTATION

The teaching materials in the Public Issues Series take the form of pamphlets. Each pamphlet comprises a unit of study and targets a specific historical or political problem. Each pamphlet opens with a vignette, story, film, piece of literature, picture, etc., that provides a discrepant event(s) or situation. All the units are interdisciplinary, drawing vignettes not only from primary sources but also from literature, and statistical data and factual information from economics, sociology, and political science. Some of the pamphlets include games (simulations) with careful instructions about how to effectively manage the simulation, including a Review, Reflection, and Research section of the unit which integrates the simulation experience with the readings to ensure that students understand the underlying concepts of the simulation.

The list of pamphlets covers a variety of social studies courses—U.S. history, government, civics, sociology, law studies, and, to a lesser extent, geography and world history. Teachers were to select those materials most germane and applicable to their particular curriculum. Thus, teachers did not have to adopt the entire program but could pick and choose the units most appropriate for their courses and students.

In order to facilitate the use of the materials in different courses, Oliver and Newmann (1967a) present ways in which teachers can make use of the pamphlets via a historical topic approach, a chronological-historical approach, a social science approach, a values- or issue-oriented approach, a current problems approach or a simplicity-complexity dimension (p. 8). Thus, while considerable leeway is given to the teacher for independent action, structures are provided throughout the units and the teacher's guides to make implementation of the materials possible.

The focus of the pamphlets in the *Public Issues Series* (attributed to Oliver & Newman, 1967a) were extremely eclectic, and included, for example, the following: *The American Revolution: Crisis of Law and Change* (1967); *Religious Freedom: Minority Faiths and Majority Rule* (1967); *The Rise of Organized Labor: Worker Security and Employer Rights* (1967); *The Immigrant's Experience: Cultural Variety and the Melting Pot* (1967); *Negro Views of America: The Legacy of Oppression* (1967); *The New Deal: Free Enterprise and Public Planning* (1968); *Rights of the Accused: Criminal Procedure and Public Security* (1968); *Communist China: Communal Progress and Individual Freedom* (1968); *Nazi Germany: Social Forces and Personal Responsibility* (1968); *20ᵗʰ Century Russia: Agents of the Revolution* (1968); *The Civil War: Crisis in Federalism* (1969); *Race and Education: Integration and Community Control* (1969); *Revolution and World Politics: The Search for National Independence* (1970); *Population Control: Whose Right to Live* (1971); and *Jacksonian Democracy: The Common Man in American Life* (1971).

Each of the titles of the pamphlets clearly establishes the dilemma to be examined *and* how the dilemma relates to the values of the American Creed. Oliver and Newmann remained conscious at all times of the underlying message they were trying to explore: values necessary to understand and promote democratic citizenship. Even more important was their belief that this was best accomplished via the analysis of complex issues that are of immense interest to large numbers of the population *and* constitute issues which people perceive differently and have legitimate concerns about.

Many, if not most, teachers have often preferred to avoid controversial issues—and that remains true through today. It is quite possible that such tentativeness is due to a lack of expertise in handling these issues in the classroom. In order to help offset such a lack of expertise and/or discomfort, Oliver and Newmann developed two works: an extensive teacher's guide entitled *Cases and Controversy: Guide to Teaching The Public Issues Series/ Harvard Social Studies Project* (1967b), and a unit prepared for students entitled *Taking a Stand: A Guide to Clear Discussion of Public Issues* (1967i).

In the teacher's guide, Oliver and Newmann (1967b) demonstrate to teachers how to lead their students to identify issues distinguishing among prescriptive, descriptive and analytic issues and the subcategories therein (pp. 4–5). Prescriptive issues constitute judgments about what should or ought to be done. Thus, they are concerned with personal beliefs and conscience, public policy, ethics, and law. Descriptive issues focus on problems of fact—describing, interpreting, and explaining—and include focusing on the truth of events and/or conditions and the relations among them. Descriptive claims generally try to explain why an event has (or will) occur[red]. Lastly, analytic issues focus on meaning. They ensure that everyone is viewing an issue using the same definitions for problems and concepts.

Additionally, Oliver and Newmann (1967b) delineate how teachers can lead their students to distinguish between "knowledge claims" (that is, problems of fact and meaning) and "values claims" (that is, judgments about what should or ought to be done). They also include instructional strategies that provide the teacher with ways to get the students to provide a justification for their positions as well as ways to help the students clarify their positions. The latter is often accomplished by having teachers and students use analogies to aid in defining terms and making distinctions.

Socratic discussion and other less confrontational formats were included for those teachers or students uncomfortable with the directness and focus of Socratic method. The teachers guide is substantive and provides ample strategies for evaluating discussions effectively.

Another instructional strategy that is recommended is the jurisprudential or legal-ethical model of instruction (see Chapter 8 Using a Jurisprudential Framework in the Teaching of Public Issues, Oliver & Shaver, 1966b, 1977). The jurisprudential, or legal-ethical, approach focuses on a contemporary issue stated in concrete terms (i.e. a current event). Using this strategy the teacher "relates the contemporary case to cases which range widely in time and space, appealing especially to historical analogies to broaden the context of the discussion" (Oliver & Shaver, 1966, p. 145). Oliver and Shaver (1966) go on to say that this approach is the:

> amalgamation of law-government, ethics, contemporary, and historical factual questions developed around perennial issues of public policy that we refer to as *jurisprudential teaching*.... Our approach emphasizes the clarification of two or more legitimately held points of view as they bear on a public policy question. In general there is much less concern with rhetorical devices or the logic of deductive reasoning than with the anatomy of legitimate communication and persuasion (italics in the original) (p. 146).

The key here is on dialogue: either between student and teacher or among students. The role of the teacher is "complex, requiring that he think on two levels at the same time" (Oliver & Shaver, 1966d, p. 146). The teacher is required to "double think" both about the issue(s) under discussion and the intellectual process(es) by which the issue(s) can be clarified or resolved. This is analogous to the explanation of two levels of thinking expected of the students in the *Taking a Stand* (Oliver & Newman, 1967i) discussion unit. (See the discussion below of *Taking a Stand*.)

In the conclusion of their discussion of the jurisprudential model of teaching, Oliver and Shaver (1966) delineate their underlying assumptions in regard to a social studies curriculum based on political controversy:

1. It is useful to distinguish facts from values.
2. It is useful to describe political controversy in terms of values rather than simply in terms of specific controversial cases.
3. It is useful to differentiate the general values of the Creed from the ultimate concern of a democratic society, the dignity of man.
4. The process of using comparative cases or analogies has the value of clarifying one's value positions and leading one toward an empirical statement of political disagreement.

The methods of history, journalism, and the social sciences are appropriate ways of dealing with empirical disagreements (pp. 164–165).

Taking a Stand could be used by the teacher prior to implementing any of the other units because it clearly delineates the process of using discussion as a technique for rational decision making for effective citizenship. Thus, simply stated, it instructs students in the art and skill of taking part in a discussion. Students are alerted to the fact that it is possible that a discussion might conclude without coming to an "acceptable solution." The authors note that a:

> discussion [is useful] if it brings increased clarity about the complexity of the problem and mutual awareness of difference in opinion. Students are expected to apply ideas and they are cautioned that none of the exercises in the book contain "absolutely correct" answers. The exercises are intended to provoke discussion about which of the answers can be considered most reasonable (Oliver & Newmann, 1967i, p. 6).

They also note that "it is often just as useful for people to know why they disagree with one another as it is for them to know why they agree" (Oliver and Newmann, 1967i, p. 6). Thus, for both teachers and students, practice with rational discussion and the strategies for making this a classroom reality are available.

Part Four of the unit is entitled "Types of Issues." The section opens with a definition central to the entire program:

A PUBLIC POLICY ISSUE is a question involving a choice or decision for action by citizens or officials in affairs that concern a government or community. Policy Issues can be phrased as general questions:
Should the United States stay in Vietnam?
Should capital punishment be abolished?
Should Government regulate automobile design?
　　Public issues can also be phrased as choices for personal action:
Should I write to my congressman to protest draft laws?
Should I petition the Government to commute a criminal's death sentence?
Should I write to a candidate asking him to pledge support for auto design regulations?
(Oliver and Newmann, 1967i, p. 29).

It is worth noting the parallel nature vis-à-vis public policy questions and the personal action questions. The latter is significant in light of the fact that the authors had repeatedly asserted that there was no call for social action within the program they had developed. Clearly part of being an effective citizen is being able to take action and the unit certainly makes that clear.

Taking a Stand would certainly be a good place for a teacher to begin if he or she felt insecure moving away from lecture and towards discussion. The sample discussions in the pamphlet could be easily updated and the strategies are as pedagogically sound and effective now as when the pamphlet was written.

Even if teachers could not find the time to implement this short unit on discussion, most of the pamphlets open with an introduction that challenges the students to ask questions and to see questions as more important than answers. The authors' aim is to make history more than a passive intake of content. It is the authors' premise that history/social studies courses cover too many answers and too few questions. As the authors note, this results in students thinking that history *had* to happen just the way it did, leading to the conclusion that what took place was inevitable—when that certainly was not the case. As the authors also note, such a belief and/or attitude is one of disempowerment and non-engagement causing students to believe that they can neither understand nor influence the "rushing stream of political, economic, and social events" in the world or their nation's reaction to them (Oliver & Newmann, 1967b, p. 1).

Oliver and Newmann strongly make the case that the past and the present are matters for Americans to think about, not merely observe and memorize. The authors assert that they have "a vigorous belief that each student is part of our national past and present, [and that their program] is intended to take [the students] into a *living dimension of history*" (italics in original) (Oliver & Newman, 1967b, p. 1). More specifically, they state:

The Public Issues series is intended to involve you as something more than a spectator; as more of a thinking, acting participant in history and modern life.

It does not provide ready-made, right-and-wrong answers to social problems of the persisting questions of history. Rather it challenges you and your fellow students to develop your own positions and to resolve conflicting views that face citizens in a free society. (Oliver and Newman, 1967a, p. 3)

RATIONAL DECISION MAKING: A FAILED MODEL?

What happened to the *Public Issues* series? The problems associated with the continuance of the Public Issues series varies widely from school to school across the nation. Possibly the greatest barrier was teacher resistance to such radically different material. Not far behind, and in some cases at the forefront of such resistance, were school boards, administrations, and/ or parents due to the introduction of such controversial materials in the classroom. Oliver, of course, was aware of how critical each of these groups were in the successful implementation of the Public Issues series, but did little to nothing to ensure their support. Many do not believe that history is open to question and interpretation. To pursue such a course would mean that the United States had made mistakes and some may have feared that admitting such could result in a decrease in patriotism and loyalty to the government—a mission that some perceive as paramount in a social studies program.

Likewise, many might not agree that the "most just" path vis-à-vis an issue (which, ideally, the students would have concluded after ample debate) should be taken in all cases. Indeed, some might see the most just path as inconvenience or even a contradiction to tradition or their own personal beliefs.

Another problem may have stemmed from the materials themselves. Oliver assumed that students would have mastered basic history, economics, geography, and government concepts and materials in prior schooling. Unfortunately, that was not the case. As a result, many, if not most, students did not have the basic foundation of knowledge that Oliver assumed they would have.

There was also the problem that the materials are broadly interdisciplinary and require a high reading level. For example, *Taking a Stand*, the pamphlet that is used to introduce students to discussion methods, uses excerpts from Herman Melville's *Billy Budd*. Such material is not only difficult to read, it is subject matter that may prove uninteresting to large numbers of students. For the materials to have been truly viable, there would have needed to be more materials that were not so heavily focused on advanced literacy levels.

And then there was Oliver's personality. Oliver, known in his early career for his abrasiveness (Stern, 2006), may have alienated his potential audience by his criticism of what and how history and social studies were being taught in the nation's schools. Mark Krug for example, criticized Oliver in *The History Teacher,* stating that there was no need for Donald Oliver to justify the need for a new approach to social studies by an ill-informed attack on history and history teachers. More specifically, Krug (1968) objected to the Oliver-Shaver approach on the grounds that it builds an entire program on conflict and controversy. Continuing, Krug (1968) asserted, "A more serious point to be raised with the Oliver-Shaver approach is whether it would be advisable to build an entire social studies course on the study of public conflicts and controversies. This may well lead to a distorted Darwinistic view of history," thus omitting periods of "general contentment and relative tranquility, often marked by great intellectual and technological creativity" (p. 26), which Krug, asserted, were worthy of student attention and study.

It is also true that federal funding in the form of grants dried up. As a result, the principal investigators were no longer guaranteed funding to cover the time needed to develop and field test the materials for the Public Issues series.

Then there was the issue of the career trajectories of the principal writers. For example, Oliver, the primary force behind the project, moved off in an entirely different direction. According to Polly Oliver, Oliver's wife, student unrest at Harvard in 1968 had a deep impact on him. He saw the 1960s as a revolutionary period, a time when students rejected obedience and awe of authority and he came to see that as real learning. Communal schools teaching non-violent protest were preparing individuals to stand up for their individual rights. Some of the latter individuals became Oliver's students and, over time, he became more interested in rural and adult education.

Interestingly, and tellingly, as early as 1967, Newmann and Oliver published an article entitled *Education and Community,* and followed it up with a *Proposal for Education in Community* in 1975. It seems clear that Oliver was searching for something missing from his life and that it was not going to be remedied solely through rational discussion.

Oliver's 1976 book, *Education and Community: A Radical Critique of Innovative Schooling* is perceived by Newmann as Oliver's most important (and difficult) work. The preface of this volume explains the change in Oliver's thinking at the time. His faith in Jeffersonian democracy becomes replaced with a vision of small communal societies and systems thinking. The thesis of the book searches for an understanding of how to create a balance between primal and modern aspects of human community, thought systems, and personality, including "creating a balance between efforts to maximize the potential development of each individual and recognizing the necessity and value of diversity among humans, even in such sensitive areas as intelligence, motivation, and social responsibility" (Oliver, 1976, p. ix). Oliver was working toward developing a metatheory (p. x) that included the relationship between education and community. He ends his preface by stating "It is our hope that the book might provide a new conceptual basis for a social studies and humanities curriculum" (p. x).

As the years passed, Oliver studied more deeply the works of Alfred North Whitehead and became engaged in process philosophy. The guiding principle of process philosophy concerns itself with "terms of processes versus things—of modes of changes versus fixed realities" (Rescher, 2002, n.p.). Gradually Oliver moved to a more holistic, affective place in his life. In terms of curriculum in general, and the social studies curriculum in particular, Oliver lost faith in the school system as a way of educating people. He also seemed to lose faith in purely rational discussion in classrooms as a means to improving citizenship (see Oliver, 1980, 1992).

Oliver no longer focused on the problem-solving approach, believing that people could discuss things *ad infinitum* and it wouldn't really change anything because people do not really listen to each other. He no longer believed in the secular state as a solution to social problems—people, he believed, need community and churches with their moral codes to provide structure. The adherence to an abstract set of values, such as The American Creed, cannot work. Human beings as a species, he concluded, simply aren't all that rational.

Finally, Shaver and Newmann, two of the principal authors, completed their studies at Harvard under Oliver, obtained their doctoral degrees, and moved on to the next stage of their careers. That, in turn, resulted in a geographic distance between them that became problematic.

For all of these reasons, and no doubt others as well, despite the excellence of the Public Issues series materials, they were never widely implemented. That, unfortunately, was to the detriment of our students' education.

That said, Shaver continued work along the same line at Utah State University, where he took a tenure-track professorship. Three of his main publications were: *Decision Making in a Democracy* (Shaver & Larkins, 1973); *Rationales for Citizenship Education* (Shaver, 1977); and *Facing Value Decisions* (Shaver & Strong, 1982). These publications all focus on the same problems and ideas that underlie the Public Issues series. Shaver also worked with Houghton Mifflin to publish *The Analysis of Public Issues Program* (Shaver & Larkins, 1973–1974), which included such units as: *Women: the Majority-Minority* (Chapin & Branson, 1973); *Progress and the Environment: Water and Air Pollution* (Shaver & Larkins, 1973); *The Police and Black America* (Shaver & Larkins, 1973); *Race Riots in the Sixties* (Larkins & Shaver, 1973) and *Student's Rights: Issues in Constitutional Freedoms* (Knight, 1974). All of these units contain, just as the Harvard Social Studies Project did, an extensive set of materials in the Instructor's Manuals. Shaver was also involved in teacher development to assist with the implementation of the series (see Shaver, 2006).

Newmann largely moved in three major directions. First, Newmann appears to have become concerned not only with social education but also social action. Illustrative of this focus is his highly regarded book, *Education for Citizen Action: Challenge for Secondary Curriculum* (Newmann, 1975). For years, he also focused on the issue of depth over coverage within the high school curriculum (Newmann, 1988), and on authentic pedagogy (assessment and learning, see Newmann, 2006). Finally, another major concern was that of school change; that is, how does a large, conservative social institution—school—go about making deep and significant changes in its curriculum and instruction program. These concerns are clearly vestiges of the research base and underlying messages in the Public Issues series.

CONCLUSION

I would maintain that *Public Issues Series* did not fail completely. The Social Science Education Consortium (SSEC), recently incorporated into the work of the National Council for the Social Studies, has reprinted several of the pamphlets (see Geise, 1989; Schott, 1993; or Singleton, 1991). Models of instruction texts (see, for example, Joyce & Weil, 2004) and social studies methods texts include jurisprudential instructional teaching strategies and Socratic discussion techniques. And, while Problems of American Democracy courses, a natural place for these materials, seem to have faded into the background, social education for social justice is still a concern for social studies teacher educators and social studies teachers nationwide. As for the pamphlets themselves, the original units are now out of print, but the revised units are available from SSEC. That said, any interested social studies teacher could order any and all of the pamphlets that are out of print through interlibrary loan or purchase them from an out-of-print internet vendor. They could also update the content integrating today's multimedia and internet sources. Finally, there is no reason why they could not use the original instructional strategies suggested for use with the Public Issues series.

While Oliver may have lost faith in rational discussion and decision-making as a tool for improving society, it seems evident that most Americans, and most social studies teachers, are still believers in the founding documents and the Jeffersonian beliefs enunciated in Myrdal's American Creed.

Finally, when looking at today's world, it appears that the current accountability push for standards based curriculum and high stakes, closed ended tests in the U.S. public schools will not yield significantly more civic knowledge or civic engagement than there has been in the past. Indeed, the lack of relevance of the current curricula found in our nation's schools—even in states where the standards purport to be based on essential questions (e.g. the Virginia Standards of Learning)—will be found wanting when all that is tested is the accumulation of unrelated factual knowledge. Our students and our nation deserve better. A revision of the content of the *Public Issues Series*, while maintaining the pedagogy found in the original series, seems like a plan that could work.

REFERENCES

Chapin, J. R., & Branson, M. S. (1973). "Women: The majority-minority." In J. P. Shaver & A. G. Larkins (Eds.), *The analysis of public issues program*. Boston, MA: Houghton Mifflin Company. [This is a booklet and it is 17 pages in length.]

Geise, J. R. (1989). *The progressive era: The limits of reform*. [Public Issues Series adapted from the Harvard Social Studies Project.] Boulder, CO: Social Science Education Consortium.

Griffin, A. (1942). *A Philosophical approach to the subject matter preparation of teachers of history*. Accessed at ERIC Document Reproduction. Number: ED237 377.

Jefferson, T. (1824). *Letter to David Harding*. Retrieved on January 2, 2008 from http://etext.virginia.edu/jefferson/quotations/jeff0700.htm

Joyce, B. R.; Weil, M., & Calhoun, E. (2004). *Models of teaching* (7th ed.). Boston, MA: Allyn and Bacon.

Knight, R. S. (1974). Student's rights: Issues in constitutional freedom. In J. P. Shaver & A. G. Larkins (Eds.), *The analysis of public issues program*. Boston, MA: Houghton Mifflin Company. [This is a booklet and it is 17 pages in length.]

Krug, M. M. (1968). The Oliver-Shaver approach to social studies. *The History Teacher* 1(4) 22–26.

Larkins, A. G., & Shaver, J. P. (1973). *Race riots in the sixties*. Boston, MA: Houghton Mifflin

Larkins, A. G.; Shaver, J. P., & Houghton Mifflin Company (1973). *Police and Black America*. Boston, MA: Houghton Mifflin.

National Center for Learning and Citizenship (2004). *Citizenship education in 10 U.S. high schools*. Retrieved on January 2, 2008 from http://www.ecs.org/html/projectsPartners/nclc/citizenship_ed.htm

National Council for the Social Studies (1992). A vision of powerful teaching and learning in the social studies: Building social understanding and civic efficacy. Washington, D.C. : Author. Retrieved on July 19, 2007 from http://www.socialstudies.org/positions/powerful/?print-friendly=true

Newmann, F. M. (1975). *Education for citizen action: Challenge for secondary curriculum*. Berkeley, CA: McCutchan Publishing Corporation.

Newmann, F. M. (1988). Can depth replace coverage in the high school curriculum?" *Phi Delta Kappan, 69*, 345–348.

Newmann, F. M. (2006). My experience with social issues and education, . In S. Totten & J. Pedersen (Eds.) *Researching and teaching social issues: The personal stories and pedagogical efforts of professors of education* (pp. 121–130). Lanham, MD: Lexington Books.

Newmann, F. M., & Oliver, D. W. (1967). Education and community. *Harvard Educational Review.* Accessed at: ERIC Document Reproductions. Number: ED 011 327.

Newmann, F. M., & Oliver, D. W. (1970). *Clarifying public controversy: An approach to teaching social studies.* Boston, MA: Little, Brown.

Newmann, F. M., & Oliver, D. W. (1975). A proposal for education in community. *National Elementary Principal, 54*(3), 48–49.

Oliver, D. W. (1962). *The analysis of public controversy, a study.* Accessed at ERIC Document Reproduction. Number: ED 003 364.

Oliver, D. (1966a). The selection of content in the social sciences. In E. Fenton (Ed.), *Teaching the new social studies in secondary schools* (pp. 98–113). New York: Holt, Reinhart and Winston.

Oliver, D. W. (1966b). A jurisprudential approach to citizenship education. In J. C. McLendon (Ed.), *Readings on social studies in secondary education* (pp. 99–105). New York: The Macmillan Company.

Oliver, D. W. (1968). The selection of content in the social studies. In J. Shaver & H. Berlak (Eds.) *Democracy, pluralism and the social studies: Readings and commentary, An approach to curriculum decisions in the social studies* (pp. 17–42). New York: Houghton Mifflin Company. [Reprint of 1966 article.]

Oliver, D. W. (1976) *Education and community: A radical critique of innovative schooling.* Berkeley, CA: McCutchan Publishing Corporation.

Oliver, D. W. (June, 1976). *Education and community: A radical critique of innovative schooling.* Berkeley, CA: McCutchan Publishing Corporation.

Oliver, D. W. (1978). Reflections on Peter Carbone's *The social and educational thought of Harold Rugg. Social Education, 42*(7), 593–597.

Oliver, D. W. (1990). Grounded knowing: A postmodern perspective on teaching and learning. *Educational Leadership, 48*(1), 64–69.

Oliver, D. W. (1992). Teaching public issues in the secondary school classroom. *Social Studies, 83*(3), 100–103.

Oliver, D., & Baker, S. (1959). The case method. *Social Education,* (January, *23*, 1): 25–28. \

Oliver, D. W., & Keen, J. (1978). Global issues and community. *History and Social Science Teacher, 13*(4), 229–236.

Oliver, D. W., & Newmann, F. M. (1967a). *The American Revolution: Crisis of law and change.* Public Issues Series/Harvard Social Studies Project. Middletown, CT: American Education Publications.

Oliver, D. W., & Newmann, F. M. (1967b). *Cases and controversy: Guide to teaching the public issues series/Harvard social studies project, and supplement. Public issues series/ Harvard social studies project.* Middletown, CT: American Education Publications.

Oliver, D. W., & Newmann, F. M. (1967c). *The immigrant's experience: Cultural variety and the "melting pot."* Public Issues Series/Harvard Social Studies Project. Middletown, CT: American Education Publications.

Oliver, D. W., & Newmann, F. M. (1967d). *Municipal politics: Interest groups and the government.* Public Issues Series/Harvard Social Studies Project. Middletown, CT: American Education Publications.

Oliver, D. W., & Newmann, F. M. (1967e). *Negro views of America: The legacy of oppression.* Public Issues Series/Harvard Social Studies Project. Middletown, CT: American Education Publications.

Oliver, D. W., & Newmann, F. M. (1967f). *The railroad era: Business competition and the public interest.* Public Issues Series/Harvard Social Studies Project. Middletown, CT: American Education Publications.

Oliver, D. W., & Newmann, F. M. (1967g). *Religious freedom: Minority faiths and majority rule.* Public Issues Series/Harvard Social Studies Project. Middletown, CT: American Education Publications.

Oliver, D. W., & Newmann, F. M. (1967h). *The rise of organized labor: Worker security and employer rights.* Public Issues Series/Harvard Social Studies Project. Middletown, CT: American Education Publications.

Oliver, D. W., & Newmann, F. M. (1967i). *Taking a stand: A guide to clear discussion of public issues.* Public Issues Series/Harvard Social Studies Project. Middletown, CT: American Education Publications.

Oliver, D. W., & Newmann, F. M. (1968a). *Colonial Kenya: Cultures in conflict.* Public Issues Series/Harvard Social Studies Project. Middletown, CT: American Education Publications.

Oliver, D. W., & Newmann, F. M. (1968b). *Communist China: Communal progress and individual freedom.* Public Issues Series/Harvard Social Studies Project. Middletown, CT: American Education Publications.

Oliver, D. W., & Newmann, F. M. (1968c). *Community change: Law, politics, and social attitudes.* Public Issues Series/Harvard Social Studies Project. Middletown, CT: American Education Publications.

Oliver, D. W., & Newmann, F. M. (1968d). *Nazi Germany: Social forces and personal responsibility.* Public Issues Series/Harvard Social Studies Project. Middletown, CT: American Education Publications.

Oliver, D. W., & Newmann, F. M. (1968e). *The New Deal: Free enterprise and public planning.* Public Issues Series/Harvard Social Studies Project. Middletown, CT: American Education Publications.

Oliver, D. W., & Newmann, F. M. (1968f). *Rights of the accused: Criminal procedure and public security.* Public Issues Series/Harvard Social Studies Project. Middletown, CT: American Education Publications.

Oliver, D. W., & Newmann, F. M. (1968g). *20th century Russia: Agents of revolution.* Public Issues Series/Harvard Social Studies Project. Middletown, CT: American Education Publications.

Oliver, D. W., & Newmann, F. M. (1968h). *The lawsuit: Legal reasoning and civil procedure.* Public Issues Series/Harvard Social Studies Project. Middletown, CT: American Education Publications.

Oliver, D. W., & Newmann, F. M. (1969a). *The Civil War: Crisis in federalism.* Public Issues Series/Harvard Social Studies Project. Middletown, CT: American Education Publications.

Oliver, D. W., & Newmann, F. M. (1969b). *Organizations among nations: The search for world order.* Public Issues Series/Harvard Social Studies Project. Middletown, CT: American Education Publications.

Oliver, D. W., & Newmann, F. M. (1969c). *Race and education: Integration and community control.* Public Issues Series/Harvard Social Studies Project. Middletown, CT: American Education Publications.

Oliver, D. W., & Newmann, F. M. (1969d). *Science and public policy: Uses and control of knowledge.* Public Issues Series/Harvard Social Studies Project. Middletown, CT: American Education Publications.

Oliver, D. W., & Newmann, F. M. (1969e). *Status: Achievement and social values.* Public Issues Series/Harvard Social Studies Project. Middletown, CT: American Education Publications.

Oliver, D. W., & Newmann, F. M. (1970a). *Diplomacy and International law: Alternatives to war.* Public Issues Series/Harvard Social Studies Project. Middletown, CT: American Education Publications.

Oliver, D. W., & Newmann, F. M. (1970b). *The limits of war: National policy and world conscience.* Public Issues Series/Harvard Social Studies Project. Middletown, CT: American Education Publications.

Oliver, D. W., & Newmann, F. M. (1970c). *Revolution and world politics: The search for national independence.* Public Issues Series/Harvard Social Studies Project. Middletown, CT: American Education Publications.

Oliver, D. W., & Newmann, F. M. (1971a). *Privacy: The control of personal information.* Adapted from the Harvard Social Studies Project. Middletown, CT: American Education Publications.

Oliver, D. W., & Newmann, F. M. (1971b). *The progressive era: Abundance, poverty and reform.* Adapted from the Harvard Social Studies Project. Middletown, CT: American Education Publications

Oliver, D. W., & Newmann, F. M. (1971c). *Population control: Whose right to live?* Adapted from the Harvard Social Studies Project. Middletown, CT: American Education Publications.

Oliver, D. W., & Newmann, F. M. (1971d). *Jacksonian democracy: The common man in American life.* Adapted from the Harvard Social Studies Project. Middletown, CT: American Education Publications.

Oliver, D. W., & Newmann, F. M. (1971e). *Moral reasoning.* Adapted from the Harvard Social Studies Project. Middletown, CT: American Education Publications.

Oliver, D. W., & Newmann, F. M. (1971f). *Social action: Dilemmas and strategies.* Adapted from the Harvard Social Studies Project. Middletown, CT: American Education Publications.

Oliver, D. W., & Shaver, J. P. (1963). The use of content analysis of oral discussion as a method of evaluating political education. ERIC Database Number: ED 229285.

Oliver, D. W., & Shaver, J. P. (1966). *Teaching public issues in the high school.* Boston: Houghton Mifflin.

Oliver, D. W., & Shaver, J. P. (1966d). Evaluating the jurisprudential approach to social studies. In J. C. McLendon (Ed.) *Readings on social studies in secondary education* (pp. 300–305). New York: The Macmillan Company.

Oliver, D. W., & Shaver, J. P. (1968a). Evaluating the jurisprudential approach to the social sciences. In J. P. Shaver & H. Berlak (Eds.) *Democracy, pluralism, and the social studies* (pp. 429–438). Boston, MA: Houghton Mifflin Company.

Oliver, D. W., & Shaver, J. P. (1968b). Selected analytic concepts for the clarification of public issues. In J. P. Shaver & H. Berlak (Eds.), *Democracy, pluralism, and the social studies* (pp. 393–414). Boston, MA: Houghton Mifflin Company.

Oliver, D. W., & Shaver, J. P. (1974). Using a jurisprudential framework in the teaching of public issues. In D. W. Oliver & J. P. Shaver (Eds.), *Teaching public issues in the high school* (2nd ed., pp. 145–169). Logan: Utah State University Press.

Oliver, D. W., Sharver, J. P., Berlak, Lh., & Seaholes, E. (1962). *The analysis of public controversy: A study in citizenship education.* Boston: Harvard Graduate School of Education.

Pickeral, T. (2000). *Integration and sustainability of quality citizenship education in U.S. Schools: How policy and quality practice lead to student citizenship knowledge, skills and dispositions.* Denver, CO: National Center for Learning and Citizenship, Education Commission of the States. Retrieved on July 19, 2007 from http:// www.cpce.gov.hk/national education/pdf/Mr._Terry_Pickeral

Rescher, N. (2002). Process philosophy. *Stanford Encyclopedia of Philosophy.* Accessed at: plato.Stanford.edu/entries/process/philosophy.

Schott, J. C. (1991). *Religious freedom: Belief, practice, and the public interest.* Public Issues Series adapted from the Harvard Social Studies Project. Boulder, CO: Social Science Education Consortium.

Shaver, J. P. (1977). *Building rationales for citizenship education.* Arlington, VA: National Council for the Social Studies.

Shaver, J. P. (2006). A happenstance-based social issues career. In S. Totten & J. Pedersen (Eds.). *Researching and teaching social issues: The personal stories and pedagogical efforts of professors of education* (pp. 161–180). Lanham, MD: Lexington Books.

Shaver, J. P., & Larkins, A. G. (1973). *Decision-making in a democracy.* Boston, MA: Houghton Mifflin.

Shaver, J. P., & Larkins, A. G. (1973). *The analysis of public issues program, instructor's manual.* Boston, MA: Houghton Mifflin.

Shaver, J. P.; Larkins, A. G., & Anctill, D. E. (1973). *Progress and the environment: Water and air pollution.* Boston, MA: Houghton Mifflin.

Shaver, J. P., & Oliver, D. W. (1965). The structure of the social sciences and citizenship education. Accessed at ERIC Document Reproduction. Number: ED 004 348.

Shaver, J. P., & Oliver, D. W. (1968). The structure of the social sciences and citizenship education. In J. P. Shaver & H. Berlak (Eds.), *Democracy, pluralism, and the social studies* (pp. 326–334). Boston, MA: Houghton Mifflin Company.

Shaver, J. P., & Oliver, D. W. (1968). *The effect of student characteristic-teaching method interactions on learning to think critically.* Accessed at ERIC Document Reproduction. Number: ED229284.

Shaver, J. P,, & Strong, W. (1982). *Facing value decisions: Rationale-building for teachers* (2nd ed.). New York: Teachers College Press.

Singleton, L. (1993). *Science and public policy: Uses and control of knowledge.* Public Issues Series adapted from the Harvard Social Studies Project. Boulder, CO: Social Science Education Consortium.

SSEC (1971). *Social studies curriculum data book.* Boulder, CO: Social Science Education Consortium.

Stern, B. S. (2007). Donald Oliver: The search for democratic community. In S. Totten & J. Pedersen (Eds.), *Addressing social issues in the classroom and beyond: The pedagogical efforts of pioneers in the field* (pp. 267–289). Charlotte, NC: Information Age Publishers.

CHAPTER 4

THE REFLECTIVE CLASSROOM ENVISIONED IN "INQUIRY IN SOCIAL STUDIES" BY MASSIALAS AND COX

Jack Zevin

The reflective classroom...is characterized by its consideration of problems and hypotheses which give it a continuing focus. While the problem defines the general field for the venture, the hypothesis, devised as the instrument of inquiry, establishes specific focus and direction. (Massialas & Cox, 1966, p. 113)

PREFACE/INTRODUCTION

A word or two of personal reflection is in order. Since I am a living representative and participant in the approach and book being revisited, this chapter represents an interesting approach to the historical roots of social studies. My views are deeply shaped by my participation in the writing, publication, and application of *Inquiry in Social Studies* since I not only used the book in my graduate class, but also contributed to the examples of classroom lessons on exhibit, and went on to write a hands-on guide to inquiry teaching with my mentor, Byron Massialas, while serving as a secondary

Teaching and Studying Social Issues: Major Programs and Approaches, pages 67–86
Copyright © 2011 by Information Age Publishing
All rights of reproduction in any form reserved.

school teacher. Byron Massialas was my methods professor at the University of Chicago and later my Ph.D. advisor at the University of Michigan.

I was Byron Massialas' graduate student and teacher-experimenter for most of his work on *Inquiry in Social Studies*. I was teaching high school in Chicago when Massialas and Cox began writing their now famous book, going on to teach middle school in Ann Arbor just as the book was completed.

Byron Massialas and I also co-authored a book, *Creative Encounters in the Classroom* (Massialas & Zevin, 1967) in order to test inquiry ideas in the classroom. We tested the ideas out in several local schools in Chicago, finishing the manuscript at the start of my doctoral studies. As I recall, there was no line between theory and practice for me, both were fused into the lessons I planned, created, and field-tested (during which we recorded classroom dialogues that we excerpted and studied that resulted in several articles and books). All of the experiments we conducted were classroom applications of inquiry ideas.

Inquiry was a deeply-held set of values that I applied or tried to apply in my daily practice, perhaps somewhat obsessively at the beginning, at least in the eyes of my students who used to complain about "thought exhaustion" from too many days and weeks of driving reflective activity and relentless examination of values.

My association with Byron Massialas, and with the work of Massialas and Benjamin Cox, provided me with the intellectual rationale for teaching that has carried on through my entire career. So, although Byron could be a cross between "Zorba the Greek" and "The Emperor Paleologus IV," we got along quite well, and my instructional sophistication improved by leaps and bounds, giving me a lifelong interest in instructional theory and methods. My own methods book (Zevin, 1992, 2001, 2007) looks back to *Inquiry in Social Studies*, using many of its best ideas that are relevant to today's education.

Massialas, Cox, and I united because we all agreed that John Dewey's and Jerome Bruner's criticisms of education—Dewey's dating back to as far as 1901—still fit the typical classroom we all observed almost daily. This was a social studies classroom that might be called the "dry as dust school of facts," and the "avoid the issues school of instruction," a program that very much controlled what most teachers were pretending was an education in social studies and history.

In our collective view, very little of what we saw in classrooms dealt with anything real. Furthermore, they all failed to call upon students to do anything by themselves. There was no struggle intellectually and little critical thinking, and the affect level for history and social studies could be abysmal.

DESCRIPTION/FOCUS/PURPOSE

The focus of this chapter is developed around Byron Massialas and Benjamin Cox's book, *Inquiry in Social Studies*, and the "New Social Studies" movement that developed after Sputnik was placed in orbit by the Soviets in 1957—an event that set off a wave of concern about academic quality and achievement in the US. Massialas and Cox became part of a broad effort to create and consolidate an innovative approach to learning, curriculum, and teaching methods sharply different from the "chalk and talk" classroom ways that characterized American education in the 1950s. A review of the key ideas contributed by Massialas and Cox will form the heart of what follows, and that will be accompanied by a discussion of several issues centered around the critical need to change instructional roles to promote problem-solving and values examination rather than stressing knowledge acquisition alone. Setting the book in a social and historical context, accompanied by a discussion of its strengths and weaknesses, as well as its impact, will form a significant part of this chapter, leading to a series of overall assessments and conclusions.

THE HISTORICAL CONTEXT

Massialas' and Cox' book, unlike many "nuts and bolts" methods books of yesterday or today, offered quite a serious philosophical view of social studies education, one that grew out of a Deweyan tradition favoring *active* and *reflective* teaching and learning. Dewey's philosophy was transmogrified by the work of Jerome Bruner, whose psychological and social theories of education were all the rage in educational circles at the time (1960s), and whose views were seen as both liberating and provocative, providing new and powerful goals while guiding the development of engaging methodologies (Bruner, 1960).

Massialas and Cox (1966) proposed a clear and precise set of goals for the social studies, which reverberates in the many watered-down versions now circulating under the guise of imaginative "new" directions in teaching:

1. It should furnish the forum for analysis and evaluation of normative propositions or value judgments;
2. It should operate within the requisites of inquiry that relate the development of hypotheses...about social relationships to supporting evidence;
3. The end result of inquiry should be the production of a body of tested principles and generalizations; and
4. The social studies classroom should afford the student the avenue for the creative venture (p. 24).

One must understand that the post World War II era was rather repressive on a number of fronts, not politically as such, but socially and intellectually. Schools pretty much performed their civic duty and most teachers lectured while students performed their time-honored rote learning activity absorbing but not thinking much about science, social studies, language, and all the other subjects. Bruner's arguments for teaching through discovery, for engaging students with hands-on work, for treating subject matter as structures, flexible and limitless, were seen as a "breath of spring" in a repressive or perhaps conformist atmosphere. Then, when the Russians launched Sputnik, all hell broke loose in the political and educational communities, motivated by the view that the US was being "beaten" in math and science education by the "Red" Russians, an intolerable situation.

This scare led to perhaps the most innovative, generous, and carefully thought-out funding of curricula in science, math, and social science education ever witnessed in American educational circles. *Inquiry in Social Studies* came at just the right time, just at the point when "the new social studies" movement was getting under way, just when the National Science Foundation funded a wide range of incredibly imaginative "alphabet soup" programs in science and social science, just as the civil rights movement was upending the restrictive written and unwritten social and political rules of our great Republic. The book was part of a revolution in thinking about many of the persisting educational issues of the 60s that have continued (and, at best, partially solved) unto our own days. As the authors themselves stated:

> The authors take the point of view that in an age of crisis, the social studies teacher must locate his authority to teach in those postulates related to inquiry, decision making, and adjudication.

> Within this context of crisis and necessary choice, education can no longer play the role of culture preserver, mediator, and innovator, but must make its most important contribution within the area of intelligent choice and decision on the part of the individual.

> Education's major function is to create the conditions for the individual to inquire into beliefs, values, and social policies and to assess the consequences and implications of possible alternatives (Massialas & Cox, 1966, p. 5).

Thus, Massialas and Cox saw social studies as involving decision-making and adjudication as part of reflective inquiry, perhaps as its ultimate objective, and spoke against education as the "culture preserver," which I took to mean carrying on the traditions and myths that we usually believe and teach such as the "perfect balance between the three branches of government" or that "Congress has the right to declare war," just to use two past but certainly relevant examples in today's world. Furthermore, the teacher's role was seen as vitally important not by conveying facts, but by setting up an atmosphere in which students would feel comfortable about discussing controversial issues, testing the evidence, and making judgments about what actions would be best.

CONTROVERSIES

Inquiry as a method, particularly as presented by Massialas and Cox, provided several intense controversies about what we would now call knowledge construction, interpretation, and the formation of values.

First and foremost, Massialas and Cox thought a teacher's role was to create conditions for students to inquire into problems in an open, fully negotiable manner. In the 1960s, openness to student thinking was an extremely difficult and thorny issue. Teacher authority was located in their skills as negotiators and devil's advocates, and only in part due to their grasp of a knowledge base. Most teachers are used to viewing knowledge as a body of facts, a set of expert interpretations, and a list of widely accepted socially-sanctioned values and beliefs. Few step into a classroom and open up volatile topics, or even challenge boringly accepted givens in history. The time-honored bottom-line approach, safe and sound, guarded and ritualized, is to give information, usually with the aid of a textbook (Cuban, 1996). That is basic to the profession, across most subjects, although once in a while you can observe a simulation game in progress, a debate, a mock election or trial, or well-designed cooperative learning groups in action. We could easily arouse considerable controversy among and between teachers simply by challenging historical conclusions, much less the methods by which these were developed, or the underlying philosophical principles (Hoetker, 1982).

Second, Massialas and Cox proposed that interpretation is grounded on evidence (itself negotiable and testable) and that the central power of discussion is reasoned inquiry, *whatever the outcome*, which has the potential to shake up notions of immutable truth, decades of cultural conditioning, and accepted historical mythology. This revolutionary idea is drawn from the social science disciplines that demand scientific inquiry for all of us—parents, students, and teachers—and was probably viewed with great suspicion by the majority of teachers who saw themselves as socializing agents, storytellers, and superiors. They did not act as Socratic questioners and group leaders working to stir up minds. The hemlock was probably not considered in this metaphor, but surely many worried about losing their bearings and jobs if they wandered out of the tightly woven web of US history shibboleths.

Third, Massialas and Cox wanted to have it all: raise questions and issues about knowledge and knowledge formation, about the process of interpretation and validation, and about the values we hold dear. Of the three, it is hard to say which was the most potentially explosive, but perhaps values has the edge over philosophical inquiry into knowledge bases or the problems of competing interpretations of history and human behavior. Just as evidence claims could be challenged or interpretations questioned, so could values be examined in the cold light of reason, or through application, and/or through a testing of consequences. In the atmosphere of the Civil Rights Movement, the Sexual Revolution, and massive political protests against the Vietnam War, it felt quite right to challenge accepted and oppressive beliefs about race, gender, authority, and propaganda. However, as more typically conservative values reassert themselves, this type of discussion can place a teacher who is unused to negotiating competing views in a very difficult position particularly if they have not themselves thought through the problem and how it plays out in a spectrum of cultural, political, and religious beliefs.

KEY IDEAS AND ARGUMENTS

Massialas and Cox offered a strong and consistent approach to teaching and learning in a period of great change and upheaval, and it was centered on several key features or big ideas:

a. encouragement of student-initiated ideas;
b. integration of theory and practice;
c. devotion to evidence as a grounding for conclusions and decisions;
d. scientific method; and
e. imagination and creativity

Above all in importance was the generation of ideas by learners and teachers, freely expressed, exchanged, and examined, carefully and systematically. Theory was married to practice in a harmonious way, with each modifying the other through instruction that was commanded to take student feedback seriously, and shift with the audience reaction, up to a point. That point and the bottom line was a devotion to "evidence," not "facts," much like the concept of evidence in a court of law. It had to be collected, proposed, defended, cross-examined, and tested before settling into belief—a very conservative and revolutionary notion at the same time.

Inquiry meant a return to looking at raw data, and not necessarily taking anyone's word for what it meant, not even the experts. In the classroom, conversations between teacher and students, as well as students and students, served to cross-check errors and unusual or tangential conclusions. It was not the teacher's role to serve as judge and jury on student conclusions, right or wrong, but to direct attention to the data itself, and the logic behind public reasoning. Inquiry required that 'error' had to be corrected publicly for clearly stated reasons, based on evidence and/or logic, so all could understand the evolution of a conclusion, generalization, or hypothesis. It was a strongly "scientific" attitude of "let's find out for ourselves" adopted from science education leaders and programs created a few years earlier than "the new social studies" movement.

The student and teacher had to make, repeat, and recognize their own errors as part of the inquiry method, and only then would it count properly as real learning. In this regard, Massialas and Cox (1966) had the following to say:

> In the past error was tolerated because error would only corroborate an already known and consistent body of truth, or because persecution of error would simply satisfy its proponents, or because error could never defeat invincible truth. But the modern rationale takes the view that all beliefs are tentatively true or false and only verifiable through a continuous process of inquiry. Therefore, all errors must be tolerated as tentative hypotheses in the search for reliable knowledge and valid belief. (p. 295)

This concept is closely allied to the idea of scientific method, which is espoused by Massialas and Cox at many points in the book, and treats history and the social sciences as bodies of evidence to be analyzed with a view to formulating tested generalizations about human behavior. There is more science here than art and this did not sit well with many history teachers in the schools because they favored storytelling and drama, both of which may be viewed as art rather than scientifically based instructional methods (Cuban, 1996).

Along with the value placed on ideas and free discussion, *Inquiry in Social Studies* went so far as to fully include students in the investigative process. In this regard Massialas and Cox (1966) wrote: "The climate of the reflective classroom is *psychologically open and permissive* (italics added). All points of view and statements are solicited and accepted as propositions which merit examination" (p. 112).

Speaking your mind, not just spouting off, should be part and parcel of each and every classroom. Massialas and Cox viewed students as full partners in teaching and learning rather than passive small-brained sponges soaking up vast quantities of myths, facts, values, stories, and data without reflection. To engage students, inquiry promoted the concept of teaching through discovery, using imagination and creativity that engaged students in role-play and game-like encounters with a wide variety of raw data that they were asked to make sense of themselves. This is all done with a little help and guidance, but NOT answers, from their teachers. The following statement in *Inquiry in Social Studies* serves to illustrate the combination of psychology and scientific discovery that Massialas and Cox (1966) viewed as most desirable:

> It is claimed that the highest state of human autonomy and perfection is achieved when the individual begins to discover for himself regularities or irregularities in his physical and sociopolitical environments. In this sense the process of discovery also serves as a potent motivational device. When the individual is involved in discovery, motivation for learning comes from within, rather than being imposed from without. (p. 137)

"Discovery" was one component of a greater sphere of creativity where students and teachers got to exercise their imaginations and draw insights rather than simply have the teacher ask the questions, direct the lesson, summarize the data, and lead students to drawing the ("correct") final conclusions.

For the most part, students reacted naturally and enthusiastically to "discovery" lessons, not even understanding why, just being swept away by intellectual interests they didn't even know they had in themselves—all because of the structure of the presentation, the turning of the tables from teacher centered to student centered problem-solving. Of course, the teacher had to resist direct answers, otherwise the mystery of discovery would be lost.

THE PROBLEM OF VALUES AND ISSUES IN SOCIAL STUDIES EDUCATION

Special credit should be given to *Inquiry in Social Studies* for trying to deal with the knotty problem of teaching values and taking action in the social studies classroom. Massialas and Cox were acutely aware that the world was changing, and that there was growing recognition of a much more pluralistic society in which many minorities and ethnic groups were left out of the story, so to speak, and could not find themselves or their folks in the textbooks of the time: "The authors endorse the position that in a democratically oriented community characterized by cultural pluralism every person should be given a chance to contribute his views on controversial social issues" (Massialas & Cox, 1966, p. 174).

The inquiry method took on the problem of teaching values four square, strongly endorsing the *examination* of values and issues, but not the actual promotion or demotion of any values and beliefs in particular. Along with this approach, they argued for much more attention to classroom discussion of personal values and beliefs, and argued in favor of a greater activism in making decisions and taking positions, strongly influenced by the work of Oliver and Shaver (1967), who promoted social studies as a process of negotiation "adjudication" using the law as a process model. "What is needed at this time is to direct our conscious effort to deal systematically, in our classes, with questions of value and with pressing personal and social issues" (Massialas & Cox, 1966, p. 157).

Massialas and Cox faced the problem of moving students from simply taking sides and expressing positions to taking action. Implicitly, Massialas and Cox opposed the "what are your values, what are mine" game that was often played out in values clarification classrooms during the 60s and 70s for they saw such as lacking both sincerity and real affect. The latter was more like a parlor game versus an intellectual endeavor. Serious inquiry sought to confront the problems of the time—like war, poverty, education, welfare, world conflict, and so forth—not just make personal small talk.

In an "age of crisis," timidity about expressing values and beliefs was particularly problematical since many teachers and students had very strong feelings and opinions on a wide range of political, social, and economic issues that characterized the times, and did not want to be left out of the process. However, in an inquiry model, to simply impose views on students was misguided, even for those who could be clueless, aggravating, silly, or pigheaded. A '"devil's advocate" method was proposed (Massialas & Cox, 1966), in which the teacher would switch sides repeatedly, undermining whoever was winning arguments in class, only to switch again when someone else seemed to get the upper hand. This definitely produced a lot of argument, often heated, and sometimes resulted in frustration.

On the issue of the teacher's stance toward value imposition, Massialas and Cox (1966) came through with one of their many clever ideas, the "doctrine" of "defensible partisanship":

> We accept the concept of "defensible partisanship" as an appropriate position for the teacher to assume in dealing with value-laden propositions. Defensible partisanship assumes that the teacher inevitably makes preferential choices among competing ethical alternatives and creates conditions in the classroom for choices based on the most rational criteria (Massialas & Cox, 1966, p 175).

The teacher could express his/her own views, but there were rules for doing so. First, the teacher had to respect and encourage student views first, and help them to formulate their, often inchoate, ideas into something resembling a position. As the students began to develop an understanding of position taking, the teacher could tentatively inject him/herself into the discussion. If the students quailed and backed off of their views, then the teacher had to withdraw for a while into anonymity, encouraging feedback and discussion from them, and then try again. But always, one had to announce views as one's own, and provide the "most rational criteria" in defense, noting that no ideas were endorsed by any public, private, or international agencies, and then see if the students could handle it.

Interestingly, social action was left for later, only after the process of analysis and formulating a stance had taken place in the classroom or some other public forum.

Thus, the process of inquiry moved inexorably from evidence to reflection to affect and values, slowly, circling the big issues, testing reactions, repeating ploys for discussion, and moving up the scale of Bloom's taxonomy to the heights of evaluation and judgment. This inquiry process, as conceived by the authors, was part of the whole orientation toward scientific method with its inherent skepticism about claims and beliefs unsupported by evidence or reasons. It was respectful, careful, reasoned, based on evidence to support claims, and in its way, very enlightened, very democratic, and very demanding, but stopped short of recommending specific actions for change. That, apparently, was left to the inquirers to discover!

RESEARCH BASE

Strengths

Inquiry in Social Studies as an idea draws from a strong and well-developed base that was growing rapidly at the time of its publication, one that harkens back to earlier work in education by John Dewey, Maurice Hunt and Lawrence Metcalf, and Ralph Tyler. John Dewey (1912) strongly supported democratic education in the schools through the practice of democracy, doing it, rather than simply learning about its formal and legalistic rules. The notion of decision-making in Massialas and Cox come from Dewey through the work of Shirley Engle, Massialas' professor at Indiana University, who argued that decision-making and values examination should lie at the heart of social studies education (Engle, 1960). To this was added an element of activism and social challenge from George S. Counts, several decades prior, who sought to create activist schools that would make a difference in how people lived, basing the curriculum on problem-solving and social issues in daily life (Rugg, 1923). In this view, everyone could and should participate in the democratic process of reasoning and testing evidence, setting out to develop and check positions on a wide range of social, political, and economic issues.

From Bruner came a strong dose of the social science commitment to scientific inquiry that respected the structure of the disciplines and promoted the collection, synthesis, and fusion of evidence into a theory or interpretation (Bruner, 1960). The introduction of science projects actually started well before social science or history projects, and often served as models for social studies to follow (Wiley, 1967). Fenton (1967) offered a version of this for the teaching and learning of history, an approach that emphasized active learning and testing of evidence, with attention to primary sources that makes its current rediscovery amusing. Vast amounts of government funding flowed into the field from the National Science Foundation and to a lesser extent the US Office of Education and other agencies, resulting in a wave of scientifically minded projects on anthropology, sociology, geography, all producing materials for teachers in the schools. The National Council for the Social Studies recognized the movement toward social science structural disciplinary teaching by offering a yearbook on the subject that covered many of the projects and positions set forth at the time (Herbert & Murphy, 1968). This very scientific notion of procedure, discovery, and subject matter was deeply interwoven into the methods advocated by Massialas and Cox throughout their work, and was bolstered by the work of many other scholars, each of whom had a slightly different bent on methodology, with greater or lesser emphasis on subject matter or values examination.

Hunt and Metcalf proposed looking into "hidden agendas" in their earlier methods book (Hunt & Metcalf, 1955). Opening hidden agendas was succeeded by a new book that developed a sophisticated approach to teaching multiple perspectives on issues in high schools (Hunt, 1962). These books were joined by a "jurisprudential method" of negotiation and debate, and supplemented by a whole series of inexpensive paperbacks of case studies that supported the proposed method (Oliver & Shaver, 1968–1973). To this heady advocacy of law education and value examination in the classroom was added a very popular approach called "values clarification," which was touted across the country as a free and open way of encouraging students and teachers to express their deepest values and understand each other more fully, thereby learning both to deal with value differences and build tolerance for other viewpoints (Simon, et al., 1972). All of these approaches were widely debated across the country, sometimes accompanied by accusations of moral relativism and attacks on traditional American values (Massialas & Cox, 1967).

In the social studies world of the 1960s, inquiry, values, and breaking free was seen as needed to combat oppressive conditioning to authority and exclusion of minorities, women, and alternative sexual orientations from the curriculum (Kohlberg & Gilligan, 1971). Inquiry, discovery, the scientific method, and values clarification were taken very seriously throughout the US and Canada, and that awakened other latent issues such as multiculturalism, racism, gender, and economic discrimination (Banks, 1971). There has probably never been such an upwelling of interest in the subject of values, and how to teach about beliefs in ways that do not privilege or deny any school of thought over any other.

Weaknesses or Limitations

Several weaknesses became apparent as the movement developed, particularly in two areas: the developmental needs of youth, and school populations.

While many were proposing exciting new ways to teach social studies and advocating strongly for decision-making, position-taking, values clarification, jurisprudential debate, etc., relatively little was known about what students actually believed or how they acquired their political values. Furthermore, school populations had very different needs, varying greatly geographically, and by social class. Scientific-based instruction that stressed the structure of the disciplines, inquiry and discovery, as well as values analysis and debate, might do well in certain kinds of communities but be met with wonder or worse yet, hostility, in other communities. The whole idea of student needs seemed to diminish in importance compared to the joys of curriculum innovation and design for all, often overlooking the work of predecessors in education who argued that courses and materials had to be tailored to audiences needs and wants rather than imposed from above (Tyler, 1950). To answer questions about student preferences and attitudes, a sub-field developed in social studies that borrowed heavily from political science and sociology; it was called political socialization (Patrick, 1969). How personal, parental, peer, and media influenced value formation added to the overall picture of the ways in which political and social values developed with maturation (Greenstein, 1965).

Research on the Massialas and Cox version of the inquiry method was conducted by Massialas and Zevin in order to learn more about students' views of inquiry instruction, subject matter, and the impact of debate and discussion in the classroom (Massialas & Zevin, 1967, 1969–1973). Classroom lessons in a wide range of subjects, science, mathematics, language, geography, and social issues were presented and recorded in local Chicago secondary classrooms. Discovery techniques dominated teacher presentations, generally applied to average students in urban public school classrooms. Based on recorded and transcribed conversations in a dozen or more classrooms, students were found to react enthusiastically to the inquiry approach, significantly increasing their level and amount of participation across subjects. Playfulness and thinking out loud characterized a majority of the recorded conversations, with many moving from a typical teacher to student, and student to teacher response pattern, toward student initiated expressions of ideas, and student exchanges of analyses, viewpoints, and positions on issues. Although many students expressed frustration with the lack of answers provided by their teachers, nearly all forged forward inquiring into the problems presented and providing tentative, grounded conclusions (at least by the end of lessons). Students began to display more self-confidence and independence than was common in a typical Chicago public school social studies classroom at that time (Massialas & Zevin, 1967). The classroom recordings supported the view that "average" students could master inquiry learning, and demonstrate progress in thinking at higher levels, moving from didactic toward reflective and affective modes of thought.

Slowly, gaps in knowledge to support the new social studies programs were filled in, but by the time the research was well under way, the programs were already under attack and their popularity dying out.

IMPLEMENTATION

Strengths

A wave of social science and social studies projects, including history initiatives, swept the educational community in the 1960s lasting well into the late 1970s. Funding largely from federal sources kept the machinery of invention and dissemination going, and most college faculty were quite familiar with at least two or three of the "alphabet soup" projects and with the new methods books in the field. The stress on discovery or inquiry learning combined with strong social science and history scholarship led to the creation of a range of exciting, intriguing, and thought-provoking programs in history, anthropology, sociology, geography, leading a bit later to cross-disciplinary efforts. All tended to share the commitment to scientific thinking and inquiry, and as time went on, also to some form of values examination process. This tended to bifurcate into those with a more psychological, clinical bent, and those with a distinctly activist, political and civic education focus.

After the rather dull and conformist 1950s, the new attention to scholarship, thinking for oneself, and evidence- rather than authority-based philosophy of teaching and learning was well received, if not fully understood, in school systems throughout the country. Even more impressive was the higher education embrace of the new social studies and inquiry methods. In fact, college faculty in the sciences and social sciences spearheaded the drive to create programs and were aided by social studies education professors from all regions of the country. The National Council for the Social Studies became a forum for sharing ideas about teaching and for learning about National Science Foundation, National Endowment for the Humanities, US Office of Education and other projects.

Almost every school had some version of a decision-making, values clarification, jurisprudential or law education program, emphasizing participation, active school government (in places), and multiculturalism. The temper of the times combined with the innovative and civic-minded programs merged in many places to makeover the curriculum. Modular courses, and courses like women's studies, race relations, multicultural topics, and African-American history were sprinkled in schools across the nation. The standard curriculum inherited from the 19th Century consisting of US and European history, along with civics and government, was challenged by more contemporary courses focusing on pertinent issues and problems.

Weaknesses or Limitations

The wave of change and innovation began to sag in the mid-1970s, perhaps earlier (this is arguable), and certainly declined in terms of implementation and popularity. There were many reasons for this. Perhaps the principal being the sophistication and complexity of the materials created. Most teachers needed intensive mentoring to prepare them to implement nearly all of the social science curricula, perhaps less so the values approach. While the government seemed to have large sums for curriculum development by the social science societies, it gave relatively paltry sums for pre- or in-service workshops and institutes. There were important National Defense Education Act and National Science Foundation seminars and institutes, but these often tended to a pattern of scholarly input in the morning and educational applications in the afternoon. Input of data tended to be stressed although the goal of changing teaching and learning styles was widely professed.

Second, although highly creative, many of the projects, such as "Man: A Course of Study," or the, "High School Geography Project," did not fit the extant curriculum very well. New courses had to be created to accommodate these programs, or they had to be added or infused into existing courses. Combined with what was often cursory teacher preparation, this led to negative perceptions of the programs as largely aimed at the elite students, or as demanding a great deal of additional work in preparing lessons and units.

While some projects like Sociological Resources for the Social Studies tried to join sociology faculty with teachers and education professors in creating units, many did not even contemplate such a mutually supportive plan, and the academics tended to drive almost the entire program from content to process to evaluation, often without considering student needs, or social problems. Massialas and Cox's methods book aimed to provide teachers with a way of dealing with the new programs, specifically detailing the steps toward the formation and testing of generalizations about human behavior. Note that while this language mimicked the scientific, structural goals of the movement, Massialas' and Cox's intent was to translate those goals into clear pedagogical actions.

Barriers

In some ways, it is amazing that such a rigorously scientific approach—one advocating that *all* ideas and values should be open to debate, combined with an opening of hidden agendas of beliefs—should have been as widely adopted as it was by methods' faculty at colleges and universities. In education circles, a variety of methods books provided well-developed theories and guides to practice, affecting most, if not all, future social studies education professors. But ultimately these theories and guides to practice came up against several important barriers that were probably underestimated at the time. Changing professors' ideas was a lot easier to accomplish than changing schools, curriculum, or teachers.

One key barrier was the force of traditional conceptions of teaching as focusing on the delivery of information about history and government (Hoetker & Ahlbrandt, 1969). Inquiry and discovery methods, including the Massialas and Cox version, tended to destabilize teachers' views of themselves as content-driven and directive, demanding a dramatic shift in their goals and daily behavior. The questioner role trumped the old delivery role, and this represented a barrier to change unless accompanied by considerable amounts of in-service training and mentoring, and even then this had limited success (Thompson, 1966).

Looking back, it is clear that a transformation of philosophy was called for, not simply a change in teaching methods, with the more imaginative elite teachers taking the forefront in trying out the new methods and the new materials (Hahn et al., 1977). Furthermore, not nearly enough attention was given to urban schools, below average students, and those schools directed by administrations to implement the programs with just bare-bones familiarity of the theoretical and practical aspects of the new programs (Hahn, et al., 1977). That said, there were a few notable projects that attempted to reach the masses (Oliver & Newmann, 1969–1973) and "slow learners" (Knowslar, 1970). Some would say that the inquiry approach and projects "oversold themselves" by promoting claims for improving learning and social skills that did not materialize, most especially for "typical teachers of typical classrooms" (Fenton, 1991).

A second major barrier was the heavy institutional investment in textbooks and curricula that basically supported traditional transmission goals rather than inquiry. (That said, over the years, there has been great improvement due to the movement's impact. For example, most current textbooks include at least some primary sources, give attention to historical and social science methods of investigation, and promote better questioning techniques, more higher level thinking.) After a period of widespread experimentation with many aspects of inquiry, course structures, topics, and special programs, the US curriculum pattern has more or less reverted to mainly history courses taught with large (though improved) narrative text-books. Meanwhile, many college faculty members continue to pursue topics that have grown out of inquiry approaches and still conduct research in political socialization, pursuing goals that are quite in line with the period of re-examination of teaching and learning goals in social studies. Values examination in the form of citizenship goals and democratic classrooms is very much in evidence in recent issues of *Theory and Research in Social Education*, demonstrating historical continuity, e.g., (the advocacy of democratic classroom behavior, Boyle-Baise, 2003).

RESOURCES DEVELOPED OR MADE AVAILABLE

Inquiry in Social Studies produced a considerable number of college faculty and teachers who entered the educational system, and has inspired many, including this author, to develop and extend their own "methods" books (Zevin, 1992, 2001, 2007), but produced no official curriculum or teaching programs. Massialas and I did create, over a long period, a series entitled, "World History Through Inquiry" that embodied inquiry principles and practices, but that was developed through a private publisher, not a government funded program (Massialas & Zevin, 1969–1973). At the time, we viewed world history courses as a relatively neglected sub-field compared with government or US history courses, and tried to develop a program based on the ideas of Dewey, Bruner, Engle, and other seminal thinkers in education. *Inquiry in Social Studies* was closely connected to many of the National Science Projects and US Office of Education programs. Many other approaches and subjects were developed, most notably, Man: A Course of Study, The High School Geography Project, The Anthropology Curriculum Study, and the Indiana Political Science Program. Most were supported by National Science Foundation grants.

IMPACT OF—WHEN FINALLY IMPLEMENTED

Inquiry in Social Studies had a generally positive reception in the field, particularly since its authors represented a continuity of opinion begun in the 1950s and early 1960s. Central to the positive reception was that Massialas and Cox (1966) recognized the earlier contributions and built on those in a more systematic way than had previously been done, while grappling with difficult issues of knowledge definition and values examination. The classroom as a forum of inquiry has been widely adopted as an idea in many courses and curricula, especially those dealing with civics, government, and politics. Despite the commitment to inquiry, the idea that all knowledge and values are ultimately negotiable—and there are no real errors in thinking—was pushed aside as upsetting and unworkable by most teachers. It must be kept in mind that this was but one of many influential methods and curriculum books mostly written in the late 1950s through the 1960s that transformed social studies education. "Democratically conducted" classrooms continue to be a popular idea, although perhaps honored more in the breach than in actual practice.

Finally, the struggle against conformist thinking and the call for creativity and discovery have largely withered away. Although it stills pops up now and then in the literature and in school programs, it is probably diminished by the drive for standards-based programs that hold the promise of significant increases in largely knowledge based standardized test scores. And yet, there are those nagging demands for critical thinking, comprehension, and analysis represented by Document Based Questions and other forms of testing. So the old pressures and contradictions are still very much in play, though the pendulum right now is on the side of transmission and accumulation of knowledge.

IMPACT OF LONG TERM

It is difficult to measure long-term impact, but Massialas and Cox certainly influenced several generations' worth of teachers and college faculty in the social studies, bolstering the strong commitment of college and university faculty in the field to some form of inquiry teaching, values examination, civic action, and curriculum development. Many of their graduates, including myself, went on to occupy college positions in social studies education, educational research, and political science departments around the country. Many produced noteworthy research studies, curriculum projects, and treatises on pedagogy. Some college faculty became unusually creative and imaginative, some disappeared from the public exchange and production of knowledge. Overall, in terms of the total functioning of the American social studies curriculum, the influence was probably marginal, with a small percentage of instructors actively pursuing inquiry/discovery instructional goals and methods, while the majority remained or settled back into the standard methods, "chalk and talk." For most teachers, the preference is for approaches best suited to the transmission of knowledge, still regarded as the central function of teaching by most teachers (Larson, 1997). However, there has been steady growth in attention to primary sources in history and to social science methods combined with higher level, critical thinking, and the development of essential questions and backward design (Wiggins & McTighe, 1998).

CONCLUSION

Inquiry in Social Studies represents one of several influential attempts to significantly alter the way teachers conceptualize instruction. Its authors provided a systematic approach to instruction in social studies based on a marriage of theory and practice, and a scientific method of questioning and reasoning that leads to the formation of tested generalizations about human actions and which offers positions and roles for teachers to play in a largely student-centered classroom where the give and take of ideas is deeply valued.

The book and its ideas were evolutionary, if viewed in the context of the times, and built on predecessor "methods" books which increasingly demanded honest and open conversation and debate about values as a key to reforming the way people think about each other and about subject matter. The dramatic events of the 1960s—the Civil Rights Movement, the assassination of beloved leaders for change, the War in Vietnam, and shifting values and beliefs about human equality, sexuality, race and gender, created a fertile ground for analyzing human behavior, examining values and taking action. Scientific method began the wave of curriculum invention and change, but fused with social studies and history centering on concerns about citizenship, and social action as well as with political pressures for greater participation, equality, and economic opportunity.

This general inquiry approach was supported, with interesting variations, by many other researchers and writers in social studies, all of whom attempted to shape teaching goals and methods in the direction of challenging students to discuss social issues, solve problems, make decisions, and come to their own conclusions in a democratic classroom atmosphere (Allen, et. al, 1968). While most of the briefly popular project materials in the 1960s and 1970s have disappeared from elementary and secondary classrooms to be replaced by 20 pound standard textbooks, the scholarship and interests of the social studies education profession, as a group, still exhibits the powerful influence of the inquiry movement on its teaching, writing, and research interests.

REFERENCES

Allen, R. F., Fleckenstein, J. V., & Lyons, P. M. (Eds.) (1968). *Inquiry in the social studies*. Washington, D.C.: National Council for the Social Studies

Banks, J. (November, 1971). Teaching Black history with a focus on decision-making. *Social Education*, 35, 740–745, 820–821.

Bruner, J. (1960). *The process of education*. Cambridge, MA: Harvard University Press

Boyle-Baise, L. (2003). Doing democracy in social studies methods. *Theory and Research in Social Education*, *31*(1), 51–72.

Cuban, L. (1996). *How teachers taught*. New York: Columbia Teachers College Press.

Dewey, J. (1901) *How we think*. New York: The Macmillan Co.

Dewey, J. (1912). *Democracy and education*. New York: The Macmillan Co.

Engle, S. H. (1960). Decision-making: The heart of social studies instruction. *Social Education, 24*, 301–304.

Fenton, E. (1967). *The new social studies.* New York: Holt, Rinehart, & Winston.

Fenton, E. (1991). Reflections on the "new social studies." *The Social Studies, 82*(3), 84–91.

Fenton, E. (1966). *Teaching the new social studies in secondary schools.* New York: Holt, Rinehart, and Winston.

Greenstein, F. (1965). Children and politics. New Haven, CT: Yale University Press

Hahn, C. L., Marker, G. W., Switzer, T. M., & Turner, M. J. (1977). *Three studies on perception and utilization of "new social studies" materials.* Boulder, CO.: Social Science Education Consortium.

Herbert, L. J., & Murphy ,W. (Eds.). (1968). *Structure in the social studies.* Washington, D.C.: National Council for the Social Studies.

Hoetker, J., & Ahlbrandt, W. P. (1969). The persistence of recitation American. *Educational Research Journal, 6*(2), 145–167

Hunt, E. M. (1962). *High school social studies perspectives.* Boston, MA: Houghton-Mifflin

Hunt, M. P., & Metcalf, L. E. (1955). *Teaching high school social studies.* New York: Harper & Row

Kohlberg, L., & C. Gilligan. (1971. The adolescent as philosopher: The discovery of the self in a postconventional world." *Daedalus, 100,*1050–1086.

Knowslar, A. O. (Ed.). (1970). *The Americans: A history of the US.* New York: American Heritage.

Larson, B. (November, 1997). Influences on social studies teachers' use of classroom discussion. Paper presented at the annual meeting of the college and university faculty association of the National Council for the Social Studies, Cincinnati, OH. ERIC: ED428009

Massialas, B. G., & Cox, B. (1966). *Inquiry in social studies.* New York: McGraw-Hill

Massialas, B. G., & Zevin, J. (1967). *Creative encounters in the classroom.* New York: John Wiley & Sons

Massialas, B. G. & Zevin, J. (1969–1973). *World history through inquiry* (9 units and multimedia supplements). Chicago, IL: Rand McNally

Oliver, D. W., & Newmann, F. M. (1968–1973). *Public issues series american education publications.* Columbus, OH: Education Center.

Oliver, D. W., & Shaver, J. P. (1962) The analysis of public controversy: A study of citizenship education. Cooperative Research Project, 8145 U.S. Office of Education. Cambridge, MA: Harvard University

Oliver, D., & Shaver, J. (1967). *Teaching Public Issues in the High School.* Boston, MA: Houghton-Mifflin

Patrick, J. J. (1969). Implications of political socialization research for the reform of civic education. *Social Education, 33*(1), 15–21.

Rugg, H. O. (1923). Problems of contemporary life as a basis for curriculum-making in social studies. In H.O. Rugg (Ed.), *Twenty-second yearbook of the National Society for Social Education. The social studies in elementary and secondary school, vol. II.* (pp. 260–273). Bloomington, IN: Public School Publishing Co.

Simon, S. B., Howe, L. W., & Kirschenbaum, H. (1972). *Values clarification: A handbook of practical strategies for teachers and students.* New York: Hart

Thompson, J. M. (1966). *Teachers, history, and NDEA institutes.* New York: Council of Learned Societies.

Tyler, R. W. (1950). *Basic principles of curriculum and instruction.* Chicago, IL: University of Chicago Press.

Wiggins, G., & McTighe, J. (1998). *Understanding by design.* Alexandria, VA: Association for Supervision and Curriculum Development.

Wiley, K. B., & Superka, D.P. (1967). *Evaluation studies on "new social studies" materials.* Boulder, CO: Social Science Education Consortium.

Zevin, J. (1992, 2001, 2007). *Social studies for the 21ˢᵗ century.* (3ʳᵈ ed.). New York: Erlbaum/Routledge/Taylor and Francis.

CHAPTER 5

HUMAN RIGHTS EDUCATION

Felisa Tibbitts and William R. Fernekes

Give to every human being every right that you claim for yourself.—Robert Ingersol

INTRODUCTION

Human rights education (HRE) is an international movement to promote awareness about the rights accorded by the Universal Declaration of Human Rights and related human rights conventions, and the procedures that exist for the redress of violations of these rights (Amnesty International, 2005; Tibbitts, 1996; Reardon, 1995). Beginning with the adoption of the Universal Declaration of Human Right in 1948, the United Nations and its specialized agencies formally recognized the right of citizens to be informed about the rights and freedoms contained in the documents ratified by their countries—the right to human rights education itself (UNESCO, 2005). Since then, numerous policy documents developed by United Nations (UN) affiliated agencies, international policymaking bodies, regional human rights bodies and national human rights agencies have referenced

Teaching and Studying Social Issues: Major Programs and Approaches, pages 87–117
Copyright © 2011 by Information Age Publishing
87

HRE, proposing that the treatment of human rights themes should be present in schooling (Pearse, 1987).[1]

The U.N. Office of the High Commissioner for Human Rights defines human rights education as "training, dissemination and information efforts aimed at the building of a universal culture of human rights through the imparting of knowledge and skills and the molding of attitudes directed to:

a. the strengthening of respect for human rights and fundamental freedoms;

b. the full development of the human personality and the sense of its dignity;

c. the promotion of understanding, tolerance, gender equality and friendship among all nations, indigenous peoples and racial, national, ethnic, religious and linguistic groups; and,

d. the enabling of all persons to participate effectively in a free society (United Nations, Office of the High Commissioner for Human Rights, 1997, p. 5).

This definition is not specific to the school sector and, in fact, the United Nations proposes human rights education for all sectors of society as well as part of a "lifelong learning" process for individuals (United Nations, Office of the High Commissioner for Human Rights, 1997, pp. 113–14). The human rights referred to cover a broad range, including those contained in the Universal Declaration of Human Rights, as well as related treaties and covenants, such as the International Covenant on Economic, Social and Cultural Rights, the International Covenant on Civil and Political Rights, the Convention on the Rights of the Child and the Convention for the Elimination of All Forms of Discrimination Against Women, among others.[2] Which human rights are addressed in learning situations, and how, has become of increasing interest as the worldwide human rights movement has grown. As the worldwide movement to expand human rights protections has grown, how to effectively develop and integrate human rights education programs within both formal and informal learning environments has also become a topic of increasing interest around the world.

This interest has not come without critical reflection on the nature of human rights itself. Human rights education programming necessarily raises questions about the universality of human rights and the viability of the

---

[1]During the 1990s, several important international documents on human rights education were developed. These were: *The World Plan of Action on Education for Human Rights and Democracy* (1993); *The Declaration and Integrated Framework of Action on Education for Peace, Human Rights and Democracy* (1995); *The World Conference on Human Rights* (1993); and *Guidelines for Plans of Action for the United Nations Decade for Human Rights Education 1995–2004* (1995).

[2]The full set of human rights documents as well as related General Comments can be found on the website of the UN Office of the High Commissioner for Human Rights at www.ohchr.org .

framework in relation to national legal and cultural norms (in particular, norms that appear to be in conflict with human rights). As with the human rights field in general, HRE is a dynamic area of work that invites self-reflection and the recognition that human rights are evolving and, in some circumstances, can even be in conflict with one another. The principles of universality and indivisibility espoused by the United Nations are intended to be respected but understanding their implications are part of the agenda for a human rights education program.

THE EXPANSION OF HUMAN RIGHTS EDUCATION IN SCHOOLS

Although still a developing field, there is increasing evidence that HRE is emerging in the work of non-governmental organizations working at the grassroots level as well as in national systems of education (Buergenthal & Torney, 1976; Claude, 1996; Elbers, 2000; HREA, 2005a; IIDH, 2002). The only study on this subject indicated that the number of organizations dedicated to human rights education quadrupled between 1980 and 1995, from 12 to 50 (Ramirez, et al., 2006, p. 3). These numbers are likely to be much higher as the secondary sources only documented those organizations that had either an Internet presence or were already networked in international circles. An International Bureau of Education (IBE) study that examined the number of times the term "human rights" was mentioned in their documents, found a mean of 0.70, 0.82, and 0.64 for countries within the regions of Sub-Saharan Africa, Eastern Europe and the former USSR, and Latin American and the Caribbean, respectively (Ramirez, et al., 2006, p. 3). Interestingly enough, the lowest means were for Asia and Western Europe and North America at 0.11 (Ramirez et al., p. 3), although the range of response rates across regions—from 31% to 74%—suggests that these results are approximate at best. A review in 1996 showed that through the cooperative efforts of NGOs and educational authorities, human rights courses and topics had been introduced into the national curricula in Albania, Australia, Brazil, Canada, Denmark, Norway, the UK and Ukraine (Kati & Gjedia, 2003; Tibbitts, 1996). The IBE study and other less formal data gathering suggests that the number of educational systems including human rights in their formal curricula is now higher.

As of 2000, Banks' study revealed that less than half of all fifty states had mandates for the inclusion of human rights content in compulsory education, and many of these mandates were linked to curriculum subtopics (for example, study of the Holocaust and genocides) that were more narrowly focused than the definition offered by the U.N. Office of the High Commissioner for Human Rights. In a subsequent study conducted in the United

States, Banks (2001) provided evidence that human rights education was evident in statewide curriculum standards in twenty U.S. states, although it remains unclear how much time individual classroom teachers actually devote to human rights instruction, or the degree to which such instruction is informed by accurate and current information on the topic. A recent study of teaching practices about the Holocaust in the United States, commissioned by the U.S. Holocaust Memorial Museum, found that engendering "respect for human rights" was a very prominent rationale for study of the Holocaust offered by teachers throughout the nation (Donnelly, 2006). The decentralized structure of educational governance and policy-making in the United States mitigates against national mandates for curricular integration, thus making state-level policy making the most influential "leverage" for inclusion of human rights education.

In the last five years, national and regional HRE networks have been established in many parts of the world (HREA, 2005a). In 2005, with the conclusion of the UN Decade for HRE, the Office of the U.N. High Commissioner for Human Rights launched an ongoing and more focused World Programme with a Plan of Action for Human Rights Education (UN General Assembly, 2005), which promises to elicit improved cooperation from governments, as well as cross-cutting support from UN bodies. The first phase of the World Programme is focused on promoting human rights education in schools. Some countries have gone as far as to design or implement a national plan for human rights education (e.g., Brazil, Colombia, Ecuador, El Salvador, Mexico, and Dominican Republic).

The signatory states-parties to the Convention on the Rights of the Child are obligated to address the need for human rights education through development of action plans concerning children's rights, and a number of states parties have taken action to examine current national efforts regarding education dealing with human rights. For example, on July 6, 2007, the National Human Rights Commission in India recommended that a comprehensive human rights education plan should be enacted "as a main subject at all levels from primary to post-graduate" (quoted in *The Hindu*, as reported on the Global HRE Listserv, HREA, 2007). This recommendation was the outcome of a study by a task force on human rights education created by the National Human Rights Commission of India in 2006.

CIVIC AND HUMAN RIGHTS EDUCATION

Education for citizenship is a universal mandate for schools in representative democracies and is traditionally incorporated as both a formal subject as well as an objective for school life and school-based activities. The specific learning agenda of citizenship education is largely determined by the state educational system, with some attention to global trends. Currently, in European societies, for example, there is an interest in the idea of "compound citizenship" because of the advent of the European Union and intra-state relationships (Tschoumy, 1993).

Citizenship—or civic—education has several core concepts, including civic knowledge and cognitive civic skills (such as understanding the principles of representative democracy, constitutionalism/rule of law, and rights responsibilities of citizens (Hamot, 2003). The goals of citizenship education most closely related to "learning to live together" relate to participatory civic skills and civic dispositions.

These skills and dispositions can be summarized as follows:

a. helping students become self-confident, well-informed citizens who are able to think rationally and who are committed to the values of human dignity and human rights;

b. fostering a willingness and capacity to participate in political affairs on local, national and international levels; and

c. developing a strong recognition of the need to balance individualism and self-interest with human interdependence and social as well as environmental responsibility (Schuetz, 1996, p. 1).

Human rights education in many countries intersects with democratic citizenship education, by taking the core concepts of citizenship education and applying them both more universally and more critically. In that way, knowledge about key concepts and facts and issues of civic dispositions and civic skills are applied to the areas of global social responsibility, justice and social action.

In the school setting, human rights education places a relatively stronger emphasis on values acquisition and cognitive skill development. However, human rights education is also intended to foster social responsibility and action among students (Tibbitts, 2002). This is critically important in the development of values and dispositions focused on addressing social problems and facilitating student empowerment to engage in social action. As Shiman and Fernekes argued in a 1999 essay regarding the intersections between human rights, the study of the Holocaust, and education for global citizenship, five capacities require development to foster the growth of responsibility and caring, which are two critical themes in the design of human rights education programs:

1. critical analysis of social conditions fostering human rights violations and those that impede such violations;

2. identifying social conditions that make the realization of human rights guarantees difficult to realize;

3. identifying and publicizing human rights violations or assaults on human rights;
4. proposing actions to redress human rights violations and protect against future violations; and
5. organizing and acting on behalf of human rights as individuals and within groups (p. 57).

Because the study of human rights naturally takes a critical stance towards governments and institutional abuses of power, topics of study are influenced by problem areas such as child labor, genocide, refugees and/or issues germane to the international, national, state, local and school communities. The organizing values of the Universal Declaration of Human Rights (UDHR) and other key human rights documents are used to examine the sources of violations of rights and to encourage action to resolve them. A "critical human rights consciousness" is a key goal for human rights educators (Meintjes, 1997, p. 68).[3] Ideally, human rights education supports the proposition of "learning to live together" by promoting an agenda of international justice (as a precondition for peace) and by encouraging the development of personal power, group support and critical awareness (Adams & Schniedewind, 1988, pp. 48–50).

These goals are integral to a conception of citizenship education that places the study of critical social issues at the center of curriculum design. As Hahn (1996) noted in a comprehensive review of the literature on issues-centered social studies in the United States:

> ...social studies educators who make a commitment to issues-centered instruction are likely to find that their students become more interested in the political arena, develop a greater sense of political efficacy and confidence, and become more interested in the issues that they have studied as well as knowledgeable about them. (Hahn, 1996, p. 37)

These findings correlate well with the skills and dispositions noted by Schuetz (1997) for human rights education, and are reinforced by the findings from the 1999 IEA study on civic education demonstrating that classroom instruction which fostered broad-based student participation with an

---

[3]According to Meintjes, critical human rights consciousness may constitute the following:
*   the ability of students to recognize the human rights dimensions of, and their relationship to, a given conflict- or problem-oriented exercise;
*   an expression of awareness and concern about their role in the protection or promotion of these rights;
*   a critical evaluation of the potential responses that may be offered;
*   an attempt to identify or create new responses;
*   a judgment or decision about which choice is most appropriate; and,
*   an expression of confidence and a recognition of responsibility and influence in both the decision and its impact.

open classroom climate and the in-depth consideration of issues facilitated greater student commitment to political participation and tolerance (Torney-Purta, et al, 1999).

IMPLEMENTATION

Strengths

The two primary strengths of HRE, as a developing area of education are (1) the critical role of pedagogy and (2) its diversity of form.

Pedagogy of HRE

Since 1995, elaboration by the U.N. and other agencies has clarified that inherent in human rights education are components of knowledge, skills and attitudes consistent with recognized human rights principles that empower individuals and groups to address oppression and injustice (Amnesty International, 2007; Asia-Pacific Regional Resource Center for Human Rights Education, 2003).

Human rights education has both legal and normative dimensions. The legal dimension deals with content about international human rights standards as embodied in the UDHR and other treaties and covenants to which countries subscribe. These standards encompass civil and political rights, as well as social, economic, and cultural rights. In recent years, environmental and collective rights have been added to this evolving framework. This law-oriented approach recognizes the importance of monitoring and accountability in ensuring that governments uphold the letter and spirit of human rights obligations.

At the same time, HRE is a normative and cultural enterprise. The process of human rights education is intended to be one that provides skills, knowledge, and motivation to individuals to transform their own lives and realities so that they are more consistent with human rights norms and values. For this reason, interactive, learner-centered methods are widely promoted. The following kinds of pedagogy are representative of those promoted by HRE advocates:

- *Experiential and activity-centered*: involving the solicitation of learners' prior knowledge and offering activities that draw out learners' experiences and knowledge;
- *Problem-posing*: challenging the learners' prior knowledge;
- *Participative*: encouraging collective efforts in clarifying concepts, analyzing themes and doing the activities;
- *Dialectical*: requiring learners to compare their knowledge with those from other sources;

- *Analytical*: asking learners to think about why things are and how they came to be;
- *Healing*: promoting human rights in intra-personal and inter-personal relations;
- *Strategic thinking-oriented*: directing learners to set their own goals and to think of strategic ways of achieving them; and
- *Goal and action-oriented*: allowing learners to plan and organize actions in relation to their goals (ARRC, 2003, n.p.).

Human rights education in school settings is adapted to the age of learners and the conditions of national/local educational policies and schools. Developmental and conceptual frameworks for HRE have been developed by the United Nations and several NGOs. These frameworks assist in settings goals for HRE, illustrating both what it shares and what it contributes to other educational approaches that address values such as social justice (see Table).

Diversity of Approach

Human rights themes and content in schools can be found as a cross-cultural theme within educational policy or integrated within existing subjects, such as history, civics/citizenship education, social studies and the humanities. Human rights education can also be found in the arts and in non-formal clubs and special events that take place in the school setting.

In addition to taking place in schools, HRE is also part and parcel of a variety of other educational settings; in training programs for professionals such as the police, prison officials, the military, social workers; for potentially vulnerable populations such as women and minorities; as part of community development programs; and in public awareness campaigns.

The broad normative framework of human rights education and the wide spectrum of potential learners have resulted in a great deal of variation in the ways in which human rights education has been implemented. Although human rights education is defined by the universal framework of the international, and, in certain cases, regional, standards, the specific topics and their application is contingent upon local and national contexts. Adaptation to local contexts is essential to help to ensure relevance and meaning and for refuting the potential criticism that HRE's promotion of international standards is primarily symbolic.

Human rights education in post-conflict or post-colonial countries tends to be associated with the rule of law and efforts by authorities attempting to establish their legitimacy. Among groups that experience a high amount of discrimination, particularly within countries that are highly repressive and undemocratic, HRE tends to be focused on popular empowerment and resistance. Human rights education in countries that are democratic but struggling with development is often oriented towards the infusion of

Methodologies: Development and Conceptual Framework for HRE (Flowers, 1998) Levels

	Goals	Key Concepts	Specific Human Rights Problems	Education Standards and Instruments
Early Childhood Preschool & Lower primary Ages 3–7	Respect for self Respect for parents and teachers Respect for others	Self Community Responsibility	Racism Sexism Unfairness Hurting people (emotionally, physically)	Classroom rules Family life Convention on the Rights of the Child
Later Childhood Upper primary Ages 8–11	Social responsibility Citizenship Distinguishing wants from needs from rights	Individual rights Group rights Freedom Equality Justice Rule of law Government Security Democracy	Discrimination/ prejudice Poverty/hunger Injustice Ethnocentrism Passivity	UDHR History of human rights Local, national legal systems Local and national history in human rights terms UNESCO, UNICEF
Adolescence Lower secondary Ages 12–14	Knowledge of specific human rights	International law World peace World development World political economy World ecology Legal rights Moral rights	Ignorance Apathy Cynicism Political repression Colonialism/ imperialism Economic globalization Environmental degradation	UN Covenants Elimination of racism Elimination of sexism Regional human rights conventions UNHCR NGOs
Older Adolescents and Adults Upper secondary Ages 15 and up	Knowledge of human rights standards Integration of human rights into personal awareness and behaviors	Moral inclusion/ exclusion Moral responsibility/ literacy	Genocide Torture	Geneva Conventions Specialized conventions Evolving human rights standards

human rights principles vis-a-vis sustainable development (Yeban, 2003). In countries that enjoy both democratic and economic development, HRE is often focused on issues of discrimination (e.g., problems faced by migrants, minorities or women). In any country at any given time, HRE can take on different forms and purposes depending upon the context of the program.

Several explanations have been proposed for the increased presence of human rights education in schools since the 1990s. One explanation relates to increased globalization, a term still being defined, but recognized as one emphasizing "world citizenship and the strong assumption of personal agency required for global citizenship" (Suarez, 2007, p. 49). Moreover, authorities are increasingly calling on schools to promote respect among peoples, democratic governance and viable civil societies.

Democratic citizenship, including human rights education, is often seen by regional human rights agencies as a way to "manage diversity," with human rights education incorporated into processes such as the Graz Stability Pact in South Eastern Europe (Council of Europe, 2001; South House Exchange, 2004). In contemporary Europe, education for democratic citizenship, including human rights education, is often a way of promoting young people's active participation in democratic society, in promoting social cohesion and in fighting violence, xenophobia, racism, intolerance and aggressive nationalism (Froumin, 2003). In the early 2000s, human rights education was linked in inter-governmental circles with a variety of global phenomena, including development and poverty, religious freedom, and globalization in general (UNESCO, 2005). Europe's regional human rights agency, the Council of Europe, is working on developing a culture of religion, "which takes an 'ethics' and 'human rights' based approach to religious teaching in order to provide an alternative to governments that currently offer required religion classes that can be a source of division and ethnic nationalism, as in Serbia-Montenegro (Tibbitts, 2003).

Since the 1940s, issues-centered approaches to curriculum design in social studies programs in the United States have emphasized the importance of reflective thought among learners, a process which has most often been linked to the examination of social problems that have defied easy solutions, or which represented "closed areas" of discourse in the society (Hunt & Metcalf, 1955). Social studies theorists such as Alan Griffin, Erling Hunt and Lawrence Metcalf, Donald Oliver and James Shaver, Fred Newmann, and Shirley Engle and Anna Ochoa have elaborated conceptual frameworks for the design of curricula that promote the development of critical reflection by students about pervasive social problems, many of which juxtapose democratic ideals and their incomplete realization as core curricular content for classroom instruction.[4] Problems such as racial/ethnic relations, patterns of prejudice, discrimination and intolerance, poverty, sexism and others directly related to human rights have been integral in issues-centered curricula, and continue to be present in social studies education throughout the USA today (Evans & Saxe, 1996; Totten & Pedersen, 2007).

Non-governmental organizations from different countries and regions periodically initiate meetings in which they identify strategies for applying the human rights framework to global challenges. One such symposium,

---

[4] To explore the works of issues-centered theorists further, consult these sources: Engle and Ochoa, 1988; Griffin, 1942; Hunt and Metcalf, 1968; Newmann and Oliver, 1970; and Oliver and Shaver, 1966.

which took place in South Africa in 2001 in a meeting organized in concert with the World Conference Against Racism, identified human rights education in schools as a key strategy for combating racism (Flowers, 2001).

LIMITATIONS

The authors see two primary limitations to HRE: diverse approaches; and an identity that can overlap with other educational approaches focused on social justice.

1. Diverse Approaches

The very features of HRE that make it possible for human rights education advocates to promote (and claim) that they are integrating HRE in schools makes it difficult to categorize HRE. The diverse approaches of HRE are evident in at least three ways: the learning goals of HRE, the content of HRE (meaning the topics that are emphasized), and the ways in which HRE is introduced in schools (for example, as a cross-curricular theme or through informal education activities). Moreover, such diverse approaches make it difficult for comparative research to be carried out.

2. Overlapping Identity

As noted earlier, human rights education has been linked in many school systems with civic or citizenship education. Other approaches that share the normative goals of HRE and, in some cases, shared methodologies, include peace and conflict resolution, global education, intercultural education, tolerance education, anti-racist education and Holocaust education, and genocide education.

Educators highly familiar with human rights education are able to recognize components that are shared by these approaches. However, those less familiar with the field may find these distinctions relatively theoretical and unclear. As Totten and Fernekes (2004) noted in regard to the problematic relationship between Holocaust education, genocide education, and human rights education:

> While it is admirable that the Holocaust is no longer a subject that is either ignored by teachers and professors, it is disturbing that is frequently taught with minimal reference to the history of human rights violations in the twentieth century. It is also disturbing that the ongoing problem of genocide and its direct connection to human rights violations is given little attention. (p. 262)

The lack of ongoing dialogue about what constitutes human rights education, and how effective relationships between HRE and other curriculum topics can be strengthened in classroom instruction contributes, unfortunately, to the invisibility of human rights education in the pre-collegiate school program.

For the purposes of promoting knowledge, skills and attitudes related to social justice, these differences may seem largely irrelevant, but that is hardly the case. In fact, two potential and significant consequences are that the human rights dimension can either be completely overlooked in a social justice approach or it may be integrated unknowingly (and possibly, not as strongly as it could or should be). Both tend to keep HRE invisible.

BARRIERS

Lack of Opportunity to Implement HRE

The primary challenges for HRE as a growing field are (1) to be formally recognized by educational policymakers, and (2) to become an integral component of national curricular frameworks. Although the presence of HRE has expanded tremendously over the last fifteen years, as noted earlier herein, there are numerous educational systems that make no formal reference to the topic of human rights.

Even in those systems that include human rights topics and HRE-related themes within their policies, the question of what is actually implemented in the classroom remains. The presence of HRE in curricular frameworks does not guarantee that teachers actually address such topics in their classrooms. To help make that a reality, it is necessary to provide teachers with solid and ample staff development, not to mention key resources.

In the United States, Banks (2001) found that 40 percent of the nation's fifty states mandated the study of human rights in the school curriculum through either legislative mandates or statewide curriculum standards (p. 7). At the same time, little reliable data exists on how such mandates are implemented in individual classrooms, and the few case studies that do exist include such small samples that they preclude broad generalizations about the effectiveness of classroom instruction vis-à-vis human rights.

One study dealing with the implementation of Holocaust education, conducted by SRI Associates in conjunction with the U.S. Holocaust Memorial Museum, found that the most prominent rationale offered by classroom teachers in the United States for study of the Holocaust was from the perspective of human rights. Eighty-eight percent of the representative sample of 327 educators who responded reported "they had taught the topic [the Holocaust] from the perspective of human rights (Donnelly, 2006, p. 52). This was far greater than the 56 percent who stated they taught the topic from the perspective of American history, the second most prominent stated rationale (Donnelly, 2006, p. 52). While this would seem to suggest that human rights content is more pervasive than previously noted in the Banks study, the SRI study does not reveal what these teachers know about human rights, nor does it provide encouraging data on professional development about the topic. As Donnelly (2006) noted, "The majority of teachers nationwide had not received any kind of formal professional development on the topic [the Holocaust]" (p. 53). There is little reason to believe the findings would be any different about human rights education, since study of the Holocaust has a much higher national profile (largely as a result of there being a major national museum in Washington, DC devoted to research and study) than does human rights education in the United States.

Stone (2002) found that while the majority of states reference human rights in their teaching standards, there was little evidence that systematic integration of human rights education was occurring in the nation's classrooms. Those educators who do make human rights education a priority in classroom instruction are largely already committed to promoting this approach and often locate resources and support independently of the school system.

In post-conflict and post-totalitarian societies, HRE resources and training are often promoted through inter-governmental and non-governmental organizations, with the blessings of the national educational apparatus, but with little sustainability.

HRE Seen as "Political"

A barrier to implementation can be partly attributed to the reluctance of school systems to address topics that can be construed as "political" or potentially "oppositional." Human rights education's critical stance towards authority and power and its emphasis on advocacy can make it an uncomfortable bedfellow for the standard curriculum of schools, not to mention the generally "conservative climate" of most school districts across the United States. In some contexts, human rights education is specifically associated with a leftist or Marxist agenda. Within certain national contexts, for example those experiencing massive human rights violations, HRE can be viewed as oppositional.

For these reasons, as well as others, a common tendency within those school systems offering HRE is to focus more on content knowledge and values related to human rights education versus content *and* advocacy. This can dilute the message of human rights education, although advocates contend that even a basic consciousness about human rights can eventually serve as a foundation for a fuller embracing of the human rights framework.

Academic Territoriality

Because of the breadth of topics encompassed in the UDHR and the significant connections evident between human rights education, citizenship education, peace education, and other curricular initiatives, human rights education must be eclectic in drawing its content from a variety of academic subject fields. While this constitutes a strength in developing the theory and practices of human rights education as an interdisciplinary initiative, it faces the problem of academic territoriality. Theorists, and to some degree practitioners as well, too often are reluctant to examine the core concepts and ideas from other subject fields, preferring to maintain contacts with scholars and teachers trained in the same academic background. Totten and Fernekes (2004) found this to be a significant problem in exploring potential pedagogical relationships between the study of the Holocaust and genocides and human rights. As they noted,

> Most scholars who study human rights issues only touch on the issue of genocide in peripheral ways and many in the field of genocide studies, while focusing on the antecedents to genocide, do not seem to invest as much time and thought into the critical need to avert human rights violations–other than massacres and genocide–as need be" (Totten & Fernekes, 2004, p. 266).

Similarly, while the study of human rights in colleges and universities typically is found in history, political science and other social science departments, there appears to be little evidence of cross-disciplinary coursework or study about human rights education with schools or faculties of education. Human rights majors and minors, when they are offered at universities, may incorporate coursework from various disciplines, but rarely are they integrated. Promoting inter-disciplinary research through university-based human rights centers may be a promising agenda for the future (Tibbitts, 2006).

Education as Nationalism

An electronic discussion held in 2005 on the Global Human Rights Education list-serve (HREA, 2005b) raised important issues about the relationship between citizenship education and human rights education. In one of the electronic postings, Ed O'Brien of Street Law Inc., a respected leader in the field of human rights education in the United States, raised concerns about educating young people to be "good citizens," particularly if that meant educating them to be non-critical when addressing issues of justice and morality, particularly regarding the conduct of governments. In the ensuing and wide-ranging discussion, many contributors discussed the problematic relationship between education about citizenship and human rights education, particularly since human rights education has as a core goal the development of skills in young people "needed to promote, defend and apply human rights in daily life" (World Programme for Human Rights Education, Plan of Action, 2005–2007). The latter may result in placing educators and students in an oppositional stance to the actions of the state and other powerful institutions in society, particularly those which justify the continuation of patterns of injustice and inequality. That, of course, is controversial, and many school administrators, school board members, and parents look askance at teaching controversial issues—and especially contemporary issues. For example, in the field of social studies education in the United States, the inclusion of national history as a curricular requirement has been justified in many instances as a way to promote patriotism, loyalty to the state and the continuity of a national mainstream historical narrative that for decades marginalized the experiences of minority groups, minimized the presentation of critical perspectives and provided little attention to the interconnections between the history of the United States and other world societies (Fernekes, 1985). Given that the core foundation documents of the modern human rights movement are international in design and application (UDHR, CRC, International Bill of Human Rights, the United Nations Convention on the Prevention and Punishment of the Crimes of Genocide, and many others), and because the United Nations and other intergovernmental organizations are the primary agencies for their implementation, the content of human rights education often results in raising challenges to the supremacy of a nationalist perspective in the social studies classroom. This raises serious questions for classroom teachers who seek to juxtapose the universalist orientation of human rights education with the nationalist focus of much required social studies coursework in the United States. To the degree that other societies require national history as a core component of citizenship education, educators in those countries will face comparable problems in reconciling teaching about national history with the universalist perspective of human rights education. How this challenge is met in classrooms around the world may yield much relevant information about the extent to which human rights education makes inroads in national and decentralized federal compulsory education systems in the coming decades.

TEACHING AND LEARNING MATERIALS

Hundreds of human rights-related teaching materials have been developed worldwide for use in classrooms and schools, and many of these are widely available free of charge on the Internet (e.g., through the On-Line Resource Centre of Human Rights Education Associates [HREA] and other on-line resource centers [ARRC, 2005; HREA, 2005; IIDH, 2005]. Moreover, bibliographies and descriptive databases of human rights education materials are available through key human rights organizations as well as United Nations-related agencies (Amnesty International, 2005; HREA, 2005a; Council of Europe, 2005; United Nations, Office of the High Commissioner for Human Rights, 2005).

This explosion of learning materials marks a stark departure from the situation in the early 1990s, when the primary materials available for use in schools was a document called "ABC, Teaching Human Rights," published by the U.N. Office of the High Commissioner for Human Rights, a primary-school national curriculum on HRE that had been developed in New Zealand by Ralph Pettman (which was not yet widely available), and a smattering of booklets developed by human rights NGOs.

In the early 1990s, it was the post-authoritarian contexts of Central and Eastern Europe and South Africa that provided a primary impetus for the idea that HRE could be integrated on a national scale and within a state curricula. These regional political changes were complemented by the U.N. Decade for Human Rights Education (1996–2005) which, although it had limited impact on national educational systems, validated and encouraged the ongoing work of NGOs in this area.

As human rights education has become more widely practiced and accepted, there has been a burgeoning of new learning materials and resources throughout the world, and their dissemination has been facilitated through the World Wide Web. Many resources are explicitly designed for youth, in both formal and informal learning environments. Typically, learning materials are in the form of teacher manuals, leaving it to the discretion of educators to integrate human rights themes at their own discretion. In many countries, including the U.S., human rights themes are included within subject-specific standards or as cross-curricular themes, but there is no mandated human rights curriculum per se. These materials often include background information on the history of human rights and key international human rights treaties (including the Convention on the Rights of the Child); the adaptation to the local learning environment is through the selection of specific themes or skill areas considered relevant for the learners (including issues that make the news, such as the increase of slavery in Africa, "slave wages" in the United States, and the outbreak of genocide).

NGOs continue to be the primary developer of HRE learning materials, even for HRE programs encouraged by national ministries of education. However, since the early 2000s, these NGOs are no longer exclusively human rights organizations, but educational agencies with an interest in social justice and human rights issues. Thus in the U.S., since 2000, organizations such as Teaching Tolerance, Facing History and Ourselves, and even the U.S. teachers' union—the National Education Association—have incorporated a human rights perspective into some of their suggested teaching and learning activities.

Internet-based resource centers and many international and national human rights groups, such as those previously mentioned, provide teachers with ready access to free learning materials. Learning materials designed for teachers can also be purchased from publishers' catalogues, such as the online Human Rights and Peace Store run by the University of Minnesota Human Rights Center. Additionally, educators can draw on primary human rights documents and a small but increasing body of work that examines the impact of HRE programs. Through consulting works such as these, and methodological frameworks (which specify relevant human rights concepts and instructional strategies at appropriate developmental levels for students) such as those developed by Nancy Flowers (1998), educators can select or adapt lessons most suited for their students. Although there is no single journal dedicated to the topic of human rights education, articles and special issues on this topic have appeared in numerous journals, as well as a variety of books.[5] Many of these resources are included in the reference section of this chapter.

Ironically, a primary challenge for educators is sifting through the wide range of materials currently available to them. For teachers new to human rights education, locating and assessing the appropriateness of such materials is a major undertaking, which many may not have the time to do. The combination of time required to develop tailored programs for students and the personal motivation teachers need to address human rights issues has meant that HRE has remain a fairly specialized undertaking in the school environment.

A relatively recent and promising development has been the recognition that the understanding, respect, and practice of human rights should not be restricted to the classroom but should constitute a school-wide event. School-wide efforts to integrate HRE frameworks are taking place through small schools such as The School for Human Rights in Brooklyn, NY and national HRE efforts, such as those being undertaken in India, Ireland, Colombia, New Zealand, and South Africa. School-wide efforts, which not only involve a cross-disciplinary integration of human rights themes within the curriculum but also draw attention to school culture, decision-making and relationships with the community, are bringing the normative framework of HRE to a new level in terms of its influence on the range of human relationships within schools and their environments. These schools, still

---

[5]Journals that have carried articles or devoted entire issues to the topic of human rights education include *Human Rights Quarterly, Intercultural Education, Journal of Social Science Education, European Journal of Education, Comparative Education Review, International Review of Education, Journal of Social Issues, Moral Education,* and *Social Education.*

in relatively nascent form, are just beginning to receive attention from the research community.

RESEARCH BASE AND FUTURE RESEARCH EMPHASES

The research base for HRE has begun to evolve, but, for all intents and purposes, it is still in its stage of infancy. Only a very small number of studies have focused explicitly on human rights education as a separate and independent field of study. The primary barriers to developing a solid research base for these fields are related to conditions already described in this chapter: a diversity of (non-standardized) approaches; and a tendency towards cross-curricular, short-term and even superficial programming. These attributes make it methodologically difficult to separate out the impact of HRE programming from other educational programming that is taking place. Moreover, the lack of long-term HRE programming makes it less feasible to expect long-term impacts on students.

Over the last five years, HRE-related studies have begun to emerge, although much more is needed in order to understand the implementation of human rights education programming and its impacts on learners. The research referenced in this chapter draws from human rights education and studies on related topics. Critical areas for future research in the field of human rights education are integrated within this section.

The authors have divided research studies related to HRE in schools and with young learners into two categories: (1) the impact of HRE curricular programs and classroom environments on young learners, and (2) environmental and personal characteristics associated with HRE occurrences and impacts.

1. Impact of HRE Curricular Programs and Classroom Environments on Learners

Knowledge

The IEA Civic Education study carried out in 1975 included seven (of 48) questions related to the United Nations and human rights. Fourteen-year-old students in ten countries were asked about the purpose of the United Nations, the role of the Universal Declaration of Human Rights and to rate the U.N. in terms of its realization of a series of values, such as "settles arguments and disagreements" (Buergenthal & Torney-Purta, 1976, p. 111). The results revealed substantial support among adolescents for equality of treatment of racial and religious minorities, although there was less consistency between countries vis-à-vis tolerance for women's rights (Branson & Torney-Purta, 1982, p. 37).

Various studies in the U.S. and Western Europe on children's beliefs and concepts related to human rights have demonstrated support for the universality of human rights. Research carried out in the 1970s with youth from the U.S., U.K., and the Federal Republic of Germany revealed that although children could not necessarily define human rights, they had a certain philosophy of rights that reflected an acceptance of human rights by virtue of being human (Gallatin, 1976, as quoted in Branson & Torney-Purta, 1982, p. 36; Torney-Purta & Brice, 1979).

Although students believe that human rights ought to be universally respected, their level of knowledge about this subject is not as high as one might wish. In the Educational Testing Service survey of college students in 1976, for example, half of the items regarding human rights appeared in the list outlining serious misconceptions on the part of students. Whereas only about half the students knew that the United Nations promulgated the Universal Declaration of Human Rights (UDHR), more than three-quarters of the freshmen overestimated the number of human rights treaties that the United States had ratified (Klein & Ager, 1981, as cited in Branson & Torney-Purta, 1982, pp. 38–39). These findings were actually more positive than a poll conducted by Peter D. Hart Research Associates in 1997 with U.S. 11th and 12th grade students that showed only a 4 percent awareness of the existence of the UDHR as an official document that set forth human rights for everyone across the globe; moreover, 59 percent of the youth surveyed did not believe that any such document existed (online document, n.p.).

Several studies have been carried out from a developmental perspective to examine adolescents' and children's knowledge about their own rights. Melton (1980, 1983) was one of the first to provide an account of the development of children's reasoning about their rights in hypothetical situations as well as their general knowledge of children's rights. The results of these studies show that the development of reasoning by children regarding children's rights is dependent on two variables: age and socio-economic background. Older children and children from high-status families think about rights in more abstract terms, based on moral considerations, while younger children, particularly those from a lower status background display more egocentric reasoning in which rights are defined in terms of what one can do or have.

Ruck, Abramovitch, and Keating (1998) have criticized this developmental framework, asserting that a stage framework, in fact, does not characterize adolescents' and children's conceptions about children's rights. Instead, they argue, such knowledge is highly influenced both by the social content (home or school) in which the right is embedded and by the type of right under consideration (cited in Molinari, 2001, p. 232).

Continuing efforts to document and analyze growth in knowledge about human rights content are critical, particularly those which examine how human rights concepts bring new perspectives to bear on critical social problems and issues.

Values, Attitudes and Feelings

Values associated with HRE include: accepting differences, respecting the rights of others (especially members of less powerful groups), and taking responsibility for defending the rights of others (Bernath et al, 1999; Claude 1998; Dupont et al., 1999; Matus, 1996; Mertus et al., 1998; Mihr, 2004; Partners in Human Rights Education, 1996). Certain authors have suggested that learners should be encouraged to develop empathy and multiple perspectives in order to understand human rights and the import of this value system for interpersonal behavior, such as being considerate of others (Glover & O'Donnel, 2003, pp. 15–17).

The effect of children's rights education on the attitudes and behaviors of children has been assessed in empirical studies by Decoene and De Cock (1996) and Covell and Howe (1999, 2001). The evaluation data gathered in these studies indicate that children's rights education is an effective agent of moral education. Children who learn about the Convention on the Rights of the Child and about the rights of children show more rights-respective attitudes toward other children and toward adults. In particular, students who learn about children's rights indicate more positive attitudes toward minority children (Covel & Howe, 1999; Decoene & De Cock, 1996 as quoted in Covell, O'Leary & Howe, 2002). A study of the Facing History Program—which emphasizes moral behavior and individual decision-making through a reflective examination of the Holocaust showed that that young people who participated in the program grew in psychosocial competencies in their interpersonal and intrapersonal skills (Barr, 2005).

One human rights-oriented curriculum implemented at Hunterdon Central Regional High School in Flemington, New Jersey, beginning in 1990 involved classroom instruction that introduced students to case studies of human rights abuses followed by the use of simulations of United Nations human rights monitoring bodies and their efforts to address violations brought forward within the United Nations human rights treaty framework. In addition to providing students with relevant information about the operation of the U.N. international human rights system, a major goal of this curriculum emphasizes the development of empathy among students regarding the victims of international human rights violations, such as torture, disappearances, and other examples of state-sponsored violence (Gaudelli & Fernekes, 2004, pp. 18–21). An action research study conducted with student and teacher participants in this curriculum over a three-year period confirmed this impact for a majority of the students. At the same time only a very small number of students indicated any interest in taking social action, leading the researchers to conclude that "most students view caring and empathy as internal responses, rather than social ones" (Gaudelli & Fernekes, 2004, p. 22).

As with other educational approaches that seek to affect the values, attitudes and feelings of young people in pro-social ways, research might explore the connections between HRE programming and the development of attitudes of caring, empathy and social responsibility. Moreover, and ideally, researchers should investigate whether such programming impacts young people's interest in social issues in general and their sense of political efficacy and confidence. A disposition towards social problems might lead us to expect outcomes in terms of student behavior.

Participation

Academics interested in education for democracy have commented that both HRE and social justice-oriented approaches should lead students to "change the existing political domain rather than just participate in it" (Oesterreich, 2002) and pursue a liberation agenda that looks at power, knowledge and authority (Hawes, 1998).

Surveys have shown that people have a natural understanding of injustice and become active participants if they (a) have a sense of self-esteem and (b) have had experiences of great injustice either personally or through stories being told to them (Müller, 2002 as quoted by Mihr, 2004, p. 6). Civic involvement in adulthood is traced to experiences of group membership and engagement in the adolescent years (Verba et al, 1995; Youniss, McLellan & Yates, 1997 as quoted by Flannagan & Sherrod, 1998, p. 452).

Significantly, one of the main messages of the 1999 IEA Study is that there are multiple modes of citizenship. These certainly include knowledge, voting and volunteering, but also encompass other types of psychological engagement with society (sense of confidence in one's ability to make a different in the groups to which one belongs) and/or a willingness to protest non-violently against injustice.

The latter has been termed social movement-related participation and includes beliefs that adult citizens should join human rights and environmental organizations or participate in groups acting to benefit the community. Interestingly, students differ across countries in the types of political engagement they anticipate being involved in (Torney-Purta & Richardson, 2002, p.197).

The 1999 IEA Civic Education Study showed that only 10 percent of U.S. 9th graders reported participating in youth organizations affiliated with a political party, and six percent participated in human rights organizations. The latter statistic was consistent with the international average across all 28 countries participating in the study (National Center for Education Statistics, 2003, p. 110). These statistics demonstrate that schools do not appear to be environments where human rights activism in an integral component of the curriculum or overall school program. Rather, there appears to be some ambivalence among educators about whether schools "should be in the business of promoting political activism" (Campbell, 2005, p. 28).

Future research might investigate how educational programming influences students' skills in terms of analyzing social conditions that foster or impede human rights violations. Research might also be carried out to help us understand the type of educational programs that are most likely to encourage youth to identify, propose and participate in organized actions against human rights violations.

Environmental and Personal Characteristics Associated with HRE Occurrences and Impacts

Certain personal characteristics and backgrounds of learners have been associated with HRE. These can be divided by gender, learning environment, and country predictors.

Gender

Gender-based differences are emerging as an area of special interest in human rights education and warrants additional research as a cross-cutting dimension of such programming.

A German study of the impact of human rights education programming on students at 43 schools showed that the results—as demonstrated through personal engagement with human rights concepts—were highest for those students profiled as "emotionally oriented/social." This profile included characteristics such as "cooperative," "emotionally sensitive," "feeling troubled when witnessing human rights violations," and "actively engaged for human rights." This contrasted with other student profiles the researcher labeled "rational/skeptical" and "self-concentrated/impulsive." Reinforcing the finding that those students (predominantly female) who are more "emotionally oriented" will have greater engagement with human rights concepts, teachers in these schools confirmed that they had found most effective those teaching methods that permitted the most emotional involvement of their students (Müller, 2002). Other sources have found gender differences more generally in attitudes relating to social justice, with females more likely to express empathy towards vulnerable persons and groups (Atkeson, & Rapoport, 2003; Hess & Torney, 2005; Sotelo, 1999; Verba, Schlozman, & Brady, 1995).

Higher empathy is one of the characteristics of adolescents that has been associated with political tolerance (Avery, 2001). The importance of developing greater empathy among students was also emphasized by Staub (1992), who in his analysis of the roots of genocide and massive human rights violations in various countries, argued for the need to "teach children about the shared humanity of all people," particularly by helping them "learn about the differences in customs, beliefs and values of different groups of individuals while coming to appreciate commonalities in desires, yearnings, feelings of joy and sorrow and physical and other needs" (Staub, 1992, p. 405).

The issue of gender as it relates to political knowledge also emerged in the International Education Association (IEA) studies. For example, the 1999 IEA Civic Education Study, which surveyed 88,000 14-year-olds, revealed gender differences in relation to political activity. More specifically, at age fourteen, the most striking gender difference was observed in the Support for Women's Political Rights Scale, with females more supportive than males in every country. Females were also substantially more supportive of immigrant's rights, more likely to collect money for a social cause, less likely to express general interest in politics and less likely to say they would block traffic as a form of protest (Torney-Purta, 2004, pp. 472–473).

Learning Environment

A major emphasis of the 1976 IEA Civic Education Study, which extensively examined the issue of classroom environment (Torney et al, 1975), was the relationship between civic instruction and knowledge of civic processes, democratic values, efficacy, and interest in participation. Concepts of democratic values overlapped with those of human rights. Data were collected from 30,000 students and teachers. The study focused on such democratic values as freedom to criticize the government, equal rights for all citizens, tolerance for diversity, freedom of the mass media, respect for others, equality in voting, belief in the freedom of the individual, the right to vote, and the right to be represented. The results from all ten countries affirmed the importance of sustaining an open atmosphere as a foundation for developing democratic values and enhancing civic participation among young people.

Similarly, results from the 1999 IEA Civic Education Study, showed that students' experiences of democracy at school and with international issues have a positive association with their knowledge of human rights (Torney-Purta, 2004). Looking at rights-related attitudes, students with more knowledge of human rights, more frequent engagement with international topics, and more open class and school climates held stronger norms for so-cial-movement citizenship, had more positive attitudes toward immigrants' rights, and had a higher sense of personal efficacy about political activities, such as participating in governance activities.

Another study, conducted in the U.S. that compared methods of instruc-tion on the Universal Declaration of Human Rights showed that knowledge of international law was greater for that subset of students who engaged in cooperative learning (Branson & Torney-Purta, 1982, p. 44). Numerous studies have confirmed the value of student-to-student interactions for en-hancing cognitive learning, as well as perspective taking and more positive interactions with peers (Branson & Torney-Purta, 1982, pp. 44–45; Furth, 1980). Although little work has been done specifically on human rights education, one can conclude that a teacher trained to facilitate cooperative learning, to value student opinions, to present a role model of one who re-spects rights and opinions of others, to encourage students to reflect upon their experience and play with new ideas, and to provide students with at least some responsibility for control over the learning process can facilitate many of the learning outcomes that are important to human rights educa-tion (Branson & Torney-Purta, 1982, p. 45).

Country-level Predictors

Data from the 1999 IEA Civic Education Study was also used to exam-ine country differences in students' knowledge pertaining to human rights compared with other forms of civic knowledge, and students' attitudes to-ward promoting and practicing human rights. The results show that coun-tries with governments that pay more attention to human rights in intergov-ernmental discourse have students who perform better on human rights knowledge items (Torney-Purta et al., forthcoming).

The International Bureau of Education/UNESCO and David Suarez and colleagues Ramirez and Meyer at Stanford (forthcoming) have recent-ly carried out a series of studies on the growth of human rights education worldwide, with special attention to Latin America. Suarez has looked both at globalization in relation to transnational "policy borrowing" in the area of HR and a range of country-level predictors in understanding what may be contributing to this expansion. Factors associated with its dissemination include country history in relation to human rights abuses/human rights ratification and civil society human rights advocacy as well as local educa-tional reform efforts. As we might have intuitively imagined, the presence of HRE in the national curricula was associated with post-totalitarian or post-conflict countries, where heightened sensitivity to human rights norms has followed massive human rights abuses and changes in educational lead-ership have brought about revisions of citizenship education curricula.

Similarly, the research of Keet and Carrim (2006) in South Africa examined the interaction between the transnational efforts to promote HRE (for example, through U.N. agencies) and the context for selective acceptance and adaptation of HRE in national curricula on the basis of the South African educational context. The question about the universality of HR and cultural relevance is thus being played out academically through critical questions about whether "universal" approaches to HRE result in "symbolic politics" (a primarily symbolic reference to human rights rather than in-depth treatment) in national educational systems and how programming can be designed that is both relevant to the national and local situations and intended to forward the full range of empowerment and action-oriented goals that HRE is intended to carry. This is an area deserving of additional examination, using national case studies, regional approaches and perhaps sub-sets of countries with similar political histories (e.g., post-conflict).

The degree to which the creative tensions between human rights education as a set of universal norms and values and human rights education that is designed to address culturally-specific norms and values remains an area requiring much greater research and study. Whether a universal and generic set of human rights norms and values can serve as the foundation for human rights education in all world cultures is unclear at this time, given the brief history of human rights education and the recent emergence of systematic plans to implement national human rights education programs under the auspices of the World Programme for Human Rights Education and the Convention on the Rights of Child.

CONCLUSIONS

At this point in time, human rights education is an emergent field of educational theory and practice gaining increased attention and significance across the globe. The international human rights movement, spurred by the efforts of non-governmental organizations, the United Nations and other regional human rights bodies, has broadened its focus since the late 1970s by seeking to integrate human rights concepts, norms and values within the mainstream educational systems of world states. This effort, which has gained momentum since the early 1990s under the auspices of the U.N. Decade for Human Rights Education and its successor, the U.N. World Programme for Human Rights Education, has spawned a growing body of educational theory, practice and research that often intersects with activities in other fields of educational study, such as civic education, peace education, anti-racism education, Holocaust/genocide education and education for intercultural understanding.

REFERENCES

Adams, B.S., & Schniedewind, N. (1988). System-wide program of human rights education. *Educational Leadership, 45*(8), 48–50.

Amnesty International (1996). *Human rights education strategy.* See http://www.amnesty.org/ailib/aipub/1996. Accessed May 18, 2001.

Amnesty International (2005). *Human rights education: building a global culture of human rights. Circular 25.* Developed for 27th International Council Meeting, 14–20 August, pp. 13–14.

Amnesty International (2007). What is human rights education? Accessed March 17, 2007. www.amnesty.org

ARRC [Asia-Pacific Regional Resource Center for Human Rights Education] (2003). What is human rights education. *Human rights education pack.* Bangkok: ARRC.

ARRC [Asia-Pacific Regional Resource Center for Human Rights Education] (2005). http://www.arrc-hre.com Accessed July 18, 2005.

Atkeson, L. R., & Rapoport, R. B. (2003). The more things change the more they stay the same: Examining differences in political communication, 1952–2000. *Public Opinion Quarterly, 67*(4), 495–521.

Banks, D. N. (2001). What is the state of human rights education in K–12 schools in the United States in 2000? A preliminary look at the national survey of human rights education. Paper presented at the Annual Meeting of the American Educational Research Association, Seattle WA, April 10–14, 2001. ERIC Document ED 454 134.

Barr, D. J. (2005). Early adolescents' reflections on social justice: Facing history and ourselves in practice and assessment. *Intercultural Education, 16*(2), 145–160.

Barrows, T. (Ed.) (1981). *What college students should know about their world.* New Rochelle, NY: Change Magazine Press.

Bernath, T., Holland, T., & Martin, P. (1999). How can human rights education contribute to international peace-building? *Current Issues in Comparative Education. 2*(1), 14–22.

Branson, M. S., & Torney-Purta, J. V. (Eds.) (1982). *International human rights, society, and the schools.* Washington, DC: National Council for the Social Studies.

Buergenthal, T., & Torney-Purta, J. V. (1976). *International human rights and international education.* Washington: U.S. National Commission for UNESCO.

Campell, D.E. (2005). *Voice in the classroom: How an open environment facilitates adolescents' civic development.* Circle Working Paper 28. College Park, MD: University of Maryland.

Chiarroti, S. (2005). Learning and transforming reality: Women from Rosario's neighborhoods demand access to public health services free of discrimination. *Intercultural Education, 16*(2), 129–136.

Claude, R. P. (1996). *Educating for human rights: The Philippines and Beyond.* Quezon City: University of the Philippines Press.

Claude, R. P. (1998). Human rights education: Its day has come. *American Society of International Law, Human Rights Interest Group Newsletter,* pp. 13–23.

Council of Europe. (2001). *Education for democratic citizenship and management of diversity in southeast Europe.* DGTV/EDU/CTT: 30. Strasbourg. 11 July, p. 8.

Council of Europe (2005). http://www.coe.int/T/E/Cultural_Co-operation/education/E.D.C/Documents_and_publications/ Accessed July 18, 2005.

Covell, K., & Howe, R. B. (1999). The impact of children's rights education: A Canadian Study. *International Journal of Children's Rights, 7,* 171–183.

Covell, K., & Howe, R. B. (2001). Moral education through the 3Rs: Rights, respect and responsibility. *Journal of Moral Education, 30*(1), 31–42.

Covell, K., O'Leary, J. L., & Howe, R. B. (2002). Introducing a new grade 8 curriculum in children's rights. *The Alberta Journal of Educational Research, 48*(4), 302–313.

Decoene, J., & DeCock, R. (1996). The children's rights project in the primary school 'De Vrijdagmarkt.'" In E. Verhellen (Ed.), *Monitoring children's rights* (pp. 627–636). The Hague: Kluwer Law International.

Donnelly, M. B. (2006). Educating students about the holocaust: A survey of teaching practices. *Social Education, 70*(1), 51–54.

Dupont, L., Foley, J., & Gagliardi, A. (1999). *Raising children with roots, rights and responsibilities. Celebrating the United Nations convention on the rights of the child.* Minneapolis: Human Rights Resource Center, University of Minnesota.

Elbers, F. (Ed.) (2000). *Human rights education resourcebook.* Cambridge, MA: Human Rights Education Associates.

Engle, S. H., & Ochoa, A. S. (1988). *Education for democratic citizenship: decision-making in the social studies.* New York: Teachers College Press.

Evans, R. W., & Sake, D. W. (Eds.) (1996). *Handbook on teaching social issues.* Washington, D.C.: National Council for the Social Studies.

Fernekes, W. R. (1985). *Critical curriculum inquiry and teaching of American History in U. S. secondary schools.* Unpublished doctoral dissertation, Rutgers University-New Brunswick.

Flanagan, C. A., & Sherrod, L. R. (1998). Youth political development: An Introduction. *Journal of Social Issues, 54*(3), 447–456.

Flowers, N. (Ed.) (1998). *Human rights here and now: Celebrating the Universal Declaration of Human Rights.* Minneapolis, MN: Amnesty International USA and University of Minnesota Human Rights Resource Center.

Flowers, N. (2001). *Summary report of human rights education symposium.* August 25–27. Durban, South Africa. Internal report. Accessed at: http://www.hrea.org/lists/wcar/alliance.html

Froumin, I. (2003). *Education for democratic citizenship activities 2001–2004. All-European study on policies for education for democratic citizenship (EDC) regional study eastern Europe Region* (p. 3). DGIV/EDU/CIT), 28 rev. Strasbourg: Council of Europe,

Furth, H. (1980). *The world of grown-ups.* New York: Elsevier.

Gallatin, J. (1976). The conceptualization of rights: psychological development and cross national perspectives. In R. P. Claude (Ed.), *Comparative Human Rights* (pp. 51–68). Baltimore, MD: Johns Hopkins University Press.

Gaudelli, W., & Fernekes, W. R. (2004). Teaching about global human rights for global citizenship. *The Social Studies, 95*(1), 16–26.

Glover, R. J., & O'Donnel, B. K. (2003). Understanding human rights. *Social Studies and the Young Learner, 15*(3), 15–17.

Griffin, A. F. (1942). *A philosophical approach to the subject matter preparation of teachers of history.* Unpublished doctoral dissertation, Ohio State University.

Hamot, G. E. (2003). *Civic education trends in post-communist countries of central and eastern Europe.* November, University of Indiana website.

Hahn, C. L. (1996). Research on issues-centered social studies. In Ronald W. Evans & David Warren Saxe (Eds.), *Handbook on Teaching Social Issues* (pp. 25–41). Washington: National Council for the Social Studies.

Hawes, L. (1998). *Going against the grain: The promises and predicaments of emancipatory pedagogy and research.* Doctoral dissertation, The University of Utah.

Hess, R., & Torney, J. (2005). *Development of political attitudes in children.* Edison, NJ: Aldine Transaction.

HREA [Human Rights Education Associates]. (2005a). Website: http://www.hrea. org. Note: This website contains over 3,000 downloadable training documents in human rights education as well as an archived Global HRE listserv that contains announcements and threaded discussions beginning in 1998.

HREA [Human Rights Education Associates]. (2005b). Re: Relationship between HRE and citizenship education, Ed O'Brien. 31 January 2005. Global Human Rights Education Listserv, http://www.hrea.org/lists/hr-education/markup/maillist.php

HREA [Human Rights Education Associates]. (2007). India: National Human Rights Commission Recommends HREA from School to Post-graduate Level. 6 July 2007. Global Human Rights Education Listserv. Original source *The Hindu,* http://www.hindu.com/thehindu/holnus/002200707061550.htm .

Hunt, M., & Metcalf, L. (1968). *Teaching high school social studies: Problems in reflective thinking and social understanding* (2nd ed.). New York: Harper and Row. Original work published 1955.

IIDH [Inter-American Institute of Human Rights]. (2005). *Inter-American report on human rights education, A study of 19 countries: Normative Development.* San Jose, Costa Rica: Inter-American Institute of Human Rights.

Ikkaracan, P., & Amado, L. (2005). Human rights education as a tool for grassroots organizing and social transformation: A case study from Turkey. *Intercultural Education, 16*(2), 115–128.

Intercultural Education. (2005). Special issue on human rights education and transformational learning, *16*(2).

Journal of Social Science Education. (2006). Special issue on International Perspectives on Human Rights Education. http://www.jsse.org/2006-1/index.html

Kati, K., & Gjedia, R. (2003). *Educating the next generation: Incorporation of human rights education in the public school system* [Albania]. Minneapolis, MN: New Tactics in Human Rights Project.

Keet, A., & Carrim, N. (2006). Human rights education and curricular reform in South Africa. *Journal of Social Science Education.* Accessed at: http://www.jsse. org/2006-1/keet_carrim_s-africa.htm.

Kehoe, J. (1980). An examination of alternative approaches to teaching the Universal Declaration of Human Rights. *International Journal of Political Education, 3*(2), 193–204.

Klein, S. F., & Ager, S. M. (1981). Knowledge. In T. Barrows (Ed.), *What college students know about their world* (pp. 56–77). New Rochelle: NY: Change Magazine Press.

Matus, V. (1996). *Women's human rights in daily life together: A manual for women's human rights.* [Prepared for Chilean Commission for Human Rights.] New York: People's Decade for Human Rights Education.

Meintjes, G. (1997). Human rights education as empowerment: Reflections on pedagogy. In G. J., Andreopoulos, & R. P. Claude (Eds.). *Human rights education for the twenty-first century* (pp. 64–79). Philadelphia: University of Pennsylvania Press.

Melton, G. B. (1980). Children's concepts of their rights. *Journal of Clinical Child Psychology, 9,* 186–190.

Melton, G. B. (1983). *Child advocacy: Psychological issues and interventions*. New York: Plenum Press.

Mihr, A. (2004). *Human rights education: Methods, institutions, culture and evaluation.* Discussion papers. Magedburg, Germany: Institüt fur Politikwissenschaft Otto-von-Guericke-Universität.

Molinari, L. (2001). Social representations of children's rights: The point of view of adolescents. *Swiss Journal of Psychology, 60*(4), 231–243.

Müller, L. (2002). *Human rights education at school and in postsecondary institutions.* Occasional Paper #6, Working Group on Human Rights, University of Trier. Trier, Germany: Arbeitsgemeinschaft Menschenrechte. Unpublished English language translation.

National Center for Education Statistics (2003). *The condition of education 2003. Indicator 16. International participation.* Washington, D.C.: U.S. Department of Education.

Nazzari, V., McAdams, P., & Roy, D. (2005). Using transformative learning as a model for human rights education: A case study of the Canadian Human Rights Foundation's International Human Rights training program. *Intercultural Education, 16*(2), 171–186.

Netherlands Helsinki Committee. (1996). *Human rights education: Planning for the future.* Soesterberg, The Netherlands: Author.

Newmann, F., & Oliver, D. W. (1970) *Clarifying public controversy: An approach to teaching social studies.* Boston, MA: Little, Brown and Company.

Oesterreich, H. (2002). 'Outing' social justice: Transforming civic education within the challenges of heteronormavity, heterosexism, and homophobia. *Theory and Research in Social Education, 30*(2), 287–301.

Oliver D. W., & Shaver, J. P. (1966) *Teaching public issues in the high school.* Boston, MA: Houghton Mifflin Company.

Partners in Human Rights Education (1996). *Training manual.* Minneapolis, MN: Partners in Human Rights Education.

Pearse, S. (1987). *European teachers' seminar on 'human rights education in a global perspective'* (p. 2). Strasbourg: Council of Europe.

Peter D. Hart Research Associates (1997). *Final youth survey data.* Washington, D.C.: Author. Accessed at: http://wwwl.umn.edu/humanrts/edumat/youthsurvl.htm.

Ramirez, F. O., Suarez, D., & Meyer, J. W. (2006). The worldwide rise of human rights education. In A. Benavot & C. Braslavsky (Eds.), *School knowledge in comparative and historical perspective: Changing curricula in primary and secondary education* (pp. 35–52). Hong Kong: Comparative Education Research Centre (CERC) and Springer.

Reardon, B. (1995). *Educating for human dignity.* Philadelphia: University of Pennsylvania Press.

Richter, F. D., & Tjosvold, D. (1980). Effects of student participation in classroom decision making on attitudes, peer interaction, motivation and learning. *Journal of Applied Psychology, 65,* 74–80.

Ruck, M. D., Abramovitch, R., & Keating, D. P. (1998). Children and adolescents' understanding of rights: Balancing nurturance and self-determination. *Child Development, 64:* 404–417.

Schuetz, P. (1996) *Political culture in the school and classroom: Preparation for democratic citizenship.* Paper presented at the International Conference on Individualism and Community in a Democratic Society, Washington, DC.

Shiman, D. A., & Fernekes, W. R. (1999). The holocaust, human rights and democratic citizenship education. *The Social Studies, 90*(2), 53–62.

Sotelo, M. J. (1999). Gender differences in political tolerance among adolescents. *Journal of Gender Studies, 8*(2), 211–217.

South House Exchange (2004). *Education for peace, human rights, democracy, international understanding and tolerance. Report of Canada.* Prepared for The Council of Ministers of Education, Canada in collaboration with the Canadian Commission for UNESCO.

Staub, E. (1992). The origins of caring, helping and nonaggression: Parental socialization, the family system, schools and other cultural influences. In P. M. Oliner, S. P. Oliner, L. Baron, L. A. Blum, & D. L. Krebs (Eds.), *Embracing the other: Philosophical, psychological and historical perspectives on altruism* (pp. 390–412). New York: New York University Press.

Stone, A. (2002). Human rights education and public policy in the United States: Mapping the road ahead. *Human Rights Quarterly, 24*(2), 537–557.

Suarez, D. J. (2007). Creating global citizens: Human rights education in Latin America and the Caribbean. *Comparative Education Review, 51*(1), 48–70.

Tibbitts, F. (1996). On human dignity: A renewed call for human rights education. *Social Education, 60*(7), 428–431.

Tibbitts, F. (2002). Understanding what we do: Emerging models for human rights education. *International Review of Education, 48*(3–4), 159–171.

Tibbitts, F. (2003). *Report from the United Nations Office of the High Commissioner subregional meeting on human rights education in south-eastern Europe.* Skopje, Macedonia, 7–8 July 2003.

Tibbitts, F. (2006). *Universities and human rights education: Mapping growth and opportunities worldwide.* Paper presented at Human Rights Education in Asia Conference, organized by Oslo University and Norwegian Human Rights Centre, 16 November, Oslo.

Torney-Purta, J. V. (2004). Adolescents' political socialization in changing contexts: An international study in the spirit of Nevitt Sanford. *Political Psychology, 25*(3), 465–478.

Torney-Purta, J. V., Barber, C. H., Wilkenfeld, B. (forthcoming). How adolescents in twenty-seven countries understand, support and practice human rights. *Journal of Social Issues.*

Torney, J., & Brice, P. (1979). Children's concepts of human rights and social cognition. Paper presented at the American Psychological Association, New York City.

Torney, J. V., Oppenheim, A. N. & Farnen, R. F. (1975). *Civic education in ten countries: An empirical study.* New York: Wiley.

Torney-Purta, J. V., & Richardson, W. K. (2002). An assessment of what fourteen-year-olds know and believe about democracy in twenty-eight countries. In W. C. Parker (Ed.), *Education for democracy: Contexts, curricula, assessments. Volume 2. Research in social education* (pp. 185–210). Greenwich, CT: Information Age Publishing.

Totten, S., & Fernekes, W. R. (2004). Human rights, genocide and social responsibility. In S. Totten, (Ed.), *Teaching about genocide: Issues, approaches, and resources* (pp. 249–274). Greenwich CT: Information Age Publishing.

Totten, S., & Pedersen, J. (Eds.). (2007). *Addressing social issues in the classroom and beyond: The pedagogical efforts of pioneers in the field.* Charlotte, NC: Information Age Publishing.

Tschoumy, J. A. (1993). *Montee en Puissance d'une Europe des Citoyennetes Composees* [The coming into force of a Europe of compound citizenships.] Neuchatel, Switzerland: Institut Romand de Recherches et de Documentation Pedagogiques (IRDP).

UNESCO. (1978). *Final document: International congress on the teaching of human rights.* SS-78/Conf.401/Col.29. Vienna, 12–16 September, p. 2.

UNESCO. (2005). *Education—Human rights education.* http://portal.unesco.org/education/en. Accessed April 11, 2005.

United Nations, General Assembly (2005). *Draft plan of action for the first phase (2005–2007) of the proposed world programme for human rights education,* 25 October. A/59/525.

United Nations, Office of the High Commissioner for Human Rights (2005). http://www.ohchr.org Accessed July 18, 2005.

United Nations, Office of the High Commissioner for Human Rights (1997). *International plan of action for the decade of human rights education.* Geneva: United Nations.

Verba, S., Lehman S. K., & Brady, H. E. (1995). *Voice and equality: Civic voluntarism in America politics.* Cambridge, MA: Harvard University Press.

Yeban, F. (2003). Building a culture of human rights: Challenge to human rights education in the 21st century. *Human rights education pack.* Bangkok: ARRC.

Youniss, J., McLellan, J. A., & Yates, M. (1997). What we know about engendering civic identity. *American Behavioral Scientist, 40,* 620–631.

CHAPTER 6

FACING HISTORY AND OURSELVES

Noble Purpose, Unending Controversy

Karen L. Riley, Elizabeth Yeager Washington, and Emma K. Humphries

INTRODUCTION

Over the past several decades, both historians and educators have voiced various concerns about the way the Holocaust is taught in secondary schools in the United States (Dawidowicz, 1992; Lipstadt, 1995; Newmann, Marks, & Gamaron, 1996; Riley & Totten, 2002; Shawn, 1995; Totten & Parsons, 1992; Totten 1998; Totten & Riley, 2005). Most articles that analyze Holocaust curricula confine their criticism to issues surrounding the selection of content materials and historical inaccuracies (Riley & Totten, 2002; Totten & Parsons, 1992). Few offer a comprehensive examination of a Holocaust program from mission statement to teacher support/inservice to user evaluation, and most important of all, student impact.

Of available Holocaust curricula, *Facing History and Ourselves* is perhaps the most well known and is considered by many as the "grandfather" of Holocaust curricula. Its longevity, popularity, and extensive organizational

Teaching and Studying Social Issues: Major Programs and Approaches, pages 119–138
Copyright © 2011 by Information Age Publishing

structure as a vehicle for the dissemination of Holocaust history have made it a likely target for any number of critics. However, rather than simply criticize *FHAO* for what it does or doesn't do, the authors of this chapter seek to examine *FHAO* on the basis of its stated mission, how its materials, especially its flagship text *The Holocaust and Human Behavior,* have been implemented in secondary classrooms, the nature and extent of criticism and controversy, and the extent to which the curriculum has made an impact upon student learning, understanding, or, moral development.

We, the authors, use the terms *FHAO* and *Facing History* interchangeably in order to facilitate reader interest. This chapter is largely based upon an analysis of actual classroom studies and multiple dissertations. What has proved problematic in rendering the "story" of *Facing History and Ourselves* has been the overwhelming amount of controversy attached to a curriculum endeavor that on the surface appears noble in its effort to confront conflict and engage students in moral reasoning. As scholars, we perceive the need to go beyond a simple explanation of what is and what has been to why *FHAO* has experienced such a high level of controversy. After examining numerous scholarly articles and at least six doctoral dissertations on *Facing History,* what became apparent to us as renderers of this "story" are the issues surrounding the nature of school culture and curricular expectations. In terms of the genesis of *FHAO,* it may have been the proverbial "right time" for a curriculum program that dealt with current problems such as racism, sexism, or other isms, albeit within the context of history, but it was, in our estimation, the wrong place (history classrooms). *FHAO's* trajectory seems eerily similar to that of social reconstruction's social studies endeavors of an earlier vintage.

THE GENESIS AND CONTROVERSY OVER *FHAO*

Facing History and Ourselves (*FHAO*) originated as a result of two Massachusetts junior high teachers' (William S. Parsons and Margot Stern Strom) attempt to introduce the concept of genocide to students in 1976, and to give students a vehicle for examining current societal problems in relationship to past events. It was one of the first major Holocaust curriculum projects developed and implemented in the United States.

Just two years earlier, under the Nixon administration, the National Diffusion Network was established as a discretionary fund of the Department of Education in order to make high quality educational programs accessible across the country. Upon its introduction, *FHAO* was labeled "exemplary" by the National Diffusion Network on the basis of its contribution to cognitive growth in seventh and eighth graders. Subsequently, the program was funded with Federal Elementary and Secondary Education Act (ESEA) Title IV monies (Fine, 1991, p. 154). Newsletters from 1983, housed at the *Facing History and Ourselves* Resource Center, indicate that its program was considered by the National Endowment for the Humanities to be one of the four leading Holocaust programs in the country and the most effective one with teachers and students (Feingold, 1984, p. 11). *FHAO's* outreach efforts included summer institutes for teachers, follow up seminars, and resource experts in offsite locations, as well as curriculum print material. In 1982, *FHAO* revised the curriculum (the newly revised curriculum moved much farther away from the actual history of the Holocaust than the 1976 version). The new curriculum, which later became the source of attacks against *FHAO* pedagogy, reached more than 270,000 students throughout the U.S. and Canada and over 14,000 educators from 46 states and Canada. Moreover, no less than 280 communities adopted the program. The success of *FHAO* may have been based, in large part, on the special recognition it received in 1981 from the U.S. Department of Education.

Once in power, Reagan and the New Right began to "shore up" what they considered to be a leaky liberal education boat, meaning a federal department (Department of Education) dominated by liberals bent on leaking funds for "affective" education programs. With battle lines drawn, Strom attempted to marshal support for *FHAO* only to be denied funding in 1986. Eventually, following a heated battle, *FHAO* was awarded a $60,000 grant (Fine, 1991, p. 162)[1].

During the aforementioned battle perhaps the most crushing blow to *FHAO* came from distinguished Holocaust scholar Lucy Dawidowicz when, in 1990, she published an article in *Commentary* on the state of Holocaust teaching in the United States. In her article, Dawidowicz refers to the 1980s funding debacle and states the following:

> The editor of an educational newsletter invited me to write a piece defending *Facing History*. I never did so, for my own reading of the curriculum persuaded me that the Department of Education had ample reason to turn down the grant application. Putatively a curriculum to teach the Holocaust, *Facing History* was also a vehicle for instructing thirteen-year-olds in civil disobedience and indoctrinating them with propaganda for disarmament. (pp. 25–31)

In fairness to *FHAO*, Dawidowicz offered her comments based upon her reading of the curriculum resource guide alone and not upon any class-

---

[1] As Fine (1991) pointed out, funding issues plagued *FHAO* throughout the 1980s. In the early 1980s, funding for *FHAO* initiatives dried up as a result of changed federal priorities (Feingold, 1984, p. 12). In the late 1980s, conservatives appointed to important positions within the U.S. Department of Education undermined funding for *FHAO* through an elaborate review process, while the Dawidowicz article published in 1990, which played into the argument launched by Department of Education conservatives, served as a major barrier to private fundraising initiatives.

room observations, although it is unlikely that as an historian she would have been swayed by teenage enthusiasm over the discussion of opinions or attitudes despite any stated moral purpose.

A SOCIOLOGY PROGRAM
VERSUS A HISTORY PROGRAM

In the curricular sense, *FHAO* or *Facing History* belongs in a sociology classroom rather than the history classroom. Its curriculum involves societies and their social problems. The sociology curriculum focuses on inequalities and inequities. As a discipline under the umbrella term of social studies, sociology offers teachers and students the opportunity to examine social issues such as racism, sexism, and the like either through current events or through the lens of historical examples e.g. the Holocaust. Therefore, the content of *Facing History and Ourselves* is consistent and compatible with the goals and aims of sociology programs. In the sociology classroom, human behavior is explored along with human rights. Moral dilemmas are embraced, discussed, and evaluated.

Education for moral development is a noble endeavor and is well served through programs such as *Facing History*. Few teachers or parents would argue against a curriculum designed to encourage moral reasoning, whose outcomes aim to result in "right" or ethical behavior on the part of adolescents.[2] However, the history classroom relies on the consistency of evidence and the use of tools of the discipline in order to construct a faithful narrative of past events. When *FHAO* purports to teach the history of the Holocaust that has special meaning for historians and/or teachers of history. While the discipline of history may indeed lead readers of history to moral conclusions or understandings on any number of topics, its purpose is not rooted in teaching moral philosophy. Rather, the discipline of history chronicles events and/or the lives of individuals; it relies on a particular methodology that seeks to resist attempts to manipulate historical evidence for social or moral purposes. While historical accounts of this or that event may convince readers of certain moral truths, the goal of the historian is to remain faithful to the evidence and not to convince readers of anything. History is not an exercise in behavior modification, propaganda, or indoctrination, although critics of *FHAO*, including renowned historian Lucy Dawidowicz (1990), in "How They Teach the Holocaust," claim that indoctrination is exactly what the program accomplishes.

---

[2]*FHAO* has cooperated (supplied material, information, and given interviews) with a number of doctoral candidates, most of whom have interviewed teachers and students, created scales, pre and post tests, and statistical measures, in their pursuit to qualify and quantify the impact of *FHAO* as a worthy curriculum in the area of moral development.

So, while the goals and mission of *Facing History*—to teach civic responsibility, tolerance, and social action to young people, as a way of fostering a moral adulthood—are laudable, its methods and materials are not rooted in historical inquiry. The study and teaching of history, above all, must be predicated on historical accuracy. To be accurate with dates, places, times, and, the names of historical actors, is the first requirement in a faithful interpretation of the past. In crafting an historical account, the historian must assign weight to all of these elements and more. Only those with ulterior motives would claim otherwise.

In their 2002 article analyzing Holocaust curricula, Riley and Totten describe this process as being consistent with authentic pedagogy as tasks that require both teachers and students to use the tools of the discipline for teaching, learning, and assessment.

Riley and Totten (2002) note that authentic pedagogy, according to Newmann (1991) and Newmann and Marks (1996), necessarily includes powerful activities that:

1. encourage deep thinking related to the topic at hand;
2. direct students to examine a wide array of material from which they construct meaning; and
3. encourage students to clarify orally or in writing how they formed their perspective.

Additionally, the learning that occurs should not only relate to the topic under discussion, but should be transferable beyond the classroom.

Tellingly, six PhD dissertations examining various aspects of *FHAO* (Feingold, 1984; Fine, 1991; Lowenstein, 2003; Morse, 1981; Ward, 1986) covering various aspects of *FHAO* all concluded that the program was more firmly rooted in moral development and reasoning than in "historical thinking" (or, that is, one that assists students to construct meaning of the historical past).

So, what is the heart of the matter in terms of course location? Simply put—expectations. Within a generalized understanding of school culture most hold that history classrooms are places where students are supposed to encounter a certain canon of information and not a place where students explore feelings, attitudes, or opinions. Sociology and psychology classrooms, on the other hand, are places where one might expect feelings and attitudes to take center stage, in a curricular sense. The *FHAO* controversy then seems to revolve around the notion of target audience—history students. Had the program's originators targeted sociology or psychology classrooms, the controversy may have been less strident.

DISSERTATIONS ON *FHAO*: STRENGTHS, WEAKNESSES, AND UNANSWERED QUESTIONS

In Melinda Fine's (1991) doctoral dissertation, *The Politics and Practice of Moral Education: A Case Study of Facing History and Ourselves,* the author refers to *FHAO* as a "moral education curriculum" in which students go "back and forth between a historical case study and reflection on the causes and consequences of present-day prejudice, intolerance, violence, and racism" (p. 8). At the outset it should be noted that Fine, a supporter of the *FHAO* curriculum, is a biased participant. In her 1991 dissertation she shares the following:

> I have developed a professional collaboration with *Facing History and Ourselves* over the past three years. As a research consultant to the organization, I have examined its classroom practice (in settings other than the one described in this thesis); reviewed its teacher training program; and assisted in the development of a long-term research agenda. Through this professional engagement I have become deeply committed to *FHAO's* pedagogy as well as friendly with several staff members and teachers (Fine, 1991, p. 14).

Fine (1991) also admits that she developed loyalties to the organization and its staff, which caused her to struggle with the issue of critical perspective as well as giving voice and serious consideration to the viewpoints of *FHAO's* opponents and critics.

Despite these challenges, Fine's (1991) portraiture study of 7th and 8th grade classrooms within the Boston area offers readers a glimpse into the dynamics of classrooms that implement *FHAO's* co-curricular (history and sociology) program. What becomes readily apparent is that the teacher fails to engage students in historical inquiry in favor of asking students to offer up their opinions on various readings such as the Boy from Old Prague.

At one point in Fine's observation, one teacher was unable to deal with a class conflict over the introduction of the *Protocols of the Elders of Zion,* a highly inflammatory monograph that claims the existence of a Jewish conspiracy to control the world's economies. The teacher called in a resource person from the local *FHAO* office to "set the record straight." His (the resource person) presence in the classroom effectively stopped further speculation or discussion on the topic.

The inclusion of fictional accounts within the body of material that also contains non-fictional accounts is problematic in terms of student understanding. For example, one common social studies skill covered in most mainstream textbooks and listed in most state standards of learning is fact versus fiction. Social Studies teachers are largely responsible for teaching students how to discern whether information is either fact or fiction. The acquisition of this skill is challenging enough without the introduction of fictional accounts of an historical event within (in the case of the resource book *Facing History and Ourselves*) a body of literature that contains non-fictional accounts. For students trying to grasp the enormity of a sweeping historical event such as the Holocaust, changing the focus from historical inquiry to moral inquiry using non-historical sources can prove to be, as stated above, more than a little problematic.

According to Fine (1991), once Strom grasped the political landscape of government funding, her letters asking for support focused on *FHAO's* Holocaust "connection," thus downplaying its contested pedagogy in a sort of "whatever works" strategy. Fine (1991) suggests

> *Facing History's* decision to frame the issue in different ways for different audiences may well have been strategically sound. But it also signifies something more problematic: an appeal to some allegedly neutral notion of democracy; a disinclination to define its educational endeavor in political terms; an unwillingness to acknowledge that the values it espouses have the potential to challenge the powers that be. (p. 225)

In the end, Fine (1991) believes that *FHAO* offers students critical reflection in the classroom rather than indoctrination. However, by her own admission, classrooms are not places of equality. The teacher always has the position of power. His or her words are always taken seriously. The findings of her dissertation fail to clarify if moral development in her classroom subjects has truly been influenced via engagement with *Facing History and Ourselves*. Perhaps statistical studies will illuminate the dark corners of uncertainty.

One such statistical study is Morse's (1981) dissertation entitled *Studying the Holocaust and Human Behavior: Effects on Early Adolescent Self-Esteem, Locus of Control, Acceptance of Self and Others, and Philosophy of Human Nature*. Like Fine, Morse collaborated with Strom and *FHAO* staffers on her project. Morse (1981) sought to discover whether or not a program (*FHAO*) that was deliberately designed to be developmentally appropriate for early adolescents could promote personal and social growth through its effect on students' attitudes toward themselves and others, an approach similar to Fine's some ten years later. Morse's study, while not exhaustive, is one researcher's attempt to quantify the effects of *FHAO* on student attitudes. Although not as rich in description as Fine's (1991) classroom observation and interview study, Morse's dissertation is important owing to its appearance of objectivity (statistical studies are generally viewed as authoritative).

The study involved 92 eighth-grade students from three public schools in a large northeastern suburban community. Four scales and their subscales were administered. The treatment protocol called for 10–12 weeks of study using *FHAO* materials and pedagogy. When the treatment group was compared to the control group, the "statistical analyses of the data did not reveal any significantly greater increase in the adjusted post-test mean scores of the experimental group than in the comparison group (Morse, 1981, p. 151). Morse speculated that perhaps if *FHAO* material and methods were introduced again and again over time, one might find an attitudinal shift. Whether or not this is true, another study on adolescents and their engagement with the Holocaust rendered similar results.

Bardige (1983) some three years later studied the reflective thinking and prosocial awareness of adolescents after their engagement with *Facing History and Ourselves*. Like Morse (1981) and Fine (1991), Bardige developed a personal relationship with the program's chief architect, Margot Strom. In her acknowledgements, she thanked Strom "for helping me to think about the process of thinking and its moral impact." Bardige's (1983) findings revealed "adolescents are capable of deep moral concern and intense reflective thinking" (p. 195). Her study consisted of student journaling and coding. She found that student remarks fell into three categories: concrete, early formal, and fully formal. While a description of each category may be of interest to developmental theorists, what the authors of this chapter find compelling is Bardige's (1983) assessment that:

> [t]he moral development revealed by these journals could not be characterized as either movement to or toward a new "stage," or within-stage increases in empathy and social responsibility. Rather, student's expanding awareness simultaneously revealed both greater cognitive complexity and greater prosocial sensitivity. (p. 195)

In other words, when presented with moral dilemmas students demonstrated more awareness that the situation was not one-dimensional, but in the end, students showed no movement in terms of empathy or social responsibility.

One year later, Feingold (1984) completed her dissertation on the change process and the dissemination of *Facing History and Ourselves*. Like the others in this section, Feingold's general appraisal of *FHAO* is flattering. Her assessment of the *FHAO* curriculum is that it is designed to "raise questions, not to answer them" (p. 13). At the time of Feingold's study, she claimed that the Holocaust was a subject that was "too emotionally and intellectually difficult to confront, or to understand," and that perhaps this "closed area" was an educational taboo because it raised questions and issues about anti-Semitism (p. 15). Feingold (1984) suggests that its status as a "closed area" may have resulted in the development of *FHAO*. For those intimately familiar with the work of Hannah Arendt, they will undoubtedly recognize its connection to the *Facing History and Ourselves* program: Arendt asks 'Could the activity of thinking, as such, be among the conditions that make men abstain from evil-doing or actually condition them against it?'" (p. 16).

In any event, Feingold's (1984) study, unlike the others so far, does not seek to describe *FHAO*'s program in terms of student achievement, teacher preparedness, or adolescent moral development. Rather, her focus was on how effective programs are best disseminated. Hence, Feingold's findings have implications for other programs with similar organizational patterns as *FHAO*.

The most recent dissertation (Lowenstein, 2003), an exploration of the influence of *FHAO* on teachers' beliefs about citizenship and civic education, asks the following essential question: "What do teachers actually understand about the subject matter and curricular purposes of civics education?" (p. 6) Lowenstein's focus on *FHAO* was based upon his belief that:

> it embodies what the literature indicates to be "best practice" in the field for professional development—it is subject specific, claims to integrate content and pedagogy, provides an intense learning opportunity away from school and then follows up with network support during the year. Second, it also seeks to provide teachers with an overarching conceptual framework for civics instruction. Third, *FHAO* was chosen because it draws teachers from a wide variety of personal experience and teaching contexts and thereby allows me to examine the nature of the impact of these contexts on teacher understandings. Finally, and not insignificantly, I could not find another widely-used organization that met the above described criteria, and I already had a trusting relationship with *FHAO* staffers from my prior experience as a participant in the summer institute[3] (p. 60).

Lowenstein's findings of the eight teachers he interviewed and observed were not particularly startling. In other words, teachers did not seem to be highly influenced by the *FHAO* program in terms of their beliefs about citizenship and/or civics. The most central filter that helps to explain this is teacher biography. According to Lowenstein (2003):

> [t]his study points to the possibility that the biographical roots of teachers' understandings of citizenship resist being easily torn out and rearranged by experiences in professional development, even when these experiences are aimed at facilitating intense and focused reflection on citizenship. (p. 314)

Although Lowenstein (2003) claims that teachers' understanding of citizenship was changed in subtle ways, he never explains what he means. Instead, he points to pedagogical content knowledge as the component that made the most significant impact (p. 313).

In the final description of his teacher participants, Lowenstein found that the *FHAO* program made only a limited impact in most cases. One of

---

[3]As with all of the dissertations surveyed for this chapter, the doctoral candidate had a personal relationship with the organizers and staffers of the *FHAO* organization. This begs the obvious question: to what extent do these personal relationships affect the interpretation of evidence or data?

the major problems experienced by teachers was their inability to transfer *FHAO* to their particular content area and that "[n]etwork support during the year, although supporting and encouraging teachers' work in some cases, in most cases did not lead to major changes in their understandings of civic education" (p. 324). Moreover, chronological history programs—a mainstay in most secondary schools—are resistant to incorporating the type of pedagogical strategies called for in a program like *FHAO*.

What can be said for the impact of *FHAO* as a curriculum program? According to these doctoral candidates, who examined at least six dimensions of *FHAO*, the impact of this storied program in terms of attitudinal change within students, moral development and reasoning, reflective thinking, and prosocial awareness has been minimal. Even Ward's (1986) dissertation exploring the thinking of urban youth and violence following a *FHAO* course admitted that:

> [i]t is clear to me now that the kind of analysis necessary to measure change within and between those who did and did not take the course would be quite complex and would have required a different research design and possibly another thesis. (p. 158)

These results, however, may not have as much to do with the failure of *FHAO* as a curricular program as they do with the enduring legacy of positionality and early learning patterns. In other words, by the time adolescents engage a program such as *FHAO*, they have experienced thirteen plus years of molding and shaping within a particular environment. This environment always mediates or filters what is absorbed.

FACING HISTORY AND OURSELVES IN THE CLASSROOM: CRITIQUES FROM THE FIELD

In a 2006 article, Schweber explored how the *Facing History* course was taught in a large, urban California high school. In this setting, the teacher went through two "phases" before covering specific Holocaust content. In the first phase, he did "community building" through storytelling and sharing of personal stories related to racism and discrimination; in the second, "identity phase," students shared aspects of themselves creatively through art, poetry, rap, etc. The teacher's third phase incorporated more Holocaust content, but according to Schweber (2006), this was not focused on key events and was not enough to give the students a sense of what the Holocaust really was. The Holocaust served as a "thematic link" between activities or as a "historical backdrop" to the teacher's stories, but it remained largely unexamined and uninvestigated.

Schweber saw evidence of the results of this approach when a local reporter visited the class and asked the students whether the Holocaust "could happen here." According to Schweber (2006), the students' answers demonstrated their unpreparedness for drawing careful comparisons; "they did not know how the Holocaust was unprecedented and how it was not" (p. 15). Also, the teacher showed at least 100 videotaped testimonies of people he hoped would serve as positive role models for the students, but the testimonies were not all from Holocaust survivors, and the students began to confuse the individuals in the videos (for example, confusing a Holocaust rescuer with a battered women's advocate).

Schweber (2006) makes a key point with implications for pedagogy: In this course, students were not taught history on its own disciplinary terms, but rather harnessed history to the heavy yoke of identity formation. Indeed, the teacher rejected both textual narration and disciplined inquiry as integral to history study and did not incorporate any primary documents into the course. Schweber also observed that the teacher's emphasis on the individual as a moral being with agency, acting alone, was a barrier to understanding the Holocaust because it did not help to explain group behavior, either of the perpetrators or the victims. One student, upon finding out that Schweber was herself Jewish, remarked, "I still don't understand how y'all let yourselves be gassed like that" (Schweber 2006, p. 17). Schweber (2006) reflected that in this teacher's classroom

> ...Holocaust memory was eviscerated...It was stretched so thinly that it posed no challenge to students—intellectually, spiritually, or ethically. With the laudable goal of empowering his students morally, "breaking down the psychological barriers" between them, and not "blocking" them academically, (the teacher) regularly focused on the behavior of individuals, the roles of their decisions in shaping experience, and, conversely, the roles of their experiences in making decisions...He focused so exclusively on individuals—acting heroically or not, but in either case terrifyingly alone—that he neglected the larger forces of history in which individuals' decisions deserve to be contextualized. (p. 17)

Schweber (2006) also observed that Holocaust memory was "democratized and morally leveled....The pain of Holocaust survivors was likened, structurally if not substantively, to the trials of the students" (Schweber, 2006, p. 17). In a sense, the "Americanization" of the Holocaust (Flanzbaum, 1999; Ozick, 1996; Rosenfeld, 1995) in this classroom turned the story of the Holocaust into one of individual, universal moral triumph.

As a quasi-therapeutic experience, the teacher seemed to be engaging in what Schweber (2006) termed "reflexive affirmation," through which a particular version of the self is projected onto the mirror of the Holocaust, reflecting—and even enhancing—that same image of the self. Moreover, "the process of reflexive affirmation demanded de-judiazation, the glossing over of Jewishness as a category central to Holocaust history" (Schweber, 2006, p. 29). In other words, through this teacher's pedagogical approach, Jews were removed from the prominent role they played in Holocaust history. Schweber (2006) concluded as follows:

> Forced through the narrow funnel of reflexive affirmation, Holocaust memory… was sweetened for easy ingestion, stripped of its horror, impotency, grandeur, and contingency…The Holocaust occurred in a world where actors act autonomously, unrestricted by historical forces, where individuals always triumph, redeemed through or despite their suffering, and where the plotline always ends well. (p. 29)

Schweber is not the only critic of *Facing History*. Katula (1996), for example, stated in the *English Journal* that "[t]eachers would be wise to look carefully at the underlying motives of curricular movements such as *Facing History and Ourselves* until such time as the proponents of this movement demonstrate that their materials are intended for education rather than propaganda" (p. 9). In another article in *The English Journal*, Klein (1993), who provides a positive appraisal of the *Facing History* program, perhaps serves as an unintentional yet effective spokesperson for the position of the authors of this chapter in regard to their critique of *Facing History*. Klein's experience with the *Facing History* program occurred when he worked with an English teacher based in a Boston-area school. The teacher he observed was a veteran teacher who regularly used the Holocaust as a springboard for teaching about racism and discrimination in the United States. During the course of his work, Klein (1993) observed that

> [f]ifteen students sat in clusters by race and gender on my first day. Ordway [the English teacher] was starting the *Facing History* unit and wrote on the board, "Describe one time you were a victim of peer pressure. How did you respond and why?" In a pattern often repeated, the lesson started with a short writing activity that asked students to think about an issue in their own lives, in this case, conformity, that also played a role in the Holocaust or some other genocide (p. 16).

The teacher's emphasis on the student's own experiences as a lens for understanding greatly diminishes the critical role that Holocaust victims played in this watershed event. Even Klein's (1993) above remarks, "…conformity, that also played a role in the Holocaust or some other genocide" (p. 16) are telling. The Holocaust, or "some other genocide," simply becomes the thinking prompt for student reflections about personal affronts. After this type of exercise, one might rightfully ask, "What did the student learn about the men, women, and children, of the Holocaust and their lived experiences?"

Klein (1993) essentially makes our case for us when he writes, "*The Facing History* philosophy is to move students gradually from literary and historical examples of genocide back to present-day experiences of intolerance and racism" (p. 16). As the week progressed, the teacher asked students to read from *The Bear that Wasn't* (1946), a story about what happens through repeated propaganda. The story does for the role of propaganda in society what Orwell's story *Animal Farm* did for understanding the mechanics and dynamics of communism. They both put readers in touch with a general impression of the event or action in an entertaining pigs-rule-way, but in no way can either be considered works that explore the complex issues at hand. Klein admits in his article that the essence of the *Facing History* program (methodology and pedagogy) is to have students identify with the victimized (Holocaust victims). This approach is as one dimensional as teachers distilling the Holocaust down to Adolf Hitler as the cause of the Holocaust. By not employing historical methods or authentic pedagogy (using the tools of the discipline) in teaching and learning about the Holocaust, students remain largely ignorant of the historical actors, antecedents, dynamics, actions, interactions, and essence, of the event itself.

In an exploration of human rights education, Ely-Yamin (1993) discusses conflicting visions of human rights education such as the utopian model and pragmatic model. The goal of the pragmatic model of human rights education, she asserts, is to prevent historical tragedies such as the Holocaust (p. 658). Ely-Yamin uses the *Facing History* curriculum as her central model of the pragmatic approach. In doing so, she concludes that:

> [u]nfortunately, the pragmatic model can allow circumstance to inform the values of human rights education rather than the other way around. It is perhaps appropriate for a grassroots training course in human rights, but could in fact be counterproductive as the only foundation of a human rights education program in secondary school. At worst, this unreflective imposition of human rights in primary and secondary school curricula threatens to empty rights of their normative content. When a human rights education program sets about choosing presentations of rights only to address specific social problems, the international documents become tool kits of applicable rights and obligations to be shuffled by the social engineer. Such a completely instrumentalist view of rights leaves open the possibility of their manipulation from the highest echelons of the state to the level of the individual classroom (Ely-Yamin, 1993, p. 659).

Ely-Yamin's selection of *Facing History* as a model curriculum for her pragmatic model is noteworthy and underscores Schweber's (2005) assessment of *Facing History* as a program and approach that is designed to "democratize and morally level" (p. 17) the experiences of Holocaust survivors with those of anyone else (usually at the individual level rather than as a group) who has faced personal trials and tribulations.

EVALUATION OF *FHAO* AS A CURRICULAR PROGRAM

Few educators will argue with the noble purpose of the latest edition of the *Facing History* resource text: to teach that "history is largely the result of human decisions, that prevention is possible, and education must have a moral component if it is to make a difference" (*Facing History and Ourselves*, 1994, p. xvi). The approach taken by *FHAO* organizers is to instruct teachers in workshop settings on how to use the tools of the humanities: inquiry, analysis, and interpretation. Following these workshops, teachers are expected to return to their classrooms as social educators, charged with the responsibility of shaping the moral fiber of their students. Moreover, *FHAO* is clear about its program's aims: commitment to content that furthers democratic values and beliefs (*Facing History and Ourselves*, 1994, p. xxi). *Facing History* basically takes an inoculation or prevention approach to the issue of the Holocaust (and other genocides), albeit most historians would likely grimace at the thought of "history as therapy."

However, *FHAO*'s concern about current social problems prevents it from engaging teachers and students in seeking historical understanding. While the 1982 version of *Facing History and Ourselves* confines itself more or less to the time period of the Holocaust, the organization's stated and implied goals are evident in the curriculum product's structure: to help shape a society whose ultimate goal is to eliminate social inequity by shaping a morally responsive individual. In the 1982 version, the *FHAO* authors/curriculum writers take a connect-the-dots-approach to developing the themes of the Holocaust. For example, they ask students to read about the Milgram experiment at Yale University—an experiment whereby test subjects willingly inflict pain on other test subjects from behind a curtain or wall (Totten, 2001)—along with an account of the *The Wave* experiment (for a week students were led to believe that they were special through their membership in a new student movement) by a California teacher. These two readings are supposed to "connect" to the experience of Germans who were conditioned to feelings of superiority and hatred of Jews (*Facing History and Ourselves*, 1982, Section 6). Students are supposed to come away from this reading experience with an understanding that humans have an innate ability to hurt others and can be manipulated into blind obedience. This over-simplistic interpretation lies outside the parameters of the historical truth and leads students away from historical understanding. Later editions of the *Facing History and Ourselves* resource guide go even further in their quest to manipulate history for the sake of achieving moral "rightness" in terms of decision-making.

While the quest of *FHAO* is to "build a community of thinkers," the primary endeavor of the program is to help teachers and their students to formulate moral principles. As such, moral education is the goal and purpose of *Facing History*. More than anything else, *FHAO* is a forum for teaching the skills of decision-making and not the skills of history making. While *Facing History and Ourselves* may find advocates in sociology or psychology classrooms, it may not appeal to many teachers of history.

Without guidance, most teachers would be unable to effectively use the *Facing History* text for the purpose of inquiry. The scope of the Holocaust is vast and requires sustained study. Despite its 500 plus pages, teachers must wade through pages of text that have little to do with the actual events of the Holocaust. For example, centuries of anti-Semitic behavior which laid the groundwork for European attitudes regarding Jews are dealt with in only four pages, while some forty pages contain readings on the individual's relationship to society. Furthermore, while the writers fail to use non-fictional accounts from the historical actors of the Holocaust in the discussion on the "individual and society," they introduce others whose historical experiences have nothing to do with the Holocaust. For example, following the reading entitled "Harrison Bergeron," (*Facing History and Ourselves*, 1994, pp. 58–64), the guide asks students to read *First Encounters in North America,* which describes European explorers and how they understood the peoples of the New World with whom they came into contact. This reading has no direct bearing on the Holocaust. Hence, this curriculum product takes the approach that one historical understanding or moment will apply to others, regardless of time, context, or circumstance. The writers follow this reading with one on slavery in colonial and early America. Why include a piece on slavery if the Holocaust is the historical event under discussion? Do the authors regard slavery in the same sense they regard the Holocaust? The employment of comparative pain leads the student to confuse historical events and simply lump them all together as holocausts.

Perhaps most illuminating is the resource text's lack of depth concerning the identity of the victims. For example, Jewish life in Europe before the war is sorely neglected. The victims—Jews, Roma, religious dissenters, the infirmed, and others—have little voice. We have little idea of who they were or what their world was like. Their stories only appear as support for the writers' over-arching concept of *being different*, and not for understanding them or their historic moment. Thus, the number six million fails to connect real men, women, and children to the study of the Holocaust. This lack of connection goes back to the goal and purpose of *FHAO*, which is to use the Holocaust as a platform for teaching moral behavior and shaping attitudes, rather than to help students acquire an understanding of the Holocaust as an historical event in its own right. Even the questions at the end of each chapter direct students to consider how the reading applies to their world today, not to the past.

By the end of the text, the Holocaust becomes diffused into a web of human rights issues and messages. Under the theme Bystanders and Rescuers (Chapter 8), the authors discuss Holocaust rescuers such as Raoul Wallenberg (pp. 408–409), a Swedish diplomat credited with protecting more than 70,000 Jews. However, woven into the topic of rescue are excerpts from a teacher and his students from Bosnia who make a plea to the world to stop war and hate. Their plea is followed by an excerpt from Liv Ullman's autobiography in which she speaks of traveling to Somalia and encountering children who have no choices in life. Reading #18 concludes with the following questions: "What are ways individuals can help to bring more choices to children in places like Somalia and Bosnia?" and "What roles in particular can American students play in this process?" (p. 411). The implications of this chapter are clear: students will not understand the nature of altruism in the face of war and terror during World War II. Instead, the *FHAO* approach to the theme of altruism seems to be more along the lines of: "we can instill the altruistic spirit in American youth today if we put them in touch with stories of rescuers of the Holocaust." Yet, teaching American students how they can act in an altruistic way will not ensure that they will transfer that learning and understand the role of rescuers during World War II.

What *Facing History* does, like other instructional materials with particular agendas, is discount the importance of words in the construction of understanding. For example, the authors pose two questions about the definition of genocide. One, "How important is a precise definition?" and two, "Can such a definition get in the way of our ability to identify and acknowledge inhumanity and suffering?" They follow these questions with an observation that "others" place their own meaning on the word genocide, which includes "the destruction of the native American population by various European colonial powers and later the United States; the enslavement of Africans in the United States; Iraq's treatment of the Kurds after the Gulf War; Serbia's policy of ethnic cleansing in what was once Yugoslavia; the anarchy in Somalia that has led to mass starvation (*Facing History and Ourselves*, 1994, p. 461).

FHAO's inclusion of these definitions implies approval for understanding the meaning of genocide driven by relativism, despite its opening remarks that *Facing History* "is not a program that is mired in relativism" (See the preface, *Facing History*, 1994, p. xxi)· Moreover, its persistent use of present-day analogies seems an added contradiction to their disclaimer.

The final two chapters, Historical Legacies and Choosing to Participate, press at the heart of *FHAO*'s implied and stated goal: moral education for American youth. No less than twelve readings are excerpts concerning the plight of African Americans and their struggle for acceptance, while numerous others are devoted to events such as the atrocities perpetrated by the Khmer Rouge in Cambodia, violence in urban America, and the Asian struggle for acceptance. Accordingly, most would agree that *FHAO* succeeds in its mission of sensitizing students to domestic issues of racial intolerance, violence, and the perceived spiraling effects of personal and emotional detachment in a post-modern world. Yet, one might rightly question the notion of history as therapy. This philosophy may serve psychology and sociology programs well, but what about the history classroom?

For some, *doing history* will require little more than memorizing a shopping list of names, dates, and assorted facts. This collection without analysis or sustained study leaves the student unconnected to the historical record and creates a distance between the past and present which is difficult to bridge. For others, *doing history* means viewing the themes or outcomes of historical events for the purpose of righting present-day wrongs. However, for social studies teachers charged with the responsibility of guiding students to higher levels of understanding or *critical thinking*, they must first help students to acquire the tools of the discipline. Teachers thus must provide a historical context, select sources or evidence for examination, present multiple perspectives, and help students to construct a reasonable explanation of a particular historical event. Hence, the outcome of this latter approach or authentic pedagogical understanding of the event gleaned through sustained study stands in sharp contrast to the use of history as a curative for social ills.

CONCLUSION

While *FHAO* staff and supporters may believe that students have a better understanding of themselves and/or their particular situation (racism, chauvinism, etc.) as a result of studying the Holocaust, enough evidence exists to demonstrate that this is not exactly the case. While many students who have engaged *Facing History* may come away from the experience with a changed attitude about racism in the United States, they may know little about the history of anti-Semitism and the elements of genocide during the Third Reich.

Few Holocaust curricula provoke the level of controversy, loyalty, or criticism experienced by *Facing History* writers and outreach staff. One might rightly ask: What is there about *Facing History* that educators like or dislike (love or hate) about *Facing History's* seemingly noble endeavor of teaching one of history's most horrific events? Answers to this question are elusive despite the fact one is rarely neutral on the topic of *Facing History*. Since its founding, this "grandfather" of Holocaust curricula has endeared itself to tens of thousands of middle and high school teachers for its delivery of a curriculum of terror, inhumanity, and death, all of which is aimed at challenging students' pre-existing notions of justice and equality in a post-Holocaust world. At the same time, *Facing History* has been the subject of controversy and criticism for its alleged a-historical approach to one of the 20th century's most pivotal historical events. Historians in particular question *Facing History* as an authentic approach to teaching the history of the Holocaust, as the contents of its flagship curriculum/resource textbook seem to wander away from the historical event itself and into exercises of the psycho-social.

One of the challenges faced by the writers of this chapter was to uncover the purpose of *Facing History* both as a history curriculum project and as an organization by examining the *Facing History and Ourselves* resource book, as well as other textbooks/resource books published by the *Facing History* organization. In particular, the authors were challenged by the changing nature of *Facing History*'s curriculum materials, which is not unlike other social studies curriculum projects developed in the second half of the 20th century. In other words, the second half of the 20th century has often been "plagued" with curriculum reform measures that have exploded onto the educational stage only to fizzle out with the first efforts of implementation (the New Social Studies for example).

Despite the organization's claims of teaching the history of the Holocaust, *Facing History* never convinced the writers of this chapter that its real mission was teaching the history of the Holocaust, albeit its 1982 curriculum resource book came closer to this end than educational products of more recent vintage (*Facing History and Ourselves*, 1994). The educational products, approaches, and pedagogy, developed by the *Facing History* organization have, over time, come to rely heavily on the "history as a social therapy" approach to understanding the history of the Holocaust. However, rather than impose what we, the authors, believed to be the goals and purpose of the *Facing History* program, we have attempted to bring to the reader what the authors of *Facing History* sought to do in their own words, from the inception of the organization until the present.

Facing History, while admittedly well intentioned, lacks authenticity in terms of historical understanding. Its connect-the-dots-approach along with a certain history-as-therapy-approach "feels" like propaganda. The moral purpose of *Facing History* is unquestioned. However, the suitability of *Facing History* as a program that teaches about the history of the Holocaust is questionable. As one observer of the *Facing History* program in action in a classroom put it:

> [t]he Holocaust occurred in a world where actors act autonomously, unrestricted by historical forces, where individuals always triumph, redeemed through or despite their suffering, and where the plotline always ends well. (Schweber, 2006, p. 29)

REFERENCES

Bardige, B. L. S. (1983). *Reflective thinking and prosocial awareness: Adolescents face the Holocaust and themselves.* Unpublished Dissertation. Harvard University.

Davidowicz, L. S. (1990). How they teach the holocaust. *Commentary,* (Dec.), 25–31.

Dawidowicz, L. (1992). *What is the Use of Jewish History?* New York: Knopf.

Ely-Yamin, A. (1993). Empowering visions: Toward a dialectical pedagogy of human rights. *Human Rights Quarterly, 15*(4), 640–685.

Facing History and Ourselves. (1994). *Facing History and Ourselves:* Holocaust and human behavior. Brookline, MA: Author.

Feingold, M. B. (1984). *The change process and the dissemination of facing history and ourselves, A Holocaust education project.* Unpublished Dissertation. Boston University.

Fine, M. (1991). *The politics and practice of moral education: A case study of facing history and ourselves.* Unpublished Dissertation. Harvard University.

Flanzbaum, H. (Ed). (1999). *The Americanization of the Holocaust.* Baltimore, MD: Johns Hopkins University Press.

Katula, R. A. (1996). Using the Holocaust. *English Journal, 85*(5), 9.

Klein, T. (1993). *Facing History* at South Boston High. *English Journal, 82* (2), 14–20.

Lipstadt, D. (1995). Not facing history. *The New Republic, 12*(19), 26–29.

Lowenstein, E. (2003). *Teachers transformed? Exploring the influence of facing history and ourselves on teachers' beliefs about citizenship and civics education.* Unpublished Dissertation. New York University.

Newmann, F. M. (1991). Promoting higher order thinking in social studies: Over view of a study of 16 high school departments. *Theory and Research in Social Education, 9*(14), 323–339.

Newman, F. M., & Marks, H. (1996). Authentic pedagogy: Standards that boost student performance. *Issues in Restructuring Schools, 8*(1), 1–6.

Newmann, F. M., Marks, H. W., & Gamaron, A. (1996). Authentic pedagogy and student performance. *American Journal of Education, 104,* 280–312.

Morse, D. O. (1981). *Studying the Holocaust and human behavior: Effects on early adolescent self-esteem, locus of control, acceptance of self and others, and philosophy of human nature.* Unpublished Dissertation. Boston College.

Ozick, C. (1996, October 6). Who owns Anne Frank? *The New Yorker,* pp. 76–86.

Riley, K., & Totten, S. (2002). Understanding matters: Holocaust curricula and the social studies classroom. *Theory and Research in Social Education, 30*(4), 541–562.

Rosenfeld, A. H. (1995). The Americanization of the Holocaust. *Commentary, 99*(6), 35–40.

Schweber, S. (2006). "Breaking down barriers" or "Building strong Christians": Two treatments of Holocaust history. *Theory and Research in Social Education, 34*(1), 9–33.

Shawn, K. (1995). Current issues in Holocaust education. *Commentary, 96*(2), 15–18.

Stern Strom, M., & Parsons, W. S. (1978). *Facing history and ourselves: Holocaust and human behavior.* Watertown, MA: Authors.

Stern Strom, M., & Parsons, W. S. (1982). *Facing history and ourselves: Holocaust and human behavior.* Watertown, MA: Intentional Educations, Inc.

Tashlin, F. (1946). *The bear that wasn't.* New York: E. P. Dutton and Co.

Totten, S. (1998). A Holocaust curriculum evaluation instrument: Admirable aim, poor result. *Journal of Curriculum and Supervision, 13*(2), 148–166.

Totten, L. (2001). *Teaching Holocaust literature.* Boston, MA: Allyn and Bacon.

Totten, S., & Parsons, W. (1992). State developed teachers' guides and curricula on genocide and/or the Holocaust: A review and critique. Inquiry in the social studies: Curriculum, research and instruction. *The Journal for North Carolina Social Studies, 28*(1), 27–47.

Totten, S., & Riley, K. L. (2005). Authentic pedagogy and the Holocaust: A critical review of state sponsored Holocaust curricula. *Theory and Research in Social Education, 33*(1), 120–141.

Ward, J. V. (1986). *A study of urban adolescents' thinking about violence following a course on the Holocaust.* Unpublished Dissertation. Cambridge, MA: Harvard University.

CHAPTER 7

TEACHING ABOUT THE HOLOCAUST IN U.S. SCHOOLS

Thomas D. Fallace

The Holocaust—the murder of nearly six million Jews and millions of others by Nazi Germany during the Second World War—is one of the most significant events of the modern era. Accordingly, educators have been teaching about the event for over half a century, and have employed a number of different pedagogical approaches. Although the idea of teaching the Holocaust received some initial resistance, it has for the most part been, in the words of sociologist Alan Mintz (2001), "a point of moral consensus between the right and left" (p. 33). However, while Holocaust education has been a source of political consensus, it has been a forum for fierce curricular debate. In other words, while everybody may agree that the Holocaust should be taught, they cannot agree on how it should be done. For some the Holocaust should be cast in the broader context of human rights and genocide education and used to make connections to current issues and events. For others, learning about the Holocaust should be a means of moral development, interpersonal growth, and inspiring social justice. For still others, the Holocaust should be studied in its historical context and viewed as a particularly Jewish event. And then, there are those who believe it should be used to understand the particulars of past and the complexities of historical investigation. There are, of course, certain overlaps among and between various groups; but while they all believe that the teaching about

Teaching and Studying Social Issues: Major Programs and Approaches, pages 139–152
Copyright © 2011 by Information Age Publishing

the Holocaust can inspire students' critical thinking, they disagree about the objectives and means of doing so.

In this chapter, I will briefly outline the origins of Holocaust education in U.S. schools. I then provide an overview of the empirical research on the extent, manner, and results of Holocaust education in the classroom. I conclude with the long-term impact of Holocaust education and consider the future of the movement. Throughout this discussion, we will see how different educational objectives have been put into practice.

THE ORIGINS OF HOLOCAUST EDUCATION

Since the Second World War, Holocaust education in the United States has had a long steady history of increased interest and popularity with teachers. However, the NBC miniseries *Holocaust* in 1978 and the production of Steven Spielberg's film *Schindler's List* in 1993 both provided substantial boosts to the movement. So, of course, did the opening of the U.S. Holocaust Memorial Museum (USHMM) in 1993. Despite the significance of events in popular culture and the establishment of the USHMM, the success of Holocaust education can ultimately be attributed to the ambition and dedication of a handful of teachers at the grassroots level. They directly questioned and confronted the neglect of the Holocaust in the curriculum.

Jewish educators addressed the Holocaust throughout the 1950s, although they initially did so through the uplifting paradigms of commemoration, heroism, and ethnic pride. Accordingly, educational materials on the Second World War focused on Jewish resistance, rescue, and escape. The Holocaust was referred to indirectly and ambiguously, but never confronted directly as a catastrophic event. In light of the founding of Israel and the successful assimilation of Holocaust survivors (called "displaced persons" in the U.S.), many Jews in the 1950s did not want to draw attention to their alleged passivity and weakness during the Second World War. As a result, the Holocaust was used to foster Jewish pride in the present, not to question the past. By the early 1960s, this approach slowly began to change (Sheramy, 2000).

The capture of former Nazi Adolf Eichmann in 1960 in Argentina and his subsequent trial in Jerusalem, Israel, in 1961, awoke the memories of Jewish suffering and victimization and shifted the Holocaust towards the center of Jewish consciousness. The trial also fuelled a sense of frustration among many older Jews about the lack of concern and knowledge of the event by the younger generation of Jews. In addition, many educators questioned the value of the putting a positive spin on such a horrific event. Concentrating on the heroic aspects of the event, Meir Ben-Horin (1961) argued was "an effort to apologize, to falsify through unwarranted prettification of the record" (p. 5). Instead, he suggested, Jewish children needed to be confronted with the horrific facts of the Nazi assault on the European Jews.

A major turning point in addressing the Holocaust in Jewish schools was the 1964 Annual Conference of the National Council for Jewish Education, which hosted a symposium on the "Shoah and the Jewish School" (*shoah* is the Hebrew word for destruction). The symposium's three speakers demonstrated how, from its inception, there were divergent views on how to teach the Holocaust to Jewish students. One progressive-minded presenter thought that the Holocaust should be explored through analogous examples of discrimination in contemporary society, particularly that against "our fellow Negro Americans" (Feinstein, 1964, p. 166). Another thought that the event should be taught through a traditional fact-based approach. A third suggested that the event should be taught as an incomprehensible mystery. Jewish theologians, teachers, and theorists continued to argue these points through the 1960s and 1970s. One of the more creative and controversial curricula designed for Jewish students was Rabbi Raymond Zwerin's *Gestapo* simulation board game, which was also used by some public school teachers (Fallace, 2007).

The major turning point for the introduction of the Holocaust in U.S. public schools was a 1972 *New York Times* article by Elie Wiesel, a Holocaust survivor, journalist, and novelist, in which he reviewed a number of children's books on the Holocaust. In the article he expressed how for years Holocaust survivors "did their best to shield their children from a subject they considered too depressing" (Wiesel, 1972, p. G3). They had left the past behind and moved on with their lives. They didn't think anyone would listen or understand. "Suddenly," Wiesel (1972) reflected, "the situation has changed" (p. G3). He pleaded that all children, not just Jewish, "be exposed to yesterday's grief and memories which, unbeknownst to them, are part and parcel of their daily experience" (Wiesel, 1972, p. G3).

Wiesel's essay was subsequently cited in the first Holocaust curriculum intended for distribution in public schools, *The Holocaust: A Case Study of Genocide*. In 1973 the Commission on Jewish Studies in Public Schools of the American Association for Jewish Education published the curriculum "in response to a wide demand by public schools for supporting curricula on the subject of genocide." Its author, Albert Post, assistant director of social studies for New York Public Schools, undertook the project "as a community service" (Post, 1973, foreword, n.p.). A Holocaust curriculum was also implemented in Philadelphia schools.

In 1975, the Jewish Community Relations Council hosted a pedagogical conference on teaching the Holocaust. The conference inspired Ezra Staples, Franklin Littell (a noted theologian and professor of religion at Temple University), and the Philadelphia school system to design and distribute its own Holocaust curriculum (Littell, 1998). In both New York City and Philadelphia, Holocaust education was mandated over the objections of certain German-American and Arab-American groups (Fallace, 2008).

In the 1970s, certain educational and cognitive researchers began focusing their attention on the previously neglected domain of students' values, emotions, and identities. Educators aimed to make historical content relevance to the lives of their students. Lawrence Kohlberg's "cognitive-developmentalism" and Louis E. Raths' "values clarification" provided an impetus to this movement by offering alternative theoretical moral frameworks for exploring areas of value conflict in the classroom. These theorists asserted that to move through the stages of moral development students had to engage in meaningful discussions that challenged their values. This curricular context, along with numerous examples and accusations of genocide domestically and globally, created an environment conducive to the introduction of the Holocaust as a topic of study in the 1970s (Fallace, 2005).

In fact, three of the first (and, at that time) most influential Holocaust curricula in the U.S. directly cited the work of Lawrence Kohlberg as rationales for their pedagogical approaches to the Holocaust: Roselle Chartock and Jack Spencer's *Society on Trial* (1978), Richard Flaim and Edwin Reynolds' *The Holocaust and Genocide: A Search for Conscience* (1983), and William Parsons and Margot Stern Strom's *Facing History and Ourselves* (1982). All of these curricula were first designed independently at the grassroots level in mid-1970s.

An abridged version of *Society on Trial* was published in National Council for the Social Studies' (NCSS) 1978 *Social Education* special issue on the Holocaust, designed to correspond with the airing of the popular NBC *Holocaust* miniseries. Through its publication in *Social Education*, it reached thousands of teachers across the United States.

In New Jersey, Flaim's and Reynolds' *The Holocaust and Genocide: A Search for Conscience* gained popularity and political support throughout the 1980s and 1990s. In 1982, New Jersey Governor Thomas Kean established the Holocaust Advisory Council, the goal of which was to promote Holocaust education throughout the state. In subsequent years, the advisory council would help organize and finance a Holocaust memorial, Holocaust awareness sessions, and summer workshops for teachers, and demonstration sites at local high schools and colleges. New Jersey would eventually become the first state to mandate the teaching of the Holocaust in its schools in 1994.

In 1980, the U.S. Department of Education recognized *Facing History and Ourselves* (Stern, Strom, & Parsons, 1982) as an exemplary model education program and added it to its National Diffusion Network for use in schools across the nation. By 1995, Facing History and Ourselves Foundation had established satellite offices in Chicago, Los Angeles, Memphis, and New

York and had trained an estimated 30,000 teachers nationwide. Its curriculum has become the most widely used in the country (Fallace, 2008).

Pedagogically speaking, the aforementioned curriculum designers employed different orientations. Post used a traditional approach that basically traced the events of Holocaust chronologically. On the other hand, Roselle Chartock and Rabbi Zwerin used affective-progressive approaches to engage their students on a visceral and emotional level through graphic images and simulations. Flaim and Reynolds (1983) and Stern Strom and Parsons (1982) approached the topic through a behavioral-progressive orientation by comparing analogous examples of genocide in the past and present. They approached the Holocaust through an investigation into human behavior. Each of these approaches has had its critics.

Leading Holocaust historians Lucy Dawidowicz (1992) and Deborah Lisptadt (1995) critiqued the progressive approach of *Facing History and Ourselves* for subsuming German anti-Semitism within the broader concepts of discrimination or prejudice. Samuel Totten (2000) and Karen Shawn (1995) directly attacked Holocaust simulations such as Zwerin's *Gestapo*, (Zwerin et al., 1976) considering such activities pedagogically unsound and disrespectful of Holocaust victims and survivors. In addition, throughout his life, Elie Wiesel has defended the historical and metaphysical uniqueness of the Holocaust, most significantly as the chair of the President's Holocaust Commission, which planned the United States Holocaust Memorial Museum (USHMM) (See Linenthal, 1995). In that regard, Elie Wiesel (1978) suggested that the Holocaust is not history at all, rather it "transcends history" (p. B1). He argued that the event should be approached as an impenetrable sacred mystery without any meaning or explanation. Wiesel (1985) explained, "I know that as teachers we are called upon to transmit some certainties.... But no certainty is eternal; only the quest is. The quest is human, all the rest is commentary" (p. 158). For Wiesel and other particularist theorists, the facts of the Holocaust can be related, but there should be no attempt to understand the feelings of the victims or actions of the perpetrators; rather, they believe (and argue), students should simply remain in a state of awed incomprehensibility.

As an alternative to the progressive approaches, in 1993 the United States Holocaust Memorial Museum's (USHMM) "Guidelines for Teaching the Holocaust," co-written by Samuel Totten and William Parsons, took more of a disciplinary perspective. The suggestions highlighted the particular historical aspects of the Holocaust, such as the importance of emphasizing Jewish culture prior to the Holocaust and the centrality of racial-based German anti-Semitism. The guidelines encouraged teachers to engage students directly with primary sources and survivor testimonies to complicate their thinking about the event (USHMM, 1995). In fact, in recent years the disciplinary approach to Holocaust education has become the preferred orientation for scholars and pedagogical critics (Riley, 2001; Riley & Totten, 2002; Schweber, 2006; Totten & Riley, 2005). Tellingly, in the *Disciplined Mind,* Howard Gardner (1999) used the Holocaust as an example of how to teach history effectively to students from a disciplinary perspective.

The original designers of Holocaust curricula for public schools formulated their units to engage students' individual values, address students' immediate concerns, and connect the material to relevant current events—all central concerns of the social studies and in accordance with the contemporaneous educational research. Therefore, when historians, interest groups, and various educational researchers attacked these specific curricula, they were not critiquing an "Americanized" Holocaust curriculum, but rather an "educationalized" Holocaust curriculum. That said, Holocaust education not only survived the various critiques hurled at it, but the movement actually flourished during this period.

RESEARCH ON HOLOCAUST EDUCATION

Not only has Holocaust education in the United States been approached from different pedagogical orientations throughout its history, but it has been evaluated from different perspectives as well. Researchers from a traditional perspective assess what facts students learn about the Holocaust and what lessons they derive from these facts. Researchers from a progressive perspective explore the moral and social growth of students who engaged with the Holocaust and how this growth has been transferred to other real world situations. Finally, researchers from the disciplinary perspective explore how the Holocaust develops historical thinking and how preexisting narrative structures shape and distort the historical context of the event.

Facing History and Ourselves (Stern, Strom, & Parsons, 1982) has been the most studied curriculum in the country, due in part because of its proximity to the Harvard Graduate School of Education and its dissemination through the National Diffusion Network. An early study of the curriculum by Lieberman (1981) found that students who were taught the unit increased significantly in their interpersonal understanding as well as factual knowledge about the event. A comparative study by Glynn, Bock, and Cohen (1982), which researched the effects of Holocaust curricula in New York City, Philadelphia, Great Neck, NY, and Brookline, Massachusetts (where *Facing History and Ourselves* is based) confirmed these findings. The researchers found the latter to be the most effective of the four in terms of learning lessons from the event and understanding its factual and historical components. However, they reported that there was no significant change in students' moral reasoning as a result of the unit. On the other hand, Brabeck et al. (1994) found that *Facing History and Ourselves* significantly increased eight-grade students' moral reasoning, and a study by Bardige (1981) reported that the curriculum increased students' social awareness and frequency of reflective thinking. In addition, Shultz, et al. (2001) found that students of the curriculum increased relationship maturity and decreased racist attitudes and self-reported aggressive and combative behavior. However, they only found minimal gains in moral reasoning.

In 1993, Melinda Fine (1993a, 1993b) published a pair of ethnographic studies on the implementation of *Facing History and Ourselves* in inner-city schools. She argued that the curriculum fostered democratic deliberations and created a climate "wherein students were able to recognize that there were a variety of viewpoints, identities, and interests in the world, all of which have some social grounding, and all of which must be understood if not necessarily accepted" (1993a, p. 786). Although *Facing History and Ourselves* was originally written from a behaviorist-progressive perspective, Boix-Mansilla (2000) analyzed the curriculum from a disciplinary orientation. She was less concerned with the content of student answers than she was with process of constructing understanding during a unit on the Holocaust and genocide in Rwanda. Boix-Mansilla found that most students were able to distinguish between the different historical conditions surrounding the two genocides, the incremental steps involved in both, and actions and dilemmas faced by individual rescuers and victims. However, with few exceptions, "students failed to recognize the constructed nature of the very accounts on which they were grounding their hypotheses and interpretations about contemporary Rwanda" (p. 410). That is, according to Boix-Mansilla, they failed to appreciate that "narratives are humanly constructed, that they embody particular worldviews, that they are written with a contemporary audience in mind, that that they seek to be faithful to the life of the past" (p. 410).

Simone Schweber's (2004) study of a California teacher confirmed that the *Facing History and Ourselves* curriculum failed to convey important aspects of historical context. By focusing on the affective elements of the Holocaust, the teacher left his students ignorant of important historical facts. As a result, Schweber reflected, the Holocaust was "discussed as a symbol rather than understood as events" (pp. 57–58). In another case study, Schweber (2004) analyzed the efforts of an instructor who raced to cram in as much information about the Holocaust as he could. This traditional approach, Schweber suggests, "effectively transmitted the factual knowledge of the event, but "razed complex moral/historical terrain" (p. 17). A similar outcome occurred with another teacher, whose Holocaust unit concentrated on a series of dramatic reenactments that Schweber described as "emotionally rich...but intellectually thinner than it might have been" (p. 140).

Ironically, the most effective unit of the four Schweber explored in the comparative study was the one for which the author had the greatest initial reservations: Ms. Bess's Holocaust experiential simulation game. Schweber entered Ms. Bess's classroom with "elaborate biases against simulations"— a bias she shared with Totten (2000) and the USHMM "Guidelines for Teaching about the Holocaust" (1994). But, to her surprise, she discovered that the simulation was effective at transmitting the historical particularities of the event as well as forcing students to wrestle with its moral implications. The simulation, she writes, was "impressive enough to change this researcher's biases against the possibilities of the genre" (p. 109). Despite the success of the simulation, Schweber (2004, 2003) still felt that Ms. Bess had failed to address adequately the particular context of anti-Semitism.

In another provocative study, Schweber (forthcoming-b) researched the Holocaust being taught in a third-grade classroom. She was weighing in on a debate between Totten (2002) and Sepinwall (1999) about the appropriateness of teaching the event to such young children. Overall Schweber was impressed by the ability of the students to distinguish between real and fictitious violence and, to an age-appropriate degree, be able to sympathize with the victims, and unlike the many of the other teachers Schweber had observed, this one had depicted the event accurately by covering the hasher aspects of the event adequately and ending the unit on a non-redemptive note. However, despite the successes of the unit on a factual level, Schweber agreed with Totten that the emotional effects of the Holocaust were too much for these young students to handle.

Beyond overall assessments of *Facing History and Ourselves* and other curricula, researchers have focused on the impact that the teacher has on the framing of the event and its reception by students. Schewber and Irwin (2003) explored how the Holocaust was taught at a fundamentalist Christian school. Instead of focusing on the role of Christians in orchestrating or tolerating the persecution of German Jews, the teacher used the Holocaust to teach students about persecution "that we, as Christians may someday face" (p. 1700). Rather than trying to inspire students to take action on behalf of social justice or genocide prevention, the teacher aimed to strengthen her students' Christian identities, an objective she successfully achieved.

Similarly, Schweber's (forthcoming-a) study of the teaching of the Holocaust at an Orthodox Jewish school for girls confirmed that fundamentalist faith, whether it be Christian or Jewish, prevented open-ended inquiry into the event by providing predetermined answers and/or mystifying the secular events of history. Like the Christian teacher, the Orthodox Jewish instructor taught the Holocaust to reaffirm her students' religious identities, not to convey specific moral lessons or to inspire social action. Over the course of the unit, students directed numerous questions at the teacher, which she deflected with particularist claims about the incomprehensibility of the event. The question of "why," Schweber pointed out, so central to the disciplines of history and the social sciences was considered superfluous.

The effects of religious belief in the framing of the Holocaust was even more pronounced in Spector's (2007) study of students in two Midwestern public schools who had just read Elie Wiesel's *Night*. The majority of these students (69%) used religious narratives of supernatural intervention to impose order on the events of the Holocaust in one of three ways. First, some students suggested that both God and Satan were historical actors engaged in a struggle of good and evil; Hitler embodied Satan, and God ultimately saved the Jews by stopping the extermination before it achieved it ultimate goal. Second, students expressed how there were certain ways in which individuals should act, and if they do not, there may be supernatural consequences. Third, students employed narratives of "the cross" in relation to Jesus—that He was either suffering at Auschwitz alongside the Jews, or that the Jews were being punished for their rejection of Him. Overall these narratives, according to Spector, blamed the victims for their suffering, moved cause-and-effect from the natural to the metaphysical realm, and justified God's lack of intervention in the event.

In another study of student responses to the Holocaust, Wegner (1996) analyzed the essays of 200 eight-graders, who responded to the prompt, "What lessons from the Holocaust are there for my generation today?" The vast majority of responses addressed moral prescriptions about what students should not be doing. The most popular response (82%) was to not allow the Holocaust to happen again. The second most common lesson (64%) was not to dehumanize others. The third most common response (60%) was not to be a bystander.

Taken together this research demonstrates that the lessons of the Holocaust are not obvious or convergent. Teaching the event, even in great depth, can but will not automatically lead to greater tolerance, historical understanding, or civic virtue. Teachers can, and do, employ their knowledge of the Holocaust towards a number of different pedagogical objectives and ends. However, under the right circumstances learning about the Holocaust can have a number of positive and measurable effects on students.

IMPACT OF HOLOCAUST EDUCATION

Holocaust education has been one of the most successful grassroots educational movements in U.S. history. In 1970, Holocaust education was barely being addressed in any public schools, yet by the 1990s several states had mandated the study of the Holocaust, and a majority of students were at least being exposed to the event. A 1987 National Assessment of Education Progress (NAEP) survey found that, although only 32 percent of 17-year-olds could place the Civil War in the correct half-century, 76 percent could identify the term "Holocaust" as reference to the Nazi genocide during WWII (Ravitch & Finn, 1987, pp. 49, 61).

Over the course of the 1980s and 1990s, state legislatures took a number of different approaches to demonstrate their support of teaching the event. By 2007, Illinois, New Jersey, and Florida directly mandated the teaching of the event in their public schools. California, New York, and Massachusetts embedded the Holocaust in the broader spectrum of human rights and genocide education, and required that teachers address a list of group atrocities in their classrooms in some manner. Connecticut, Indiana, Ohio, Pennsylvania, and Washington, "encouraged" or "recommended" teaching the Holocaust and created commissions to support it. Georgia, Alabama, Maryland, Nevada, North Carolina, South Carolina, Tennessee, Rhode Island, and West Virginia also appointed Holocaust and genocide and/or human rights commissions to develop resources and support teachers, but did not in any way push the topic into classrooms.

Although state mandates, the content of textbooks (Friedlander, 1973; Kanter, 1998; Pate, 1980), and the amount of teacher training all impact the extent to which the Holocaust will be taught, the most influential factor is teacher's "Holocaust profile" (Ellison, 2002; Mitchell, 2004). In other words, teachers with a personal interest in the event are more likely to do research, track down resources, and enthusiastically attend Holocaust workshops than those have no intrinsic interest. There is not a single example of a teacher who became interested in the topic as result of a mandate. In fact, all the exemplary teachers covered in the ethnographic studies above had been teaching the event for years before the mandates were even implemented. In addition, teachers with "Holocaust profiles" tend to agree with the suggestions put forth by leading Holocaust educational organizations such the USHMM and Facing History and Ourselves Foundation, mainly because they have often participated in professional development with these very organizations (Linquist, 2002; Mitchell, 2004).

Facing History and Ourselves Foundation and the USHMM are the two most pervasive forces in Holocaust education. This is interesting because the two organizations offer conflicting approaches to teaching the event. Facing History and Ourselves supports an agenda of social justice and social activism, and frames the Holocaust in a progressive manner that will further these goals. On the other hand, the USHMM places more emphasis on the particularities of the Holocaust and seeks to impart an appreciation of the historical and definitional uniqueness of the event by focusing on anti-Semitism and engaging directly with survivor testimonies (although the museum also provides materials on other victims). Both organizations receive funding from the federal government, and both support grassroots efforts to improve and spread Holocaust education. Teachers do not seem to be cognizant of these subtle differences between the two organizations, and many ambitious teachers have attended professional developments sessions for both (Mitchell, 2004).

Holocaust education seems to be most popular in two areas—suburban districts with substantial Jewish populations and urban areas with high non-white ethnic populations (Ellison 2002; Holt, 2001). The Holocaust is relevant to both these areas, but for different reasons. Obviously, areas with high Jewish populations are more likely to have teachers with "Holocaust profiles," who have greater knowledge and interest in the event. Teachers of inner city minority students frequently teach the event as an indirect way to deal with the prejudice and discrimination that their students experience on a daily basis (Ellison, 2002; Schweber, 2004; Fine, 1993a). The context of the school, to a large degree, seems to impact the pedagogical approach. Teachers with large Jewish populations seem to emphasize the particular aspects of the event. On the other hand, teachers with either high minority ethnic populations or with ambition goals of furthering social justice seem to employ a more progressive approach (Ellison, 2002). Undoubtedly, there are certainly exceptions to this pattern (see Schweber, 2003; Brabeck, et al, 1994).

Finally, teachers at the university, secondary, and middle school levels all seem to be relying heavily on three resources: Elie Wiesel's *Night, The Diary Anne Frank*, and *Schindler's List* (Donvito, 2003; Ellison, 2002; Haynes, 1998; Mitchell, 2004). The former two texts have been popular with teachers for decades. So, despite the numerous books, films, and memoirs published on the event and the extensive efforts of the USHMM and the Facing History and Ourselves Foundation, the major content and lessons of the Holocaust may simply be boiled down to these three major sources. Much more research is needed on what students and teachers actually learn from these texts. In addition, more research is needed on ordinary Holocaust teachers, those who have not necessarily been recognized as exemplary, particularly those who have just started teaching it in response to a state mandate.

CONCLUSION

A 1992 study by the American Jewish Committee reported that 36 percent of adults and 59 percent of students listed schools as their primary source of Holocaust education (cited in Baron, 2003). This survey, conducted before many states had mandated the teaching of event, demonstrates that schools have done much to spread awareness and knowledge of the event. If we consider Holocaust education as an educational movement or pedagogical innovation, its success has been remarkable.

However, it is difficult to determine to what extent the Holocaust has become just a topic to be taught instead of a more broadly-conceived pedagogical and moral intervention. The founders of the movement certainly designed it to be a transformative experience. But in recent years, some researchers (Schweber, 2006, Shawn, 1995) have worried that the proliferation of Holocaust education may be leading to "Holocaust fatigue" or to diluting the potential impact of the event. I, on the other hand, worry less about overexposure of Holocaust education and more about how it is being transformed by the impact of high-stakes testing. The future of Holocaust education as a topic may be healthy, but I wonder if the kind of Holocaust education envisioned and enacted by the founders of the movement is becoming endangered by the encroachment of the one-size-fits all curriculum that values breadth over depth. Either way the topic of the Holocaust is now safely embedded in the curriculum of U.S. schools.

REFERENCES

Bardige, B. (1981). Facing history and ourselves. Tracing development though analysis of student journals. *Moral Education Forum*, 6(2): 42–48.

Baron, L. (2003). The Holocaust and American public memory, 1945–1960. *Holocaust and Genocide Studies, 17*(1), 62–88.

Ben-Horin, M. (May 5, 1961). Teaching about the Holocaust. *Reconstructionist, 27*(6), 5–9.

Boix-Manilla, V. (2000). Historical understanding: Beyond the past and into the present. In P. Sterns, P. Seixas, & S. Wineburg (Eds.), *Knowing, teaching and learning history: National and international perspectives* (pp. 390–418). New York: New York University Press.

Brabeck, M., Maureen K., Sonia S., Terry T., & Stern-Strom, M. (1994). Human rights education through facing history and ourselves programme. *Journal of Moral Education, 23*(3), 333–347.

Chartock, R. (1978). A Holocaust unit for classroom teachers. *Social Education, 42* (4), 278–285.

Dawidowicz, L. (1992). How they teach the Holocaust. In L. Dawidowicz (Ed.), *What is the use of Jewish history?* (pp. 65–83). New York: Shocken.

Donvito, C. (2003). A descriptive study: The implementation of the 1994 New Jersey Holocaust/genocide mandate in New Jersey public middle schools. Unpublished dissertation, Seton Hall University.

Ellison, J. (2002). From one generation to the next: A case study of Holocaust education in Illinois. Unpublished dissertation, Florida Atlantic University.

Fallace, T. D. (2007). Playing Holocaust: Origins of the Gestapo Holocaust simulation game. *Teachers College Record, 109*(11), 2642–2665.

Fallace, T. D. (2008). *The emergence of Holocaust education in American schools.* New York: Palgrave Macmillan.

Feinstein, S. (1964). The Shoah and the Jewish school." *Jewish Education, 34*(2), 165–6.

Fine, M. (1993a). "You can't just say that the only ones who can speak are those who agree with your position": Political discourse in the classroom. *Harvard*

Educational Review, 63(4). Accessed May 21, 2007 from www.edreview.org/harvard93/wi93/w93fin.html).

Fine, M. (1993b). Collaborative innovations: documentation of the facing history and ourselves program at an essential school. *Teachers College Record, 94*(4), 771–789.

Flaim, R., & Reynolds, E. (Compilers). (1983). *The Holocaust and genocide: A search for conscience: A curriculum guide.* New York: Anti-Defamation League.

Friedlander, H. (1972). *On the Holocaust: A critique of the treatment of the Holocaust in history textbooks accompanied by an annotated bibliography.* New York: Anti-Defamation League of B'nai B'rith.

Gardner, H. (1999). *The disciplined mind: Beyond facts and standardized tests, the K–12 education that every child deserves.* New York: Simon and Schuster.

Glynn, M., Bock, G., & Cohen, K. (1982). *American youth and the Holocaust: A Study of four major Holocaust curricula.* New York: National Jewish Resource Center.

Haynes, S. R. (1998). Holocaust education at American colleges and universities: A report on the current situation. *Holocaust and Genocide Studies, 12*(2), 282–307.

Holt, E. (2001). *Implementation of Indiana's resolution to Holocaust education by selected language arts and social studies teachers in middle schools/junior high and high schools.* Unpublished dissertation, Indiana State University.

Kanter, L. (1998). *Forgetting to remember: Presenting the Holocaust in American college social science and history textbooks.* ERIC-CRESS ED 439 039: 1–59.

Lieberman, M. (1981). Facing history and ourselves: A project evaluation. *Moral Education Forum, 6*(2), 36–42.

Lindquist, D. H. (2002). *Towards a pedagogy of the Holocaust: Perspectives of exemplary teachers.* Unpublished dissertation, Indiana University, Bloomington.

Linenthal, E. (1995). *Preserving memory: The struggle to create America's Holocaust Museum.* New York: Columbia University Press.

Lipstadt, D. E. (March 6, 1995). Not facing history. *The New Republic,* 26–27, 29.

Littell, M. S. (1998). Breaking the silence: A history of Holocaust education in America. In D. F. Tobler (Ed.), *Remembrance, repentance, reconciliation: The 25th anniversary volume of the annual scholars' conference on the Holocaust and churches* (pp. 195–212). New York: University Press of America.

Mintz, A. (2001). *Popular culture and the shaping of Holocaust memory in America.* Seattle: University of Washington Press, 2001.

Mitchell, J. P. (2004). *Methods of teaching the Holocaust to secondary students as implemented by Tennessee recipients of the Betz-Lippman Tennessee Holocaust educators of the year awards.* Unpublished dissertation, East Tennessee University.

Pate, G. S. (1980). *The Treatment of the Holocaust in United States history textbooks.* New York: Anti-Defamation League of B'nai B'rith.

Post, A. (1973). *The Holocaust: A case study in genocide: A teaching guide.* New York: American Association of Jewish Education.

Ravitch, D., & Finn, C. E. (1987). *What do our 17-year olds know? A report on the first national assessment of history and literature.* New York: Perennial Library.

Riley, K. (2001). The Holocaust and historical empathy. . In O.L. Davis, Elizabeth A. Yeager, & Stuart Foster (Eds.), *Historical empathy and perspective taking in the social studies* (pp. 139–166). Lanham, MD: Rowman and Littlefield.

Riley, K., & Totten, S. (2002). Understanding matters: Holocaust curricula and the social studies classroom. *Theory and Research in Social Education, 30*(4), 541–562.

Schultz, L. H., Barr, D., & Selman, R. (2001). The value of a developmental approach to evaluating character development programmes: An outcome study of facing history and ourselves. *Journal of Moral Education, 30*(1), 3–27.

Schweber, S. (2004). *Making sense of the Holocaust: Lessons from classroom practice.* New York: Teachers College Press.

Schweber, S. (2006). Holocaust fatigue in teaching today. *Social Education, 70*(1), 44–49.

Schweber, S. (forthcoming-a). Holocaust education at Lubavitch girls yeshiva, Unpublished manuscript version. *Jewish Social Studies,* 1–55.

Schweber, S. (forthcoming-b). What happened to their pets?: Third graders encounter the Holocaust, Unpublished manuscript version. Forthcoming *Teachers College Record,* 1–72.

Schweber, S., & Rebekah, I. (2003). "Especially special": Learning about Jews in a fundamentalist Christian school. *Teachers College Record, 105*(9), 1693–1719.

Sepinwall, H. (1999). Incorporating Holocaust education into K–4 curriculum and teaching in the United States. *Social Studies and the Young Learner* (Jan/Feb 1999), 5–8.

Shawn, K. (1995). Current issues in Holocaust education. *Commentary, 96*(2), 15–18.

Sheramy, R. (2000). *Defining lessons: Holocaust education and American Jewish youth from World War II to the present.* Unpublished dissertation, Brandeis University.

Spector, K. (2007). God on the gallows: Reading the Holocaust through narratives of redemption. *Research in the Teaching of English, 42*(1), 7–55.

Stern Strom, M., & Parsons, W. (1982). *Facing history and ourselves: Holocaust and human behavior.* Brookline, MA: Facing History and Ourselves Foundation.

Totten, S. (2000). Diminishing the complexity and horror of the Holocaust: Using simulations in an attempt to convey historical experiences. *Social Education, 64*(3), 165–171.

Totten, S. (2002). *Holocaust education: Issues and approaches.* Boston: Allyn and Bacon.

Totten, S., & Riley, K. L. (2005). Authentic pedagogy and the Holocaust: A critical review of state sponsored Holocaust curricula. *Theory and Research in Social Education, 33*(1), 120–141.

United States Holocaust Memorial Museum. (1995). *Teaching about the Holocaust: A resource book for educators.* Washington DC: USHMM.

Wiesel, E. (5 November 1972). Telling the war. *The New York Times,* Sec. 7, p. 3.

Wiesel, E. (16 April 1978). Trivializing the Holocaust: Semi-fact and semi-fiction. *New York Times,* p. B1.

Wiesel, E. 1985. *Against silence: The voice and vision of Elie Wiesel* (Vol. 1, I. Abrahamson, Ed.). New York: Holocaust Library.

Zwerin, R., Marcus, F. &, Leonard, K. (1976). *GESTAPO: A learning experience about the Holocaust.* Denver: Alternatives in Religious Education.

CHAPTER 8

ENVIRONMENTAL EDUCATION

Mindy Spearman

Ever since environmental education's informal origins in the early twentieth century, the field has been plagued by what some scholars call a "continuing definitional dilemma" that shows few signs of resolution (Disinger, 1997, p. 29). One reason for the difficulty is that environmental education is, by nature, an interdisciplinary line of inquiry. As such, scholars tend to filter it through whatever "major" discipline in which they are personally grounded. A biologist with an interest in environmental education, for example, might prefer a definition that stresses the science of biophysical systems while a sociologist might stress the socio-cultural aspects of human-environment interaction. Where there is any sort of tentative consensus in the characterization of environmental education, it reflects elements of William Stapp's 1969 definition. Stapp, a University of Michigan professor who is often nicknamed the Father of Environmental Education, defined environmental action in the following manner: "Environmental Education is aimed at producing a citizenry that is knowledgeable concerning the biophysical environment and its associated problems, aware of how to help solve these problems, and motivated to work towards their solution" (Stapp 1969, pp. 30–31). Significantly, Strap was one of the first to include an element of praxis in his characterization of environmental education.

Teaching and Studying Social Issues: Major Programs and Approaches, pages 153–168
Copyright © 2011 by Information Age Publishing

While many contemporary definitions echo Stapp's description (see, Archie & McCrea, 1998), more recent iterations also tend to stress a skill set of "critical thinking, problem solving, and effective decision-making" and include, in one way or another, "responsible" or "informed" environmental actions (Disinger, 1997, p. 30). Be that as it may, no one definition seems to be completely embraced by either scholars or practitioners.

THE OBJECTIVES AND PURPOSES OF ENVIRONMENTAL EDUCATION

The objectives of environmental education present another ambiguity. Harold R. Hungerford (2005) laments the lack of "agreed on goals for the field" (p. 5). In an attempt to streamline pedagogical efforts, Hungerford, along with Ben Peyton and Richard Wilke, wrote the *Goals for Curriculum Development in Environmental Education* (*GCDEE*) in 1980. The framework operationalizes the Tbilisi Declaration (1978), a policy statement created at the Intergovernmental Conference on Environmental Education in October of 1977. The Tbilisi Declaration states that environmental education would be best served by focusing on awareness, knowledge, attitudes, skills and participation. *GCDEE* states similar objectives: ecological foundations, conceptual awareness, issue investigation/evaluation and citizenship action. One important distinction between these two goal sets is that *GCDEE* places these objectives in a hierarchy. The first goal level, ecological foundations, ensures that students have the knowledge base necessary for intelligent decision-making. Learners then progress to an awareness level, where they perceive connections between life and the environment. Goal level three, the investigation and evaluation level, guides learners through processes that will allow them to inquire and assess environmental solutions. The final goal level, action, prompts learners to take action to further a quality relationship between life and the environment.

Hungerford and his supporters insist that *GCDEE* remains as applicable to current practice as when it was first written over twenty-five years ago (Simmons & Volk, 2002). In fact, *GCDEE* seems to be well-accepted by environmental education scholars (Culen, 2005). Still, Hungerford himself bemoans that these goals do not always manifest themselves in classroom practice. Rather than utilizing *GCDEE*, individuals, groups, and administrators tend to rely on an "intuitive impression" of what they perceive of as being important to address (Hungerford, 2005, p. 5). Often, this results in teachers who support their students at the first two *GCDEE* levels, but never address the investigation and action levels of environmental education curriculum (Paul & Volk, 2002).

A popular means of expressing *GCDEE* in a concise phrase is to say that environmental education is education *for* the environment. Yet, as Mappin and Johnson (2005) point out, the preposition *for* might mean different things to different educators. First, one might conceptualize "education for the environment" as education *for behavioral change*. When guided by this purpose, teachers may hope that students will change their attitudes, knowledge and behavior to act in ways that respect the human relationship to the environment; for example, driving fuel-efficient vehicles, recycling, voting green or providing financial contributions to environmental organizations. Often tagged as "environmental responsibility" or "environmental literacy," this purpose is one that is frequently embraced by educators (Mappin & Johnson, 2005). In fact, promoting environmental responsibility has been referred to as the ultimate goal for environmental education (Simmons, 2005). Hungerford's *GCDEE* goals are, in fact, structured to support this purpose.

Second, "education for the environment" might mean education *for personal change*. According to such a perception, teaching about environmental issues becomes something that might lead students to a personal transformation and the creation of a new philosophical basis for living. This perspective is often associated with the naturalistic approach of American nature writers like Henry David Thoreau, Aldo Leopold, John Muir and Edward O. Wilson. With this sort of naturalistic learning purpose, educators teaching about environmental issues highly regard place-based learning (i.e., connecting curriculum to a student's immediate surroundings), critical thinking and the interconnectedness of knowledge (Greenfield, 2005). This purpose is also connected to a transcendental, spiritual model of human/nature relations and concepts of eco-theology.

Finally, some educators perceive "education for the environment" as education *for social change*. Those who adhere to this notion believe that a revolution must take place in socio-economic and political systems worldwide in order to foster long-term, dramatic social change. Eco-justice, environmental racism, and ecological advocacy are some of the chief concerns focused on by those who teach environmental issues for social change. Educators who hew to this notion eschew the previous two perspectives—education *for behavioral change* and education *for personal change*—for focusing too heavily on the individual rather than on the global (Mappin & Johnson 2005).

Each of these different perspectives/purposes necessitates different content and pedagogical strategies in the classroom. For example, environmental education *for behavioral change* might focus more heavily on the science of ecology; environmental education *for personal change* often stresses content derived from literature, philosophy and religion; and environmental education *for social change* might pull most heavily from sociology and politics. Consequently, it is important that teachers who plan on incorporating environmental issues into their curriculum reflect upon which of these three goals they perceive as fundamental—in the words of Mappin and Johnson (2005, p. 20), is one's purpose in teaching about the environment "explanation, enlightenment, or emancipation"?

THE EVOLUTION OF ENVIRONMENTAL EDUCATION

Education *for* the environment was not always the central purpose of the field. Rather, the nineteenth and twentieth century antecedents of environmental education first focused on education *about* the environment. This sort of inquiry-based discovery education was first called "nature study." It was a popular subject matter for all grade levels, although particularly with young learners in primary school. At the 1892 meeting of the National Education Association, the Committee on Secondary School Studies (colloquially referred to as the Committee of Ten) recommended that biology and zoology "ought to be taught as early as possible, even in kindergarten" (Kohlstedt 2005). Progressive educators consequently heralded nature study as an important form of "new education" that would replace traditional, rote book learning.

Early nature study included subject matter from natural science fields like botany, zoology, and mineralogy. Children involved in nature study lessons might classify plants, collect insects, or draw maps of rivers. Several organizations established themselves as aids for teachers wishing to organize this sort of learning for young students. The Audubon Society, for example, created special Junior Audubon Clubs for primary classrooms; participating teachers paid ten cents per student and received a variety of curricular materials, many based in ornithology ("Editorial", 1927, p. 486). The American Nature Study Society, organized in Chicago in 1908, also distributed curricular materials to teachers. The society's first charter included a goal "to promote critical investigation of all phases of nature-study (as distinguished from technical science) in schools, especially all studies of nature in elementary schools" ("The American Nature Study Society", 1908, p. 433). Although the nature study movement waned in popularity as the twentieth-century progressed, both the American Nature Study Society and the Junior Audubon Clubs (recently revived) still operate today (Braus and Disinger, 1996, p. 10).

During the mid twentieth-century, education *in* the environment was another popular purpose for environmental education. Educators coined the term "outdoor education" to refer to organized learning that took place outside of the physical school building. Students involved in some of the first outdoor education experiences hiked, walked, gardened, and camped while studying different curricular areas. During these experiences, the environment acted more as a vehicle for education than it did a subject of education. Thus, outdoor education traditionally has been more of "an approach rather than an educational goal or a content area" (Braus & Disinger, 1996, p. 11). Because of this focus on process, outdoor education during the mid twentieth-century often focused on objectives that were not related to broader environmental education goals. During World War I, for example, President Woodrow Wilson and the Bureau of Education commissioned the "United States School Garden Army" (USSGA). As part of the program, urban children cultivated small garden plots using rural techniques and produced fruits and vegetables to supplement the American public's food supply during wartime. While much of the program took place *in* the environment, the educational purpose of the garden army was not an environmental one; rather, the enlisted children learned lessons about "thrift, patriotism, service and responsibility" (Davis, 1995, p. 118).

Outdoor education remains a productive curricular field during the twenty-first century. Different purposes still underlay environmental education and outdoor education. Programs like Outward Bound and Project Adventure have become the new face of outdoor education; sometimes referred to as "Adventure Education" or "Expeditionary Studies," these programs focus chiefly on goals relating to teamwork, leadership and problem solving. Although the fields of outdoor education and environmental education have historically informed each other, Hungerford insists that they not be confused:

> To deal with the two fields as synonymous does serious injustice to both. Much in environmental education can be subsumed within the precepts of outdoor education because it is usually (not always) outside the classroom where environmental problems exist. But, outdoor education, much as science and social studies, goes far beyond the domain of environmental education (1975, p. 22).

Still, despite such differences, Hungerford and other scholars readily acknowledge that outdoor education programs have done much to call attention to environmental concerns over the last century (Palmer and Birch, p. 127).

RESEARCH BASE

The history of the field of environmental education has shaped the progression of scholarly research in the discipline. In the early twentieth-century, at the height of "nature study" popularity, scholarly research was firmly grounded in the sciences. As Palmer and Birch (2005) importantly note,

...although environmental education research has moved away from its roots in the scientific paradigm toward a broader base of qualitative methodologies, the quantitative approaches continue to be a powerful influence in environmental education research and practice. (p. 120)

Most of these earlier quantitative studies—especially those published in the 1970s and 1980s—tend to reflect a behaviorist paradigm. With the progression of environmental education into the social sciences, research has become "increasingly diverse and complex" (Palmer & Birch, 2005, p. 114). More recent studies tend to embrace constructivist and, more rarely, critical research paradigms. They include data analysis techniques like "discourse analysis, critical ethnography and action research" (Palmer & Birch, 2005, p. 120).

Future directions in environmental education research must deal with some critical weaknesses in the current research base. As a result of an analysis of major environmental research articles published from 1993 to 1999, Mark Rickinson (2001) suggests several avenues that are in need of attention. One of Rickinson's conclusions demonstrates that the research base focuses more heavily on student knowledge and attitudes than on students' educational experiences. Rickinson also notes that scholars frequently attend to environmental education goals and outcomes, but less often investigate the process of environmental learning itself. Although the field is continually reshaping and refocusing, there is a general need for longitudinal case studies that focus on learning experiences and classroom practice.

ENVIRONMENTAL EDUCATION, ADVOCACY OR INDOCTRINATION

Probably the most significant theoretical-level controversy surrounding environmental issues involves the appropriateness of advocacy in the classroom. Is the classroom an appropriate place for the transmission of values and, perhaps, pushing a particular political stance? Can teachers teach a subject that they feel passionate about without proselytizing? With environmental education, the anti-advocacy argument is exacerbated by the claim that students are not given the opportunity to form counter-opinions. Eco-education critics assert that environmental education curriculum contains one-sided arguments that, essentially, indoctrinate students into a pro-environment stance. William Grigg, in a Libertarian critique of the environmental education movement called "The Global Children's Crusade" (1993), expresses serious concerns about environmental education practices. Grigg's chief criticisms center around the idea that environmental education is about politics rather than citizenship and encourages children to take actions that might disrespect their parents. That is, Grigg expresses concern that "environmentally-conditioned" children might manipulate their parents to take a pro-environmental stance and that the act of this manipulation consequently degenerates traditional family values. Additionally, Grigg objects to curricula that promotes ideas related to the Gaia Hypothesis—a theory which reasons that the complex connections between Earth systems necessitate that the planet itself be conceptualized as a living being. He argues that the Gaia Hypothesis promotes a secular religion into which young learners are indoctrinated.

Other critics of environmental education, while perhaps not as extreme as Griggs, echo similar concerns. One renown critique of the environmental education movement is a 1996 publication by the Alabama Family Alliance entitled *Facts Not Fear: A Parent's Guide to Teaching Children About the Environment* (Sanera and Shaw, 1996). The authors warn that many reports on environmental issues are exaggerated, that activists are too gloomy about the future of the planet, and that, like Grigg's argument, many young children are scared into a particular mindset. Marilyn Quayle, former Vice President Dan Quayles' wife, in her foreword to the book, places blame on the shoulders of activists:

> To some extent, I think that the treatment of these issues reflected a wave of misinformation that has spread across the country, introduced by environmental activists and disseminated by the press. Some of the people who perpetuate these exaggerated versions of reality are genuinely misinformed. Others, I think, deliberately scare the public and, ultimately, our children. (Sanera & Shaw, 1996, ix–x).

Sanera and Shaw's book has proved to be a popular resource for environmental education critics. Many environmental educators have taken the criticism seriously. In an article that responds to many of Sanera and Shaw's concerns, Gregory A. Smith (2005) admits that anti-environmentalist arguments, while "shallow," will likely continue to persist in the coming decades (p. 395).

Yet activist educators warn that teachers who completely avoid advocacy in the classroom might encounter another spectrum of problems. For example, environmental ethicist Bob Jickling (2003) argues that:

> In leaning away from advocacy, educators risk implying through their programs and actions that a) participation in controversial issues and adoption of a position are unimportant, b) work of environmentalists should not be valued, and c) much "radical" thinking and actions should be avoided. (p. 24)

Indeed, one of the goals paramount to structuring a curriculum around social issues is to "encourage students to actively participate in the improvement of society" (Ochoa-Becker, 1996, p. 1). It would stand to reason, then, that completely removing the element of praxis from environmental education would fail to meet broader social education goals. Advocating such a praxis position is a common stance for many social educators. E. Wayne Ross, for example, goes so far to argue that both social studies educators and the National Council for the Social Studies (NCSS) need "to take a risk" and not succumb to pretenses of objectivity (Ross, 2001, p. 14).

Is there, one must ask, a compromise between the two positions? Richard Wilke (2000) suggests one possible solution; teachers should take care to scaffold students carefully in the decision-making process regarding whether or not action is merited. Furthermore, since students live in a democratic society, students should always have the option not to take action. Wilke suggests that teachers should refer to the fourteen questions designed by Harold Hungerford, Ralph Litherland, R. Ben Peyton, John Ramsey and Trudi Volk as part of a 6–12 environmental education curriculum entitled *Investigating & Evaluating Environmental Issues & Actions: Skill Development Program* (Hungerford, Litherland, Peyton, Ramsey & Volk, 1992). The questions are called "action analysis criteria" and involve, in part, the following: backing up action with evidence, evaluating the economic, legal, social, ecological and ethical consequences of the action, and looking at the skills, courage and time needed to complete the action successfully. Wilke (2000) explains that "students who become involved in citizen action after addressing these fourteen questions are practicing environmental education action, not environmental advocacy" (n.p.).

IMPLEMENTING ENVIRONMENTAL EDUCATION

The most significant challenge faced by educators who support environmental issues revolves around its placement in the curriculum. Many administrators are confused as to whether environmental education should be placed in the sciences, in social studies, or somewhere else. There has also been discussion over whether environmental education be treated as an additional content area. This debate is often characterized as an insertion versus infusion issue; that is, should environmental issues be inserted into the curriculum or should they be infused into existing scope and sequences? Most environmental educators acknowledge the reality of the situation by noting that while the creation of a separate environmental education subject would be ideal, an "already overloaded curriculum" in PreK–12 education does not make insertion feasible (Ramsey, Hungerford, & Volk, 2005, p. 133). Thus, infusion seems to be the only viable choice. A much more pressing problem, however, is that the "insertion versus infusion" question is one that, all too often, never gets asked in the first place.

A related problem centers around the lack of teacher preparation and awareness concerning environmental issues. Scientists complain about environmental issues that are taught by teachers who know little, if anything, about ecological concepts (Powers, 2004b). Such teachers might rely on "green slogans" (e.g., "reduce, reuse, recycle") but fail to teach the deeper concepts necessary to facilitate student understandings of those slogans (Cotton, 2006, p. 224). Without critically thinking about the meaning—and politics—behind these slogans, they can sometimes "take on a life of their own, slipping towards more advocatory positions" (Jickling, 2005, p. 96).

Educating classroom teachers unfamiliar with environmental issues presents the same sort of problems similar to any other issue. In-service teachers who are presented with entirely new programs often feel overwhelmed with any additional curricular demands (Winther, Volk, & Shrock, 2002). Frustrated with a lack of class time and specialized knowledge sets, many teachers might simply choose to push environmental education to the side.

One solution is to concentrate on pre-service teacher education. "The power of the preservice curriculum," explains Powers (2004b), "is its multiplier effect. Where one teacher has the potential to impact the number of students taught throughout a career, a methods course has the potential to impact many future teachers and, ultimately, a far greater number of students" (p. 3). However, in a parallel to classroom practice, many professors of education who teach methods courses do not attend to environmental issues in their methods coursework (Powers, 2004b, p. 10). In light of the above, Powers (2004b) suggests five potential solutions that might help increase the attention given to environmental issues in pre-service teacher preparation courses:

1. Increased faculty professional development;
2. Support for methods instructors from environmental professional organizations;
3. Emphasis on the interdisciplinary nature of environmental education;
4. Field-based classroom practice; and
5. The creation of curriculum standards and testing for environmental issues (p. 9).

CURRICULAR DESIGN AND PEDAGOGICAL RESOURCES

Researchers in environmental education suggests that teachers should employ environmental problem solving (EPS) as a pedagogical model in their classrooms (Ramsey, 2005). With an EPS model, students actively engage in inquiry about one or more environmental issues, gather information, and offer solutions. Bardwell, Monroe, and Tudor (1994) suggest that there are four different popular EPS strategies commonly in use: The Hungerford, Hammond, Stapp, and Robottom models (1996).

Bardwell, Monroe, and Tudor (1994) place these strategies on a continuum. On one end of the continuum is Hungerford, whose structured model places investigation before action. On the other end of the continuum is Robottom, whose less-structured model places action before investigation. Hammond's and Stapp's models lie in the center of the continuum. Hungerford's issue-centric model emphasizes inquiry and decision-making while Robottom's participatory action approach emphasizes social change. Teachers interested in investigating social issues involving the environment could certainly combine elements of both frameworks within their classroom practice.

The most popular pedagogical framework for environmental education involves the implementation of an issues-based curriculum. This model is closely associated with the purpose of environmental education *for behavioral change*. Students working with this type of curricular approach critically examine environmental issues from several different sides and evaluate potential solutions. This approach to the teaching of social issues is supported by nearly a century of research (Evans, Newmann, & Saxe, 1996). Students engaged in issues-centered learning must, of course, possess decision-making skills in order to avoid psychological barriers like cognitive biases, overconfidence and the poor use of heuristics. Without thoughtful decision-making, students run the risk of "crystallizing" their thinking by basing their response on ideology alone (Fluery & Sheldon, 1996). To combat this potential pitfall, Arvai, Campbell, Baird, and Rivers (2004) suggest using a "structured decision process" with students when investigating environmental social issues (p. 39). When following such a process, students would:

1. Define the decision that needs to be made through different frames of reference;
2. Identify the important objectives that relate to the issue in question and suggest alternatives; and
3. Evaluate all possible consequences and appraise the feasibility of tradeoffs.

As Fluery and Sheldon (1996) note, a variety of resources exist for teachers interested in implementing an issues-based approach to environmental issues in their classroom. They suggest, for example, taking current environmental issues from newspapers and magazines and evaluating them with a policy analysis approach. Teachers might also consider using books on environmental issues written with the classroom in mind. One example is Kerski and Ross' (2005) *The Essentials of the Environment*, an encyclopedia of over 200 global environmental issues that teachers might use to structure an issues-center curriculum. Entries ranging from "Chernobyl" to "invasive species" are written from the perspective of two or more sides and thus might prove a useful classroom resource for this sort of curricular design.

Then there is *Investigating and Evaluating Environmental Issues and Actions* (*IEEIA*), a decision-making based environmental issues curriculum that has a significant research base demonstrating effectiveness in classrooms (Paul & Volk, 2002).

IEEIA curriculum stresses instilling students with a sense of environmentally aware citizenship in order to become personally invested in environmental issues and to take action to search for solutions. The program offers instructional elements that emphasize exploration, issue identification, research and interpretation—all with a student-centered approach. It is particularly valuable in that it allows students to work relatively independently, with the teacher acting as a facilitator rather than a leader or manager.

Another approach to environmental education focuses on engaging students in community investigations through a participatory action research (PAR) framework (Mordock & Krasny, 2001). This model is closely associated with the purpose of environmental education *for social change*. PAR is primarily concerned with action and collaboration; students involved in participatory action research collaborate with the community to research local problems and propose solutions (Patton, 1990). Proponents claim a tight fit with environmental education goals because PAR emphasizes "inquiry, learning and action" (Mordock & Krasny, 2001, p. 16). One advantage of this approach is that students involved in this sort of study might combine quantitative methodologies (e.g., water testing) with qualitative methodologies (e.g., interviews with local community residents, historical investigations). Studies also suggest that students who work with ecological service-learning projects gain an enhanced sense of environmental place through community involvement (Fisman, 2005; Powers, 2004a).

Citizen Science and Student Scientist Partnerships are two K–12 programs that effectively utilize a participatory action research approach in environmental education. In both of these programs, scientists who are investigating environmental issues collaborate with volunteers ("citizen scientists") or classrooms (Student Scientist Partnerships) to reach solutions. In most cases, the issues investigated are longitudinal and broad in scope, such as global climate changes, migration patterns or population trends. Scientists who participate in such programs are able to gather larger datasets than would be possible without additional help, and young learners are able to participate in large-scale scientific investigations. Krasney and Bonney (2005) explain that these programs help balance "the scientists' need for data with the educational community's interest in improving student understanding and attitudes about science and the environment" (2005, p. 292).

THE EFFECTS OF ENVIRONMENTAL
ISSUES IN THE CLASSROOM

The immediate effect of teaching about environmental issues is an increase in the "environmental literacy," or "environmental citizenship," of students. This includes knowledge about both green issues (conservation) and brown issues (pollution), environmental racism, and healthy ecological futures. This knowledge may or may not result in immediate local action.

Significantly, a research study in Costa Rica suggests that children who learn about environmental principles (in this case, conservation) often help to change the ecological viewpoints of their parents and other adults they contact (Vaughn, Gack, Solorazano, & Ray, 2003). In this approach, infusing environmental issues into the curriculum immediately impacts not only the environmental literacy of students, but also adults. Thus, teaching about environmental issues in the classroom has the potential to impact local community knowledge as well as student knowledge.

Global sustainability is the ultimate long-term impact of teaching children about the environment. Sustainability education investigates the relationship(s) between the environment, economic systems, and human life with a focus on creating a future where all three of those players remain healthy. These elements are sometimes referred to as the "Six E's": ecology/environment, economy/employment, and equity/equality (Edwards, 2005, p. 17). In this regard, when young learners knowledgeable about environmental social issues reach adulthood, it is hoped they will be eco-citizens ultimately working for a sustainable planet. Ultimately, most environmental educators hope that teaching about environmental issues today will create a future ecosystem that is economically sound, environmentally healthy, and equitably resourced.

FINAL THOUGHTS

Although the field of environmental education is perceived as positive by many (including, classroom teachers, and environmental activists and various teacher educators/university researchers), the incorporation of environmental issues still have a "largely inadequate, relatively inconsistent and scattered presence in the curriculum" (Hungerford & Volk, 2003). Indeed, Johnson and Mappin worry that "natural scientists, social scientists, and educators have been diverging in recent decades on their idea of environmental education" (Johnson & Mappin, 2005, p. xi), and that such divergence could have a weakening effect overall. What solution, then, can save the field from gradually disappearing from the curriculum much as nature study did in the early twentieth-century?

The solution is one that is easy in theory, but difficult in practice. Recalling Mappin and Johnson's (2005) purposes for environmental education, teachers might teach environmental issues for "explanation, enlightenment or emancipation" (p. 20). A key question, though, is: might not these three purposes simply harken back to disciplinary constructs—natural scientists teaching for explanation, humanities scholars teaching for enlightenment, and social scientists teaching for emancipation? If that is the case, the solution for many of environmental education's troubles lies in the creation of a truly interdisciplinary curriculum. Since environmental education is truly an interdisciplinary line of inquiry this solution makes ultimate sense. This, it must be noted, is not a new, or even recent, idea. As far back as 1975, Harold Hungerford, asserted that "Environmental education is multidisciplinary, and, where personnel can plan and work cooperatively, a team approach would more appropriately reflect its true nature than any other strategy" (Hungerford, 1975, p. 25). Unfortunately, it is an idea that rarely surfaces in practice. Only with dialogue and compromise between the natural sciences, the humanities, social sciences, and teacher education can environmental education garner the support it needs to find a secure home in PreK-12 curricula. Then, teachers will not have to choose to educate for "explanation, enlightenment or emancipation" but, even more powerfully, might teach for all three.

REFERENCES

N/A. (1908). The American Nature Study Society. *Science, 27*(689), 433–434.

N/A. (1927). Editorial news and comment: Audubon bird pictures. *The Elementary School Journal, 26*(7), 481–492

Archie, M., & McCrea, E. (1998). Environmental education in the United States: Definition and direction. In M. Archie (Ed.), *Environmental education in the United States: Past present, and future: Collected papers of the 1996 National Environmental Education Summit* (pp. 1–8). Troy, OH: North American Association for Environmental Education.

Avari, J. L., Campbell, V. E. A., Baird, A., & Rivers, L. (2004). Teaching students to make better decisions about the environment: Lessons from the decision sciences. *Journal of Environmental Education, 36*(1), 45–52

Bardwell, L., Monroe, M. C., & Tudor, M. (Eds.) (1994). *Environmental Problem Solving: Theory, Practice, and Possibilities in Environmental Education.* Troy, OH: North American Association of Environmental Education.

Braus, J., & Disinger, J. F. (1996). Educational roots of environmental education in the United States and their relationship to its current status. In M. Archie (Ed.), *Environmental Education in the United States: Past Present, and Future: Collected Papers of the 1996 National Environmental Education Summit* (pp. 9–19). Troy, OH: North American Association for Environmental Education.

Cotton, D. R. E. (2006). Teaching controversial environmental issues: Neutrality and balance in the reality of the classroom. *Educational Research, 48*(2), 223–241.

Culen, G. R. (2005). The status of environmental education with respect to the goal of responsible citizenship behavior. In H. R. Hungerford, W. J. Bluhm, T. L. Volk, & J. M. Ramsey (Eds.), *Essential readings in environmental education* (pp. 37–46). Champaign, IL: Stipes Publishing Company.

Davis, Jr., O. L. (1995). School gardens and national purpose during World War I. *Journal of the Midwest History of Education Society, 22,* 115–126.

Disinger, J. F. (1997). Environment in the K–12 curriculum: An overview. In R. J. Wilke (Ed.), *Environmental education, teacher resource handbook. A practical guide for K–12 Environmental Education* (pp. 23–45). Corwin Press, Inc., Thousand Oaks, CA.

Disinger, J. F. (2005). Tensions in environmental education: yesterday, today, and tomorrow. In H. R. Hungerford, W. J. Bluhm, T.i L. Volk, & J. M. Ramsey (Eds.), *Essential readings in environmental education* (pp. 1–12). Champaign, IL: Stipes Publishing Company.

Edwards, A. R. (2005). *The sustainability revolution.* Gabriola Island, BC: New Society Publishers.

Evans, R. W., Newmann, F. M., & Saxe, D. W. (1996). Defining issues-centered education. In R. W. Evans & D. W. Saxe (Eds.), *Handbook on teaching social issues: NCSS Bulletin 93* (pp. 2–5). Washington, DC: National Council for the Social Studies.

Fisman, L. (2005). The effects of local learning on environmental awareness in children: An empirical investigation. *Journal of Environmental Education, 36*(3): 39–50.

Fleury, S. C., & Sheldon, A. (1996). Environmentalism and environmental issues, . In R. W. Evans & D. W. Saxe (Eds.), *Handbook on teaching social issues: NCSS Bulletin 93* (pp. 188–196). Washington, DC: National Council for the Social Studies.

Greenfield, D. (2005). *The land as the forgotten teacher: How a naturalistic land ethic, as exemplified in Thoreau, Leopold, and Wilson, informs environmental education.* Unpublished Ph.D. Dissertation, Kent State University.

Grigg, W. N. (1993). Globalist children's crusade. *New American,* (Fall), 44–47.

Hungerford, H. (1975). Myths of environmental education. *Journal of Environmental Education, 7*(2), 21–26.

Hungerford, H. (1994). Ecology: An Introduction for Non-Science Majors. Stipes Publishing Co., 10–12 Chester Street, Champaign, IL.

Hungerford, H. (2005). Thoughts on a substantive structure for environmental education. *Journal of Environmental Education, 36*(3), 5.

Hungerford, H. (2006). Book Review: The essentials of the environment. *Journal of Environmental Education, 37*(3), 44.

Hungerford, H., Litherland, R., Peyton, R.B., Ramsey, J., & Volk, T. (1992). *Investigating and evaluating environmental issues and actions: Skill development modules.* Champaign, IL: Stipes Publishing.

Hungerford, H., Peyton, B., & Wilke, R. (1980). Goals for curriculum development in environmental education. *Journal of Environmental Education, 11*(3), 42–47.

Hungerford, H., & Volk, T. (2003). Notes from Harold Hungerford and Trudi Volk. *Journal of Environmental Education, 34*(2), 3–5.

Jickling, B. (2005). Education and advocacy: A troubling relationship, pp. 91–113. In E. A. Johnson & M. J. Mapping (Eds.), *Environmental education and advocacy: changing perceptions of ecology and education.* Cambridge, UK: Cambridge University Press.

Jickling, B. (2003). Environmental education and environmental advocacy: Revisited. *Journal of Environmental Education, 34*(2), 20–27.

Johnson, E., & Mappin, M. J. (2005). Preface. In E. A. Johnson & M. J. Mappin (Eds.), *Environmental education and advocacy: Changing perceptions of ecology and education* (pp. xi–xii). Cambridge, UK: Cambridge University Press.

Kerski, J., & Ross, S. (2005). *The essentials of the environment.* London: Hodder Education.

Kohlstedt, S. G. (2005). Nature, not books: Scientists and the origins of the nature-study movement in the 1890s. *Isis, 96,* 324–352.

Krasny, M. E., & Bonney, R. (2005). Environmental action through citizen science and participatory action research. In E. A. Johnson & M. J. Mapping (Eds.), *Environmental education and advocacy: Changing perceptions of ecology and education* (pp. 292–319). Cambridge, UK: Cambridge University Press.

Mappin, M. J., & Johnson, E. A. (2005). Changing perspectives of ecology and education in environmental education. In E. A. Johnson & M. J. Mappin (Eds.), *Environmental education and advocacy: Changing perceptions of ecology and education* (pp. 1–27). Cambridge, UK: Cambridge University Press.

Mordock, K., & Krasny, M. (2001). Participatory action research: A theoretical and practical framework for EE. *Journal of Environmental Education, 32*(3), 15–20.

Ochoa-Becker, A. S. (1996). Introduction. In R. W. Evans & D. W. Saxe (Eds.), *Handbook on teaching social issues: NCSS Bulletin 93.* (p. 1)Washington, DC: National Council for the Social Studies.

Palmer, J.A., & Birch, J.C. (2005). Changing academic perspectives in environmental education research and practice: Progress and promise. In E. A. Johnson & M. J. Mappin (Eds.), *Environmental education and advocacy: Changing perceptions of ecology and education* (pp. 114–136). Cambridge, UK: Cambridge University Press.

Patton, M. Q. (1990). *Qualitative evaluation and research methods (2ⁿᵈ ed.).* Newbury Park, CA: Sage Publications.

Paul, G., & Volk, T. L. (2002). Ten years of teacher workshops in an environmental problem solving model: Teacher implementation and perceptions. *Journal of Environmental Education, 33*(3), 10–20.

Powers, A. L. (2004a). An evaluation of four place-based education programs. *Journal of Environmental Education, 35*(4), 17–32.

Powers, A. L. (2004b). Teacher preparation for environmental education: Faculty perspectives on the infusion of environmental education into preservice methods courses. *Journal of Environmental Education, 35*(3), 3–11.

Ramsey, J. (2005). Comparing four environmental problem Solving models: Additional comments. In H. R. Hungerford, W J. Bluhm, T. L. Volk, & J. M. Ramsey (Eds.), *Essential readings in environmental education* (pp. 387–398). Champaign, IL: Stipes Publishing Company.

Ramsey, J., Hungerford, H. R., & Volk, T. L. (2005). Environmental education in the K–12 curriculum: Finding a niche. In H. R. Hungerford , W J . Bluhm, T. L. Volk, & J. M. Ramsey (Eds.), *Essential readings in environmental education* (pp. 387–398). Champaign, IL: Stipes Publishing Company.

Rickinson, M. (2001). Learners and learning in environmental education: A critical review of the evidence. *Environmental Education Research, 7*(3), 207–320.

Robottom, J. (1994). Beyond the model/module mentality in Environmental Education. North American Association for EE. Ohio: Troy.

Ross, E. W. (2001). Rethinking the work of NCSS: From the editor. *Theory and Research in Social Education, 29*(1), 6–17.

Sanera, M., & Shaw, J. S. (1996). *Facts not fear: A parent's guide to teaching children about the environment.* Washington, DC: Regnery Publishing Company.

Simmons, D. A. (2005). Are we meeting the goal of responsible environmental behavior? An examination of nature and environmental education center goals, pp. 367–376. In H. R. Hungerford, W. J. Bluhm, T. L. Volk, & J. M. Ramsey (Eds.), *Essential readings in environmental education.* Champaign, IL: Stipes Publishing Company.

Simmons, B., & Volk, T. (2002). Environmental educators: A Conversation with Harold Hungerford. *Journal of Environmental Education, 34*(1), 5–8.

Smith, G.A. (2005). Defusing environmental education: An evaluation of the critique of the environmental education movement. In H. R. Hungerford, W. J. Bluhm, T. L. Volk, & J. M. Ramsey (Eds.), *Essential readings in environmental education* (pp. 387–398). Champaign, IL: Stipes Publishing Company.

Stapp, W.B. (1969). The concept of environmental education. *Environmental Education, 1*(1), 30–31.

Wilke, R. (2000). Should action be a goal? Yes. *Property and Environment Research Center* (PERC). http://www.perc.org/education.php?id=736 [Accessed July 25, 2007]

Winther, A. A, Volk, R. L., & Shrock, S. L. (2002). Teacher decision making in the 1st year of implementing an issues-based environmental education program: A qualitative study. *Journal of Environmental Education, 33*(3), 27–33.

UNESCO.SCO. 1978. *Final report of intergovernmental conference on environmental education.* Organized by UNESCO in cooperation with UNEP, Tbilisi , USSR, 14–26 October 1977, Paris: UNESCO *ED/MD/49.*

UNESCO-UNEP. (1978). *The Tbilisi Declaration: Final report intergovernmental conference on environmental education.* Organized by UNESCO in cooperation with UNEP, Tbilisi, USSR, 14–26 October 1977, Paris, France: UNESCO.

Vaughan, C., Gack, J., Solorazano, H., & Ray, R. (2003). The effect of environmental education on schoolchildren, their parents, and community members: A study of intergenerational and intercommunity learning. *Journal of Environmental Education, 34*(3), 12–21.

CHAPTER 9

AN "ECONOMIC WAY OF THINKING"

Approaches and Curricula for Teaching about Social Issues Through Economics

Phillip J. VanFossen and Christopher McGrew

INTRODUCTION

> Western industry is running on empty. The strategic petroleum reserve is nearly depleted. Spurred on by multiple economic crises created by the growing shortage of oil, the president commits the Rapid Deployment Force to seizing and holding the oil fields in Saudi Arabia...Several Army divisions are reassigned from Europe and Korea to bolster the soldiers opposing Syrian units...near the Persian Gulf.

After reading this passage, one might be tempted to think it comes as a prediction of headlines in the year 2011. Instead, it is a quote from *Economic Education for Citizenship* written by Steven L. Miller in 1988. What is interesting to note, however, is not that Miller's fictitious scenario so closely mirrors current events in 2011—as well as the issues of public policy underlying them—but that these issues have remained so remarkably similar in the

Teaching and Studying Social Issues: Major Programs and Approaches, pages 169–194
Copyright © 2011 by Information Age Publishing

intervening two decades. Indeed, issues such as globalization, oil prices, the debate over the minimum wage, tax policy, the crisis in Africa, prescription drug policy, poverty, military spending, and so on and so forth, remain as pertinent today as they were in 1988.

What do such issues have in common? Without exception, they are either rooted in fundamentally economic issues, or can be more fully understood using economic analysis; what we will refer to in this chapter as "an economic way of thinking." In relation to these issues, an economic perspective "is significant...not merely because it investigates an important slice of life in the market place, but because the (choice) phenomena which emerge... are also found in virtually all other human activities" (Boulding, 1971, p. 255). Further, "virtually all forms of human activity are amenable to economic analysis," not just those activities of the marketplace (Anderton & Carter, 2006).

Because economics and economic analysis *are* so pervasive, touching both citizens' personal and social lives, economic literacy is crucial to effective citizenship education because "most of the significant social issues confronting our society remain fundamentally economic" (Miller, 1988, p. 4). Despite this, Armento, Rushing, and Cook (1996) have noted that analysis of such complex social issues is often only superficial at best:

> Of course everyone has an opinion about such questions, but is the opinion informed, thoughtful, mindful of alternatives, trade-offs, and the short- and long-term consequences of various policy options? (p. 211)

Miller (1988), considering the same question, concluded that it was "unlikely that the general public understands what created [these problems] or how they were solved, because most citizens have no framework for economic concepts, no intellectual tools for organizing and interpreting the phenomena of the energy crisis or other economic events" (p. 2). What's more, this is not a new perspective. Indeed, it is one that has been pervasive for decades.

The publication of the widely-popular bestseller *Freakonomics* (Levitt & Dubner, 2005) highlighted this important nexus between social issues and economic analysis. Levitt and Dubner's (2005) analysis applied basic tools from neo-classical economics to questions such as "Why do drug dealers still live with their moms?" and "Where have all the criminals gone?" The subtitle of the book—*A Rogue Economist Explores the Hidden Side of Everything*—may be a bit disingenuous, however, because Levitt and Dubner's use of economics' analytical tools are anything but "roguish." What is noteworthy about *Freakonomics* is the application of economic tools to explore social issues, the result of which often lead to very different public policy conclusions—some "that turn conventional wisdom on its head" (p. xi).

Indeed, some social issues "are so 'hot,' emotional, and loaded with intensity, and often with dogmatic, pre-determined conclusions, that thoughtful classroom treatment is difficult" (Armento, Rushing, & Cook, 1996 p. 214). Without some framework for analysis—for thoughtful consideration of such issues—an issues-oriented approach could devolve into superficial debates and retrenchment of previous held viewpoints. Economics can bring such a framework to the study of these issues. Adam Smith, when writing about what would become classical economic theory, believed that economics allowed people to put themselves in the position of a third person, a sort of impartial observer, and in this way form a notion of the objective merits of one side or the other of a case (Heilbroner, 1953).

THE DISCIPLINE OF ECONOMICS AND THE POTENTIAL OF "AN ECONOMIC WAY OF THINKING"

For the purposes of this chapter, we define economics as the social science that investigates how people choose to use limited or scarce resources in attempting to satisfy their unlimited wants. At the heart of such a definition lies the act of choice. As much as anything, economists systematically analyze—while trying to be Smith's "third person"—the choices people make (whether those choices are made by individuals, by communities, or by nations) and the outcomes of those choices. Also central to this definition is the notion of relative comparison of many alternatives. Choices are rarely between "this or nothing" (an absolute comparison), but rather between "this or this or this or this or that" (a relative comparison). A common phrase used in economic analysis then is "relative to the next best alternative…" In this, economic education involves acquiring the ability to see new perspectives, and to make new comparisons. As the influential 19th century economist Alfred Marshall noted (1890/1920), economics is really:

> a study of mankind in the ordinary business of life; it examines that part of individual and social action which is most closely connected with the attainment and with the use of the material requisites of wellbeing. Thus, it is on one side a study of wealth; and on the other, and more important side, a part of *the study of man.* (emphasis added, p. 1)

The potential that economics brings to the analysis of social issues is that—as noted above—economics analysis is a "way of thinking": it tells us how incentives shape rational human behavior in all areas of life. For example, economic analysis can help diagnose social problems (e.g., the "negative externality" problem that accompanies air pollution) and show the consequences of various legal and/or political responses to those problems (e.g., regulation, taxation, enforcement). Economic analysis can also describe the costs and benefits of current and alternative policies, creating a framework for discussion of eventual policy decisions.

Harold Winter (2005) believed such use of an economic way of thinking (what Winter calls "economic reasoning") provided a "unique way of thinking about social issues, one that allows (the reader) to sidestep some of the moral, ethical, or legal arguments often used in policy debates" (p. xi). Winter (2005) believed that the benefits of such an approach are in identifying the "trade-offs—that is, the costs and benefits—of whatever issue is at hand" (p. 1). He reduced his approach to social issues to three steps:

1. Identify the theoretical trade-offs of the issue in question;
2. If possible, empirically measure the trade-offs to determine if the costs outweigh the benefits, or vice versa; and
3. Recommend (or implement) social policy based on the first two.

Thus, for Winter, an economic approach to analyzing social issues brings the analytical tools needed to identify and understand the trade-offs associated with various policy "solutions." By considering both the costs and benefits of potential policy solutions, Winter (2005) argued, real-world policy decision-making is best served by an explicit recognition of as many trade-offs as possible.

A NOTE ABOUT POSITIVE
VERSUS NORMATIVE ECONOMICS

We must note here that many would take exception to the claim that economic analysis is free from subjective (read: ideological) influence. In fact, Armento, Rushing, and Cook (1996) argued that instruction in economic analysis "must acknowledge and incorporate ideological differences and multiple interpretations about what is right or wrong when it comes to economic issues" (p. 211). While we acknowledge the rationale put forward by Armento, et al. (1996), we believe this focus on ideology to be unnecessary, and perhaps even counterproductive. We believe this because: (a) research has questioned (as will be discussed later in this chapter) whether high school students are capable of the depth of critical analysis needed to accurately and completely deal with the underlying ideologies Armento, et al (1996) refer to, and (b) the field of economics already acknowledges these larger ideological issues in two ways. For example, economic analysis is often brought to bear on fundamental questions such as "equity vs. efficiency" and "market failures."[1] In addition, the field has long divided itself

[1] For market failures, for example, economists can calculate the cost of imperfectly competitive markets. This *deadweight loss* is a loss of economic efficiency that can occur when markets are not truly competitive. Causes of deadweight loss can include monopoly pricing, externalities, taxes or subsidies.

into two branches of economic analysis: positive economics and normative economics.

As described by Nobel laureate economist Milton Friedman, positive economics is the branch of economics that focuses on the economic analysis of events and, to some degree, cause-and-effect relationships.[2] Positive economic analysis attempts to state what the economy *is actually like.* Normative economic analysis focuses on value judgments about what the economy *should be like.* Moreover, normative economic analysis often considers the desirability of certain aspects of the economy relative to others, and supports policy recommendations relative to certain societal (or governmental) goals.

To illustrate: a positive economic analysis might attempt to determine if a relationship existed between education and training and wages paid in a particular labor market and what the determinants of that relationship might be. A normative analysis might use the results of this positive analysis to build a case that—given such a relationship—funding for public schools should be seen as primarily an investment in human capital and thus should be increased. Of course, positive and normative analysis may in fact be related; the results of positive analysis about the economy may influence views of what policies should be enacted.

It is very important to recognize the importance of developing the analytical tools of *positive* economics—the analysis of "what is"—in future and current citizens. Nobel Prize winning economist Kenneth Boulding (1969) described the importance of applying positive economic analysis to political and societal issues in this way:

> An accurate and workable image...of the economic system in particular...is increasingly essential to human survival. If the prevailing images of the social system are unrealistic and inaccurate, decisions which are based on them are likely to lead to disaster...In a complex world, unfortunately, ignorance is not likely to be bliss, and a society in which important decisions are based on folk tales may well be doomed to extinction. (pp. 10–11)

Often, however, such positive analysis of social issues does not occur, leading to support for policies that fail or that have unintended consequences. Consider the long-supported (by economists, at least) policy of free trade. Dating back to Adam Smith's time, positive analysis has long demonstrated the gains associated with free international trade. Yet even today some interest groups continue to lobby for protectionism, and other trade barriers. Blinder (1987) argued that the allure of protectionism stems not from economic analysis, "but from the politics of special interests..." because "trade protection secures concentrated and highly visible gains for

---

[2]Milton Friedman, *Essays in Positive Economics.* (Chicago, IL: University of Chicago Press, 1953).

a small minority by imposing...costs on a vast and unknowing majority" (p. 112). Blinder reported the results of positive analysis of trade barriers enacted in the U.S. steel industry in the 1980s to "save" the jobs of U.S. steel workers. Eventually, the barriers did just that, but Blinder reported that those workers in the domestic steel industry who maintained their jobs did so at a cost of $750,000 per job (in 1980s dollars; in 2010—adjusted for change in the consumer price index—this would be equivalent to approximately $1,972,000)![3] It may well be the case that citizens knew the full cost of these policies and chose to support them anyway. It seems more likely, however, that citizens were unaware of these true costs as revealed through economic analysis.

AN ECONOMIC WAY OF THINKING AND SOCIAL ISSUES

What am I ever going to do with this stuff?...—7th grade social studies student in Indiana

This question or a form of this question has been asked in many classrooms containing young adolescents and adolescents alike. Issues-based social studies can provide an opportunity for students to answer this question. As noted earlier, globalization, terrorism, and environmental problems are examples of topics typically introduced in secondary social studies classrooms. Because these problems are rarely neat and orderly, students often bring incomplete (or inaccurate) prior knowledge concerning the key concepts and/or issues with these problems. As a result, students are unable "to think about the issue," or worse, they act upon the issue with ignorance.

An important question to ask is: Are high school students even ready to think about such complex social issues? In attempting to answer this question, Leming (2003) drew upon research claiming that most secondary students are *not* able to deal with such complex social issues within the context of social studies classes. He claimed that students typically use their own experiences or the position of a single expert alone to justify their own thinking (Leming, 2003). Other researchers have found that this inability to think complexly makes it very difficult to teach critical thinking about public policy or social issues (Johnston, Anderman, Milne, Klenk, & Harris, 1993).

Cognitive research has also indicated that for students to completely grasp social issues, they need to be thinking at levels higher than most students in a secondary classroom. In order to process complex, open-ended,

---

[3]Hufbauer, Gary, Diane T. Berliner, & Kimberly A. Elliot. *Trade Protection in the United States: 31 Case Studies.* Washington, DC: Institute for International Economics, 1986.

issues, students should possess thinking levels that allow them to see that "knowledge is an outcome of a process of reasonable inquiry in which solutions to ill-structured problems are constructed" (King & Kitchener, 1994). Leming (2003) claimed that adolescent students rarely achieved this level.

Given this research, it is clear that if secondary social studies students are to effectively grapple with complex social issues, they require tools to help them organize and structure these problems—preferably into levels that include elements that they can recognize; a form of instructional "scaffolding," if you will. The term scaffolding was developed as a metaphor to describe the type of assistance offered by a teacher (or peer) to support learning (Wood, Bruner, & Ross, 1976). In the process of scaffolding, the teacher provides just enough structure to allow a student to master a task or concept that the student is initially unable to grasp independently.

Here the discipline of economics, and specifically economics education, can help. Paul Heyne (1998) stated that "the discussion of social issues would be vastly improved and public policy would be much sounder if people understood the economic way of thinking" (p. 1). Economics and the economic way of thinking describe the language of decision-making and choice within a world of scarce resources. Because young people face choices and are required to make decisions on a daily basis, this approach provides tools that adolescent students can relate to. In this, economics and the economic way of thinking can help provide a framework for articulating the complex relationships that often accompany social issues. According to Paul Heyne (2000), the economic way of thinking is based on the presupposition that "all social phenomena emerge from the actions and interactions of individuals who are choosing in response to expected benefits and costs to themselves" (p. 4).

When people respond to constraints placed upon them by conditions of scarcity, they consider what will benefit them the most given a discreet set of resources and because of this, the economic way of thinking helps "clarify a lot of puzzling but important interactions" (Heyne, 2000, pp. 4–5). However, students need *not* be required to completely understand every facet of the field of economics in order to adopt an economic way of thinking (Davis, 1987). If students can understand that economics is not just about money, nor high level mathematics but about choices, they can indeed become economically literate and use this important tool to better function in society and be a more effective citizen (Miller, 1988).

Expanding on this idea to provide a framework for students to look at issues faced by society has been the focus of work by economic educators such as Mark Schug (Professor Emeritus at the University of Wisconsin, Milwaukee), John Morton (National Council on Economic Education), and Donald Wentworth (Pacific Lutheran University) who have created a list of criteria that should be addressed when applying economic analysis to the complexity of human decisions and interactions. These criteria use commonly-held beliefs from the discipline of economics that help students to organize their thinking about complex social issues. These are:

1. that people encounter limits in striving to satisfy their desires;
2. that everyone must make choices;
3. that consequences follow from our choices; and
4. that complex dynamics underlie an individual's transactions with others (Schug & Western, 2000, pp. 1–2).

THE HANDY DANDY GUIDE TO SOLVING ECONOMIC MYSTERIES

Caldwell, Ferrarini, and Schug (2006) provide clear examples of how these general criteria translate into cognitively appropriate tools (the "scaffolding") that secondary and post secondary students might use to investigate complex social issues in issues-based instruction. In a number of curriculum publications published by the National Council on Economic Education, Caldwell, et al., and others have articulated a set of principles they call the "Handy Dandy Guide (HDG) for Solving Economic Mysteries" (see Table 1).

A number of creative instructional strategies have been developed that can help teachers build upon the scaffolding outlined in the HDG. For example, the PACED model is a decision-making strategy that takes its name from the acronym created by the steps in the model (Day, Christopher, Fer-

Table 1. The Handy Dandy Guide for Solving Economic Mysteries.

1. People Choose—"...people manage their lives through making choices," and "...that, in making choices, people act rationally."

2. People's Choices Involve Costs – "Decisions come with costs, always," and "...not all costs are dollar costs."

3. People Respond to Incentives in Predictable Ways – "Incentives are rewards that prompt people to make decisions or take action."

4. People Create Economic Systems that influence individual decisions – A climate of formal and informal rules provide incentives and influence the choices that people make.

5. People Gain When They Trade Voluntarily – As long as trade is voluntary (without coercion), monetary and non-monetary gains are realized when exchange occurs.

6. People's Choices Have Consequences That Lie in the Future. – The choices and actions of people today will often benefit (or harm them) them in the future

(Caldwell, et al., 2006, pp. xii–xvi).

guson, and George, 2006). First students identify the specific (p)roblem; then they identify all possible (a)lternative solutions; then they develop a set of (c)riteria for evaluating all solutions; then they develop a means for (e)valuating how well each solution meets each criterion; and finally recommend a (d)ecision based on the results of this analysis. The PACED model is a prominent part of a number of curricula that deal with decision-making and social issues. The *Energy, Economics, and the Environment* series (Christopher, et al., 2006) and the *Handy Dandy Guide to Solving Economic Mysteries* (Schug & Western, 2000) are two of many curricula based on this approach. In each of these curricula, students start by applying the PACED model and an economic way of thinking to decisions from their own lives. Students then move onto more complex social issues and experience decisions that they might face as citizens or as policy-makers. The PACED model isn't the only tool that has been used to promote an economic way of thinking, but it is an important component and can serve as integral part of issues based instruction, especially at the middle and high school levels.

An extension of the basic principles outlined in the HDG came from Harvard University economist Greg Mankiw, former chairman of the President's Council of Economic Advisors. Mankiw (2006) has expanded the HDG principles to be more useful for advanced high school students or for introductory economic students in a college classroom. His "Ten Principles of Economics" add more detailed discussions of markets and the economic role of government to an economic way of thinking (Mankiw, 2006).

Table 2.   The Ten Principles of Economics.

1. People face trade-offs.

2. The cost of something is what you give up to get it.

3. Rational people think at the margin.

4. People respond to incentives.

5. Trade can make everyone better off.

6. Markets are usually a good way to organize economic activity – History shows that buyers and sellers interacting in the market are more efficient at allocating scarce resources than government planners.

7. Governments can sometimes improve economic outcomes – Although markets may be efficient, they fail at times. Government can sometimes correct for these failures.

8. A country's standard of living depends on its ability to produce goods and services – The productivity of the resources of a country influences the standard of living enjoyed by people in that country.

9. Prices rise when the government prints too much money.

10. Society faces a short-run trade-off between inflation and unemployment.

(Mankiw, 2006, pp. 3-13))

All of these tools allow students to organize their thinking about complex social issues, and teachers to scaffold student analysis within a common framework and—as research has suggested—this may help students reach higher levels of cognitive development. Through this use, students are able to apply an economic way of thinking to analyze decisions that they make, and can eventually transfer that model to more complex social issues.

CURRICULUM THAT EMPLOYED AN "ECONOMIC WAY OF THINKING" ABOUT SOCIAL ISSUES

The Senior Economist

Designed for high school economics and social studies teachers and published by the National Council on Economic Education four times a year from 1985 to 1995, *The Senior Economist* regularly provided classroom teachers with economic analysis of various current events. Under the editorship of Mark Schug, each issue featured an essay on a particular issue by a prominent economist and three complete lesson plans written by practicing classroom teachers. The intellectual quality of the *Senior Economist* was particularly high as, over the years, a number of very noteworthy economists contributed introductory essays. Among the contributors were Alan Blinder (Princeton), Jeffery Sachs (Harvard), William Baumol (New York University), Paul Heyne (University of Washington), (Stanley Fischer (Massachusetts Institute of Technology), and Nobel Laureates Douglass North (Washington University) and Gary Becker (University of Chicago).

Of the more than 30 issues of the *Senior Economist,* more than two-thirds focused on economic analysis of a social issue or problem. Indeed, an important feature of the journal was its attempt to bring economic analysis to bear on timely issues that were being debated by politicians and in the popular press. Among the social issues examined were:

- "The Changing Economic Condition of Women"
- "Why is Good Economics Bad Politics?"
- "Time for a National Energy Policy?"
- "Choice in Education"
- "Why So Much Food? Why So Much Famine?"
- "A New Look at Poverty and Welfare"
- "Trade and Peace in the Middle East"
- "The Economics of Crime"
- "Can Market Forces Protect the Environment?"
- "Immigrants and the Economy"
- "Overpopulation?"

While the topics addressed in the *Senior Economist* varied widely, the essays and lesson plans all shared one feature: the goal of helping students "think outside the box" by applying an economic way of thinking to current political and social issues. Indeed, many of the lesson plans utilized some form of the Handy Dandy Guide described above. For example, the essay and lessons in the issue entitled "Can Market Forces Protect the Environment?" (1990) introduced teachers and students to an economic incentives approach to environmental protection. In his introductory essay, economist Thomas Tietenberg (1990) argued that increased attention to economic incentives (e.g., rewarding firms that pollute less) and market forces (e.g., "pollution credits" that can be bought and sold in a private market) "offer(ed) a practical way to achieve environmental goals more flexibly and at a lower cost than traditional regulatory solutions" (p. 5). The lesson plans in this issue examined: (1) the role of incentives for firms and the costs and benefits of government regulation; (2) the economic concept of externalities and the role of well-defined property rights in pollution; and (3) the case of Brazil in the 1980s and the trade-offs (or costs) associated with various Brazilian environmental policies.

In "Immigrants and the Economy," economist George Borjas (1992) brought an economic perspective and market analysis to the issue of immigration to the United States. At the heart of Borjas' (1992) analysis was the idea of choice: that immigrants made a rational choice to leave one nation and that such choices were made in an immigration "market." Borjas (1992) went on to say that in this market, nations "compete" for "immigrants' human and physical capital" and that by "presenting a specific set of economic opportunities and by pursuing a particular set of immigration policies...the United States makes a particular offer, relative to the offers of other countries, in the immigration market" (p. 3). The lessons in this issue examined: (1) the incentives that influence potential immigrants; (2) the way in which the Immigration Act of 1990 (the "rules of the game" at the time for the U.S. the immigration "market") influenced individual choices and incentives to emigrate and also the costs and benefits of those rule changes; and (3) analysis of immigration statistics to determine which country wins (and which loses) when people immigrate.

National Council on Economic Education (NCEE) Curricula

In the National Council on Economic Education (NCEE) publication *Focus: Understanding Economics in U.S. History,* an economic way of thinking and the HDG are used to help students analyze how various historical policy decisions were made and how such decisions influenced people throughout United States history. For example, several lessons ask students to examine the importance of property rights and how the "rules of the game" were established in the United States Constitution. Students also use economic reasoning and the economic way of thinking to examine reasons for the Civil War and how some of President Franklin D. Roosevelt's New Deal Policies may have actually extended the Great Depression (Caldwell, et al., 2006).

Use of this economic way of thinking also has the potential to give teachers and high school students a new way of examining environmental issues. The *Energy, Economics, and the Environment* series (Day, Christopher, Ferguson, & George, 2006) constitute a collection of lessons—developed by classroom teachers for classroom teachers—that use the economic way of thinking to analyze environmental issues concerning land and water use, as well as solid waste disposal and energy resources. One manifestation of the economic concepts embedded in the Handy Dandy Guide was the use of two critical thinking decision models: the decision tree and the decision-making grid. These allow students to break down possible solutions and develop evaluation criteria when making decisions about environmental issues. As noted earlier, such decision models are a staple of curriculum material developed using an economic way of thinking.

Two other important economic concepts used by the teacher committee that developed these materials were the concept of marginalism, and the idea of spillover costs (and benefits) of negative and positive externalities. To illustrate these concepts, the authors introduced the problem of a dirty river in the lesson "Cleaning Up the River." They begin by discussing the incentives firms and individuals have for shifting some of the costs of production and consumption to others. They explain how "spill-over costs" are shifted to society through the production process and through consumption of goods and services by individuals. Figure 1 provides a graphic representation of this spill-over process.

Through this introduction, teachers, and ultimately, their students, are able to see how people's choices, their incentives for making those choices, as well as the consequences associated with such choices, lead to environmental market failures.[4] Students begin to understand how market failures lead to overproduction and over consumption of certain resources at a cost to innocent bystanders (Day, et al., 2006), and why the local community must consider possible solutions to these environmental market failures. They also begin to appreciate how communities must decide how best to protect these innocent bystanders, and to balance this with the impact on the income earning abilities of the firms and workers in the local community.

---

[4]Market failure refers to a situation in which markets fail to efficiently allocate goods and services. If the inefficiency is significant, non-market institutions (e.g., government provided goods, or government regulation) may be more efficient and increase social welfare relative to market solutions.

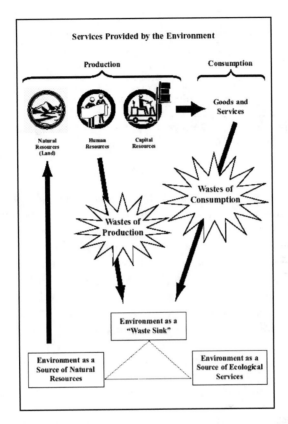

Figure 1. Example of spill-overs from "Cleaning up the River" (Day, et al., 2006, p. 14).

How government responds to these market failures becomes the main focus of student analysis. Marginalism provides students with a tool to use when analyzing the solutions for cleaning up the dirty river created by the choices people make. Students review data about *both* the total costs and benefits of each of these various levels of clean-up, *and* the marginal (or incremental) costs and benefits of each level. Day, et al. (2006) point out that without an understanding of economics and the economic way of thinking, students make choices based on the total cost analysis alone. They forget that for every decision, there is a cost represented by the missed opportunity, measured as "marginal cost." Because opportunity cost may be captured when using marginal analysis, policy-makers can evaluate each solution based on the benefit to the community of one additional level of cleanliness compared to the cost of that additional level. Figures 2 and 3 illustrate these comparisons.

Degree of Cleanup	Marginal Cost	Total Cost	Marginal Benefit	Total Benefit
25%	$10,000	$ 10,000	$100,000	$100,000
50%	$15,000	$ 25,000	$ 70,000	$170,000
75%	$25,000	$ 50,000	$ 50,000	$220,000
100%	$50,000	$100,000	$ 20,000	$240,000

Figure 2. Marginal Cost/Benefit Data from "Cleaning up the River" (Day, et al., 2006, p. 14).

Students begin to see, through this example, that solutions can be analyzed using this kind of marginal cost benefit analysis, because resources that could be used to correct for the spill-over (in this case, the pollution in the river) have alternative uses (Day, et al, 2006). Marginal analysis could reveal that resources might benefit the community more if used in these alternative ways (e.g., for environmental education).

In *Energy, Economics, and the Environment,* students are provided with a number of case studies that allow them to demonstrate an understanding of these economic concepts and to use the economic way of thinking. Certainly, for current and future citizens — and potential policy-makers — this type of analysis is one important tool for preparing students to participate in a civic society.

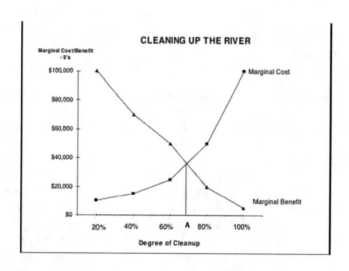

Figure 3. Graphic Representation of Marginal Cost/Benefit Data from "Cleaning up the River" (Day, et al., 2006, p. 15).

Trade-offs: An Introduction to Economic Reasoning and Social Issues

The last example presented here is not really curriculum per se, but rather an economic primer. In *Trade-offs: An Introduction to Economic Reasoning and Social Issues,* economist Harold Winter (2005) laid out a case for using economic reasoning when examining social issues (one that we examined briefly above) because such analysis "allows economists to detach themselves not only from their personal views, but also from favoring one side or the other of whatever social issue is at hand" (p. x). This view echoes Adam Smith's claim that economic analysis acts as a "third person," detached from the outcome. As is the case with the Handy Dandy Guide, Winter (2005) does not claim such an approach will provide a "cure-all for real-world problems" but rather provides a framework for examining them (p. xi). His goal in *Trade-offs* is to present:

> ...a unique way of thinking about social issues, one that allows you to side-step some of the moral, ethical, or legal arguments that are often used in public policy debate. Keep in mind that in no way am I claiming these other concerns are unimportant...I only want to present economic reasoning as *a* way of thinking about social issues, not *the* way of thinking about them. I do believe, however, that economic reasoning is an important and valid way of thinking about social issues (emphasis in original) (Winter, 2005, p. xi).

In *Trade-offs,* Winter (2005) brings insightful economic analysis to issues such as intellectual property and music piracy; organ transplantation and stem cell research; the pharmaceutical industry; product regulation; and insurance, safety and risky behavior. Any of Winter's analyses could be used to begin study of a specific social issue in a high school class. In one of his more unique analyses, Winter examined the issue of smoking and the social regulation of smoking by starting with the unique assumption that (a) smokers choose to smoke because they benefit from the act, and that (b) smokers are rational decision-makers. Winter (2005) began by asking, if smoking carries no benefits to the individual, "why are smokers willing to pay so much for something that provides them with no benefits?" (p. 55). He went on to explain that smokers obviously receive gains to trade—i.e., benefits beyond the price cost—for each pack they smoke, or they would not voluntarily consume them. Winter then tackled the common "yeah, buts..." to this line of reasoning. Yes, Winter (2005) conceded "there is evidence to suggest that smokers *don't* understand the risks of what they are doing" but, he argued, evidence showed smokers actually *overestimate* those risks (p. 56). Yes, Winter conceded, many smokers are addicted, but, he argued that even in addiction, consumers make choices based on past and future consumption. In other words, it is possible to be a "rational addict" for whom consumer sovereignty holds. Winter (2005) argued "consumers decide what is in their best interest, even when purchasing products that may be addictive" (p. 58).

Finally, Winter (2005) examined the concept of the negative externality (that private consumption of a good such as cigarettes has third-party costs) associated with second-hand smoke in restaurants and bars. As we have seen from the HDG, all decisions have costs and involve trade-offs, and so "an efficient outcome may involve some trade-off between the benefits smokers receive and the costs they impose on the non-smokers" and what is meant by the efficient outcome "will depend on the definition of social welfare" (Winter, 2005, pp. 73–74). The Coase Theorem in economics postulates that if property rights can be assigned (e.g., to the bar owner), and if negotiation costs are low (e.g., patrons can freely choose to come in or go down the street to another bar), then the parties can agree on a solution under which both would benefit (Coase, 1960).

Winter (2005) conceded that he had "no idea if the costs of smoking grossly exceed the benefits or vice versa" but offered his personal conclusion that "the costs of smoking have probably been overstated, while the benefits of smoking have definitely been understated" (p. 84). Regardless of his conclusions, Winter—through his economic analysis—has provided a compelling new lens through which to view an issue that is very often viewed from one side alone. This, in summary, is the overarching goal of economic analysis: to propose and analyze alternate (and often counterintuitive) hypotheses in order to explain human decision-making behavior.

The Research Base Supporting Pre-Collegiate Economic Education

Miller and VanFossen (2008) argue that "with few exceptions, no single area in the social studies has been as rigorously and quantitatively analyzed as the teaching and learning of economics at the pre-college, and especially high school, level." They claim this is due—in no small part—to the development and use of measurement tools such as the Test of Economic Literacy (hereafter, TEL). First developed in 1976 by the then Joint (later National) Council on Economic Education, the TEL was revised in 1985 by a committee of economists, high school economics teachers, and test experts, and then administered to more than 3,000 students from across the United States and from various socio-economic backgrounds. This norming process confirmed that the TEL could "differentiate between students with more (economic) knowledge and those with less" (Lynch, 1994, p. 63). The TEL was subsequently revised in 2001 and once again normed using a sample of more than 7,200 high school students in 36 states (Walstad & Rebeck, 2001).

While by far the most widely-used achievement test in pre-collegiate economic education, the TEL has been criticized for apparent ideological bias, for a naïve macroeconomic view (Nelson & Sheffrin, 1991), and for failing to address the value of fiscal policy in a Keynesian framework (Galbraith, 1987). Lynch (1994), however, concluded that these and other criticisms of the TEL may result more from the "state of macroeconomic thought today than it does any bias in the TEL" (p. 68). Despite these criticisms, the TEL has been widely used in the study of pre-collegiate economic education.

In his exhaustive review of hundreds of research studies on pre-collegiate economic education—many that employed the TEL or variants thereof—Watts (2006) summarized the major findings in the field across four areas:

1. "At both the elementary and secondary levels, students of teachers who know more economics, who spend more time teaching economics…learn more economics" (p. 1).
2. "A formal secondary (9-12) course in economics is the safest way to improve student's knowledge of economics…" (p. 1–2).
3. "Most secondary students today will never take a college course in economics. In fact, most U.S. high school students…do not take an economics course in high school…" (p. 2) Coupled with this finding is one that the "more economics adults (including teachers) know" (p. 3), the closer their opinions match those held by economists.
4. "Good instructional materials also make a difference…major sets of instructional materials, including video and computer components as well as good textbooks and other printed materials, can have a greater effect than a few individual lessons scattered over a course or school year" (p. 5).

Barriers to Economic Education in Schools

Because nearly half of all students in U.S. high schools do not take an elective or required course in economics (Walstad & Rebeck, 2001), it seems safe to conclude that economic education is not a high priority. Only fifteen states require a course in high school economics for graduation (NCEE, 2005); down from a high of sixteen in 1993 (Lynch, 1994). As states try to increase the rigor in college prep diploma programs, more students are taking a stand-alone economics course. However, the course is usually combined with a course in U.S. government and taken in the senior year (Walstad, 2001), and is often the last social studies course taken by students in high school. Efforts are also being made to integrate economic concepts into existing social studies or social science curriculum. The assumption is that simply adding economic concepts to existing social science content will provide students with the knowledge and skills that they need to fully understand complex social issues; however, research has indicated that this "integration approach" actually hinders a student's ability to understand the economic concepts so important to issues-based instruction (Walstad, 2001).

In 2004, seven states required students to take a personal finance economics course, with nine states requiring that students test in personal finance knowledge (NCEE, 2004). While personal finance and business economics are indeed important, a separate economics course for students headed directly into the job market or to post-secondary education may improve student basic knowledge they need to function in the "real" world (Walstad, 2001).

The standards movement—beginning with *A Nation at Risk: An Imperative for Education Reform* in 1983—has provided teachers with blueprints for social studies and discipline-based courses in economics, history, civics and government, geography, and the behavioral sciences (Buckles, Schug and Watts, 2001). While the standards created as a result of this movement led to curriculum reforms across the country, Buckles, Watts, and Schug (2001) expressed great concern over the degree of economic content knowledge teachers would be required to possess in order to meet these standards.

Indeed, studies have called into question the economic knowledge of social studies teachers, and a final barrier to implementing economic education is this lack of preparation on the part of social studies teachers. Research has long suggested a positive relationship between teacher background in economic content and student knowledge of economics (Allgood and Walstad, 1999; Lynch, 1994; Schug and Walstad,1991; Walstad 1991), but this relationship emerges only when teachers take *at least* 12 semester hours of college-level economics (Lynch, 1994). Walstand and Kourilsky (1999) found that only 20% of social studies teachers had at least this level of coursework in economics. Dumas, Evans, and Weible (1997) found that state licensure standards for the social studies required, on average, only *four* semester hours in economics. Eisenhauer and Zaporowski (1994) discovered that 86% of the economics courses in New York state high schools were taught by 'cross-disciplinary' teachers—broad field social studies teachers who taught economics as a small proportion of their teaching load and who had significantly less economic content preparation.

FINAL THOUGHTS

Armento, et al. (1996) concluded their chapter on issues-oriented economic education by stressing that social studies should help students engage in "informed reflection on important economic matters...instill dispositions of thoughtfulness and inquiry...and foster awareness and appreciation for the validity of alternative interpretations of complex issues" (p. 218). We strongly agree with this conclusion. As we have delineated herein, we believe that introducing students to an economic way of thinking about social issues encourages students to question assumptions, pursue alternative hypotheses, and use valid data to answer questions raised in the process. Armento, et al. (1996) also noted that students learn best when "they are intimately involved in the identification of a problem and in the construction of its...'solution'" (p. 218). Fostering an economic way of thinking provides the necessary cognitive scaffolding so that students who may not possess the higher order thinking skills needed to grasp social issues—as research would indicate—may still be involved in the construction of meaningful "solutions."

We disagree, however, with the final conclusions of Armento et al. (1996) that at "present, most economics educators will find themselves developing their own issues-oriented lessons, and will need to identify and gather the available data sources" (p. 219). We have presented a number of examples of curricula that employed an economic way of thinking about social issues. We feel confident that should a classroom social studies teacher wish to develop his/her students' ability to bring an economic analysis to social issues, he/she will find a variety of materials and resources to accomplish this task.

Research is clear: a stand-alone course in economics is the most effective way to teach economic ideas and the economic way of thinking (Lynch 1994; Walstad & Rebeck, 2001; Watts, 2006) and, therefore, perhaps the best place to integrate issue-oriented economic education. Although some progress has been made in the number of states that require a stand-alone course in economics (NCEE 2005), that progress has been sporadic (Walstad, 2001). Some scholars argue that the high school course should be offered earlier in the student's social studies experience (Buckles, Watts, & Schug, 2001). In addition, teachers of high school economics should be provided with more training. Significant improvements in student scores on standardized assessments of economic concepts are seen if the teacher has more than four courses in economic education (Lynch 1994, pp. 65–66). As studies have indicated, teachers can improve their economic knowledge via solidly planned and implemented economic in-service programs. In fact, such programs have resulted in gains in economic knowledge of both teachers and students (Miller & VanFossen, 2008).

As we write this chapter, the Reauthorization of the Elementary and Secondary Education Act ("No Child Left Behind") is being considered. It has become clear from recent research (Heafner, Lipscomb, & Rock, 2006; VanFossen, 2005) that No Child Left Behind's (NCLB) emphasis on accountability and adequate yearly progress in reading, math, and science has served to "crowd out" social studies instruction (the home of economics in the curriculum) generally, and at the elementary level specifically. Moving to make economics an explicit focus of the accountability and adequate yearly progress that NCLB demands would go a long way toward increasing the amount of economics taught across the K-12 curriculum.

Indeed, it is clear that knowledge of the concepts and skills of economics are important for *all* students. Citizens of the United States and other democratic republics need a core of economic knowledge and economic literacy in order to analyze and make sense of complex questions of public policy. In order for citizens to fully participate in our democratic society, they will also need to understand the complex issues that they will face in the global economy. All citizens need this core of economic knowledge and economic literacy (an economic way of thinking) because decisions they make regarding public policy will have significant consequences for them as individuals and for society at-large. Perhaps James Tobin (1986), Nobel Laureate in Economic Science, put it best when he described the importance of economic literacy for citizens in this way:

> High school graduates will be making economic choices all their lives, as breadwinners and consumers, as citizens and voters. A wide range of people will bombard them with economic information and misinformation for their entire lives. They will need some capacity for critical judgment. They will need it whether they go to college or not. (p. 22)

NOTES

The following list of works provides the reader with additional detail vis-à-vis research on the economic education:

Allgood, S., & Walstad, W. (1999). The longitudinal effects of economic education on teachers and their students. *Journal of Economic Education, 30*(2), 99–111.

This longitudinal study focuses on the impact the Nebraska Economic Fellow Institute had on teachers' knowledge of economics, their ability to think like economists, and the teachers' impact on their own students' knowledge of economics. The study purports to overcome the limitations of past research and to offer new insights. The authors provide evidence for three key findings: 1) economic understanding of fellows improved; 2) fellows thought more like economists after participating in the Institute; and, 3) economics teachers with more economic knowledge, and who thought more like economists, were more able to improve student learning.

Cargill, T. F., Wendel, J., & Jurosky, J. (2006). Implementing economics standards: A pilot transition program. *The Journal of Economic Education, 39*(2), 126–134.

The authors developed a pilot program in a school district to address obstacles of implementing economics standards. In doing so, the authors addressed the obstacles of developing a stand-alone course versus imbedding economics instruction in existing courses. The study focused on six components: 1) economics training for the teachers; 2) module development by the teachers (assisted by graduate students in economics); 3) identification of control group and pilot classes; 4) presentation of the nine-week economics modules in the high school senior pilot government class; 5) post-testing in the pilot and control group classes; and 6) analysis of the pre- and post-test results. The authors found that limited test score improvement was comparable to the results reported in other studies for students who had participated in stand-alone economics courses, thus addressing the obstacle of having only stand-alone economics courses.

Clark, J. R., Schug, M. C., & Harrison, A. S. (2009). Recent trends and new evidence in economics and finance education. *Journal of Economics and Finance Education, 8*(1), 1–10.

In the first part of this article, the authors provide an overview of two reviews of the literature regarding economics education. The majority of the article focuses on the results of the National State Survey and the National Assessment of Education Progress in Economics. The authors conclude that there is ample good news, including the fact that young people can learn economics, when they learn it best, and that twelfth graders may know more economics than do most members of the U.S. Congress. They go on to state, though, that there are major barriers to overcome, including poorly-prepared teachers (when it comes to economics) and over-reliance on high school economics courses to provide economic and financial literacy required in today's society.

Cohn, E., Cohn, S., Balch, D.C., & Bradley, J. (2001). Do graphs promote learning in principles of economics? *Research in Economic Education, 32*(4), 299–310.

In this study, Cohn et al. examined the use of graphs in an economics course and the impact of the use of graphs on student achievement. The authors were clear that they fully expected the use of graphs would increase achievement for their students. However, the use of graphs appeared to reduce learning. Controls were implemented for ability and other student characteristics and no differences were found in learning. Only students with high math abilities were found to benefit from the use of graphs. The authors conclude that if graphs are complicated and little time is given to analyze or ask questions about the graphs their use may be counterproductive.

Knoedler, J. T., & Underwood, D. A. (2003). Teaching the principles of economics: A proposal for a multi-paradigmatic approach. *Journal of Economic Issues, 37*(3), 697–725.

Knoedler and Underwood provide a brief analysis of why there is a decline in undergraduate enrollment in economics. The main focus of their paper presents an alternative hypothesis arguing that it is important to consider the "subject matter of modern mainstream principles to understand student disinterest in the course." (p. 697) The authors then provide three key questions they asked themselves regarding the current state of economics education: 1) what is the role of principles in the general education curriculum; 2) how does principles as defined by the most popular textbooks go about fulfilling that role; and, 3) why do students' schemata lead them to follow other general education avenues? In their final analysis, the authors provide an alternative set of economic principles that offers a "foundation for a principles course that provides a richer understanding of the real economy." (p. 725)

Leming, J. S., Ellington, L., & Schug, M. (2006). The state of social studies: A national random survey of elementary and middle school social studies teachers. *Social Education, 70*(5), 322–327.

This national study of elementary and middle school teachers focused on a variety of issues related to the teaching of social studies. Key findings from the study included evidence to suggest that teachers don't perceive their schools putting a priority on teaching social studies in general or in areas such as civics, economics, geography and history. The authors conclude that given the importance of citizens' knowledge of history, civics, geography and economics to the effective functioning of our republic, it is troubling to see how little time and importance is attached to the social studies in comparison to other areas of the school curriculum.

Miller, S. L., & VanFossen, P. J. (2008). Recent research on the teaching and learning of pre-collegiate economics education. In L. Levstik & C. Tyson (Eds.) *Handbook of research in social studies education* (pp. 284–306). New York: Routledge.

Miller and VanFossen provide an updated summary of research on the status of precollegiate economic education. The authors begin with a brief overview of the rationale for economic education and its history in K–12 classrooms. The authors then provide a comprehensive review of the literature since 1991 (the year the Schug and Walstad published their review of the literature in the *Handbook of Research on Social Studies Teaching and Learning* [Shaver, 1991]). Updated topics include research on technology and economic education and economic education in other nations, including the former Soviet Union.

Morton, J. (2007). Economic education: Is the glass half full or half empty? *Education Report*. Retrieved from *http://www.educationreport.org/pubs/mer/article. aspx?id=9100*.

This article examines the results of the National Assessment of Educational Progress (NAEP) as it relates to economics education. Morton indicates that 79 percent of high school students performed at the basic level and 42 percent at the proficient level or higher. He attributes these results to students taking economics in high school (two-thirds of high school graduates have taken an economics course). Morton indicates that NAEP results for economics are better than expected, however there remains a need for more widespread economic literacy.

VanFossen, P. J. (2000). Investigating teacher rationales for the high school economics course: A preliminary study. *Theory and Research in Social Education. 28*(3), 391–410.

VanFossen investigated the rationales for economic education held by eight veteran high school economics teachers. Results suggested that teachers held a range of goals and objectives for the high school economics course. Three broad themes emerged: (1) high school economics serve as a preparation for college economics; (2) economics constitute an important "life skill"; and (3) economics is equated with good citizenship education.

VanFossen, P. J., & Herman-Ellison, L. C. (2006). Internet-based economic education: The case of EconEdLink. *Social Education, 70*(3), 151–155.

According to the authors, even though the Internet includes a proliferation of economic information, few teachers take advantage of it. This is true, the authors assert, even though research has shown the benefits of the Internet for economics classrooms. They argue that EconEdLink is one way to address the concerns of teachers who are reluctant to use the internet. EconEdLink is a part of the MarcoPolo network (ww.marcopoloeducation. org/home.aspx). EconEdLink provides lessons and classroom learning activities for teachers based on economic concepts and topics. It also provides real-time economic data. In this article, the authors provide sound advice and practical examples on how to use EconEdLink.

Walstad, W., & Rebeck, K. (1999). How does economic education impact economic literacy?" *The Region, 13*(3), 18–21.

This study compared the economic knowledge of individuals who had an economics course in high school or college with those who did not have economics in high school or college. Results indicate that individuals who had an economics course in high school or college performed better as adults than those who did not have a course(s). This was true even when the authors controlled for age, gender, & level of education and the matriculation of economics courses. Walstad and Rebeck conclude that these are encouraging findings and suggest that economic education in high school or college does make a difference regarding adult understanding of economic issues.

Watts, M. (2004). What the empirical research tells us about precollege economic education. Paper presented at the International Symposium: Partnerships for Professional Development in Economic Education in Kiev, Ukraine.

This article provides an overview of the empirical research regarding precollege economic education. Watts begins by stating that "few economists take coursework in education, including psychometrics, while few educators take courses in economics, including econometrics." (p. 1) His point here is that "researchers in the fields of education, economics and economic education…don't know enough about what both groups of researchers are doing." Watts indicates that there are few empirical studies available regarding economics education at the precollege level, and most studies that have been done lack solid methodology. Watts outlines five key findings from empirical research: 1) Teachers who have more training in economics and use good resources spend more time teaching economics and, as a result, students learn more economics; 2) A separate course in economics at the high school level is important to economics learning; 3) The instructor has a very important role in the learning of economics; 4) The more economics one takes as a student the more one is likely to think like an economist; and 5) Little empirical research exists as to those teaching methods that work most effectively with precollege students or whether a particular order of teaching concepts works better than others.

REFERENCES

Allgood, S., & Walstad, W. (1999). The longitudinal effects of economic education on teachers and their students. *Journal of Economic Education, 30*(2), 99–111.

Anderton, C., & Carter, J. (2006). Applying intermediate microeconomics to terrorism. *Journal of Economic Education, 37*(4), 442–457.

Armento, B., Rushing, F., & Cook, W. (1996). An approach to issues-oriented economic education. In R. Evans & D. W. Saxe (Eds.), *Handbook on teaching social issues* (pp. 211–219). Washington, DC: National Council for the Social Studies.

Blinder, A. (1987). *Hard heads, soft hearts.* Menlo Park, N.J.: Addison-Wesley Publishing Company.

Boulding, K. (1969). Economic education: The stepchild too is father of the man. *Journal of Economic Education, 1*(1).

Borjas, G. (1992). Immigration and the economy. *The Senior Economist, 7*(3), 3–5, 12.

Boulding, K. (1971). Is economics necessary? In F. Glahe (Ed.), *Kenneth Boulding: collected papers, Vol. II.* Boulder: Colorado Associated University Press.

Buckles, S., Watts, M., & Schug, M. (1997). How well do the US standards work together? *Children's Social and Economic Education: An International Journal*, 2 (3): 145–157.

Buckles, S., Watts, M., & Schug, M. (2001). A national survey of state assessment practices in the social studies. *The Social Studies*, *92*(4),141–146.

Caldwell, J., Ferrarini, T., & Schug M. (2006). *Focus: Understanding economics in U.S. history*. New York: National Council on Economic Education.

Coase, R. (1960). The problem of social cost. *Journal of Law and Economics, 3*, 1–44.

Davis, J. E. (1987) *Teaching economics to young adolescents: A researched-based rationale*. Davis, CA: The Foundation for Teaching Economics.

Day, H., Christopher, D., Ferguson, K., & George, P. (2006). *Energy, economics, and the environment: Case studies and teaching activities for high school* New York: National Council on Economic Education.

Dumas, W., Evans, S., & Weible, T. (1997). Minimum state standards for secondary social studies teacher licensure: A national update. *The Social Studies, 88*(3), 163–166.

Eisenhauer, J., & Zaporowski, M. (1994). Cross-disciplinary teaching in high school economics. *Social Education, 58*(4), 226–229.

Galbraith, J. (1987). On teaching fractured macroeconomics. *Journal of Economic Education, 18*(2), 213–226

Heafner, T., Lipscomb, G., & Rock, T. (2006). To test or not to test?: The role of testing in elementary social studies: A collaborative study conducted by NCPSSE and SCPSSE. *Social Studies Research and Practice*, (2), 1.

Heilbroner, R. (1953). *The worldly philosophers: The lives, times and ideas of the great economic thinkers*. New York: Simon & Schuster

Heyne, P. (1998). Limitations of the economic way of thinking. *Religion and liberty*, (Vol. 8, No. 4). Grand Rapids, MI: Acton Institute.

Heyne, P. (2000). *The economic way of thinking*. Upper Saddle River, NJ: Prentice Hall.

Johnston, J., Anderman, E. M., Milne, L., Klink, L., & Harris, D. (1993). *Improving civic discourse in the classroom: An experiment*. Ann Arbor: Institute for Social Research, University of Michigan.

King, P. M., & Kitchener, K. S. (1994). *Developing reflective judgment: Understanding and promoting intellectual growth and critical thinking in adolescents and adults*. San Francisco, CA: Jossey-Bass Publishers.

Leming, J. (2003). Ignorant activists. In J. Leming, L. Ellington, & K. Porter (Eds.) *Where did the social studies go wrong?* Washington D.C.: The Thomas Fordham Foundation.

Levitt, S., & Dubner, S. (2005). *Freakonomics: A rogue economist explores the hidden side of everything*. New York: William Morrow/HarperCollins.

Lynch, G. (1997). High school economics: Separate course vs. the infusion approach. *The International Journal of Social Education, 8*(3), 59–69.

Mankiw, G. (2006). *Essentials of Economics: 4th edition*. Mason, OH: Thompson Higher Education.

Marshall, A. (1890/1920). *Principles of economics*. London: Macmillan and Co., Ltd.

Miller, S. L. (1988) *Economic education for citizenship*. Bloomington, IN: ERIC, the Foundation for Teaching Economics and the Social Studies Development Center.

Miller, S. L., & VanFossen, P. J. (2008). Recent research on the teaching and learning of pre-collegiate economics. . In L. S. Levstik & C. Tyson (Eds.), *Handbook of research on teaching and learning in social studies* (pp. 284–306). Mahwah, NJ: Lawrence Erlbaum Associates.

National Council on Economic Education (2005). *Survey of the states: Economic and personal finance education in our nation's schools in 2004.* New York: Author.

Nelsen, J., & Sheffrin, S. (1991). Economic literacy or economic ideology? *Journal of Economic Perspectives, 5*(3), 157–165.

Schug, M., & Western, R. (2000) *The great economic mysteries book: A guide for teaching economic reasoning grades 4–8.* New York: National Council on Economic Education.

Shaver, J. (Ed .) (1991). *Handbook of research on social studies teaching and learning.* New York: MacMillan Reference Books.

Tientenberg, T. (1990). Harnessing the power of the market to enhance environmental protection. *The Senior Economist, 6*(1), 3–5.

Tobin, James (1986). Economic literacy isn't marginal investment. *Wall Street Journal,* July 9, 22.

VanFossen, P. J. (2005). "Reading and math take so much of the time…": An overview of social studies instruction in elementary classrooms in Indiana. *Theory and Research in Social Education, 33*(3), 376–403.

Walstad, W. (2001). Economic education in U.S. high schools. *The Journal of Economic Perspectives, 15*(3), 195–210.

Walstad, W., & Kourilsky, M. (1999). *Seeds of success: Entrepreneurship and youth.* Dubuque, IA: Kendall-Hunt.

Walstad, W., & Rebeck, K. (2001). Assessing the economic understanding of U.S. high school students. *The American Economic Review, 91*(2), 452–457.

Watts, M. (2006). *What works: A review of research on outcomes and effective program delivery in precollege economic education.* New York: National Council on Economic Education.

Winter, H. (2005). *Trade-offs: An introduction to economic reasoning and social issues.* Chicago, IL: The University of Chicago Press.

Wood, D., Bruner, J. S., & Ross, G. (1976). The role of tutoring in problem solving. *Journal of Psychology and Psychiatry, 17.*

CHAPTER 10

TEACHING SOCIAL ISSUES FROM A GLOBAL PERSPECTIVE

Merry M. Merryfield

As never before, the lives of students in our classes today are shaped by the outcomes of globalization. Students download music from Mexico onto I-pods developed by a U.S. company and made in China as they eat hamburgers made from Brazilian beef that grazed on land that was once primary rainforest. Their families may drive Japanese or European cars made in Ohio or South Carolina as they worry about the price of gas that originated in the oil fields of Saudi Arabia, Nigeria, or Venezuela. Today's students have grown up watching news beamed nightly from correspondents in Israel, Russia, or Iraq, and many watched the 2008 Olympics live from Beijing. Along with millions of other young people around the world, they have shared the trauma of terrorist attacks on their fellow citizens and the anguish of having people in their community die in a foreign war. Unlike previous generations, many are accustomed to hearing languages other than English spoken and personally know immigrants, exchange students, or refugees from Latin American, Asia, Africa or Europe. Things international—be it styles, technologies, entertainment, religious conflicts, health, or environmental issues—are inextricably situated in their lives.

This chapter is about global education, a field of study developed to increase student knowledge about their connections to people, events, and

Teaching and Studying Social Issues: Major Programs and Approaches, pages 195–216

issues across the world and to prepare students to participate locally and globally as members of the world community. Global educators aim to "develop in youth the knowledge, skills, and attitudes needed to live effectively in a world possessing limited natural resources and characterized by ethnic diversity, cultural pluralism, and increasing interdependence" (National Council for the Social Studies, 2005). This chapter focuses on the historical development of global education and examines relevant research, implementation and resources for infusing global perspectives into programs and classrooms today.

HISTORICAL CONTEXT

In the period following World War II, the world experienced dynamic change as European empires dissolved, global trade increased, and multinational corporations, international institutions (e.g., the United Nations, the World Bank and The International Monetary Fund) and private voluntary organizations (e.g., Greenpeace, CARE, The Palestinian Liberation Organization) became actors on the world stage. The forces of globalization became more salient every year as new consumer goods entered global markets, multinational companies exploited opportunities for cheap labor worldwide, and environmental destruction and toxic waste disposal became global issues. The Cold War created proxy conflicts, political entanglements, economic, and military interventions—all of which fed into an escalating arms trade across the planet. By the 1960s and 1970s, various scholars and educators began to discuss how education needed to change to meet the challenges of a global age (Adams & Carfagna, 2006; Anderson, 1979; Becker, 1979).

In the United States, the movement for global perspectives in education grew out of the perceived obsolescence of two traditional approaches to teaching about people and places beyond the U.S.: international relations and Eurocentric histories/geographies/literature. The traditional international relations approach focused on political and economic interaction of nation-states and was often taught through nationalistic points of view. Global educators believed students should study a variety of actors on the world stage—from individuals and local groups to new regional and global organizations that had no national base or alliance, such as multinational companies, terrorist organizations, environmental organizations, religious groups, and self-help groups (Boyer, 1983; Council on Learning, 1981; National Governors' Association, 1989). There was recognition that many new problems—the OPEC cartel and energy crisis, nuclear proliferation, desertification, over-fishing, the plight of refugees, and new pandemics—were affecting people across nations. They could only be solved if people worked together across borders and regions (Adams & Carfagna, 2006; Diaz, et. al, 1999).

Eurocentric approaches to the study of world cultures, literature, geography, or history tended to ignore or marginalize the experiences and voices of people in Africa, Asia, the Middle East, and Latin America. In a globally interconnected world, global educators believed that students needed to learn firsthand from Africans, Asians, Latin Americans, and people in the Middle East (who together make up the vast majority of the world's peoples) in order to understand and address issues facing the planet.

The grandfathers of global education—Lee Anderson (a political scientist), Chadwick Alger (a political scientist), James Becker (an educator), and Robert Hanvey (an anthropologist)—saw the need for students to become well informed, world-centered citizens. Recognizing the outcomes of globalization long before the term developed the connotations it has today, they believed students should see the world as a whole, where events and issues in one part of the world frequently affect people in another part. Indeed, they had a vision of students seeing the world from a global perspective instead of such divisions as "us and them," rich and poor, or First World/Third World (Alger, 1974; Anderson, 1979; Becker 1979, Hanvey, 1975).

Global education was initially grounded in two constructs that set it apart from traditional ways of teaching about the world: global interconnectedness and perspective consciousness (Anderson, 1979; Becker, 1979; Hanvey, 1975). Initially, global interconnectedness included the study of interactions between local and global communities, between past and present realities, and between economic, political, environmental, and social issues facing the planet. Global education encouraged young people to develop a "global perspective" in which they examined the world as a closed system with finite resources (Alger, 1974; Anderson, 1979; Becker, 1979). Global interconnectedness was especially relevant for the study of history as it connected events across regions and issues across time periods.

"Perspective consciousness" was defined as "the recognition or awareness on the part of the individual that he or she has a view of the world that is not universally shared, that this view of the world has been and continues to be shaped by influences that often escape conscious detection, and that others have views of the world that are profoundly different" (Hanvey, 1976, n.p.). In order to understand the world, students needed to look at why and how people of different cultures often perceive events and issues quite differently from each other. Although patterns of thinking may change over time, culture always shapes how humans make sense of their world (Hanvey, 1976). When students acquire skills in perspective consciousness, they can begin to develop awareness, understanding and empathy for people in different circumstances, and they develop skills in deconstructing reasons for cultural conflicts (Case, 1993; Merryfield & Wilson, 2005). Perspective consciousness teaches the habit of seeking out and examining multiple perspectives and valuing primary sources from cultures under study.

Perspective consciousness and global interconnectedness contributed to the development of the concept of "worldmindedness," habits of the mind that allow students to process new knowledge within a global context and develop intercultural skills in communication and interaction with people different from themselves (Becker, 1979; Bennett, 1993). Many came to believe that perspective consciousness and global interconnectedness enriched the social studies as students learned to examine events and issues within a global framework and inquire into the perspectives and experiences of diverse people and organizations, especially those people who have little power (Adams & Carfagna, 2006; Anderson, 1979; Becker, 1979; Diaz et al, 1999).

In the 1970s and 1980s considerable debate ensued over definitions of global education as people's conceptualizations were grounded in particular geographic, political or disciplinary contexts (Lamy, 1986). In retrospect, there was general agreement that global education taught students to examine the world as a whole through knowledge of global interconnectedness, global systems (economic, political, environmental, technological) and global issues such as security, human rights, economic development, deforestation, population (Goodlad, 1986; Leetsma, 1979). Students were to come to understand the state of the planet based on the perspectives, knowledge and experiences of diverse people and the status of other species across world regions (Hanvey, 1976; Kniep, 1986; Pike & Selby, 1988). A greater emphasis was placed on the need to understand how there had been an acceleration of interdependence between peoples over time, the many and complex antecedents to current events, and contact and the type of borrowing among cultures that took place and the impact of such (Kniep, 1986). Students also began to study causes of contemporary world problems from a global perspective. Thus, for example, lessons on the twentieth century might run the gamut from the origins of borders and reasons for ethnic diasporas to the effects of imperialism, religious conflict, movement of people and new technologies (Merryfield & Wilson, 2005). Skills in perspective consciousness, intercultural communication and interaction, critical thinking, and research were advocated along with dispositions that promoted positive attitudes towards engagement in the world (Alger and Harf, 1986; Kniep, 1986; Wilson, 1993).

Implementation of such concepts began by infusing these ideas into the existing curriculum and through projects that focused on the teaching of local/global connections. The first popular curriculum projects revolved around local communities and the world. *Columbus in the World/The World in Columbus* created by Chad Alger and teachers in Columbus, Ohio was soon followed by *Indiana in the World, the World in Indiana* and then spread to over 50 local/global projects in diverse cities and states (Alger, 1974; Becker, 1979). These projects were very popular with teachers and parents as they focused on recognizing international influences in the local community (for example, students identified where products in their homes and grocery stores came from) and involved local interactions with people from other countries (through business, cultural, religious and linguistic connections, such as an Irish priest on a fundraising tour, a Honda executive from Japan, a community health worker from India, and a refugee family from Sudan). Students learned firsthand how they are dependent on people who grow or make products they value and they came to recognize how their generation's decisions as consumers were affecting people and environments across the planet. They also came to recognize how small changes in one region (an oil spill, ethnic conflict, new technologies, political alliances) often effect changes across the world over time (Alger, 1974, Alger and Harf, 1986; Pike & Selby, 1995).

By the late 1970s and the 1980s, global education was characterized by a growing number of organizations that developed instructional materials and worked with schools and practicing teachers. Among these were: The Mid-America Program for Global Perspectives in Education in Bloomington, Indiana, the Bay Area Global Education Project in San Francisco, the Center for Teaching International Relations in Denver, the Mershon Center in Columbus, Ohio, and Global Perspectives in Education in New York City (eventually renamed the American Forum for Global Education) which provided leadership in hosting annual conferences in the 1980s and early 1990s. Although some of these new organizations were associated with universities, most survived by obtaining grants from foundations and state or federal governments. During this period, national professional associations, such as the National Council for the Social Studies, the American Council on the Teaching of Foreign Languages, and the Association for Supervision and Curriculum Development began to address global education in their conferences, publications, and position statements. In 1989, the National Governors' Conference also published a document supporting global education (National Governors' Conference, 1989).

Although all along there were people who, for various reasons, looked askance at global education, several major controversies made headlines in the 1980s over global education instructional materials and instructional practices. For example, in a 1986 article entitled "Blowing the Whistle on Global Education," Gregg Cunningham accused the Center for Teaching International Relations at the University of Denver of producing materials that seek "to ridicule our value system by suggesting that we relinquish our economic and political preeminence in the interest of some shadowy 'global justice'. Their worldview is utopian and pacifistic. They are redistributionists" (Cunningham, 1986, p. 21). Subsequently, his arguments were taken up by Phyllis Schafly (1986) in "What Is Wrong with Global Education?" published in the *St Louis Globe Democrat*. She attacked global education as an attempt to censor content about American history, culture, and heroes, to promote moral equivalence and brainwash teachers to use techniques of indoctrination. In 1988, controversy spread to Minnesota when Katherine Kersten (1988) wrote "The Radicalization of Minnesota's Public Schools," an expose of what she called the one-sided and inaccurate views on Central America that were being promoted and distributed to teachers by the Minnesota Global Education Coalition. Although her target was the Central American Resource Center in Minneapolis, which was associated with the Coalition, her critique of global education was reported nationally as it served to further various political agendas (Schukar, 1993). These and other controversies caused global educators to consider how they could go about balancing conflicting views and perspectives and reframing rationales and curricula within local political and economic contexts (Merryfield, 2006; Schukar, 1993).

At one and the same time, the 1980s and 1990s were characterized by the growth of teacher education programs in global education. Most were aimed at practicing teachers since few states required global content for initial licensure. Gene Gilliom at Ohio State University, Jan Tucker at Florida International University, Angene Wilson at the University of Kentucky, John Cogan at the University of Minnesota, Carole Hahn at Emory University, Ken Tye at Chapman College, and Don Johnson at New York University all worked on conceptualizing and implementing teacher education in global education. In 1990, Merryfield (1991) profiled 31 U.S. teacher education programs that included a global education component. In 1995, the National Council for Accreditation of Teacher Education (NCATE) standards began to mandate global perspectives for pre-service teachers. By 1996, the American Association of College of Teacher Education (AACTE) published *Making Connections Between Multicultural and Global Education: Teacher Educators and Teacher Education Programs* which profiled 115 educators and programs. In 1997, members of the AACTE Global and International Committee produced *Preparing Teachers to Teach Global Perspectives: A Handbook for Teacher Educators*, an edited volume that set forth conceptual underpinnings for infusing global perspectives across teacher education programs and provided illustrations of best practices (Merryfield, 1996; Merryfield, Jarchow & Pickert, 1997).

Over the last ten to fifteen years, global education has focused attention on such concerns and issues as perceptual learning, citizenship education, and issues of equity and social justice (Banks et al., 2005; Bigelow & Peterson, 2002; Gaudelli, 2003; Noddings, 2005). In addition *and* in contrast to the substantive dimension of knowledge about the world, the inner dimension of global education has come to focus on understanding of self, one's own beliefs and values, and habits of the mind such as open-mindedness, resistance to stereotyping, and anticipation of complexity (Case, 1993; Pike, 2003).

Furthermore, as more global educators have advocated learning from the experiences, ideas, and knowledge of people who are poor, oppressed, or in opposition to people in power, global education has increased representation of marginalized peoples, their issues and concerns through a pedagogy for social justice (Banks et al, 2005; Bigelow & Peterson, 2002; Gaudelli, 2003; Tan, 2004). Today, global educators ensure that students learn from people whose experience(s) and knowledge differ from dominant discourse (Adams & Carfagna, 2006; Apple & Buras, 2006; Pang, 2005).

Global education continues to develop in different ways across the United States as it works to ground students in local/global connections and helps to make the world relevant to their experiences and the lives of those in their community. Unlike the early years of the 1970s, global educators today have a wealth of strategies and resources available to help K–12 students understand the world as one finite and interconnected system. Introduction to global geography or world studies may begin with students examining images of Earth from space, mapping the products they use every day from other world regions, or tracing how historical events from politics in ancient Greece to trade over the Silk Road to Japanese expansionism in the 20th century still influence their lives today. New electronic technologies are often used to help students learn about diverse cultures through cross-cultural interactions and participation in worldwide discussions and problem-solving. In today's global classrooms students make connections across time periods and study local issues within a global framework (Merryfield & Wilson, 2005).

It is important to remember that throughout its short history global education has developed out of specific geographic, political and economic contexts within the United States as well as other countries. While connections with Latin America are central for Dade County Schools in Miami, connections with East Asia are much more relevant in Seattle and Hawaii. Economic realities (agri-business in the Midwest; shipping in Long Beach, California; NAFTA in many states) or political acts (such as terrorist attacks, peace-keeping and military alliances) continue to influence how global education is implemented locally (Merryfield, 1995). The goals of global education are dynamic and change over time as they are directly related to both local issues and world events. In the post-Cold War era the major goals of global education in the United States focus on understanding the complexities of today's world, the increasing interconnectedness of diverse peoples, and the search for social justice and human rights (Adams & Carfagna, 2006; Tan 2004).

RESEARCH BASE

Global education has been narrowly theorized and under-researched. Situated in centers and private organizations in the 1970s and 1980s, most leaders in global education focused on taking action in schools, state legislatures, and professional organizations in order to implement programs and legitimize the field. Their priorities were curriculum development, the dissemination of instructional resources, and work with inservice teachers. The relatively few studies from this period were from a handful of tenured professors (such as John Cogan, Jan Tucker, Ken Tye, and Angene Wilson), PhD students' dissertations, and from professors in other disciplines whose research interests overlapped to some degree with a goal or outcome of global education (such as Ken Cushner, Michael Paige, and Judith Torney-Purta).

By the early 1990s, more tenured and tenure-track professors in Research I universities began lines of inquiry into various facets of global education. Among some of the many were Margaret Crocco, Toni Kirkwood, Merry Merryfield, and Graham Pike. Since 2000, many more researchers have come to focus on diverse elements of global education and its connections with other areas of study, particularly multicultural education, technology, and citizenship education. Among such individuals are: Kathy Bickmore, Barbara Cruz, Bill Gaudelli, Elizabeth Heilman, John Myers, Walter Parker, Binaya Subedi, and Guichun Zong.

In this section, several studies are described that are indicative of the field, its goals, and its problems. For the most part, the studies focus on implementation, teacher and student thinking, and cross-cultural experiences.

Across the years, researchers have looked at how schools and individual teachers implement global education and how it affects student learning. One of the earliest studies focused on the implementation of a globally-oriented curriculum within a social studies project entitled "Family of Man." This social studies curriculum was centered on global change, understanding diverse cultures, and valuing human dignity, freedom of choice, and the role of the individual. Inquiry strategies encouraged students to learn through a discovery process and act as social scientists developing hypotheses and making generalizations. In a quasi-experimental design, Charles Mitsakos (1978) compared the learning and perceptions of an experimental group (21 third grade classes totaling 233 students who had been taught this curriculum for three years) with two control groups (220 students who had not been exposed to globally-oriented social studies). Although comparison of the pre-post tests of general knowledge showed no statistical significance, the People Pictures test in which students reacted to visuals demonstrated that the students in the experimental group had significantly more favorable perceptions of people different from themselves. Mitsakos concluded that a well-implemented global education program can have a positive effect on children's understanding and attitudes towards people from other countries.

Several smaller studies add to the literature on how globally-oriented instruction may affect student perceptions of diverse cultures and the world. Sandra LeSourd (1993) examined how ten and thirteen year old students perceived people in Thailand, Pakistan, Peru, Ghana, and the USSR. The students examined photos and then answered questions. The ten-year-olds were more concerned about the people's thoughts and feelings. The thirteen-year-olds focused more on the countries' geography, society or politics. Bickmore (1999) looked at 33 urban fourth and fifth graders who had been taught through a social education curriculum based on conflict resolution theory. The students studied the Hutu-Tutsi conflict in Rwanda and Zaire, and compared it with bullying and other conflicts in school, international conflicts over the use of water resources, and the Arab-Israeli conflict. Bickmore concluded that the integration of global conflicts with school-based conflicts allowed students to apply lessons and develop some conflict resolution skills. Helen Benitez's (2001) study focused on student attitudes that developed during a globally-oriented U.S. History course. She compared students who experienced a global version of U.S. History with those who were taught a traditional U.S. History course. From pre- and post-tests she found that the experimental group of 55 became more internationally-minded while the control group of 74 became more nationalistic. The tests measured elements of anticommunism, the role of the United States in defending democracy throughout the world, ethnocentrism, and the relative importance of domestic versus international problems. Overall, she found the experimental group recognized connections between local, national and global issues that were not recognized by the control group. In all four of the studies above there is evidence that a globally-oriented curriculum can make a difference in students' knowledge, perception, and skills.

Some studies examine global education within whole school reform. For example, Barbara and Ken Tye (1992) followed the progress of teachers through an entire school year as they implemented several reforms, one of which was global education. The researchers collected data from teachers as they made instructional decisions. Although the teachers said they supported some of the global education goals, they explained that they did not implement the new curriculum as designed because of a lack of time and the pressure of other reforms that were considered to be more important. The Tyes also found that some teachers resisted implementing the curriculum due to their concerns about global education being too ambiguous, too much work or, for a few, somewhat unpatriotic.

William Gaudelli (2003) also studied educational reform in relation to the issue of global education, following a mandate for a global curriculum.

He examined teachers' implementation of *New Jersey World History/World Cultures Curriculum*, a state-mandated global curriculum in urban, rural, and suburban high schools in New Jersey. Gaudelli looked at how the teachers who had no training in global education developed their lessons and taught the new courses. He concluded that local contextual factors beyond the control of teachers determined what changes took place. At the urban school, the teachers taught what Gaudelli called "trivial pursuit pedagogy" (facts from textbooks) while at the rural school there was interdisciplinary instruction with active learning methods. The suburban school focused on course content and used individuals as representatives of their culture. The lesson learned is that the local context of a school is critical.

There have also been studies of expert global educators. Merry Merryfield (1993, 1994, 1998) looked at the implementation of global education across sixteen teachers (four elementary, four middle school, eight high school) who were considered to be exemplary global educators by their school districts. She studied their processes of instruction and decision-making over two years. She then compared the characteristics of the exemplary group to two other groups: preservice social studies teachers and inservice teachers who had no background in global or international education. The exemplary group differed from the other groups of teachers in several ways: they taught global interconnectedness across historical periods and world regions, and they focused on the state of the planet, global issues and global systems. Unlike teachers in other two groups, they taught about global inequities and power relations, and included diverse voices.

The instruction of the exemplary teachers was at times profoundly influenced by local/world events as well as the characteristics of students who were in their classes. The study began in 1990–1991, the year of the first Gulf War, and the teachers rearranged their courses to help students understand the build-up to the war, environmental and economic implications, and cultures of the nations involved. Compared with the other groups in the study, the exemplary teachers perceived the war as a teachable moment, and as an opportunity for students to learn about the Middle East (Merryfield, 1993). These teachers often took the characteristics of students into consideration when planning lessons (Merryfield, 1994). When a class had a student from another part of the world, the teachers often developed connections to the student's country so that the rest of the class would come to appreciate their culture, history, art or music. Students' experiences or interests in another place or with a global issue were jumping off places for the whole class to learn something new. Based upon these studies, teachers highly experienced in teaching global perspectives were more likely to connect content to student lives and interests and foster student development of worldmindedness.

There have been numerous studies of how overseas experiences change teachers' and student's perceptions of themselves and the world. These include documentation of the effects of study abroad, Peace Corps experiences, or teaching abroad. Angene Wilson (1993, 1998) has written about the effects of overseas experiences on teachers' instruction, the use of international students as conversation partners, international students in American classrooms, and the lived experience of teacher educators teaching in other countries. Wilson has developed theories from her studies on how international experience leads to substantive knowledge, perceptual understanding, personal growth, interpersonal connections, and the ability to become a cultural mediator (Merryfield & Wilson, 2005).

Toni Kirkwood (2002) targeted study abroad funded by the U.S.-Japan Foundation. Thirty-three teachers from the Miami area spent two weeks of study in Japan. They came back with new knowledge and the motivation to infuse Japanese content into state-mandated social studies classes. Kirkwood found that the teachers focused on cross-cultural understanding, acceptance of human diversity, and the interconnectedness of global history. They also addressed the dropping of the atom bombs on Japan.

Martha Germain (1998) researched how teachers change when they have the experience of teaching in another country. She studied the life experiences of six veteran teachers, four who lived and taught in Japan and two who lived and taught in China. She researched their backgrounds, their experiences in other countries, and their reflections on the effects of their experiences. She found that the teachers developed a heightened sense of empathy with immigrant and ethnic minority students, and the ability to address stereotypes. She also found that they revised the resources and methods they used to make them more authentic.

Another approach to the study of cross-cultural experiences can be seen in the work of Guichun Zong (2005b), who has developed counter narratives based of her experiences growing up during Mao's China and her life journey in becoming a student and then a professor in the United States. Her work on border crossing is similar to that of Binaya Subedi (2006) who has studied how teachers born in South Asia negotiate teaching about the world to their inner city students in the American Mid-West.

Recently there has been research on using electronic technologies to develop cross-cultural awareness and intercultural competence. For example, Guichun Zong (2002) examined how a technology-enhanced global education course affected two preservice secondary teachers. The pre-service teachers participated in ICONS, a worldwide simulation network that uses both synchronous and asynchronous communication characteristics of the internet to teach international negotiation and intercultural communication to university and high school students. Zong studied the preservice teachers during their student teaching and documented how they infused global perspectives into their instruction. She concluded the global education plus the ICONS simulation boosted their understanding of global perspectives and prepared them to use the Internet to integrate global perspectives into their teaching. This study was followed up in 2005 by her two-year study of what preservice teachers learned from participating in a semester long web-based multinational discussion. She looked at how such online interaction fostered understanding of cultural diversity and global awareness. Overall findings suggested that the web-based discussions create new understandings of other countries, global issues and an appreciation of multiple perspectives. Zong concluded that the preservice teachers developed greater efficacy in taking action for a better global community. Actions included using websites that connect students to organizations that provide opportunities for intercultural cooperation and integrating primary sources into their instruction so that students developed the habit of listening to people in other countries instead of only seeing global issues through American eyes.

There have also been some studies of how experienced global educators use the world wide web. In several web-based courses, Merry Merryfield (2000) found that inservice teachers reported that the online discussions fostered more cross-cultural interactions and allowed them to ask hard questions and tackle controversial issues. For example, in one course two U.S. teachers questioned two Africans about their experiences with racism in the United States which led to an African American and a Nigerian debating the privilege foreigners have (or don't have) in the United States. In another class, a teacher from Appalachia challenged what he perceived as "hillbilly" stereotypes in a message posted by a teacher in New York. In both these instances other teachers joined in to address critical issues related to prejudice and privilege, locally and globally. Such prickly issues are raised in almost every online discussion, yet rarely emerge when the same course is taught face-to-face. That said, some perceived online interaction as artificial or difficult to believe. When asked about their use of the term "artificial," the teachers explained that it is easy for people to write anything on a computer to people they will never see, thus it is much harder to believe people are being completely genuine online than it is when you "look in their eyes."

In a later study, Merryfield (2006) found that practicing teachers expanded their teaching about the world by using websites with content from other world regions that promoted diverse perspectives on global issues, international events and news.

Based on these studies, it seems safe to say that interests continue to remain pragmatic with a focus on how to implement globally-oriented curricula in P–12 classrooms and how to open teacher and student minds to the ideas, issues and experiences of people across the planet.

Overall, there is little depth to research in global education, and studies, in general, lack long term or longitudinal data. The field needs to marshal its resources to focus on several significant research questions: What do students know about the world and its peoples? How do they develop intercultural competence? What are best practices that bring about teachers' and students' development of global perspectives and world mindedness? and, How can we assess such goals in a systemic way over time?

IMPLEMENTATION

As noted under the History and Research sections above, the implementation of units of study and curricular programs has been a priority for global educators. In the early years, curriculum and resource development dominated the field with private organizations and university centers producing instructional materials and providing inservice education to practicing teachers. Many leaders in global education—such as Jan Tucker in Florida, Jim Becker in Indiana, Dennis Lubeck in Missouri, Andy Smith in New York, Gary Howard in Washington State, and Ron Herring in California—focused on the politics of education through national professional organizations and the actions of state legislatures, state departments of education and school districts. Organizations ranging from the Association of Supervision and Curriculum Development and the National Council for the Social Studies to the World History Association wielded broad influence through their publications and conferences.

The influence of globalization on people's lives and jobs has also been a significant factor in popular support for implementation. By New Year's Eve of 2000, the twenty-first century hype was well on its way to convincing many Americans (and many American politicians) that young people needed to understand the world in order to be prepared for their future. Over the last ten years, the world has come into people's lives in profound ways from the 9/11 attacks to global environmental changes to contamination in imported toys and pet food.

Today though implementation has grown more sophisticated as there is more depth and complexity and more attention to voices from people who have been ignored or marginalized in the past. There are three areas in which trends can be seen:

1. In teaching global connections attention is generally directed towards: cultural diffusion (the process by which cultures expand and change over time and place); hybridity (the mixing of ideas, language, or ways of living that result when two or more cultures encounter each other peaceably or through conflict); historical antecedents(using historical frameworks to inform contemporary realities); economic dependence (the ways in which people across the planet depend to some degree on the economic decisions and actions of people, organization and governments in other parts of the world); and, ecological dependence (the ways in which peo-

ple's decisions and lives affect and are affected by changes in the natural or physical world—water, land, air, natural resources, and the biodiversity of plants and animals).

2. In teaching how culture affects perception and interaction, the following issues are frequently addressed: surface vs. internal culture (attributes of surface culture include clothes, music, and celebration of holidays, whereas internal culture provides a framework of beliefs and values that shape norms of behavior and styles of communication and interaction); and, cultural assumptions(people interpret new information or experiences through their cultural lenses that provide a structure for making sense of and judging events, issues, and people).

3. In examining relationships across nations and within societies, attention is also generally paid to trying to understand relationships between mainstream knowledge and power (mainstream academic knowledge is what is taught in schools and universities—think of what is included in textbooks or high stakes tests—and presented by dominant media outsets as true): Imperial world views(patterns of thinking that develop as empires expand); Mainstream academic knowledge (knowledge taught in most public institutions that is sanctioned by the government and groups in power); and contrapuntal voices (literature, speeches, films, websites, etc., by people who have been oppressed or marginalized within a society or globally).

Today, though, implementation has grown more sophisticated as there is more depth and complexity and more attention to voices from people who have been ignored or marginalized in the past. There are three areas in which trends can be seen:

1. In teaching global connections attention is generally directed towards:
    - cultural diffusion (the process by which cultures expand and change over time and place);
    - hybridity (the mixing of ideas, language, or ways of living that result when two or more cultures encounter each other peaceably or through conflict);
    - historical antecedents (using historical frameworks to inform contemporary realities);
    - economic dependence (the ways in which people across the planet depend to some degree on the economic decisions and actions of people, organizations, and governments in other parts of the world); and,

- ecological dependence (the ways in which people's decisions and lives affect and are affected by changes in the natural or physical world—water, land, air, natural resources, and the biodiversity of plants and animals).

2. In teaching how culture affects perception and interaction, the following issues are frequently addressed:
   - surface vs. internal culture (attributes of surface culture include clothes, music, and celebration of holidays, whereas internal culture provides a framework of beliefs and values that shape norms of behavior and styles of communication and interaction); and,
   - cultural assumptions (people interpret new information or experiences through their cultural lenses that provide a structure for making sense of and judging events, issues, and people).

3. In examining relationships across nations and within societies, attentions also generally paid to trying to understand relationships between mainstream knowledge and power (mainstream academic knowledge is what is taught in schools and universities—think of what is included in textbooks or high-stakes tests—and presented by dominant media outsets as true):
   - imperial world views (patterns of thinking that develop as empires expand);
   - mainstream academic knowledge (knowledge taught in most public institutions that is sanctioned by the government and groups in power); and
   - contrapuntal voices (literature, speeches, films, websites, etc., by people who have been oppressed or marginalized within a society or globally).

Today, there are also a series of generalizations that often are taught as enduring understandings in global education. These include:

- Ideas, beliefs, and values from many cultures across hundreds of years have shaped and will continue to shape our identities, our communities, and our nation;
- Our lives are connected to global systems—economic, political, social, technological, and ecological—that provide us with opportunities and place upon us constraints;
- Although we may more readily notice cultural and political differences across nation-states or world regions, there are significant commonalities shared across the human experience;

- As contributors to popular culture and consumers with considerable purchasing power, young Americans are influencing jobs, lifestyles, and environmental changes happening right now across the planet;
- Societies see their world through cultural lenses that shape how they think and take action;
- Confusion, misunderstandings, and conflict can result when people do not know or appreciate other people's beliefs, values, and norms of behavior;
- People with political, economic and social power shape a nation's mainstream academic knowledge; and
- Created within cultural and political contexts, knowledge reflects assumptions, values, and perspectives of its time and place.

These concepts and enduring understandings can be integrated into the social studies through the inclusion of multiple perspectives *and* primary sources developed by people in other countries. Above all, the recognition of the inheritance of imperial worldviews and the relationships between power and knowledge relies upon skills in critical thinking. Students need to be able to identify unstated assumptions, detect bias, and anticipate relationships between power and knowledge.

How can these ideas be integrated into social studies lessons? Below are a few examples from social studies classrooms. See the section entitled "Resources" below for more lesson ideas and materials.

Teaching Idea: Global Perspectives on Leadership

In an activity called "Campaign Manager," students researched post-World War II leadership in China, Russia, Great Britain, South Africa, the U.S. and India. Each country group was given a list of three to four political leaders along with websites and other materials to examine for background information. The groups then developed a campaign and a poster based on each leader's strengths. For example, the China group was given Mao Zedong, Zhou Enlai and Deng Xiaoping with these sites to research:

http://afe.easia.columbia.edu/china/gov/mao_zedo.htm
http://www.asiasource.org/
http://www.britannica.com/
http://www.bergen.org/AAST/Projects/ChinaHistory/HISTORY.HTM

In follow-up discussions, students mapped out how the type of government and time period influenced the qualities of leadership and then identified qualities most often found in leaders. As they examined how these leaders affected and were influenced by each other, the students found that many leaders in quite different countries had much in common, and leadership styles were often influenced by what was happening in other countries.

Teaching Idea: Direct and Indirect Patterns of Communication

Culture influences the ways in which we communicate. In this lesson students discussed cultural norms of behavior and then analyzed the dialogue below. They identified the cultural misunderstanding and then hypothesized what element(s) of internal culture needed to be understood in order to communicate well across these cultures.

Dialogue # 1: Don't Bother

Tyrone:	How is the project going with Keiko?
James:	Fine, it is going well.
Tyrone:	Did you ask her about the research?
James:	Yes, I told her that we are sorry the visuals are not ready.
Tyrone:	And what did she say?
James:	She said, "I see," and changed the subject.
Tyrone:	I guess she will deal with it.

The students' explanation: The misunderstanding is that Tyrone and James are interpreting Keiko's remarks based on their own direct communication norms. They say what they are thinking and assume Keiko is also communicating directly. Keiko, coming from a culture that values understatement and indirect styles, has played down her disappointment that they have not completed their work. She changed the subject abruptly, indicating that she finds the conversation embarrassing and uncomfortable. The boys assume Keiko will finish the work while she assumes from the statement "we are sorry" that they feel badly about falling behind and will hurry to get it done.

Teaching Idea: Terrorists or Freedom Fighters?

In order to teach complex views of European colonialism and African nationalism, a teacher had his students study both European and African constructions of independence movements in Kenya and South Africa. For example, they read Kenyatta's 1952 speech, The Kenyan African Union is not the Mau Mau (which can be accessed at: http://www.fordham.edu/halsall/mod/1952kenyatta-kau1.html) for its ideas on nationalism and self-determination and compared it with British ideas on colonial rule and "Mau Mau" insurgents. The students also examined ideas of the African National Congress in South Africa (see: http://www.anc.org.za/ancdocs/history/) with those of the apartheid regime. To increase the complexity of their understanding, the teacher also included relevant speeches and documents from Algeria and the Belgian Congo so that his students recognized that there were different outcomes of colonial rule and diverse approaches to African nationalism.

Teaching Idea: Buildings Across Time and Cultures

The study of architecture and other structures can demonstrate both connections across world regions and connections across time. In this activity, a teacher chose three global themes for students to examine across several time periods: (1) the nature of buildings that signify wealth and power (it was the website of castles in Japan that inspired this choice http://www.japan-guide.com/e/e2296.html); (2) walls (from ancient walled cities to China's Great Wall to the Berlin Wall and walls being constructed in contemporary Israel); and (3) religious buildings (Buddhist, Jewish, and Hindu temples, mosques, churches, and cathedrals). As students compiled images, the class covered a classroom wall with pictures that documented cultural universals—similarities in buildings across diverse cultures over hundreds of years. The project greatly affected student thinking in that what they originally perceived as differences changed to an appreciation of how people across cultures have shared many assumptions about buildings and walls and how ideas about building have been shaped and reshaped by cross-cultural interaction and conflict.

Teaching Idea: Timelines

Historical timelines are often used to trace events over a country or a region's history. In this lesson, students came to appreciate cultural influences on historical thinking by comparing timelines developed in different world regions. When students examined and compared (see: http://www-chaos.umd.edu/history/time_line.html), a timeline of Chinese history (see: http://www.humanities-interactive.org/splendors/timeline.htm), with a Pre-Columbian timeline, they found that different criteria were used to design the different historical timelines. This finding led to further research on how cultural values can be identified by examining past and present timelines developed in a variety of countries. This activity ended with a discussion of why timelines delineating U.S. history rarely include art, music or literature when they appear frequently in timelines developed in other parts of the world.

CONCLUSION

Global education has always been an ambiguous, contested, and complex field of study. While some associate it with the teaching of global languages, global issues, world environmental systems or world history, others perceive it as peace education or human rights education. Global education has often been defined by its content rather than its goals (Kniep, 1986). That said, experts in the field see global issues, global interconnectedness, global systems, global literature, and global history as the main thrust of global education. Skills include cross-cultural communication, taking part in conflict resolution, intercultural interaction, critical thinking, and perspective consciousness. Dispositions usually aim for open-mindedness, empathy, tolerance for ambiguity, anticipation of complexity, and rejection of stereotypes.

Social studies teachers are developing many strategies to prepare American students for the culturally diverse and interconnected world in which they live. Using 21st century technologies, students are developing the skills needed to access, evaluate and use global information from multiple points of view to inform their decisions and actions. Recognizing the implications of increasing cross-cultural interactions, teachers are teaching world cultures through content and skills that prepare young people to understand, communicate and interact with people different from themselves.

Through the study of local/global connections, the scholarship of people in other countries, attention to current issues facing the planet, students are learning to see themselves and their communities within a global context. It is hoped that in the process, they are becoming more world minded with an appreciation of the complexity, interconnectedness, and syncrety of the global human experience.

REFERENCES

Adams, J. M., & Carfagna, A. (2006). *Coming of age in a globalized world.* Bloomfield, CT: Kumarian Press.

Alger, C. F. (1974). *Your community in the world; The world in your community.* Columbus: Mershon Center at The Ohio State University.

Alger, C. F., & Harf, J. E. (1986). Global education: Why? For whom? About what? In R. E. Freeman (Ed.), *Promising practices in global education: A handbook with case studies* (pp. 1–13). New York: The National Council on Foreign Language and International Studies.

Anderson, C. (1990). Global education and the community. In K. A. Tye (Ed.), *Global education from thought to action* (pp. 125–141). Alexandria, VA: Association for Supervision and Curriculum Development.

Anderson, L. (1979). *Schooling for citizenship in a global age: An exploration of the meaning and significance of global education.* Bloomington, IN: Social Studies Development Center.

Apple, M. W., & Buras, K. L. (2006). *The subaltern speaks.* New York: Routledge.

Banks, J. A., Banks, C. A. M., Cortes, C., Hahn; C. L., Merryfield, M. M.,Moodley, K. A., Murphy-Shigematsu, S., Audrey Osler, A., Caryn Park, C., & Parker, W. A. (2005). *Democracy and diversity: Principles and concepts for educating students in a global age.* Seattle, WA: Center for Multicultural Education.

Becker, J. M. (Ed.) (1979). *Schooling for a global age.* New York: McGraw-Hill.

Benitez, H. (2001). The effects of a globalized U.S. history curriculum. *Theory and Research in Social Education, 29*(2), 290–307.

Bigelow, B., & Peterson, B. (Eds.). (2002). *Rethinking globalization.* Milwaukee, WI: Rethinking Schools.

Case, R. (1993). Key elements of a global perspective. *Social Education, 57,* 318–325.

Council on Learning. (1981). *Task force statement on education and the world view*. New Rochelle, NY: Author.

Darling, L (1994). *Global education as moral education*. Unpublished doctoral thesis. University of British Columbia.

Darling, L. (1995). Empathy and the possibilities for a global perspective: A cautionary tale. In R. Fowler & I. Wright (Eds.), *Thinking globally about social studies education* (pp. 35–50). Vancouver: Vancouver Centre for the Study of Curriculum and Instruction, University of British Columbia.

Diaz, C., Massialas, B. G., & Xanthopoulos, J. A. (1999*). Global perspectives for educators*. Boston, MA: Allyn & Bacon.

Dove, T, Norris, J., & Shinew, D. (1997). Teachers' perspectives on school/university collaboration in global education. In M. M. Merryfield, E. Jarchow, & S. Pickert (Eds.), *Preparing teachers to teach global perspectives: A handbook for teacher educators*. (pp. 55–71)Thousand Oaks, CA: Corwin Press.

Gaudelli, W. (2003). *World class: Teaching and learning in global times*. Mahwah, N.J.: Lawrence Erlbaum Associates.

Gilliom, M. E., Remy, R. C., & Woyach, R. (1980). Using the local community as a resource for global education. *Teaching Political Science, 7* , 251–264.

Goodlad, J. I. (1986). The learner at the world's center. *Social Education, 50,* 424–436.

Hanvey, R. G. (1976). *An attainable global perspective*. Denver, CO: The Center for Teaching International Relations, The University of Denver.

Johnson, D. (1993). Academic and intellectual foundations of teacher education in global perspectives. *" Theory into Practice, 32*(Winter), 3–13.

Kirkwood, T. F. (2002). Teaching about Japan; Global perspectives in teacher decision-making, context and practice. *Theory and Research in Social Education, 30*(1), 88–115.

Kniep, W.M. (1986a, October). Defining a global education by its content. *Social Education, 50,* 437–466.

Kniep, W. (1986b). Social studies within a global education. *Social Education, 50*(November/December), 536–542.

Lamy, S. (1987). *The definition of a discipline: The objects and methods of analysis in global education*. New York: Global Perspectives in Education.

Lamy, S. L. (1990). Global education: A conflict of images. In K. A. Tye (Ed.), *Global education from thought to action* (pp. 49–63). Alexandria, VA: Association for Supervision and Curriculum Development.

Merryfield, M. M. (1991). Preparing American social studies teachers to teach with a global perspective: A status report. *The Journal of Teacher Education, 42*(1), 11–20.

Merryfield, M. M. (1992). Preparing social studies teachers for the twenty-first century: Perspectives on program effectiveness from a study of six exemplary programs in the United States. *Theory and Research in Social Education, 20*(1), 17–46.

Merryfield, M. M. (1993). Responding to the Gulf War: A case study of teacher decision-making during the 1990–1991 school year. *Social Education, 57*(1), 33–41.

Merryfield, M. M. (1994). Shaping the curriculum in global education: The influence of student characteristics on teacher decision-making. *Journal of Curriculum and Instruction, 9,* 233–249.

Merryfield, M. M. (1995). Institutionalizing cross-cultural experiences and international expertise in teacher education: The development and potential of a global education PDS network. *Journal of Teacher Education, 46*(1), 1–9.

Merryfield, M. M., Jarchow, E., & Pickert, S. (Eds.). (1997). *Preparing teachers to teach global perspectives: A handbook for teacher educators.* Thousand Oaks, CA: Corwin Press.

Merryfield, M. M., & Remy, R. C. (Eds.) (1995). *Teaching about international conflict and peace.* Albany: SUNY Press.

Merryfield, M. M., & Wilson, A. (2005). *Social studies and the world.* Silver Spring, MD: The National Council for the Social Studies.

Mitsakos, C. L. (1978). A global education program can make a difference. *Theory and Research in Social Education, 6*(1), 1–15.

Muessig, R. H., & Gilliom, M. E. (Eds.) (1981). *Perspectives of global education: A sourcebook for classroom teachers.* Columbus: The College of Education, The Ohio State University.

National Council for the Social Studies. (1982). *Position statement on global education.* Washington D.C.: Author.

National Council for the Social Studies (2005). *Position statement on global education.* Silver Spring, MD: Author.

National Governors' Association. (1989). *America in transition: The international frontier.* Washington, DC: Author.

Noddings, N. (Ed.). (2005). *Educating citizens for global awareness.* New York: Teachers College Press.

Pang, V. O. (2005). *Multicultural education: A caring reflective approach* (2nd ed.). Boston, MA: McGraw-Hill.

Pike, G. (2000). Global education and national identity. *Theory Into Practice, 39*(2), 64–73.

Pike, G., & Selby, D. (1988). *Global teacher, global learner.* London: Hodder & Stoughton.

Pike, G., & Selby, D. (1995). *Reconnecting from national to global curriculum.* Toronto: International Institute for Global Education, University of Toronto.

Sassen, S. (1996). *Losing control? Sovereignty in an age of globalization.* New York: Columbia University Press.

Storti, C. (1999). *Figuring foreigners out.* Yarmouth, ME; Intercultural Press.

Tan, K. C. (2004). *Justice without borders.* New York: Cambridge University Press.

Tucker, J., & Cistone, P. (1991). Global perspectives for teachers. *Journal of Teacher Education, 42*(1), 3–10.

Tye, B., & Tye, K. (1992). *Global education: A study of school change.* Albany: SUNY Press.

Werner, W. (1990). Contradictions in global education. In D. Henley & J. Young (Eds.), *Canadian perspectives on critical pedagogy. Occasional monograph #1* (pp. 77–93). Winnipeg: The Critical Pedagogy Network and Social Education Researchers in Canada.

Willinsky, J. (1998). *Learning to divide the world.* Minneapolis: University of Minnesota Press.

Wilson, A. (1982). Cross-cultural experiential learning for teachers. *Theory into practice, 21*(1), 184–192.

Wilson, A. (1983). A case study of two teachers with cross-cultural experience: They know more." *Educational Research Quarterly, 8*(1), 78–85.

Wilson, A. H. (1993a). Conversation partners: Helping students gain a global perspective through cross-cultural experiences. *Theory into Practice, 32* (1), 21–26.

Wilson, A. H. (1993b). *The meaning of international experience for schools.* Westport, CT: Praeger.

Wooster, J. (1993). Authentic assessment: A strategy for preparing teachers to respond to curricular mandates in global education. *Theory into Practice, 32*(1, Winter), 47–51.

Zong, G. (2002). Can computer mediated communication help to prepare global teachers? An analysis of preservice social studies teachers' experiences. *Theory and Research in Social Education, 30*(4), 589–616.

CHAPTER 11

MULTICULTURAL EDUCATION REFORM MOVEMENT

Allan R. Brandhorst

INTRODUCTION

Multicultural education is a curriculum reform movement expressive of the mainstream of the American sociopolitical tradition. As a reform movement multicultural education has attempted to redress issues of power relationships as expressed in the ideology of the long-established general education program inherent in most U.S. schools, but particularly as nested in the language arts and social studies curriculum. Due in part to its narrative nature, the multicultural education reform movement has had little interest in or impact on curriculum theory in science and mathematics. The multicultural education reform movement is primarily interested in challenging the cultural narrative of American Civilization as transmitted through the general education curriculum. It developed out of recognition of a need for the American public school curriculum to include the voices of African-Americans, Native Americans, and Hispanic Americans in the American literary and historical tradition. Along the way the movement has added the voices of other marginalized groups. Thus, multicultural educa-

Teaching and Studying Social Issues: Major Programs and Approaches, pages 217–231
Copyright © 2011 by Information Age Publishing
All rights of reproduction in any form reserved.

tion has been expanded to include concerns for gender, sexual orientation, social class, and disability.

Given its narrative orientation, a paradigmatic definition of multicultural education is extremely difficult. A scholarly attempt at definition is as challenging as herding cats, because the movement is defined not in terms of a common agenda as much as it is defined in terms of opposition to the status quo. This definition by negation ultimately leads to fault lines in the movement, which will become progressively more problematic as the human race moves in the direction of a global village.

Given the disjunctive nature of multicultural education as a concept, an appropriate approach to an elaboration of the movement is to explore each strand of the movement in isolation, thereby creating a foundational clarity which can become a basis for identifying the common elements which draw its proponents to a common umbrella. Those common elements share an origin in the distinctively American traditions of individualism, progress, human rights, and American exceptionalism. The latter element may prove to be the ideological belief that splinters the coalition that currently constitutes the multicultural education movement.

CATEGORIZATIONS AND TYPOLOGIES

One of the more enduring categorizations of the multicultural tradition over the past two decades was created by Sleeter and Grant (1988). Currently in its fifth edition, *Making Choices for Multicultural Education* draws on five approaches to multicultural education identified by Gibson (1976):

1. education of the culturally different;
2. education about cultural differences;
3. education for cultural pluralism;
4. bicultural education; and
5. multicultural education.

Sleeter and Grant, however, move beyond the approach of Gibson to create their own typology:

1. teaching the exceptional and culturally different;
2. human relations approach;
3. single-group studies approach;
4. multicultural education approach; and
5. multicultural social justice approach.

The attraction of the Sleeter and Grant approach is that it attempts to capture the evolving nature of the multicultural education reform movement, as it has refocused from issues of cultural exclusion to issues of power. This historical view of the multicultural education reform movement gives directionality to the drift of reform, and accordingly provides a vantage point from which to anticipate difficulties for the movement in the future. This chapter will use the Sleeter and Grant categorization as a template for surveying the movement, and as a vantage point for looking ahead.

A second organizing principle for this chapter is the dimensional typology provided by James Banks (1995). Banks identifies five dimensions of educational outcomes of particular relevance to multicultural education. These are:

1. content integration;
2. knowledge construction;
3. prejudice reduction;
4. equity pedagogy; and
5. empowering school culture.

Drawing on these educational outcomes as they are expressed in each of the approaches of the Sleeter and Grant typology, processes of comparison across approaches will be facilitated.

TEACHING THE EXCEPTIONAL AND CULTURALLY DIFFERENT

This strand (teaching the exceptional and culturally different) most closely approximates the initial thrust of the multicultural education movement as it emerged from the civil rights movement of the 1960s. At its emergence, the multicultural education movement in the 1960s had primarily a multiethnic focus (Banks, 1973). In *Teaching Ethnic Studies: Concepts and Strategies* (43rd Yearbook of the National Council for the Social Studies), Banks (1973) laid out a series of curriculum proposals for incorporating ethnic studies into the social studies curriculum. Initially there was an emphasis on inclusion of African-American, Native American, and Hispanic American experience into the K–12 social studies curriculum for all American children. This was a departure from earlier demands for special Black Studies coursework for African-American students, demands which were met with the provision of special courses in Black history and literature and Chicano history and literature. Banks (1981) refers to this as Phase I: Monoethnic Courses. Banks refers to subsequent phases (Phase II: Multi-ethnic Studies Courses; Phase III: Multiethnic Education; Phase IV: Multicultural Education) as a progressive transformation from comparative scholarly perspectives, through education for enabling minority student success, to pluralistic education which encompassed, in addition to educational challenges of ethnic minorities, the challenges faced by women, the handicapped, religious groups, and regional groups.

All five of Banks dimensions of educational outcomes are progressively incorporated into these phases. Phases I and II clearly addressed the outcome of multi-ethnic content integration, initially for members of individual ethnic groups (Phase I), but later for knowledge construction for all students—ethnic minority and majority culture students (Phase II). Phase III clearly addressed the need for prejudice reduction and equity pedagogy. Phase IV addressed the development of empowering school culture for all at-risk student populations. Phase IV, as identified by Banks, most closely approximates the understanding of the scope of multicultural education provided by Sleeter and Grant.

HUMAN RELATIONS APPROACH

The Human Relations Approach to multicultural education is focused primarily on prejudice reduction and the development of interpersonal interaction between members of disadvantaged groups. It shares many intellectual roots with the conflict resolution literature. The target group for this curricular reform is the total school population. The goals of the human relations approach are to be reached through cooperative learning activities and real or vicarious experiences with other groups (Sleeter & Grant, 1999).

The main thrust of the human relations movement grows out of the tendency to disregard the salience of social or cultural group ideologies. The presumption is that training in and experience with inter-group relations is all that is needed to combat prejudice. This is very nearly a fatal flaw of the approach, as the broader literature from cross-cultural and ethnic studies documents. Coles (1986) documents that children in Northern Ireland are capable of suspending their antipathy during outings with children of the out-group, but may revert to that antipathy and truculence "when everyone is going home" (p. 82). Ross (2004), in discussing difficulties in bridging the antipathies between Israelis and Palestinians, references naïve realism as causal. Naïve realism is the human tendency to presume that one's perceptions are true reflections of reality. Ross is less than optimistic about the human ability to overcome naïve realism. Ultimately, human relations as an approach to multicultural education must address the problem of trust (Brandhorst, 2004). Trust, the foundation for a sense of security, originates in the earliest months of life (Greenspan, 1997). It is difficult to understand how failure to develop a sense of trust in the earliest years of life can somehow be compensated for in the institutional structure of schools.

How does the human relations approach fit Banks' dimensional typology of educational outcomes? Content integration is, at best, a marginal emphasis in the human relations approach, and this is because the focus is on process rather than content. Knowledge construction fares somewhat better under this approach because real or vicarious experiences with other groups could conceivably lead to the construction of knowledge of the other without the burden of bias, depending (of course) upon other variables. This, in turn, should sensitize students to the existence of cultural assumptions within disciplines which have shaped knowledge construction within the discipline.

Prejudice reduction is the strong suit in this approach, but, as suggested above, naïve realism may undermine this outcome. Each child or adolescent in a classroom brings a somewhat different cultural background to social interactions. When the social interactions are across cultural or ideological differences, messages intended may not be messages received.

Equity pedagogy, the emphasis on developing concepts and strategies that would help low income children achieve academically, does not seem to be a major goal of the human relations approach. It may be served by the human relations approach if cognitive style differences are central to failures of children to succeed in traditional classrooms. The human relations approach emphasis on cooperative learning draws on this theory, which assumes that learners with particular cognitive styles learn better under the cooperative learning model; and that learners from lower socioeconomic classes and some ethnic heritages disproportionately possess those cognitive styles. The caveat is that the concepts of cognitive style have not been definitively linked to particular ethnic groups. Some scholars even question the validity of many cognitive style differences (Sternberg, 1997). For an extended discussion of this issue see Irvine and York (1995).

The concept of an empowering school culture has a varied fit with the human relations model. Empowering school culture emphasizes basic skills, standardized evaluation, and teacher accountability. On the one hand, cooperative learning strategies may lead to a sense of empowerment. On the other hand, cooperative learning strategies may not provide the clarity essential to the standardized testing element associated with an empowering school culture. Moreover, learning from peers may potentially lead to reversal of progress through the zone of proximal development (Tudge, 1990), which would undermine the effectiveness of standardized testing rubrics, a central element of empowering school culture. A final concern here is the paucity of research on empowering school culture as it applies to secondary schools. The human relations model might seem to be a better fit with secondary school students than elementary school students. Yet this is precisely the level of schooling on which very little of the effective schools research has been centered.

On balance, the human relations approach does not appear to be particularly well focused on the goals of multicultural education as outlined by Banks.

THE SINGLE-GROUP STUDIES APPROACH

The single-group studies approach to curriculum reform can take as its target audience either the total school population or a single group. Single group studies begin from the premise that education is not ideologically neutral. Rather, the premise perceives educational institutions in the United States as existing to reduce cultural differences and "convert" children of immigrants to American values, the American Way of Life. Advocates of the single-group approach oppose this traditional and historical purpose of schooling. They see such approaches as necessarily discounting the values of groups who differ, in one or more significant ways, from the dominant culture. As such, the traditional approach of schools purportedly alienate those who are not white, male, and middle class.

Given the large number of disparate groups included under the umbrella of multiculturalism it is not possible to survey the range of single group studies. That is done very well elsewhere (Banks & Banks, 1995). An exploration of a particular single-group studies curriculum, however, will serve as a useful illustration of this approach.

Afrocentric, or African American immersion, schools represent a serious attempt to implement the Single Group Studies approach because of the failure of schools to successfully educate African American children (Sleeter & Grant, 1999). The philosophy of Afrocentrism has been fleshed out under the leadership of Molefi Kete Asante. Central to that philosophy is the position that American Civilization has systematically decentered African Americans from their historical heritage (Asante, 1987, 1988, 1989).

Asante's position is that African Americans need an education that reestablishes their connection to their historical and cultural roots. The experience of slavery and the deliberate efforts to separate slaves from their native languages has decentered them from their cultural roots. Only an Afrocentric education can reconnect them to their roots and prepare them for re-entry into American life as an equal partner to Euro-Americans.

Central to an Afrocentric education is the existence of an African Cultural System of which Classical Egyptian Civilization was a progenitor. It is further suggested that because classical Egyptian Civilization gave birth to Greek Civilization, the Western tradition is of African origin by way of Egypt (see Bernal, 1987). The concept of Afrocentrism, however, is not directly rooted in African culture, because the African American experience of slavery is uniquely different than the African experience. Thus Afrocentrism merges studies of African culture with the African American experience.

Afrocentric schools were established in Philadelphia, Detroit, Milwaukee, and elsewhere, and are often distinguished by separation of the sexes. Afrocentric academies often enroll only male students with instruction provided by male teachers. Early on, Afrocentric schools were successful in creating a climate of scholarly rigor. The rise in popularity of Afrocentric schools over the past two decades suggests that this success continues. Why do they succeed? Because many of the factors associated with Black student failure (Irvine, 1990) are addressed in the design of Afrocentric schools.

How does the Single-Group Studies approach fit with Banks' five dimensions of educational outcomes? Single-group studies certainly focus on knowledge construction, and, in some cases, content integration. Knowledge construction in this approach occurs because students are exposed to alternative ways of constructing knowledge, ways that lie outside the mainstream culture.

They may or may not directly address prejudice reduction, depending upon whether single group studies promote ethnic nuclei or ethnic boundaries (Higham, 1974). If single group studies support ethnic nuclei but not ethnic boundaries then the result may well be prejudice reduction.

Single group studies have the potential for a match with equity pedagogy, because they are particularly focused on differences in the affective and emotional foundations for learning. Greenspan (1997) makes a convincing case for the centrality of affective and emotional development as the basis for academic success. To the extent that single group studies provide students with affective and emotional resources for learning, they fit well with Banks' concern for equity pedagogy.

Empowering school culture is increasingly identified with the effective schools movement. As such, it can fit particularly well with single group studies approaches, given the priorities of the effective schools movement. Because of the emphasis in effective schools on basic skills (math, reading, and language), effective schools advocates suggest stealing time from other subjects such as social studies (Levine & Lezotte, 1995). If there is a poor fit between the standardized testing associated with the effective schools movement and the ethnic or class based content of the single group studies, this approach does not meet the Banks' criteria for empowering school culture. If, on the other hand, empowering school culture is seen from an ethnic perspective, perhaps single group studies provide the most empowering school culture. Some of the evidence from the Afrocentric schools movement may bear this out (see, for example, Anselmi & Peters, 1995).

MULTICULTURAL EDUCATION APPROACH

Multicultural education is a term that "educators use increasingly to describe education policies and practices that recognize, accept, and affirm human differences and similarities related to gender, race, disability, class, and (increasingly) sexual orientation" (Sleeter & Grant, 1999). The term, in fact, has mutated as a consequence of usage. It is an umbrella term that has steadily been stretched to accommodate a larger and larger array of political agendas.

There are risks in this practice. As Sleeter and Grant (1999) note, in the multicultural education approach there is a mixing of theory and ideology, and accordingly these concepts need to be carefully defined. Ideology, after Newman (1973), prescribes what ought to be. Theory, on the other hand, describes how social systems or human psychology actually work. There is clearly an imperative to use knowledge of how social systems and human psychology actually work in order to improve the prospects for student learning. To the extent that the multicultural education approach is directed toward this end, there should be no basis for challenging the approach. Multicultural education approaches, however, have focused on advocacy of some policies for which there is no national consensus. For example, the Multicultural Education approach promotes inclusion of gay and lesbian issues in the curriculum. Attempts to do so have been met with resistance from communities and from teachers' groups.

Another issue is the definition of equal opportunity as a legal right. As Sleeter and Grant (1999) observe, "advocates of the Multicultural Education approach do not see it as sufficient to remove legal barriers to access and participation in schooling. So long as groups do not gain equal outcomes from social institutions, those institutions are not providing equal opportunity" (pp. 155–156).

Concerning race and ethnicity, Sleeter and Grant (1999) note that advocates of Multicultural Education "have written much more about ideology than about theory" (p. 158). On the other hand, in regard to gender, Multicultural Education, advocates "have written more about theory of how sex roles are learned than about ideology" (Sleeter & Grant, 1999, p. 158). In the case of gender, theory becomes a foundational support for an ideological stance. There are problems with the move into the realm of ideology.

Certainly there are elements of ideology in the three previous approaches enumerated by Sleeter and Grant. The goals identified by the other approaches, however, are centered on improving the chances of education achievement success for students. The balance is in the direction of using knowledge of how social systems and human psychology actually work. With the multicultural education approach, the thrust shades toward using the schools as a tool for changing societal values. The presumption here is that the schools should determine societal goals and promote those goals through the activities of the school.

This is not the first time in American education that ideologists have captured the public education sector. For generations, American history textbooks have been ideological tools for presenting a historically inaccurate picture of the American past, with the goal of promoting American nationalism, exceptionalism, and, through manifest destiny, imperialism. The publication of *Lies My Teacher Told Me* (Loewen, 1995) is only the most recent challenge to the ideological status quo in the American History textbook industry. The continuing success of that volume (global sales from Amazon.com, reported in *The Economist,* February 10, 2007, p. 89.) attests to the general public's concern about ideologically influenced educational practices. While it may be true that the proponents of the multicultural education approach are motivated by a desire to resist blatantly biased curriculum, substituting an alternative ideology for the existing ideology does not address the core purposes of American education. The effective schools movement may well be a backlash against the efforts of the advocates of the multicultural education approach. With its emphasis on basic skills and accountability through testing, the effective schools movement is attempting to refocus the schools on what many see as their primary function, preparing children and adolescents for their roles as productive citizens and responsible decision-makers in the American future.

How does the Multicultural Education approach fit Banks' dimensional typology of educational outcomes? Content integration is an important element of this approach. Examples would include the promotion of bilingualism (a common practice elsewhere in the world), use of content drawn from multiple perspectives and multiple groups, and relating curriculum to the experiential backgrounds of students. Knowledge construction would also be addressed through emphasis on critical thinking and analysis of alternative viewpoints. Prejudice reduction, however, may be more a hoped-for outcome than a realistic goal. Advocacy of policies for which there is no national consensus means that the larger society does not reinforce those policies, thus undermining their effectiveness.

Equity pedagogy is a major focus of this approach. Using teaching strategies matched to the learning styles of students from different groups is consistent with this approach. An empowering school culture, as envisioned by the effective schools movement, emphasizes a stripped down curriculum focused on basic skills, standardized testing and teacher accountability. This may be consistent with the Multicultural Education approach in terms of intended outcomes, but at odds with it in terms of practice. In a test-driven school environment, it is difficult to see how teachers would have the time and resources to attend to all the ideological concerns of this approach, given that effective schools' ideology advocates stealing time from other curricular elements to improve basic skills instruction.

MULTICULTURAL SOCIAL JUSTICE APPROACH

The Multicultural Social Justice Approach has its roots in the social reconstructionism movement (Brameld, 1956, 1957), and is visionary and utopian. This approach is basically a critique of modern culture; and in the context of the goals of schooling, it advocates for the preparation of citizens to work actively toward social structural equality (Sleeter & Grant, 1999). Curriculum would be designed to achieve these ends through the organization of content around current social issues. Instruction would involve students in active democratic decision-making.

Much of this approach is similar to an approach proposed by Hunt and Metcalf (1968) for the teaching of social studies. As a subset of the general curriculum particularly well suited to teaching social studies, there is an established historical record for this practice. As part of the educational reform movement of the 1960s, several innovative approaches to social studies were developed. The Public Issues Series, known popularly as the Harvard Project Series, was developed by Donald Oliver and some of his graduate students at the Harvard Graduate School of Education. Issues were identified on the basis of current concerns in society, and each issue was explored in terms of its historical roots and key questions raised by the issue. The instructional approach relied heavily on classroom discussion of the issue at hand. Controversy was welcomed and critical thinking on the part of students was encouraged.

The Sleeter and Grant (1999) multicultural social justice approach has a somewhat different foundation, growing out of conflict theory, cognitive development theory, and a sociological theory of culture. Each of these theoretical strands, however, finds a nuanced expression for the advocates of the multicultural social justice approach.

Conflict theory for advocates of this approach emerges from a sociological perspective which emphasizes the role of groups in creating the basis for conflict. Conflict arises out of the competition of these groups for scarce resources. The central presumption of this understanding of conflict theory is that groups, whether they are class, gender, ethnic, or racial in origin, are the basis for the distribution of resources of wealth and power in society. Another central assumption is that the dominant group uses social institutions to maintain and increase its control of resources. Thus, the creation and maintenance of an ideology is of central importance to the dominant group. It is through the inculcation of this ideology that the populace at large comes to believe that the system is fair. Thus, an ideology of racial inferiority was critically important to the maintenance of the system of segregation in the American South, and an ideology of feminine inferiority was critically important to the maintenance of gender inequality in the economic marketplace. The schools as centers of institutional influence for all Americans thus become central to the perpetuation of these ideologies. Only by critical thinking and open discussion in classrooms of issues of inequality (ethnic, social class, racial, gender) could all Americans be freed to maximize their potential for contributing to the common good.

While there is merit in the perspective of the advocates of this approach concerning conflict theory, there are also problems. We are now living in a global community. Increasingly, the conflict experienced in American life is more pervasively rooted in the international as opposed to the intranational domain. Some observers note that the dominant groups in society have successfully shifted the conflict onto the international stage, thereby diverting attention from intranational group conflicts. Thus all Americans have a vested interest in free trade because it lowers the cost of consumer products, and the individuals on the other side of the conflict (those who have lost their jobs to outsourcing overseas, blue collar and white collar) have no coherence as groups. The issue of illegal immigration from Latin America likewise shatters group solidarity as blue collar workers in the United States lose jobs to illegal immigrants who will work (off the books) for less.

Cognitive development theory similarly finds a nuanced expression for advocates of this approach. Cognitive development theory as elaborated by Vygotsky (1986) posits human development as the intersect of the individual psyche with the language culture. Cognitive development theory as elaborated by Piaget (1952) posits human development as constructive. The child reconstructs the culture of the group in the process of acquiring the language of the group. Central to this acquisition is active involvement by the child in the creation of meaning. The term "language," as used here, is more than vocabulary, and includes the way the language is used by adult members of the group. Over time, as the language is internalized, the mind of the individual develops as an internal representation of the language. That language acquisition, however, is developmental, and depends upon the creation of a succession of structures of mind. Vygotsky's concept of the zone of proximal development poses the necessity of helping children develop meaning by building new understandings upon existing mental structures. For Vygotsky, thought is language, but language acquisition is structured and sequenced off a foundation of prior learning. For Vygotsky, all language is cultural, and therefore, all education is culturally framed. Necessarily, language differences lead to different understandings of the phenomenal universe.

Advocates of the Multicultural Social Justice Approach are concerned about cognitive development because requiring children to learn in a cultural framework that is different than their prior cultural framework creates a crisis of meaning for these children. While recognizing the problem posed by cognitive development theory for children of minority groups, the advocates of the Multicultural Social Justice Approach propose corrective strategies at variance with the nature of the problem. They propose "direct and active involvement with the group or issue of concern" (Sleeter & Grant, 1999, p. 196). This misses the Vygotskian point that current learning is always interpreted via the lens of prior knowledge. If that prior knowledge has derogated the issue or group of concern, direct and active involvement with the group or issue may not lead to a reduction of prejudice toward the other group or a reduction of dogmatic perspectives concerning the issue. Advocates of the Multicultural Social Justice Approach propose "democratizing power relationships in the classroom" (Sleeter & Grant, 1999, p. 197). This presumably will give students experience with and insight into the nature of society. The nature of society, however, may vary extensively across cultural, ethnic, and gender groups, particularly at a time of major immigration into the United States from the Third World. Thus the prior experience of members of each group may predispose them to draw very different understandings of the nature of society from the democratization of power relationships in the classroom.

The theory of culture similarly finds a nuanced expression for advocates of the Multicultural Social Justice Approach. The theory of culture advanced here is one that anthropologists may not recognize. "To them, much of everyday life is an adaptation to life's circumstances, which have been in part determined by group competition for resources" (Sleeter & Grant, 1999, p. 197). This politicization of the concept of culture is particularly American, and may be partially a response to the failure of our educational system to educate young Americans about the rest of the world. From the perspective of advocates of this approach, culture is all about power—and the varied ethnic roots of Americans no longer determine their values. Thus for Americans, "the substance of culture results directly from a group's material and political position" (Sleeter & Grant, 1999, p. 198).

While this understanding of culture may have some validity for second and third generation Americans, it may have considerably less validity for first generation Americans who still retain strong roots to their ethnic heritage. Cultural values and beliefs do not die a sudden death. Change tends to be gradual, across generations. Thus the Multicultural Social Justice Approach may not work so well with the children of the new immigration in the United States.

A further problem with this understanding of culture is that it does not address the problem of cultural differences in the global village. As the world becomes more integrated and interdependent it is not in the best interest of Americans to equip its youth with a distorted understanding of cultural differences. Failure of our educational system to provide an education which informs and inculcates respect for cultures at variance with the American Creed continues to create difficulties for Americans as they confront a world in which cultural differences are not reducible to group competition for resources.

How does the Multicultural Social Justice Approach fit Banks' dimensional typology of educational outcomes? Content integration can be addressed whenever and wherever the issues being explored are focused on conflict between defined groups. Accordingly content background for those groups would be an essential element of instruction.

The knowledge construction process clearly is central to issues-centered curricula, as exploration of issues necessarily requires the development of deep structural understanding of knowledge, including the cultural assumptions underlying knowledge construction. This particular element of Banks' dimensional typology may be one of the stronger aspects of the Multicultural Social Justice Approach.

Prejudice reduction may be a by-product of this approach, if the exploration of social issues provokes students to examine their own biases. The likelihood of this outcome probably depends upon the particular instructional strategies through which social issues are explored.

Equity pedagogy is a weaker fit with the Multicultural Social Justice Approach because children of some ethnic groups may have culturally derived values which resist participation in confrontational argumentation which is so often central to social issues' approaches to education. The very fact that social issues education, to be effective, is regularly drawn from current controversies in society may lead to reticence on the part of members of some sub-cultures to participate.

An empowering school culture is potentially a good fit with the Multicultural Social Justice Approach, to the extent that the school community provides for inclusion of all groups on an even-handed basis in all school activities. A social milieu of this nature can foster cross-group friendships and associations which will translate into a greater openness to participation in issues-centered discussions in the classroom.

WHAT ARE THE FUTURE PROSPECTS FOR MULTICULTURAL EDUCATION?

From its inception, the major concern of the multicultural education movement has been to find ways to provide equal educational opportunity for all members of society, regardless of their ethnicity, race, language, gender, and social class. The focus for much of the multicultural education movement has always been an opposition to discriminatory practices in the school. Over the past decade, however, the school as an institution may have lost much of its influence with young people, having been displaced by a media disseminated popular culture. The popular media, as a major influence on young people, has arguably been a powerful influence in reducing ethnic and racial bias among young people (Cortes, 1995). Over time, popular programming on television, popular music, and popular movies have increasingly presented a more diverse picture of American society.

Cortes (1995) notes that the way that young people process that diverse picture is strongly influenced by race and ethnicity of recipients. He further notes that the schools and researchers have done little to assess media-based multicultural knowledge construction.

This should be a cause for concern. Popular media is, for the most part, a visually based cultural tool. As such, it is impressionistic—and, as such, it does not require critical thought or reflection on meaning. As Greenspan (1997) notes, "mature empathy and morality are possible only after an individual develops the ability to connect emotions and ideas, to reflect on himself and his actions, and finally to construct an inner world of stable values alongside that of changing experiences" (p. 122). We may be seeing a surface appearance of a multi-ethnic society, when in fact there is little or no depth to the value systems that we believe have emerged. There is certainly a role for an issue-centered education to accommodate those criteria. Perhaps in the future multicultural education should focus more on the nature of the lessons and meanings that young people are extracting from their participation in mass media.

REFERENCES

Anselmi, S., & Peters, D. (1995). *School Context Effects in Block Adolescents: Perceptions of Self and the Future.* Annual Convention of the American Psychological Association. (ED 388 750).

Asante, M. K. (1987). *The Afrocentric idea.* Philadelphia, PA: Temple University Press.

Asante, M. K. (1988). *Afrocentricity.* Trenton, NJ: Africa World Press.

Asante, M. K. (1990). *Kemet, Afrocentricity, and knowledge.* Trenton, NJ: Africa World Press.

Banks, J. (1973). *Teaching ethnic studies: Concepts and strategies.* (43rd Yearbook, NCSS). Washington, DC: National Council for the Social Studies.

Banks, J. (1981). *Multiethnic education: Theory and practice.* Boston, MA: Allyn and Bacon.

Banks, J. (1995). Multicultural education: Historical development, dimensions and practice. In J. Banks & C. A. McGee Banks (Eds.) *Handbook of research on multicultural education.* New York: Macmillan.

Banks, J., & McGee Banks, C. A. (Eds.) (1995). *Handbook of research on multicultural education.* New York: Macmillan.

Bernal M. (1987). *Black Athena: Afroasiatic roots of classical civilization. Vol. I. The fabrication of ancient Greece, 1785–1985.* New Brunswick, NJ: Rutgers University Press.

Brameld, T. (1956). *Toward a reconstructed philosophy of education.* New York: Holt, Rinehart, Winston.

Brameld, T. (1957). *Cultural foundations of education.* Westport, CT: Greenwood Press.

Brandhorst, A. (2004) Identity centered conflict, authority, and dogmatism: Challenges for the design of social studies curriculum. *Theory and Research in Social Education, 32*(1), 10–23.

Coles, R. (1986). *The political life of children.* Boston, MA: Houghton Mifflin.

Cortes, C. (1995). Knowledge construction and popular culture: The media as multicultural educator. In J. Banks & C. A. McGee Banks (Eds.) *Handbook of research on multicultural education.* New York: Macmillan.

Gibson, M. (1976). Approaches to multicultural education in the United States: Some concepts and assumptions. *Anthropology and Education Quarterly, 7,* 7–18.

Greenspan, S. (1997). *The growth of the mind and the endangered origins of intelligence.* Reading, MA: Perseus Books.

Higham, J. (1974). Another American dilemma. *Center, 7*(July), 67–73.

Hunt, M. P., & Metcalf, L. (1968). *Teaching high school social studies: Problems in reflective thinking and social understanding.* New York: Harper and Row.

Irvine, J. J. (1990). *Black Students and School Failure: Policies, Practices, and Prescriptions.* Westport, CT: Greenwood Press.

Irvine, J. J., & York, E. (1995). Research on learning styles. In J. Banks & C.A. McGee Banks (Eds.), *Handbook of research on multicultural education.* New York: Macmillan.

Levine D., & Lezotte L. (1995). Effective schools research. In J. Banks & C.A. McGee Banks (Eds.) *Handbook of research in multicultural education* (pp. 525–547). New York: Macmillan.

Loewen, J. (1995). *Lies my teacher told me.* New York: Simon and Schuster.

Newman, W. (1973). *A study of minority groups and social theory.* New York: Harper and Row.

Piaget, J. (1952). *The language and thought of the child.* London: Routledge and Kegan Paul.

Ross, L. (2004). Peace in the middle east may be impossible. *APS Observer, 17*(10), 9–11.

Sleeter, C. E., & Grant, C. A. (1988). *Making choices for multicultural education: Five approaches to race, class, and gender.* Columbus: Merrill Publishing. Sleeter, C., & Grant, C. (1999). *Making choices for multicultural education.* New York: Wiley.

Sternberg, R. (1997). *Thinking styles.* New York: Cambridge University Press.

Tudge, T. (1990). Vygotsky, the zone of proximal development, and peer collaboration: Implications for classroom practice. In Luis Moll (Ed.), *Vygotsky and education: Instructional implications and applications of sociohistorical psychology* (pp. 155–172). New York: Cambridge University Press.

Vygotsky, L. (1986). *Thought and language.* Cambridge, MA: MIT Press.

CHAPTER 12

THE (UNFULFILLED) PROMISE
OF CRITICAL PEDAGOGY

Ronald W. Evans

We begin with the teacher. Every year thousands of teacher candidates enter teacher education programs full of promise, hope, and high ideals. Increasingly, in an age of standards, high stakes testing, and demands that teachers adopt scripted programs of instruction, the intellectual quality of teachers' work is being rapidly diminished. Despite these many unhealthy pressures, teachers in most schools have wide latitude to choose from several possible curricular paths (Gardner, 1999). In social studies, for example, there is the traditional path, with history and the social sciences taught from a textbook; the structure-of-the-disciplines path, in which students inquire as "little league" social scientists; the progressive or meliorist path, through which teacher and students create an interdisciplinary curriculum focused on issues and decision-making; and there is the critical path, in which students and teachers engage in a problem-posing dialogue aimed at raising questions of social transformation.

For the teacher, critical pedagogy is one of four main choices of curriculum orientation and identity. Unfortunately, in many if not most cases, teacher education programs give student teachers only a partial understanding of the choices before them, with a well-documented tendency to impose a technocratic rationality focused on methods that will "work" devoid of higher purpose, or deeper connection to possible meanings. The

Teaching and Studying Social Issues: Major Programs and Approaches, pages 233–249
Copyright © 2011 by Information Age Publishing

waters of the typical teacher education program get muddied with a mix of state and NCATE (National Council for Accreditation of Teacher Education) mandates, institutional and practical considerations. Moreover, the realities of learning to teach, and induction into the culture of schooling, means that many teachers seldom, if ever, get to consider their deeper purposes and the connection of their purposes to their classroom practices. As one esteemed colleague once remarked, there is a great deal of "mindlessness" in social studies classrooms and in schools.

I believe that it is healthy to interrupt the rush to practice with foundational questions. The choices teachers make are too important to be either imposed or left to chance—the choice of curricular path and philosophical orientation should be explicitly worked on through a dialogical process of confronting the challenge of creating a pedagogic creed, and the itinerant process of learning to teach, to work out the meaning of that creed in practice.

In this chapter, we will examine one particular creed, the critical/social reconstructionist orientation, in some depth. Moreover, we will examine that creed from several angles including its historical development; its definition; its foundations in theoretical and research literature; critiques that have been offered; its strengths, weaknesses, and limitations; and, its implementation in classrooms. Following that, we will make a few recommendations for improving the implementation of critical pedagogy in classrooms.

RESEARCH BASE

The research base for the critical/reconstructionist approach to teaching social studies and other subjects in schools is largely theoretical. That is not surprising in that the bulk of critical work in education is theoretical, with a few articles and books offering theory into practice work, and still fewer articles and books reporting empirical studies of critical practice in school classrooms.

As it exists in the 21st century, critical pedagogy has grown from numerous influences. The educational dialogue of the 1980s and 1990s contained multiple voices, from many different perspectives. One of the main camps in the long turf battles over the curriculum was the social reconstructionist group. Social reconstructionists such as George Counts, Harold Rugg, William Kilpatrick, and others, believed that schools could contribute to the transformation of the social order toward the realization of a cooperative commonwealth in which the needs and interests of the common people would be given higher priority. Teachers were to be the vanguard of the movement for change. In the latter 20th century, social reconstructionism was itself transcended by critical perspectives largely imported from outside

(Europe, Latin America), but generally sharing a similar radical orientation. The growing influence of this trend led, in part, to charges of "political correctness." For example, journalists such as Dinesh D'Souza and Roger Kimball charged that tenured radical professors were imposing their radical views on students and were not open to alternative points of view. These charges were, in fact, a reaction to two trends in the academy and society. These were the increasing influence of critical theory in academia and the growing mandate for multicultural education. Though they were ostensibly separate movements, the two trends had much in common and shared many insights and a similar orientation toward using education as one of the means for social transformation.

Critical theorists in education are far from a monolithic group and include scholars specializing in reconceptualist curricular theory, cultural studies, feminist scholarship and other forms. Critical scholarship has been strongly influenced by European theoretical perspectives including the critical theorists of the Frankfurt School, neo-Marxist social theory, structuralism and more recent developments in postmodernism and post structuralism. Many observers see in the growing influence of critical theory a delayed impact of the civil rights and human potential movements of the 1960s. Campus radicals have grown up and now hold tenured positions at major universities. Critical theory has a broad influence in academia as well as in schools of education.

In the United States, critical pedagogy has retained a strong link to the works of John Dewey and forged some direct links to social reconstructionist theory. Frequently, critical pedagogues draw on the works of European theorists including Gadamer, Gramsci, Habermas, Foucault, and Derrida. Their agenda is similar in ultimate goals to the social reconstructionists, but their work seems to focus on building a community of scholars critical of mainstream educational practice, conversant in critical theory, cognizant of the systemic and interwoven nature of educational, political, and social systems, and committed to resisting the dominant interests that control the bulk of wealth and power in the United States and whose interests the schools tend to serve.

Among the earliest and most influential was the Brazilian educational theorist Paulo Frerie. In his seminal work, *Pedagogy of the Oppressed*, Freire drew a distinction between traditional forms of education built around the "banking theory," in which knowledge is bestowed upon ignorant students by knowledgeable teachers, mirroring the oppression of capitalist society in which an elite with inordinate wealth and power dominates and oppresses, and problem-posing education (in which teacher and students cooperate in the search for understanding), which breaks this hierarchical pattern by creating a new dynamic in which the teacher is a student and the students are teachers and all are engaged in a common project. "Education," he wrote, "is suffering from narration sickness." The narration at the heart of traditional educational practices "turns students into 'containers,' into 'receptacles' to be 'filled' by the teacher..." Education then becomes "an act of depositing, in which the students are the depositories and the teacher is the depositor. Instead of *really* communicating *by* engaging in discussion and dialogue, the teacher issues communiqués and makes deposits, which the students patiently receive, memorize, and repeat. Banking education maintains this de-humanizing hold "through....attitudes and practices, which mirror oppressive society as a whole." It does so by re-creating the power relationship of owner vs. worker, master vs. slave, etc. Problem-posing education, on the other hand, creates a dialogue of teacher-student with student-teacher through which both teacher and student teach and learn simultaneously. It is an approach through which, "They become jointly responsible for a process in which all grow." What Freire was talking about, advocating and, in fact, putting into practice was not simply literacy but a process of liberation or conscientization which would provide students with the means to challenge an oppressive social order—to transform oppressive social relations (Freire, 1970).

Several other important works contributed to the growth of critical perspectives on education. One of the most important was *Schooling In Capitalist America* by Samuel Bowles and Herbert Gintis, published in 1976. Bowles and Gintis asserted that far from being the great equalizer, public schooling fostered and reproduced social-class based distinctions. In the course of their book's discussion of these issues, they introduced the terms "reproduction" and "correspondence theory" to a new generation of radical educators. "Reproduction" refers to the ways in which schools, by providing different qualities of educational experiences for different social classes, re-create and perpetuate the hierarchical social relations of capitalist society. Similarly, but from a different angle, "correspondence theory" refers to the way in which the hierarchical and class-based structure of schools replicates capitalist social structure. The central propositions of the book included, first, the idea that schools prepare students for adult work roles by socializing them to function well in the hierarchical structure of the modern corporation or institution and do this by replicating the environment of the workplace. Second, that *social* class and other aspects of economic status are passed on from parent to child by means of unequal educational opportunity. And, third, is the evolution of schooling in America best explained by a series of class and other conflicts arising through the social transformation of work. They argued, in essence, that:

> The educational system serves—through the correspondence of its social relations with those of economic life—to reproduce economic inequality and to distort personal development, thus under corporate capitalism, the objectives of liberal educational reform are contradictory: it is precisely because of its

role as producer of an alienated and stratified labor force that the educational system has developed its repressive and unequal structure (Bowles & Gintis, 1976, p. 48).

This work was very influential in the development of critical pedagogy. To varying degrees, critical pedagogues shared an affinity for reproduction and correspondence theories, often extending them to hold that not only school structures, but their hidden and overt curricula tend to mirror and reproduce the dominant social hierarchy, imposing different kinds of knowledge on different groups in accordance with their place in a stratified social order. Through intellectual and moral influence as well as direct coercion, dominant groups (the economic, political, and cultural elite) maintain the hegemony of the dominant culture and retain power over marginalized groups (women, the poor, persons of color). Somewhat more recently, "resistance theorists" accepted most of the insights of reproduction theory, but were more optimistic regarding the potential for educators to challenge the dominant interests. From this perspective, schools can best be understood as "contested terrain" and school curricula as "complex discourse that simultaneously serves the interests of domination while also providing possibilities for opposition and emancipations" (Stanley, 1991, p. 100).

Another path-breaking work was *Ideology and Curriculum* by Michael Apple, published in 1979. Among the first to establish a link between the curriculum and its implicit political ideology, Apple noted that not only the schools as institutions, but the curriculum itself served as a means of reproducing the social, cultural, and economic patterns of society. Thus, in his view, schools were engaged in preserving and distributing the symbolic property of cultural capital (as often represented in the official knowledge of textbooks and curriculum standards in which certain groups receive fuller treatment while others, i.e., persons of color, are marginalized or omitted). He argued that we needed a better understanding of, "why and how particular aspects of the collective culture are presented in school as objective, factual knowledge." How, concretely, may official knowledge represent ideological configurations of the dominant interests in a society? How do schools legitimate these limited and partial standards of knowing as unquestioned truths?" (Apple, 1979, p. 14). Apple's book was significant both for its insights, and for the fact that it marked the beginning of an emerging discourse among educational theorists, a critical and thoughtful discourse reminiscent of exchanges in the *Social Frontier*, a journal published in the 1930s and 1940s in which educational theory related to social reconstructionism was promoted and vigorously debated.

Other major contributors to the discourse of critical theory include William F. Pinar, Henry Giroux, Jean Anyon, Peter McLaren, Carmen Luke, Elizabeth Ellsworth and others. Though critical theory and social reconstructionism differ in many ways, and were developed independently and at different times, they share many of the same methods, concerns, and perspectives. And, as mentioned above, critical pedagogy is more strongly influenced by European theoretical perspectives including critical theory, neo-Marxism, structuralism, phenomenology, postmodernism, and post-structuralism, and by more recent developments such as feminist thought and scholarship. Moreover, while social reconstructionism was largely part of modernist discourse, critical pedagogy developed more recently, in what some have called the postmodern era.

Among the key propositions of the critical perspective on education are the following ideas:

1. Emancipation from domination by others should be the central aim of education. (domination could be economic, political, sexual, intellectual);
2. Knowledge itself is socially constructed and usually serves to support, legitimate, and maintain dominant interests;
3. If the quest for knowledge is addressed to understanding the significance of dominant interests, schooling can offer the possibility of emancipation;
4. Mastery of analytical skills and the tools required for reading, writing, and computation should be inspired by a commitment to work for a collectively emancipated world; and
5. Teaching must be guided by a continuous examination of fundamental beliefs, experiences, and knowledge, a critical discourse (Newmann, 1985).

These ideas *have* practical implications for the teaching of social studies *and other fields*, including: a focus on discourse analysis; the examination of language and content to determine bias; an awareness of the ways language may be shaped by dominant interests; a focus on the study of ideology; the ways of domination; and the means of emancipation. Thus, in the study of history, for example, critical pedagogy implies concentration on understanding the influence of dominant interests on the development of social institutions—*and* an accentuation on the means of emancipation—on the struggles of the oppressed to obtain their own liberation. In a sense, this focus on emancipation from domination was code for a critique of capitalism and the ways it is reflected in the broader cultural and social institutions of society.

In social studies, critical theory made a brief appearance in *Social Education,* the official journal of the National Council for the Social Studies (NCSS), in a special issue that appeared in 1985 entitled "The New Criticism: Alternative Views of Social Education." The issue included a number of articles by advocates of a critical theory stance, including Henry Giroux's "Teachers as Transformative Intellectuals," and contributions from Michael

W. Apple, Henry Giroux, William B. Stanley, Cleo Cherryholmes, Jack L. Nelson, and others (Nelson, 1985). At the time, it seemed to be the dawn of a new period in which critical perspectives might play a prominent role in social studies theory and practice. By the mid-to-late 1990s critical perspectives were a common feature of *Theory and Research in Social Education*, NCSS's research journal, with a number of works incorporating critical discourse, but made only infrequent forays into the practitioner oriented journals.

Over roughly the same period, several books were published, heavy on theory, offering or analyzing critical perspectives on social studies curricula, including, for example: *Curriculum for Utopia* (Stanley, 1991), *Democratic Social Education* (Hursh & Ross, 2000), and *Social Studies—The Next Generation* (Segall, Heilman, & Cherryholmes, 2006). Elsewhere, Bill Bigelow contributed to a growing understanding of what a critical approach might look like in schools through articles in *Rethinking Schools* and other publications. Earlier, Amy Gutman's *Democratic Education* (1987) gave voice to a thoughtful approach to schooling built around a democratic theory of education. Despite the increasing volume of rhetorical support, others wondered whether critical or postmodern theory was having much real impact in schools (Evans, 1993).

Given its political stance, critical theory was not without opponents. Many scholars asserted that it was unrealistic, naïve, or unreasonable to expect schools and teachers to act as agents of social transformation. They argued that the majority of teachers and school administrators were mainstream in their thinking, and reflected the general populace. Others charged that social reconstructionism had the potential to lead toward indoctrination of students, toward proselytizing, and propaganda. In addition, a number of feminist scholars, who shared a critical orientation, accused critical theorists of being gender blind and ignoring feminist scholarship. They accused critical pedagogues of framing their work within epistemologies that are essentially masculinist and patriarchal, and of privileging logic and rationality at the expense of emotional, intuitive, and moral ways of knowing.

Critical pedagogy as a project might learn from, and even take a page from the work of sympathetic scholars in social studies, some of whose work is described in other parts of this book. Critical pedagogues would be wise to draw on scholars in the issues-centered tradition such as Harold Rugg, Alan Griffin, Maurice Hunt and Lawrence Metcalf, Donald Oliver and James Shaver, Fred Newmann, Byron Massialis and Benjamin Cox, and Shirley Engle and Anna Ochoa, icons of issues-centered social education. Critical pedagogues can also draw both theoretical and practical insights from some of the leading critical theorists in education, such as Paulo Freire, Michael Apple, Henry Giroux, Peter McLaren, Antonia Darder, William Ayers, and from those in other fields such as Howard Zinn, Peter

Irons, and Ronald Takaki, and practical applications from teachers such as Bill Bigelow and his many colleagues at *Rethinking Schools*. Critical pedagogy can also draw strength and inspiration from icons of the broader struggle for social justice such as Eugene Debs, Michael Harrington, Clinton Jenks, Karl Marx, Fidel Castro, Jose Marti, Che Guevara, Emma Goldman, Caesar Chavez, Huey Newton, and Malcolm X.

Perhaps the most noteworthy strength of critical pedagogy may be found in the depth and power of the critical analyses it offers of capitalist schooling and society. The pervasive inequalities that persist in capitalist nations offer much to be criticized (Domhoff, 2006). A second strength may be found in the sources of critical pedagogy, in the long tradition of critical analysis of schools and society, much of which has been bold and forward looking. The focus of the critique has been on the ultimate promise of democracy and democratic schooling, and the possibility of social and cultural transformation. A third strength may be found in the deep intellectual challenge that critical pedagogy offers to teachers, teacher educators, and others concerned about the process, goals, and ultimate influence of schooling. To what extent is schooling contributing to the reification of cultural reproduction and the training of students to fit into a hierarchical and undemocratic system? On the other hand, to what extent is schooling leading students to question social injustices and to develop deep dreams of fairness and equity? A fourth strength of critical pedagogy is that the body of theory developed to this point offers powerful explanations of the functions of schooling in capitalist society, serving to reproduce inequalities and to transmit and reproduce the social system without full consideration of alternatives.

One purported weakness of critical pedagogy is that it is a "biased" and largely negative view of society and schooling based on critiques of capitalism and capitalist schooling by "tenured radicals" bred in the counterculture of the 1960s. This critique reflects the point-of-view of alternative ideologies that are not in agreement with the underlying premises of critical pedagogy. A second critique suggests, with much justification, that it is largely a theoretical stance, and that too much is left unclear regarding the meaning of critical pedagogy for teaching practice. Its theoretical stance is apparent in the frequently dense language which makes the work of many critical theorists difficult to read and ultimately alienates, or fails to connect with, many teachers.

While critical and postmodern scholars offer "fresh conceptualizations," much of their work lacks a bridge to the practical (Crocco, 2006, p. 231). As one mainstream critic wrote recently, they give "little attention ... to developing defensible curricula or instructional methods in social studies" and "can easily succumb to contentment with quoting Baudrillard" (Barton, 2006, pp. 243–244). Indeed, it is true that postmodern critics often seem content to jump up on their desks and shake their fists at the shibboleths of modernism through critical research and analysis, with too little attention to praxis. A case in point, when we read critical pedagogy in the foundational courses I teach, I ask students, "Critical of what?" Some students are stumped by the question, and often focus on the pedagogical. This suggests that many critical pedagogues are not always forthright and open in their critique of *capitalism*, though others are very direct and open about where they are coming from (i.e. Apple, 2006; McLaren, Martin, Farahmandpur, 2004; Pruyn, 1999). A third weakness may be found in the paucity of field-based research on critical teaching in K–12 classrooms. Though there is some helpful theory into practice work being done, a good deal of narrative description from teachers, and the amount of such work is growing (Ayers, Hunt, & Quinn, 1998; Darder, 2002), the small number of classroom studies suggests a major need.

IMPLEMENTATION

As suggested above, critical pedagogy has suffered from a general lack of cogent implementation. Despite the small numbers of critical teachers in our nation's schools, the potential for a stronger implementation exists, especially if critical pedagogy is cast as part of a broader struggle for democracy in schools and society (Giroux, 2004). In much of the critical literature, there is a sense of moral outrage at the ravages of capitalism, including its human and environmental costs. Critical pedagogues offer their perspectives in opposition to the dominant structures of capitalist society. They claim the moral high ground, and challenge students to do likewise. In my own work with students at various levels, I have found that students are interested in social justice issues and in an exploration of social criticism as a major focus of social studies instruction, partly because it asks them to step outside their own particular roles and context and partly because it avails them of the opportunity to examine important questions and issues that impinge on their lives.

At the university level over recent decades, we have witnessed something of a shift toward a more critical stance in the social sciences and humanities. Perhaps this shift will trickle down to schools. For social studies teachers, there are a number of people and organizations that have written and developed useful materials helpful in creating a critical approach in the classroom. Chief among them are the work of Howard Zinn, author of *A Peoples History of the United States* (1980), and Bill Bigelow and his colleagues at *Re-thinking Schools*.

Despite such works by some fine teachers and scholars who are deeply committed to education for social justice, critical pedagogy has found only a limited presence in schools. The practical literature that exists is too limited in scope and difficult reading for many teachers. A teacher who supports, and seeks to implement, a social justice orientation in social studies, must seek out these materials and purchase or borrow them. Many teachers are undoubtedly caught in the gulf between theory and practice, and succumb to the overwhelming pressure in schools to teach to the test. Moreover, critical pedagogues, whether theorists or advocates/exemplars of theory into practice, have done little to address the barriers or constraints that limit the use of critical materials and perspectives in schools. On this matter, a very helpful book from Rethinking Schools entitled *The New Teacher Book* (2004) is a step in the right direction, with many thoughtful essays on the trials and tribulations of learning to teach from a social justice framework. This book includes practical essays written by teachers on how beginning schoolteachers, especially those with a social justice orientation, can successfully navigate the school system, develop a support network, deal with standards and testing, survive the first year, meet the challenge of classroom discipline, and develop a thoughtful and multicultural curriculum. It also contains descriptions of and linkages to a wealth of resources useful for any teacher, focused on teaching about social justice concerns.

Another helpful resource may be found in the recent work of William Ayers and his colleagues, whose work with teachers aims in a similar direction, at transforming a highly theoretical critical pedagogy that sometimes seems focused on critique (and is deemed "negative" by many critics) into a discourse of "possibility" that celebrates and supports even modest successes in teaching for change, and seeks to keep some small "embers of hope burning" in the classrooms and hearts of critical pedagogues (Ayers, Hunt, & Quinn, 1998; Ayers, Michie, & Rome, 2004). Another practical resource may be found in the work of Antonia Darder, especially in her 2002 book on implementing a critical pedagogy, *Reinventing Paulo Freire*, which provides several excellent narratives from teachers and teacher educators on the implementation of critical theory in teaching practice. Another helpful resource may be found in the work of Joan Wink, especially, *Critical Pedagogy: Notes from the Real World* (2005), a very practical and down to earth primer.

Barriers to the successful implementation of critical pedagogy in school are significant, and must be addressed if advocates of critical pedagogy are to make greater progress. Sometimes it seems that the entire structure of schooling is set against any form of critical thought. Harold Rugg (1956), the great progressive educator and advocate of social reconstructionism whose social studies textbooks were the subject of great controversy, in his later years, addressed this *quite* thoughtfully:

> One of the very essential factors in the creative process, it seems to me, is the concept of integrity. It's involved in that very homely phrase, "I say what I think my way"... An authoritarian world will not permit [the following] question to be asked, "What do you think?" ... Why it's revolutionary! ... So you could generalize that, ... and you could put it into schools. And (it) consists of teachers honestly asking, "What do you think?"

I think we've seen almost a vicious expression of the very opposite of this. Not what they really think, but what ought to be said to fit in with the controlling interest, with the boss, with the owner, the employer, with the party ... And you see it at its worst in all these fascist organizations [i.e., Merwin K. Hart and the New York State Economic Council] and you see it in complete form in any authoritarian society, *whether it be the Russian one, or Hitler, or Mussolini, or the Japanese war party, or whether it be* the same kind of thing in a democratic society where the powers that be control.

Educationally, I would go back to what seems to be the heart of it, getting teachers to understand, that no matter what the board of education has prescribed, no matter what the superintendent and the principal, and the supervisor have said must be done, that basically, this group of children and I have got to explore life ... together, honestly, and confront the problems ... in spite of the possible authoritarian (reaction) ... The teacher would have to bring them right down to this village, this town, this neighborhood, this school, this class.

As Rugg suggested, too often we see a vicious expression of the very opposite, with students and teachers given little freedom to say what they think, or to develop social criticism. Perhaps this constraint on teaching goes right to the heart of the school as an institution. Part of the "grammar of schooling" has to do with the unspoken rule that students are not to challenge the thinking of their teachers, and teachers are not to challenge the thinking of their administrators. A reflection of the hierarchical structure of schooling, the imposition of authority in schools, and the growing endangerment to democratic freedoms, this is perhaps the most significant constraint on the teacher and student freedom required for critical pedagogy to flourish. And, it frequently operates insidiously, through self-censorship.

There are other important constraints. Advocates of critical pedagogy are often quite strident in their rhetoric, thus leaving one with the sense that critical pedagogy constitutes the imposition of a rather dogmatic view, critical of capitalism, militarism, sexism, etc. Unfortunately such dogmatic posturing, while understandable and linked to a sense of moral outrage, tends to alienate some, if not many, students, teachers, and administrators. Fortunately, there are many alternative ways to make critical commentaries, and many thoughtful approaches to introducing a consideration of critical perspectives in schools. A skilled teacher, much like a skilled politician, can sometimes get students and colleagues to consider difficult issues and perspectives, not by using critical perspectives like a club and figuratively hitting over the head, but by quietly posing them as alternatives and by asking students to consider value choices and their potential consequences and to make up their own minds.

This brings up another barrier, and a failing of critical pedagogy, and that is the apparent hesitance or failure of many critical pedagogues to connect with the long tradition of issues-centered education (Engle & Ochoa, 1988; Evans & Saxe, 1996; Hunt & Metcalf, 1955, 1968; Ochoa, 2007; Oliver & Shaver, 1966; Rugg, 1923). Perhaps the literature on and approaches of many of those who have advocated a reflective or issues-centered approach to teaching in social studies seem too soft or too conservative to some advocates of critical pedagogy, and it is true that the problems and issues raised by advocates of a liberal progressivism have often segmented and trivialized the treatment of social problems and issues—and have, more often than not, stopped short of examining the systemic nature of such problems. However, despite this initial reaction, the critical teacher would do well to seriously consider the relevance and usefulness of this literature, much of which is described in previous chapters of this volume. If social transformation through a critical "problem posing" process is the goal, then the process of democratic, issues-centered teaching may be one of the most effective means to reach the goal, especially in a context when even "small victories" deserve to be celebrated (Ayers, Michie, & Roma, 2004).

Another significant barrier to implementation of critical pedagogy may be seen in the periodic but regularly recurring attacks on academic freedom that have occurred in educational history. The Rugg textbook controversy, the MACOS (Man A Course of Study) controversy, and the periodic "crises" in the teaching of American history are each examples of what can happen, and what has happened (Evans, 2004). These episodes were controversial because the school materials involved asking students to question our social, cultural and economic institutions. Such episodes have served to constrain teacher freedom and the range of choices available, sometimes explicitly by casting out innovative materials, and sometimes implicitly, by creating a chill in the atmosphere and social context of schooling. The current mania for standards and high stakes testing, an outgrowth and logical extension of an era of conservative restoration in schools and society, has contributed significantly to a growing lack of teacher freedom, and to the imposition of a business mentality in schooling in which innovative approaches are no longer welcome, and through which only what is measurable on high stakes tests is valued. When we add to the mix the technocratic rationality of most teacher education programs, it is little wonder that critical pedagogy has had trouble making an impact on schools and finding its way into the school curriculum.

IMPACT

Despite the general lack of critical practice, there have been some noticeable successes. It is important to recognize, and to celebrate, these successes, because they indicate that some teachers are committed to a critical or issues oriented approach and that it is important to continue the struggle to have wider influence in schools. Perhaps the single most notable success of the past is the example of the Rugg Social Science Program. Rugg's textbooks were innovative, well written, and pedagogically advanced. They brought a questioning stance to bear on many of our world's institutions and social problems. The rationale for the Rugg program began with the notion that we have a "troubled world" and that through a meaningful examination of social issues and problems students can be educated to help overcome those problems (Rugg, 1923). Despite the fact that the Rugg books were deemed "Un-American" by conservative and business groups and eventually cast out of the schools during World War II, they remain a shining example of what is possible (Evans, 2007). Rugg's books were the most popular junior high social studies textbooks of the 1930s. His work influenced a generation of students, a generation of citizens.

There are several additional and noteworthy examples of critical or social reconstructionist pedagogy having an influence, though none have had as much influence on schools as Harold Rugg. Another example may be found in the work of Myles Horton at Highlander Folk School, which influenced many social activists of the 1950s and 1960s. Highlander, in Tennessee, was an innovative school focused on preparing community activists and was responsible for preparing many participants in the civil rights movement. Another example may be found in the era (1968–1975) of social studies focused on social issues, relevance, and student activism, which was a strong reflection of a critical orientation to the field, and had an influence for a time. During that period, which I have called the "newer social studies," there were several innovations including growing use of pamphlets and materials focused on social problems and issues *such as* Gerald Leinwand's *Problems in American Society* series (Leinwand, 1968–1969); the mini-course explosion (which focused on social issues and relevant topics such as, Bread and Roses, Is War Necessary, and Human Sexuality); and, the 1971 *NCSS Curriculum Guidelines* which were issues-centered and social reconstructionist in orientation (NCSS Task Force, 1971).

Paulo Freire's *Pedagogy of the Oppressed* (1970) came out at an opportune time when the nation's campuses and many of its cities were on fire with rebellion and a sense of revolution in the air. Critical theorists in education, and virtually all of us who were alive then, were strongly influenced by the questioning of our institutions and the explosive social issues of that time, including the direct influence of Freire.

In more recent years, other developments have had significant impact. The work of Howard Zinn has had an influence on many teachers. His book, *A Peoples History of the United States,* has sold over one million copies, more than a few of which have found their way into classrooms, and led to materials specifically created for high school students. And, the work of *Rethinking Schools* (founded in Milwaukee in 1986 and headed by a group of critical teachers) has touched many teachers through their initiatives and publications. *Rethinking Columbus* has sold over 250,000 copies and has been used in thousands of classrooms, K–12.

RECOMMENDATIONS/CONCLUSIONS

I began this essay with the teacher. If critical pedagogy and democratic schooling are ever going to make deeper inroads in the institution of schooling, I believe that our best chance is to seek to influence more teachers. In this closing portion of my chapter, I wish to posit this question: What might help strengthen the appeal and practicality of critical pedagogy so that more teachers will develop a critical practice?

First, I believe that a re-conceptualization of teacher education is in order. Teacher education in its current form occurs through a variety of avenues and practices, many of which do not embrace a problem-posing or critical stance. Even when a critical approach is present, it often takes the form of counter-imposition. An alternative that I believe may have some appeal would involve an explicit focus on problematizing the act of teaching, and asking teachers and teacher candidates to consider their philosophical options and approaches through a process of rationale-building. For this approach to be most effective, the full range of choices must be examined in some depth via an open and reflective process in which teachers engage in a deep foundational study in education and curriculum history and philosophy, identifying their own pedagogical beliefs and influences in some depth, and then developing teaching practices and materials that can help them enact their creed in the classroom. For this approach to be most meaningful, teachers will have to have a broad degree of freedom to serve not just as curricular instructional gatekeepers, but as thoughtful instructional designers as well. To deepen its influence, it will need to extend into the first several years of a teacher's service and experience in schools.

Second, under the rubric of "democratic education" and in the interest of a broader philosophical choice of approaches to teaching, it may be possible to establish greater institutional support in the form of money and materials for continuing teacher education and growth. This will probably be most effective if linked explicitly to a notion of deliberative teaching (Parker, 2003) or creating greater classroom thoughtfulness via constructivist, or authentic, pedagogy (Scheurman & Newmann, 1998).

Third, additional materials aimed at teaching for social justice would be helpful for use by teachers and students, especially if coordinated with and sequenced to be used alongside of a traditional textbook in the most commonly offered social studies courses: American history, world history, geography, government, etc. Materials are likely to reach the widest audience if they are free or inexpensive. A philanthropist or foundation with the goal of making education more broadly democratic could make a real difference by funding the infusion of such materials in schools.

Fourth, greater and more effective efforts will need to be made to help teachers overcome or at least cope with the barriers and constraints that impinge on creative and critical approaches to teaching. Paramount among these are constraints on academic freedom and the imposition of too numerous and too onerous a system of standards and high stakes assessments that create unhealthy pressure to cover vast amounts of content and that tend to favor superficial coverage over depth, understanding, and meaning.

Finally, there may be several tactics to avoid: rigid or dogmatic imposition of critical perspectives; imposition of conclusions from the teacher or text; and, a rigid neutrality in which the teacher refuses to reveal her or his own beliefs and perspectives. The teacher's point-of-view should enter the classroom as a part of the conversation, but not as the dominant or sole perspective. Critical pedagogy implemented effectively requires a teacher well-versed in creating meaningful and open dialogue through which a wide range of ideas and alternatives are considered and discussed, in which the possible consequences of a given choice, interpretation, or decision are weighed, in which considerable evidence is brought to bear, in which underlying values are explored, in which decisions are tentative, choices deliberate, and actions carefully warranted. In the end, implementing a critical pedagogy in schools will be a respectful process of educating teachers and infiltrating the institution of schooling in ways both dynamic and effective. Though we may never convince a majority of teachers to fully embrace a critical and issues-centered approach, we must never doubt that our continuing efforts can make a difference.

REFERENCES

Apple, M. W. (1979). *Ideology and curriculum.* London: Routledge & Keegan Paul.

Apple, M. W. (2006). *Educating the "right" way: Markets, standards, God and inequality.* New York: Routledge.

Ayers, W., Hunt, J. A., & Quinn, T. (Eds.). (1998). *Teaching for social justice: A democracy and education reader.* New York: The New Press, Teachers College Press, distributed by W. W. Norton.

Ayers, W., Michie, G., & Rome, A. (2004). Embers of hope: In search of a meaningful critical pedagogy. *Teacher Education Quarterly, 31*(1), 123–130.

Barton, K. (2006). After the essays are ripped out, what?: The limits of a reflexive encounter. In A. Segall, E. E. Heilman, & C. Cherryholmes (Eds.), *Social studies—The next generation: Re-searching in the postmodern.* New York: Peter Lang.

Bowles, S., & Gintis, H. M. (1976). *Schooling in capitalist America: Educational reform and the contradictions of economic life.* New York: Basic Books.

Crocco, M. (2006). The invisible hand of theory in social studies education. In A. Segall, A., E.E. Heilman, & C. Cherryholmes (Eds.) *Social studies—The next generation: Re-searching in the postmodern.* New York: Peter Lang.

Darder, A. (2002). *Reinventing Paulo Freire: A pedagogy of love.* Boulder, CO: Westview Press.

Domhoff, G. W. (2006). *Wealth, income, and power.* Downloaded from http://sociology.ucsc.edu/whorulesamerica/power/wealth.html.

Engle, S. H., & Ochoa, A. S. (1988). *Education for democratic citizenship: Decision making in the social studies.* New York: Teachers College.

Evans, R. W. (1993). Utopian visions and mainstream practice: A review essay on *Curriculum for utopia: Social reconstructionism and critical pedagogy in the postmodern era,* by W. B. Stanley. *Theory and Research in Social Education, 21,* 161–173.

Evans, R. W. (2004). *The social studies wars: What should we teach the children?* New York: Teachers College Press.

Evans, R. W. (2007). *This happened in America: Harold Rugg and the censure of social studies.* Charlotte, NC: Information Age Publishing.

Evans, R. W., & Saxe, D. W. (Eds.) (1996). *Handbook on teaching social issues.* Bulletin #93. Washington, DC: National Council for the Social Studies.

Freire, P. (1970). *Pedagogy of the oppressed.* New York: Continuum.

Gardner, H. (1999). *The disciplined mind: What all students should understand.* New York: Simon and Schuster.

Giroux. H. (2004). Critical pedagogy and the postmodern/modern divide: Towards a pedagogy of democratization. *Teacher Education Quarterly, 31*(1), 31–47.

Gutman, A. (1987). *Democratic education.* Princeton, NJ: Princeton University Press, 1987.

Hunt, M. P., & Metcalf, L. E. (1968). *Teaching high school social studies: Problems in reflective thinking and social understanding.* New York: Harper & Brothers.

Hursh, D. W., & Ross, E. W. (Eds.). (2000). *Democratic social education: Social studies for social change.* New York: Falmer.

Leinwand, G. (Ed.). (1968-1969). *Problems of American society* (series). New York: Washington Square Press.

McLaren, P., Martin, G., & Farahmandpur, R. (2004). Teaching in and against the empire: Critical pedagogy as revolutionary praxis. *Teacher Education Quarterly, 31*(1), 131–153.

NCSS Task Force on Curriculum Guidelines (1971). *Social studies curriculum guidelines. Social Education, 38* (8), 853–867.

Nelson, J. L. (Ed.). (1985). New criticism and social education. *Social Education, 49* (5), 368–405.

Newmann, F. M. (1985). The radical perspective on social studies: A synthesis and critique. *Theory and Research in Social Education, 13* 1), 1–8.

Ochoa, A. S. (2007). *Democratic education for social studies: An issues-centered decision making curriculum.* Greenwich, CT: Information Age Publishing.

Oliver, D. W., & Shaver, J. P. (1966). *Teaching public issues in the high school.* Boston, MA: Houghton Mifflin Company.

Parker, W. C. (2003). *Teaching democracy: Unity and diversity in public life.* New York: Teacher's College Press.

Pruyn, M. (1999). Social education through a Marxist postmodern lens: Toward a revolutionary multiculturalism. *Theory and Research in Social Education, 27* (3), 408–423.

Rethinking Schools (2004). *The new teacher book.* Milwaukee, WI: Rethinking Schools.

Rugg, H. O. (1923). Problems of contemporary life as the basis for curriculum-making in the social studies. In H. O. Rugg (Ed.), *The social studies in the elementary and secondary school. Twenty-Second Yearbook, National Society for the Study of Education, Part II* (pp. 260–273). Bloomington, IL: Public School Publishing Co.

Rugg, H. O. (1956). Rugg speaking to the New York Geriatric Society, Cold Spring, New York, June 15, 1956. Transcript and tape in the possession of the author.

Scheurman, G., & Newmann, F. M. (1998). Authentic intellectual work in social studies: Putting performance before pedagogy. *Social Education, 62*(1), 23–25.

Segall, A., Heilman, E. E., & Cherryholmes, C. (Eds.). (2006). *Social studies—The next generation: Re-searching in the postmodern.* New York: Peter Lang.

Stanley, W. B. (1991). *Curriculum for utopia: Social reconstructionism and critical pedagogy in the postmodern era.* Albany: State University of New York Press.

Wink, J. (2005). *Critical pedagogy: Notes from the real world,* 3rd edition. New York: Longman.

Zinn, H. (1980). *A peoples history of the United States.* Boston, MA: Beacon Press.

CHAPTER 13

EDUCATION FOR DEMOCRATIC CITIZENSHIP

Decision Making in the Social Studies

Mark A. Previte

OVERVIEW

The status of American social studies education has been and continues to be entangled in a contentious debate concerning the curricular and instructional direction of social studies education between the supporters of the teaching of the social studies disciplines and the advocates for a social studies curriculum taking an issues-centered approach. This contested conversation over the true course of social studies education has endured and apparently will not be resolved in the foreseeable future (Evans, 2004; Leming, Ellington & Porter, 2003; Ross, 2001, Thorton, 1991).

This chapter focuses on the issues-centered movement's continuing quest for mainstream acceptance of the vision put forth by Shirley Engle and Anna Ochoa's book *Education for Democratic Citizenship: Decision Making in the Social Studies.* The Engle and Ochoa book was published during the 1980s at a time when the political scene of the nation was deeply embedded in the "Reagan Revolution" ushered in by Ronald Reagan's U.S. presidency

Teaching and Studying Social Issues: Major Programs and Approaches, pages 251–275
Copyright © 2011 by Information Age Publishing
All rights of reproduction in any form reserved.

(1981–1989), and the educational pendulum was swinging back to a basics, business-oriented model of education with a focus dominated by the academic disciplines.

Engle and Ochoa's philosophy of social studies education was predicated to a large extent on the ideas found in the work of John Dewey and the Progressive Movement (1916, 1933) and the Committee on Social Studies Report (1916). The basic tenet of their philosophy is that if education is to be a reflection of life, social studies teachers must prepare their students to be able to solve problems that the students will face. Dewey (1938) believed that teachers must focus on a theory of experience that provides them with the opportunity to choose the materials, methods and experiences necessary to link subject matter and process to a student's life experience. The history of social studies education is replete with many noble efforts to develop a social studies program adhering to such goals, including the work of the Rugg brothers from the 1920s through the 1940s, Alan Griffin at Ohio State in the 1940s and 1950s, Maurice Hunt's and Lawrence Metcalf in the 1950s, Shirley Engle and the Indiana Experiment of the 1960s, and the Oliver, Shaver, Newmann Harvard jurisprudential model of the 1960s and early 1970s. The Engle-Ochoa model was the continuation of such efforts.

SWINGING BACK
TO THE RIGHT

During the 1980s, the nation's politicians, media and citizens demanded appropriate action to stem the perceived tide of mediocrity in the American educational system (National Commission on Excellence in Education, 1984). This firestorm of criticism concluded that the economic, political, and cultural implications of American students falling behind their foreign counterparts would take the United States down a road from which it may never recover. These experts proposed solutions that would reinforce student attainment and understanding of factual knowledge, which in essence, evoked the process of dominant culture transmission (Adler, 1982; Bloom, 1987; Cheney, 1987; Hirsch, 1987).

Social studies was not immune to this crisis. While the National Council for the Social Studies (1980) decided to hitch their wagon to the conservative, back-to-basics movement, Engle decided to take an oppositional stand and continue to speak out for an issues-centered philosophy. Engle's views on social studies vehemently opposed the swing towards the use of the expository mode of instruction along with the almost complete reliance upon the textbook as the dominant resource in classrooms. More specifically, he envisioned the social studies "as being properly the process of thinking about and reaching decisions about problems, rather than merely the exposition of facts and conclusions from the social sciences to be held in memory" (Engle, 1986b, p. 1). Adults/teachers playing the role of transmitters of all that is worth knowing and the students being empty vessels to be filled with important facts was totally antithetical to Engle's philosophy. More specifically, according to Engle (1982a):

> [t]he primary role of the school in a democracy is to help children to gain some distance from their society. It is to help children to gain the capacity for objectivity concerning the beliefs and institutions otherwise imposed upon them by the status quo. It is to help them gain the capacity to participate in the continual reconstruction and improvement of society. . . .Participation implies the right to reflect on one's own beliefs and those of others, the right to harbor doubt about beliefs, and full access to information whereby beliefs may be studied and validated. Education, if it is to serve the purposes of democracy, should reflect these rights at every turn and should help citizens to build the skills and the kind of ordered knowledge required for the exercise of these rights. . . . (p. 49).

If schools were to take advantage of their immense potential, then they needed to heed the idea that participation in school was a prerequisite for participation in life. This was critical if the student was to "acquire a *social* sense of their own powers and of the materials and appliances used" (Dewey, 1916, p. 40).

From Engle's perspective, the social studies had become more of an academic exercise rather than a mode of living. Furthermore, he was bothered by the fact that, for the most part, no correlation was being made between what was being studied in the classroom and what was occurring in real life. Additionally, it upset him that the classroom environment and course content were being used to indoctrinate students rather than help them make decisions (Engle, 1977). At the top of his agenda was the desire for an adequate definition of "social studies" under the rubric of citizenship education. Engle argued incessantly that schools should develop students as active, participatory citizens. Furthermore, he implored social studies teachers to assimilate the following components into their instructional and curricular philosophy:

1. Course work should focus on developing in-depth treatment of social issues and problems.
2. In order to learn how to address such issues and solve such problems, students should learn how to develop their skills and abilities as decision makers and problem solvers.

3. Social criticism, the ability to ask complex, searching questions, must become the staple of the student's repertoire of social studies skills.

4. The student must also be taught that knowledge possesses a tentative quality due to the change process that society undergoes (pp. 6–8).

Another dilemma that vexed Engle was the purpose of enculturation and indoctrination (Leming, 1981; Stanley, 1981). Engle was certainly aware that one of the roles of the school was to instruct students on the rules and norms of their society. Teachers were to transmit information so that students would discern the boundaries of their own knowledge and behavior. He was also well aware that these two concepts were not mutually exclusive (Engle & Longstreet, 1978). The problem imbedded in this conflict was whether or not it would be advisable to turn all students into social critics. What would be the consequences of this dilemma? Engle would rely upon his friendship with James Shaver to help clarify his thinking.

Shaver raised several concerns about Engle's dilemma. One took the form of a dichotomy between conformism and activism; Shaver described it as rationality versus commitment (Shaver, 1978). How can students become social critics of a society without being "indoctrinated" with the values and beliefs of that society? According to Shaver, indoctrination in the schools cannot be avoided for how else can education occur in the elementary setting. Shaver (1978) was also quick to point out that much of a child's indoctrination takes place outside of the school, from such sources as family, peers, church, and the media:

> . . . .it seems to me that the challenge is to recognize not only that the dilemma or the dichotomy between conformism and activism or rationality is not a perfect one, but that, indeed, it is a basic paradox of a democratic society; that the school curriculum should reflect that paradox; and that, in particular, adequate coping with the paradox involves a view of the curriculum based on a developmental conception of children.

> ...We need to pay much more attention to the instilling of commitment to basic democratic values during the early elementary years; and then as the children move to the concrete operational stage and to formal operational reasoning, we need to involve them in the "rationalization of those values." (p. 3)

Ultimately, the problem that Engle confronted was as follows: when does the process of socialization end and the process of "liberation" or critical thought take over and where does society strike a balance between social activism, continuity and tranquility? (Engle, 1977)

Ever since his co-authoring, with Wilma Longstreet, *A Design for Social Education in the Open Curriculum* (1972), Engle had contemplated writing another book that would coalesce his thinking about issues-centered philosophy and education. Coming out of the New Social Studies movement steeped in the social sciences, Engle and Longstreet took a non-traditional route by structuring an open curriculum anchored by a trio of ideas: a problems orientation, relevance to the student's life, and six action-concepts including conflict, power, valuing, interaction, change, and adjustment. Engle had started a two year campaign to enlist the services of Shaver to co-author the book as both were kindred spirits of a reflective issues based approach—and that was true even though Oliver and Shaver (1966) was dedicated to a public issues approach while Engle's approach was grounded in a broader sweep. Both were also past presidents of the National Council for the Social Studies. Their writings continued to focus on issues related to curriculum and instruction with a progressive bent, but each wondered whether he was still on the right track (Engle, 1982b). In a letter to Shaver, Engle outlined the sections of the book:

Part I: The Implications of the Democratic Ideal for the Social Studies
What distinguished citizenship in the democratic society from that of others? How is information, from whatever source, appropriately dealt with in a democracy? How is this process learned by children?
How are value problems appropriately dealt with in a democracy? How is this process learned by children?
What are the intellectual and social skills required of citizens in a democracy? How are these learned?

Part II: The Relationship Between the Disciplines and the Social Studies
How is a discipline appropriately used in the process of thinking about a social problem?
How can disciplines be learned so that they will be functional in thinking about a social problem?
How is (are) the social studies distinguished from the disciplines?
What is the useful interface between the social studies and the disciplines commonly associated with the social studies? How does one assimilate information gathered from direct experience or information acquired from sources other than the disciplines into this mix?

Part III: The Content of the Social Studies Curriculum
What criteria should rule the selection of content for the social studies curriculum?
What specific content will meet these criteria at each grade level?

Part IV: Teaching the Social Studies
What is the relationship of instructional procedures to the objectives of the social studies?
What is the relationship of school governance and social environment to the objectives of the social studies?
What role should the social studies teacher play in the development of the democratic character of our society? and
How should instruction be carried on in the social studies classroom in a democracy? (Engle, 1981)

In a heartfelt response, Shaver (1982) responded that other projects and feelings of "mid-career doldrums" and "burn out" had sapped his motivation for the project. Engle then turned to Anna Ochoa, a colleague at the University of Indiana during the 1970s. Ochoa had come to Indiana by way of Florida State University, where she served under the department leadership of Byron Massialas, a former graduate student of Engle's during the Indiana Experiments of the 1960s (Monteverde, 2002). Ochoa agreed to serve as a co-editor, and thus the project was undertaken. As a preview to the publication of their book, Engle and Ochoa submitted a model of their curriculum to the National Council for the Social Studies' (NCSS) Task Force on Scope and Sequence whose charge was to select several K–12 scope and sequence models (Engle & Ochoa, 1986, pp. 514–525). The other models submitted to NCSS were: Thomas L. Dynneson's and Richard E. Gross' "A Century of Encounter"; H. Michael Hartoonian's and Margaret A. Laughlin's "Designing a Scope and Sequence"; William B. Stanley's and Jack L. Nelson's "Social Education for Social Transformation," and Willard M. Kniep's "Social Studies Within A Global Education."

Engle and Ochoa had submitted their model in response to (and, essentially, as a critique of) the Task Force's 1983 model of a scope and sequence that continued the "Conservative Cultural Continuity" tradition outlined by the Project SPAN report (National Council for the Social Studies, 1984). Project SPAN suggested that in order to develop students as full participants in society, the social studies curriculum should be organized around seven vital roles basic to the lives of students: citizen, worker, consumer, family member, friend, member of social groups, and self (Superka & Hawke, 1980). Each of the aforementioned roles were to be subsumed within the individual disciplines. Engle criticized the members of the SPAN committee for their "superficial patching" of the social studies curriculum. He suggested that changes in content rather than a roles emphasis should have been the primary obligation of the committee:

> In the absence of any systematic effort to deal with the question of content, there is little likelihood that a focus on roles, grade after grade, subject after subject, will be any less boring or shallow than a focus on geographic place or

anything else. I can hear children in, say, the fifth grade groan, "Do we have to study 'friends' again?" There is little reason to believe that teachers who cannot make history and geography interesting would do any better with 'roles'" (Engle, 1980, p. 588).

Citizenship education and scope and sequence were identified as prime curriculum requirements during the early to mid-1980s (Hahn, 1985; Morrisett, 1986), and Engle's (1984) insistent voice attempted to agitate NCSS, champion of the status quo, toward the progressive left:

> I am disappointed because the scope and sequence does not really come to grips with the crisis in citizenship we are experiencing in this country. Neither does it face up to why the social studies has been so ineffectual in influencing the intelligent behavior of citizens. Ignoring the criticism leveled at the social studies in every study made in recent years, the Task Force offers us business as usual, a few inconsequential changes in sequence, a new topic here and there, but in the main the same old tired subject centered curriculum including American history three times over, which has proven so ineffectual in the past. In the almost total absence in the report of a rationale for teaching the social studies, appropriate to democracy and intelligence and appropriate to a nation and a world that is beset with problems, we are encouraged, if not actually required, to continue in the same old way with the textbook exposition of subjects, watered down and overly simple representation of disciplines and not disciplined study at all, facts, too many of them, all neatly boxed in textbooks and ready to be delivered to passive and unthinking and unquestioning students who will be expected to return them verbatim. It is as if we the teachers have all the answers. It is as if the world has no problems and above all no one should be encouraged or helped to do any thinking about them (pp. 1–2).

In addition to his appeal to the Task Force that the general tone of the scope and sequence be reversed, Engle (1984) posed four concrete alternatives to the task force's sequence:

1. that American history be studied more maturely, at a higher grade level, by organizing it around the study of "persistent problems" in American history, or by organizing the study around the validation of key truth claims made in the text or around the definitions used, or even, by organizing the study around historiographic problems in the text;

2. that geography in grades III, IV, and VII should be brought to focus on such problems as those of declining scarce resources, pollution of the world's environment and over population of the globe rather than to focus exclusively on the relationship between space, time and culture;

3.   the emphasis suggested by the Task Force in grade IX should be skewed more from describing social and economic systems as they exist, as if they were finished products about which there can be no quarrel, to an identification of the problems of justice and economy which face the United States and the entire world; and

4.   the study of broad social problems should be [integrated] into the curriculum throughout rather than to be left to incidental treatment or relegated to one of six electives in grade XII as is suggested by the Task Force. (pp. 8–9).

Two years later in their proposed scope and sequence model, Engle and Ochoa (1986) presented the following guidelines for their curriculum:

1.   *The curriculum should be confrontational rather than strictly expository.* It should confront students with important questions and problems for which answers are not readily available. The study of problems needs to be open ended, in the hypothetical mode and without the pressure for closure on a correct answer.

2.   *The curriculum should be highly selective.* The topics to be chosen should be those having the greatest potential for encouraging and supporting thinking, and even controversy, about an important social problem. Traditional topics for which no such connection can be conceived should be dropped from the curriculum.

3.   *Each unit of instruction should be organized around an important problem in society that is to be studied to the greatest depth possible, given the circumstances of schooling, as well as with as much independence from the other problems selected for study as is reasonable.* Problems may take the form of judgments of the "rightness" or "wrongness" of actions [taken vis-à-vis] important matters in the past and in the present; or they may take the form of a search for a solution, however tentative, of pressing social problems. Variations of the first form of the problem would be the verification of different versions of past events or the construction from raw data of one's own version of these events. In some cases, the very discovery within a general state of public uneasiness or concern of what the problem is, and why it exists, is in itself an important social insight.

4.   *The curriculum should utilize relatively large quantities of data from a variety of sources such as history, the social sciences, literature and journalism, as well as (and possibly most important) from students' first-hand experiences.* In all likelihood, greater quantities of materials would be used than is ordinarily possible under ground-covering techniques. The information sought, however, would be utilized as evidence in making decisions and would not require memorization (p. 515).

It should be noted that the authors did not build a scope and sequence in the traditional sense (Leming, 1994). Indeed, the most noticeable omission from this document was a specific sequence of courses. There were 24 scope and sequence criteria the aforementioned NCSS committee used to critique each model. The report went on to reveal that there exists a lack of consensus on the question of the precise nature of a scope-and-sequence model. If placed on a spectrum, the six models would constitute the gamut from those "fully developed with options" at one end to "conceptual background for a curriculum" at the other (Ad Hoc Committee, 1989).

Ultimately, the Engle/Ochoa model suffered a double setback: not only was their model rejected due to its failure to incorporate NCSS criteria but Leming (1989) utilized the Engle/Ochoa book to undergird/support his theory that university professors had lost contact with the reality of the social studies classroom. Ochoa (1991) believed that one of the reasons for the rejection of their model was the deficiency of prescribing courses at each grade level.

EDUCATION FOR
DEMOCRATIC CITIZENSHIP

Ultimately, Engle and Ochoa would enhance their model greatly in their 1988 publication *Education for Democratic Citizenship: Decision Making in the Social Studies*. In fact, it was Ochoa's recollection that the two of them were both thinking about authoring a book. She had assumed that Engle was already thinking about writing a book on the history of the social studies rather than one centering on the reflective philosophy (Ochoa, 1991).

The rationale for this curriculum was based on democratic principles. Democracy, of course, is such a relative term since any group, conservative or liberal, patriotic or revolutionary, can fashion their own definition by wrapping it around their own political agenda. That said, Engle and Ochoa took a progressive bearing by crystallizing their definition of democracy through the lenses of such luminaries as Broudy (1981) Myrdahl (1944), Niebuhr (1971), Murray (1964) and Johann (1965). According to the authors, teachers should move their students in a direction where they become aware of the rights granted to each of the nation's citizens, cherish the diversity of its citizenry and maintain the nation's democratic values through an open discussion of those issues that are deemed important. They also believed that teachers should help their students to come to an understanding and appreciation as to why and how the diversity of the American culture encourages the dominant and minority voices to deliberate over the definition of democracy and how best to make it work. The dominant voice should not be permitted to establish permanent control.

Engle and Ochoa (1988) asserted "we cannot hope to advance the development of democratic citizenship by imitating educational models based on autocracy" (p. 11). In part, what they were saying was that if schools are to cultivate and inspire democratic principles, educators must realize that schools are not erected as democratic institutions. Put another way, and Engle and Ochoa would be in agreement with this, until those inside and outside the educational arena mobilize to propel school reform toward the establishment and implementation of a true democratic model for schools, educators are bound to continue to simply pay lip service to the concept of democracy via their rhetoric and contrived actions in the classroom (Beane & Apple, 1995).

The central focus of *Education for Democratic Citizenship: Decision Making in the Social Studies* highlights the twin cornerstones of socialization and countersocialization. Socialization necessitated that students be inculcated with the existing customs, traditions, rules, and practices of the general society and subcultures to which they belong. Part of the U.S. educational prescription is to preserve the existing order. Students should possess a basic understanding and appreciation of the culture and heritage of their country and ethnic background. The elementary grades should use socialization as the primary philosophical foundation due to the student's undeveloped reflective skills. The problem that persisted throughout the authors' careers that continued to amaze and embitter them was observing social studies teachers, especially secondary teachers, who fashioned their classroom environment around the usage of the textbook and teacher dominated monologues. Hence, the creation of its counterpart: countersocialization. One problem with education was that many students were memorizing facts and principles without being asked to analyze, synthesize, and evaluate what they learned. Engle and Ochoa felt quite strongly that a constituent component of education should be one that emphasizes independent thinking and responsible social criticism. In light of that, they believed that decision-making and problem-solving skills should be implemented in order for the student to confront, deliberate and act upon situations that they will meet in real life.

Engle and Ochoa (1988) assert that the process of countersocialization "can begin at the elementary level" (p. 30). The authors refer to "the increasing maturity and intellectual capability of students" as justification to begin the countersocialization process at that time (Engle & Ochoa, 1988, p. 32). If educators are to begin to initiate their students into this model they must rely upon their professional judgment to ascertain the readiness of the students, their families, and community standards to handle such a change from a traditional educational philosophy and pedagogy. This, in turn, raises the issue of the discussion of controversial issues in the classroom, such as whether teachers should discuss with fifth grade students, for example, the pros and cons of saying the Pledge of Allegiance (Kavett, 1976)? The authors suggest that no better opportunity exists than to implement these thinking skills in conjunction with the issues-approach and social studies education. If students are to become participatory citizens and good decision makers, it is of greater importance to focus on helping people make intelligent and responsible decisions for themselves than it is to tell them what to think (Kurfman, 1977).

For Engle and Ochoa, an open curriculum is necessary to the sufficient development of the issues centered approach to social studies education as opposed to a closed curriculum determined solely by subject design. Accordingly, "the key to a curriculum that purports to prepare citizens of a democracy is its capacity to encourage young citizens to think and to make considered decisions" (Engle & Ochoa 1988, p. 127). The open curriculum features a topical design with the necessary flexibility to incorporate content pertinent to the student's life that is "related to ways of treating topics so that they are in a continuous state of change" (Engle & Longstreet, 1972, p. 27). In this regard, the proposed curriculum should provide a more probing treatment of problems, ideas, values, and materials covering fewer topics than usual, going deeper into each (Engle & Ochoa, 1986).

Obviously, in developing such a curriculum, curriculum developers and teachers would have to decide which issues are to be dealt with in the classroom and how much time should be spent on each. Materials from the social sciences and the humanities would have to be incorporated in order to furnish students the best available evidence from which decisions are to be made. Ultimately, such an approach will present curriculum developers and teachers with the problem of fitting this model into a scope and sequence pattern. Furthermore, if flexibility is the by-word for this curriculum—and it is—teachers may be ill-prepared to handle the constant stream of decisions inherent in this model (Jenness, 1990; Leslie & Lewis, 1990).

Participation is the key that unlocks the door to questioning and analyzing values and beliefs (Levitt & Longstreet, 1993). In that regard, teachers must be prepared to help students develop the skills to take an active and thoughtful part in the discussion, analysis and evaluation of issues and their potential solutions (Engle, 1986). Ideally, schools are sites "where students can learn and practice the skills of democratic participation necessary for a critical understanding of the wider political, social, and cultural processes that structure American society"(Giroux, 1985, p. 61). Social studies teachers should not be in the business of perpetuating the notion that all is right in the world, as that would be fantasy. Ultimately, it is incumbent upon teachers to attempt to present what is right and wrong; in essence, a slice of reality. In this regard, Engle (1982) had the following to say:

> . . . .the school has no business to indoctrinate. . .the task of the school is to make the student intelligent about his culture. . . . So it turns out that the right to doubt as by citing contradictory facts used to support a belief or the inducement of perplexity as by citing conflicting beliefs, become important tools in teaching (p. 49).

Positive reviews of the Engle/Ochoa book emanated from inside the social studies' "reflective camp." The praise was for the authors' commitment to democracy and reflective citizenship in the schools, a balanced approach to socialization and countersocialization that required teachers to reflect on their notions of curriculum and instruction, and its suggestions regarding diverse forms of assessment aimed at stimulating students to cultivate their critical thinking skills (Haas, 1988; M. Nelson 1988; J. Nelson 1988).

On the other hand, criticisms of the Engle/Ochoa book noted some of the flaws that have dogged the reflective tradition for years. Chamberlain's (1990) review, for example, cited the lack of development of students' skill in regard to their "exerting power and influence, or enhancing a sense of [their] political efficacy" as the major criticisms of this book (pp. 174–175). Moreover, he asserted that Engle's and Ochoa's good citizen was a "passive knower," one who is concerned about the intellectual aspects of the decision making process but lacks any responsibility or knowledge about converting that information into social action (Chamberlain, 1990). In his rebuttal, Engle admitted that more could have been articulated relevant to the "action-based component" (Engle & Ochoa 1986, p. 523; Engle & Ochoa 1988, p. 146), but countered that Chamberlain missed the entire point of the book: social action cannot take place unless you have a reflective citizenry that can evaluate evidence and use reason and judgment to reach important decisions (Engle, 1990).

In his criticism of the book, Leming (1989) suggested that conflicting agendas existed between the liberal-minded university professors and the conservative thinking classroom teachers. He contended that the university types are bound together by a code of values stipulating that the American project is beset by myriad problems that must be solved, that the role of citizenship as the primary rationale of social education has not been clearly validated and discussed, and that a balanced condition has yet to be achieved between teaching commitment and critical thought to young people (Leming, 1989). Leming's most resounding rejoinder identified one of the reflective tradition's shortcomings: "There is no evidence to suggest that critical thinking, political attitudes, or political participation are to any practical extent affected by the current curricula" (Leming, 1989, p. 407).

A year later, Engle reminded this author [Previte] that no matter how logical an educational philosophy may sound, the litmus test of that philosophy should be based on hard data:

> I am afraid you give me too much credit [for the philosophical underpinnings of the reflective tradition]. It is a little frightening to me to have such an important topic hang so much on my opinion supported as it is, by so little hard data. The Indiana Study went a short way toward establishing a relationship between exposure to problem solving and citizen behavior but this study did not afford anything like conclusive evidence. But neither do the expositor-memoritor people support their claim with really hard evidence. Short answer paper and pencil test of facts remembered have practically no validity for predicting the behavior or [sic] citizens. Both sides are talking through their hats. We have logic on our side but little else (Engle, 1989, p. 2).

Engle and Ochoa were also accused of depicting an "us versus them" mentality; that is, those of the reflective tradition (us) versus those who espouse "memorization, didactic pedagogy, chronological presentation of history, and other violations of their precepts for proper 'social studies' instruction" (them) (Reginer 1989, p. 385).

Engle and Ochoa (1988) believed that the New Social Studies movement failed due to a litany of weaknesses. If we are to learn from the lessons of the past, there are some common denominators that have restricted its move to the front burner of social studies curriculum and instruction. These include:

> . . .lack of a supportive societal context, a school bureaucracy that is extremely impermeable to change, a basic reward system for teachers that reflects the values of order and textbook knowledge, the teachers' own frames of reference in regard to content and student control, and the lack of appropriate instructional materials (Shaver, 1989, p. 195)

A decade later, Rochester (2003) criticized the progressivist philosophy of Engle and Ochoa for "subtle devaluing of positive aspects of American democracy" (p. 17), focusing on critical thinking rather than "basic familiarity"(p. 17), equating knowledge transmission with indoctrination (p. 18), anti-intellectualism, and turning students into cynics (p. 19). These criticisms have been part and parcel of the conservative mantra over the previous half-century (Bestor, 1953; Ravitch & Finn, 1987; Rickover, 1959). Such criticisms, in turn, were addressed by a number of university professors known for their staunch defense of issues-centered social studies. Ross and Marker (2005), for example, countered that the Deweyan model of social studies, with its focus on deliberation and democracy, encourages students "to engage in careful consideration and discussion of alternatives for the purpose of creating a better life" (p. 141). Kornfield (2005) admonished Rochester for creating a frightening image of "progressive university professors who are out of touch with mainstream American values" (p. 144). On a personal note, my twenty years of teaching secondary social studies was highly influenced by the Engle/Ochoa issues-centered philosophy. Indeed, my classroom was transformed into a "think tank" where students addressed past and present issues/questions from different political and ideological positions. True, this did lead to disagreement about democratic values, and involved numerous deliberations over what it meant to be an effective, patriotic citizen. Foregoing the banking method of schooling where factual information is deposited with students for future use (Friere, 1970), the Engle and Ochoa model created a classroom atmosphere that emphasized socialization, counter socialization, decision making, reflective thinking, and deliberation.

Education for Democratic Citizenship was a personal and professional triumph for the authors that would place their work alongside the other seminal works of the reflective tradition (Hunt & Metcalf, 1955; Newmann & Oliver, 1970; Oliver & Shaver, 1966).

The knowledge that the NCSS Task Force on Scope and Sequence would not recognize their model was a bitter pill to swallow, especially for Engle. Even though the Task Force did offer an olive branch by suggesting to teachers and curriculum developers that they should be aware of the important roles of socialization and social criticism (National Council for the Social Studies, 1990, p. 25), Engle was upset that content coverage instead of in-depth analysis of problems would still rule the day:

> I see this [meaning, the Task Force report's aforementioned deficiencies] as the same old stuff, backward-looking, memory-bound, and unequal to the needs of today's world. Protesting the charge given to the "Commission on the Social Studies," I see this [meaning, the curriculum models selected by the NCSS Task Force on Scope and Sequence] as being too narrow and parochial to bring about the changes so badly needed in the social studies today. Protesting the Council's inability to lead in making changes in the social studies, I see a new need for a responsive social studies in a world of nuclear power, environmental disaster, television, politics, and drugs. I hope someday that the social studies profession will grow up, eschew mere book-learning, and do something positive about the problems of the real world in which we live (Engle quoted in Holt ,1989, p. 27).

STRENGTHS AND WEAKNESSES

Engle and Ochoa (1988) specify that "teachers who are willing to admit that they do not know a particular answer or that they are not sure that their answer or that of the textbook is correct are serving as models of democratic behavior" (p. 38). Recognizing his/her content inadequacies will require some moral backbone. Increased pressure will also be placed on the teacher to identify alternative sources of information so that he/she and the students can solve such problems that arise. How will this be interpreted by the students? Will they view this as a part of democratic behavior or as an inadequate teacher who lacks a solid content background?

To integrate student criticism into the classroom environment, teachers must begin to develop in their students an open mind vis-à-vis questioning what are often perceived as sacrosanct beliefs, positions, decisions, actions, and values within our society. As for beliefs and values, they are the cement that holds the issues structure together. Therefore, it will become necessary to compare and contrast those beliefs and values that are at the core or our very being. If the role of teachers is to prepare students to take their rightful place as effective citizens to be able to face the torrent of events and experiences that life will present to them *and* to make decisions that will help them survive, beliefs and values must be questioned and deliberated over without fear of scorn or reprisal. Engle and Ochoa (1988) believe that it is through the use of definitional, evidential, policy, value, and speculative types of probing questions that help develop teacher and student reflective thinking (pp. 40–47). In accordance with Dewey, they perceive education as "that of procuring the postponement of immediate action upon desire until observation and judgment have intervened" (Dewey, 1938, p. 69) Citing Alan Griffin, Engle and Lawrence Metcalf recognized that a lack of questioning of the most basic values would lead schools down the path toward authoritarianism that is inimical to the fundamental principles of the issues approach (Engle, 1982a, pp. 48–49; Metcalf, 1963, p. 934). Engle clearly supported this concept of social criticism when he stated that "without social criticism, the student cannot learn how to question and explain what is happening around him/her. Maintaining the status quo, i.e., the expository method, renders the student effectively brainwashed and incapable of critical thought" (Engle, 1986a, p. 21).

For too many years, the social studies educator has maintained the status quo by implementing the standard operating procedures of a social studies classroom: implementing the textbook as the major, and sometimes only, source of information—and often utilizing it as an encyclopedia. Teachers should help students to recognize and use a text for what it really is: just another source with its own particular biases, vantage points, and interpretations. A second procedure teachers abuse is employing the lecture method to continue the tradition that exposing the student to information will turn him/her into the good citizen. Finally, teachers usually present knowledge following a chronological scheme. It is no wonder that students have been anesthetized by social studies practices; they feel as if they are playing "Jeopardy" or "Trivial Pursuit." Ultimately, many do not see the relevance of—nor have they been presented the opportunity to question the pertinence of—what they study in their social studies class vis-à-vis their social milieu (Van Sickle, 1990). Many educators do not seem to appreciate, let alone abide by, Dewey's (1916) point that it is the responsibility of the teacher to evaluate the applicability of the subject matter to be presented in relation to the life experiences of the pupil.

If such a reflective educational model is going to be incorporated into the public school curriculum (particularly in the social studies) then teacher education programs will have to radically alter the focus of the courses they teach. Professors and graduate students, who teach social studies methods courses, will have to become role models and integrate such theories and practices into their classroom repertoire of classroom strategies. The fact is, though, an issues-centered approach is definitely bucking against tradition. Some may just let this pass right by and continue to live by a "don't rock the boat" mentality.

Moving from a traditional to a progressive educational philosophy entails a great deal of work and reflection on the part of the teacher. Indeed, it necessitates a philosophical change of direction for those who want to become progressive educators: instead of using the language (and practice) of the status quo (transmission, imposition, exposition, and silence), the language of reflection, possibility and critique (change, hypothetical, creativity, social and active) must be employed (Dewey 1938; Oldendorf,1989). That said, it is critical to take into account Giroux's (1981) warning when he cautioned teachers that "critical reasoning becomes an empty exercise if students do not learn how to both reflect on, as well as transform, the nature and meaning of their own lived-worlds" (p. 124).

THE SIGNIFICANCE OF
ACADEMIC FREEDOM

Over 70 years ago, John Dewey (1936) asserted that:

> [t]oday freedom of teaching and learning on the part of instructors and students is imperatively necessary for that kind of intelligent citizenship that is genuinely free to take part in the social reconstructions without which democracy will die. . . . Since freedom of mind and freedom of expression are the root of all freedom, to deny freedom in education is a crime against democracy. (p. 165)

To act in accordance with Dewey's position presupposes the need for greater academic freedom in the classroom, particularly in an issues-centered classroom where many issues under discussion may be of a controversial nature.

For the problems approach to function properly, an outlet must be forged for those highly-charged and volatile issues to be identified, discussed, and resolved. In this regard, Engle (1986a) stated that "critical and controversial issues must be studied not from an objective and controversy-free treatment of the problem—one that satisfies everyone and is safe for children to hear. So far as I can see, no consideration was given to the possibility or propriety of thrusting tender minds into the center of a controversy and helping them work their way out" (p. 22). That, of course, is easier said than done; and may induce, at least in some school districts, battles of the will between teachers and parents, teachers and site administrators, and teachers and central office administrators, and teachers and school board members.

Implications of the Issues-centered Approach Classroom for the Teacher

One of the reasons children fail to remember or internalize the history they study is because too much information is taught too quickly, and little of it is reinforced (or when it is, it is done in a perfunctory manner). An issues-centered approach is capable of ameliorating this problem. Using an issues-centered approach requires serious teachers and students to conduct in-depth analyses, which, in turn, lends itself to greater assurance that the skills of analyzing, synthesizing, and evaluation will occur than that found in classrooms driven by a pedagogy focused on memorization and comprehension alone (Goodland, 1984; Mckee, 1988; Newmann, 1986).

Many teachers who are tied down to a chronology-based course of study are not only frustrated but tormented when the end of the year approaches and only half of the course content has been covered. The issues-centered approach allows for greater flexibility and thus greater discussion of both modern and contemporary issues/events in the classroom. Incorporating such an approach would make curriculum development more current, creative, dynamic and, hopefully, relevant to the lives of the students. Indeed, as VanSickle (1990) suggested, instead of waiting five to ten years to change or update the curriculum, usually precipitated by an outdated textbook, teachers need to view curriculum as an on-going process (see VanSickle, 1990, pp. 23–27, 59). The occurrence of "recent" events would require an annual review of the curriculum. This would permit the teacher to analyze and evaluate content that would have greater relevance and meaning to the student.

Since textbooks are not constructed with the issues model in mind, teachers will need to increase their efforts to incorporate eclectic and rich sources of information into their classrooms. Today, of course, this is much easier than in the past when teachers did not have ready access to the wealth of information available on the Internet.

Teachers must be ready, willing and able to move beyond addressing a single discipline in the issues-centered classroom. More specifically, the social sciences, according to Engle (1994), cannot be taken separately to teach the problem solving approach in the classroom. The humanities must also be included in order to avail students of different points of view and value judgments, and to introduce them to numerous others types and sources of information.

Teachers who wish to retain the status quo in social studies classrooms because of the need to maintain control in the classroom may well be flummoxed by an issues-centered approach. Once students receive a taste of a democratic classroom, with less teacher talk and more student talk and the introduction of controversial issues, the paradigm of the classroom begins to change. In part, this means that the "straight-forward exposition and textbooks" syndrome, with their accompanying teacher and student manuals and workbooks, will be shoved aside. In turn, this means the emergence of the use of multiple sources and various, interactive pedagogical methods that encourage open-endedness

Finally, if and when the issues centered approach is implemented, it is possible that teachers would then take the opportunity to expand the basic knowledge and comprehension type tests into evaluation instruments that challenge students to employ higher order thinking and decision making skills. In this regard, Engle and Ochoa (1988) listed six skills that evaluation instruments, combined with the teacher-based objectives, should include:

1. sizing up a problem and identifying the central conflict or the main issue, including the underlying values that are at stake;
2. selecting information that is relevant to the problem and relating it logically to proposed solutions;
3. judging the reliability of various sources of information, including firsthand experience and research based information;
4. seeing a problem in its broadest context including the value considerations involved;
5. building a scenario of likely consequences regarding any proposed solution to a problem; and
6. making reasoned judgments where the evidence is conflicting or where there is conflict between desired values (p. 180).

RESEARCH

The need for greater dissemination and interpretation of empirical data about issues centered education that was a major concern for Engle and Ochoa twenty years ago has shown some progress. Still, there is a continuing exigency for further classroom observation of issues centered education to extend Engle's and Ochoa's argument that a reflective approach would produce student intellectual and civic growth (Jerich, 1996).

John Allen Rossi's (1995) research into issues-centered classrooms provided invaluable data vis-à-vis the quest to determine if issues-centered education increases student knowledge, cognition, and civic awareness. Rossi observed and collected data on two classrooms: the first was an elective course on future studies and the second was a one semester course on contemporary issues using the Oliver, Shaver, and Newmann model. He reported only on the second classroom that contained 26 students, 14 female and 12 male, the majority of whom were from white, middle and upper class homes. Rossi selected three students to interview from a suggested list of names provided by the classroom teacher. His findings indicated that relevant issues, time to read and reflect prior to class, and time to voice positions in class did lead to more critical thinking than in a didactic classroom. He also found that some teachers and students viewed their classroom roles differently; teachers moved away from the status quo to where control of the classroom was partially relinquished in order to provide students with the freedom to think critically and speak to the issues introduced in class. Be that as it may, there were problems; students would not complete their readings assigned for homework, some felt uncomfortable speaking in such a large group, others did not enjoy the "openness" of the class and yearned for a teacher-dominated environment. Rossi concluded that "this research both confirms and disconfirms the value of in-depth study" (p. 116).

In a follow up study, however, Rossi and Pace (1998) discovered that utilizing the Engle and Ochoa model with low achieving high school students uncovered a number of dilemmas, including unit planning, harnessing student attention, student comprehension of content, student autonomy, student defense of their positions, and teacher planning time (pp. 405–406). Moving from a traditional to a progressive educational philosophy entails a great deal of work and reflection on the part of the teacher. Formulating authentic unit questions, developing imaginative and substantial activities and strategies, and allowing students to do democratic work in the classroom can be somewhat threatening to teachers who have viewed themselves as the sage on the stage. Furthermore, low-achieving high school students may not view social studies as relevant to their lives. They may also be lacking in questioning techniques and general inquisitiveness by the time they reach high school. Many are more like (a) sieves and Teflon, because very little appears to stick, and (b) bobble head dolls (where they simply accept—with little to no thought—what is presented to them) because they have not been taught or given much opportunity to play the role of citizen/critic.

Chilcoat and Ligon's (2000) study of three 5th–6th grade classes utilizing the Engle/Ochoa model concluded that issues-centered instruction can find varying degrees of teacher/student acceptance and academic success (p. 266). A majority of the students posited that the study of issues did grab their interest and the classroom work provided them with opportunities to identify problems/issues, conduct research, evaluate evidence, ask questions, analyze points of view, make decisions, write letters, vote, participate in discussions and deliberations and voice their positions. Consistent with the research conducted by Carole Hahn (1996a, 1966b), the students found issues-centered work to be enjoyable and interesting.

CONCLUSIONS

As for the impact of Engle's and Ochoa's work, it seems worth noting that Leming and Nelson's citation analysis published in the 1991 *Handbook of Research On Social Studies Teaching and Learning* indicated that *Education for Democratic Citizenship* placed third in the "most frequently cited source" category (pp. 171–172). Additionally, *Education for Democratic Citizenship* was cited 35 times in the NCSS publication *Handbook On Teaching Social Issues* (Evans & Saxe, 1996).

Ultimately, Engle was vastly disappointed with the lack of acceptance of an issues centered philosophy in U.S. social studies classrooms (Previte, 2007). Gaining acceptance of an issues centered model in the U.S. social studies classrooms continues to be an uphill struggle (Evans, 2004; Kohlmeier, Mitchell, Saye, & Brush, 2006). Ochoa-Becker (2006) believes that schools have more or less dropped the ball in fulfilling their role of citizenship education. Preserving the status quo appears to have been and continues to be the guiding light for many social studies educators. Conversely, hope continues to spring eternal as a result of the issues centered philosophy resonating with a new generation of educators who seem determined to carry on the work of their predecessors and follow in the footsteps laid down, in part, by the important work of such scholars/teacher educators as Shirley Engle and Anna Ochoa-Becker.

REFERENCES

Ad Hoc Committee on Scope and Sequence (1989). Report of the ad hoc committee on scope and sequence. *Social Education, 53*(6), 375–376.

Adler, M. J. (1982). *The Paideia proposal: An educational manifesto.* New York: Macmillan.

Anyon, J. (1979). Ideology and United States history textbooks. *Harvard Educational Review, 49*(3), 361–386

Beane, J. A., & Apple, M. W. (1995). The case for democratic schools. In M. W. Apple & J. A. Beane (Eds.), *Democratic schools* (pp. 1–25). Alexandria, VA.: Association for Supervision and Curriculum Development.

Bestor, A. (1953). *Educational wastelands: The retreat from learning in our public schools.* Urbana: University of Illinois Press.

Bloom, A. (1987). *The closing of the American mind.* Chicago, IL: University of Chicago.

Broudy H. S. (1981). *Truth and credibility: The citizen's dilemma.* New York: Longmans.

Chamberlain, C. (1990). Book review of *Education for democratic citizenship. Theory and Research in Social Education, 18*(2), 174–175.

Cheney, L. V. (1987). *American memory: A report on the humanities in the nation's public schools.* Washington, D.C.: National Endowment for the Humanities.

Chilcoat, G. W., & Ligon, J. A. (2000). Issues-centered instruction in the elementary social studies classroom. *Theory and Research in Social Education, 28*(2), 220–272.

Dewey, J. (1916). *Democracy and education.* New York: The Macmillan Company.

Dewey, J. (1936). The social significance of academic freedom. *The Social Frontier, 2,* 165–167.

Dewey, J. (1938). *Experience and education.* New York: Macmillan Publishing Company.

Engle, S. H. (1977). The search for a more adequate definition of citizenship education. Paper presented at the Fifty-Seventh Annual Meeting of the National Council for the Social Studies, Cincinnati, OH.

Engle, S. H. (1980). React to the "social roles" proposal of SPAN. *Social Education, 44*(7), 587–588.

Engle, S. H. (1981). Personal communication with James P. Shaver, October 7. Palo Alto, CA: Hoover Institution on War, Revolution and Peace, Stanford University.

Engle, S. H. (1982a). Alan Griffin, 1907–1964. *Journal of Thought, 17*(3), 45–54.

Engle, S. H. (1982b). Personal communication to James P. Shaver, January 13. Palo Alto, CA: Hoover Institution on War, Revolution and Peace, Stanford University.

Engle, S. H. (1984). Testimony in the scope and sequence in the social studies. Stanford, CA.: Hoover Institution Archives.

Engle, S. H. (1986a). Late night thoughts about the new social studies. *Social Education, 50*(1), 20–22.

Engle, S. H. (1986b). Shirley Engle (1907–). Unpublished. Document in Mark Previte's files.

Engle S. H. (1989). Letter to the author, July 6.

Engle, S. H. (1990). Response to Mr. Chamberlain's review of *Education for democratic citizenship*. *Theory and Research in Social Education, 18*(2), 181–182.

Engle, S. H. (1994). Introduction. In M. R. Nelson (Ed.), *The social studies in secondary education: A reprint of the seminal 1916 report with annotations and commentaries* (pp. vii–viii). Bloomington, IN: Eric Clearinghouse for Social Studies/Social Science Education.

Engle, S. H., & Longstreet, W. S. (1972). *A design for social education in the open curriculum*. New York: Harper & Row, Publishers.

Engle, S. H., & Longstreet, W. S. (1978), Education for a changing society. In A. Hoppe & G. V. Flannery (Eds.), *Improving the human condition: A curricular response to critical realities* (pp. 226–259). Washington, D.C.: Association for Supervision and Curriculum Development.

Engle, S. H., & Ochoa, A. S.(1986). A curriculum for democratic citizenship. *Social Education, 50*(7), 514–516, 518–525.

Engle, S. H., & Ochoa, A. S. (1988). *Education for democratic citizenship: Decision making in the social studies*. New York: Teachers College Press.

Evans, R. W. (2004). *The social studies wars: What should we teach the children* New York: Teachers College Press.

Evans, R. W., & Saxe, D. W. (Eds.). (1996). Materials and resources. *Handbook On Teaching Social Issues, NCSS Bulletin 93* (pp. 338–379). Washington, D.C.: National Council for the Social Studies.

Finn, C. E., & Ravitch, D. (1988). *What do our 17-year olds know? A report on the First National Assessment of History and Literature*. New York: HarperCollins.

Friere, P. (1970). *Pedagogy of the oppressed*. New York: Continuum.

Giroux, H. A. (1981). *Ideology, culture, and the process of schooling*. Philadelphia, PA: Temple University Press.

Giroux, H.A. (1985). Thunder on the right: Education and the ideology of the quick fix. *Curriculum Inquiry, 15*(1), 57–62.

Goodlad, J. (1984). *A place called school*. New York: McGraw-Hill.

Hahn, C. L. (1985). The status of the social studies in the public schools of the United States: Another look. *Social Education, 49*(3), 220–223.

Hahn, C. L. (1996a). Investigating controversial issues at election time: Political socialization research. *Social Education, 60*(6), 348–350.

Hahn, C. L. (1996b). Research on issues-centered social studies, pp. 25–41. In R. W. Evans & D. W. Saxe (Eds.) *Handbook on Teaching Social Issues*. Washington, D.C.: The National Council for the Social Studies.

Haas, M. (1988). Book Review: *Education for democratic citizenship: Decision making in the social studies*. *The Social Studies, 79*(5), 246.

Hirsch, Jr., E. D. (1987). *Cultural literacy: What every American needs to know*. Boston, MA: Houghton Mifflin.

Holt, E. R. (1989). *ICSS at 50: Remembering for renewal. 50th anniversary commemorative edition*. Bloomington, IN: Indiana Council for the Social Studies.

Hunt, M.P., & Metcalf, L. E. (1955). *Teaching high school social studies: Problems in reflective thinking and social understanding*. New York: Harper and Row.

Jerich, K. H. (1996). Supervision for teacher growth in reflective, issues-centered teaching practice, pp. 306–315. In R. W. Evans & D. W. Saxe (Eds.), *Handbook* on teaching social issues, Bulletin 92. Washington, D.C.: National Council for the Social Studies.

Johann, R. O. (1965). Authority and responsibility. In J. C. Murray (Ed.), Freedom and man (pp. 141–151). New York: P. J. Kenedy & Sons.

Kavett, H. (1976). How do we stand with the Pledge of Allegiance today? Social Education, 40(3), 135–140.

Kohlmeier, J., Mitchell, L., Saye, J., & Brush, T. (April, 2006). Meeting the challenges of problem-based historical inquiry in a challenging environment. Presented at the annual meeting of the American Educational Research Association, San Francisco, CA.

Kornfield, J. (2005). Framing the conversation: Social studies education and the neoconservative agenda. The Social Studies, 96(4), 143–148.

Leming, J. S. (1981). Moral advocacy and social education. Social Education, 45(3), 201, 205–207.

Leming, J. S. (1989). The two cultures of social studies education. Social Education, 53(6), 404–408.

Leming, J. S. (1994) Past as prologue: A defense of traditional patterns of social studies instruction. In M. R. Nelson (Ed.), The future of the social studies (pp. 17–23). Boulder, CO: Social Science Education Consotrium, Inc.

Leming, J., Ellington, L. & Porter-Magee, K. (2003). Where did the social studies go wrong? Thomas B. Fordham Foundation, Washington, DC.

Leming, J. S., & Nelson, M. (1995). A citation analysis of the Handbook of Research on Social Studies Teaching and Learning. Theory and Research in Social Education, 23 (2), 169–182.

Leslie,C., & Shawn, L. (1990). The failure of teacher ed. Newsweek, 116(14), 58–60.

Longstreet, W. S. (1982). Education for citizenship: New dimensions. Social Education, 53(1), 41–45.

McKee, S. J.(1988, October). Impediments to implementing critical thinking. Social Education, 52(), 444–446.

Metcalf, L. E. (1963). Research on teaching the social studies. In N. L. Gage (Ed.), Handbook of research on teaching (pp. 929–965). Chicago, IL: Rand McNally.

Monteverde, F. E. (2002). Anna Sultanoff Ochoa-Becker, pp. 137–139. In M. S. Crocco & O. L. Davis, Jr. (Eds.) Building a legacy: Women in social education 1784–1984, NCSS bulletin 100. Washington, D.C.: National Council for the Social Studies.

Morrissett, I. (1986). Status of social studies: The mid-1980s. Social Education, 50(4), 303–310.

Murray, J. C. (1964). Challenges to democracy: A tenth anniversary symposium of the fund for the republic. New York: Praeger.

Myrdahl, G. (1944). An American dilemma: The negro problem and modern democracy. New York: Harper & Brothers.

The National Commission on Excellence in Education (1984). Meeting the challenge of a nation at risk. Cambridge, MA: USA Research.

National Council for the Social Studies (1990). Social studies curriculum planning resources. Washington, DC: National Council for the Social Studies.

National Council for the Social Studies Essentials of Education Statement (1980). *Essentials of social studies.* Washington, D.C.: National Council for the Social Studies.

Nelson, J. L.(1988). Social studies and the study of controversy. *Phi Delta Kappan, 70*(3), 268.

Nelson, M. R. (1988). *Education for democratic citizenship:* Book review. *Educational Leadership, 46*(2), 86.

Newmann, F. M. (1986). Priorities for the future: Toward a common agenda. *Social Education, 50*(4), 240–250.

Newmann, F. N., & Oliver, D. W. (1970). *Clarifying public controversy: An approach to social studies.* Boston, MA: Little, Brown, and Co.

Niebuhr, R. (1971). Democracy's distinction and danger. *Center Magazine, 4*(4), 1–4.

Ochoa, A S. (1991). Interview with the author, November 23.

Ochoa-Becker, A. S. (1996). Building a rationale for issues-centered education. In R. W. Evans & D. W. Saxe (Eds.), *Handbook on teaching social issues, Bulletin 9* (pp. 6–13). Washington, D.C.: National Council for the Social Studies.

Ochoa-Becker, A. S. (2006). Social issues and decision making: A career long commitment, pp. 131–144. In S. Totten & J. Pedersen (Eds.), *Researching and teaching social issues: The personal stories and pedagogical efforts of professors of education.* Lanham, MD: Lexington Books.

Oldendorf, S. B. (1989). Vocabularies, knowledge and social action in citizenship education: The Highlander example. *Theory and Research in Social Education, 17*(2), 107–120.

Oliver, D. W., & Shaver, J. P. (1966). *Teaching public issues in the high school.* Boston, MA: Houghton Mifflin Co.

Previte, M.A. (2007). Shirley H. Engle: A Persistent voice for issues centered education. In S. Totten & J. Pedersen (Eds.), *Addressing social issues in the classroom and beyond: The pedagogical efforts of pioneers in the field* (pp. 159–185). Charlotte, NC: Information Age Publishing.

Regnier, P. (1989). Review of S. Engle and A. Ochoa, *Education for democratic citizenship: Decision making in the social studies. Journal of Curriculum Studies, 21*(4), 383–385.

Rickover, H. G. (1959). *Education and freedom.* New York: E. P. Dutton & Co.

Rochester, J. M. (2003). The training of idiots: Civics education in America's schools. In J. Leming, L. Ellington, & K. Porter (Eds.) *Where did social studies go wrong?*

Ross, E. W (2001). *The Social Studies Curriculum: Purposes, Problems, and Possibilities (Revised Edition).* Albany: State University of New York Press.

Ross, E. W. (2001). *The social studies curriculum: Purposes, problems, and possibilities* (revised ed.). Albany: State Univeristy of New York Press.

Ross, E. W., & Marker, P. M. (2005). Social studies: Wrong, right or left? A critical response to the Fordham Institute's *Where did social studies go wrong? The Social Studies, 96*(4), 139–142.

Rossi, J. A. (1995). In-depth study in an issues-oriented social studies classroom. *Theory and Research in Social Education, 23*(2), 88–120.

Rossi, J. A, & Pace, C. M. (1998). Issues-centered instruction with low achieving high school students: The dilemmas of two teachers. *Theory and Research in Social Education, 26*(3), 380–409.

Shaver, J. P. (1978). Personal communication with Shirley H. Engle. February 10. Palo Alto, CA: Hoover Institution on War, Revolution and Peace, Stanford University.

Shaver, J. P. (1982). Personal communication with Shirley H. Engle, January 27. Palo Alto, CA: Hoover Institution on War, Revolution and Peace, Stanford University.

Shaver, J. P. (1989). Lessons from the past: The future of an issues-centered social studies curriculum. *The Social Studies, 80*(5), 192–196.

Stanley, W. B. (1981). Indoctrination and social education: A critical analysis. *Social Education, 45*(3), 200, 202–204.

Superka, D. P., & Hawke, S. (1980). Social roles: A focus for social studies in the 1980s. *Social Education, 44*(5), 577–586.

VanSickle, R. L. (1990). The personal relevance of the social studies. *Social Education, 54*(1), 23–27, 59.

CHAPTER 14

THE MANY FACES OF STS

Social Issues in Science Education

Barbara Spector and Robert Yager

INTRODUCTION

The recent incorporation of social issues into science education has been labeled the science/technology/society (STS) movement. The initial thrust of introducing social issues into science learning and teaching was to make school science more relevant to students in response to their common lament in science classes, "Why do I have to know this?" and their general lack of interest in science. The National Assessment of Educational Progress (NAEP) began tracking student interest in science in 1978. And that initial study and all follow-up studies clearly indicated that student interest in science waned the longer they studied science during their K–12 school years (NAEP, 1978; Yager & Yager, 1985).

Regardless of the specific parameters one uses to identify what a social issue is, it always involves "solving human problems"—which is largely what technology is all about as well. In today's human-made world, most people encounter science through some form of technology about which they can readily see its "usefulness." The focus on the human-made world (i.e., introduction of social issues in science teaching and learning) results in the

Teaching and Studying Social Issues: Major Programs and Approaches, pages 277–311

acceptance of learning about technology as a legitimate part of school science. This is in contrast to post-sputnik reforms of the 1960s that advocated basic science to the exclusion of applied science and technology. The latter concerns were often delegated to the "shop."

Concurrently, world events and advances in cognitive science research supported changes that characterize STS—that is, using social issues in meaningful ways to gain student interest, curiosity, and involvement. Such use demands a change in intended outcomes in science in schools while also requiring altered forms of instruction and assessment. Furthermore, the shift from a focus in the 1960s on increasing the number of scientists in society to a focus in the 1980s on achieving scientific literacy for all citizens also contributed to new outcomes and new ways of teaching.

In 1999, after four years of discussion and debate, the National Science Teachers Association position paper vis-à-vis STS was accepted unanimously by its Board of Directors. A report of the committee proclaimed STS to be "the teaching and learning of science and technology in the context of human experience."

In practice, STS is an umbrella term encompassing a multitude of diverse approaches (subsequently interpretations) for developing a scientifically-literate citizenry by changing what is taught in school science and, (perhaps more importantly) how it is taught. It is interesting to note that STS is the longest-lived reform movement in the history of science education in the United States.

DEFINITIONS IMPORTANT FOR UNDERSTANDING STS

STS includes specific components associated with each of its three parts: science, technology, and society. Science has been defined by Simpson (1963) to include a series of actions. These include:

1. asking questions of nature;
2. thinking about possible answers;
3. collecting data to support proposed "answers"; and
4. sharing evidence to convince others of the validity of the explanations offered.

To "do" science requires that all four facets be experienced by students. Some refer to these steps as "inquiry." The National Research Council's (2000) publication, *Inquiry and the National Science Education Standards,* lists five *essential features* of inquiry as follows:

1. learner engages in scientifically oriented questions;
2. learner gives priority to evidence in responding to questions;

3. learner formulates explanations from evidence;
4. learner connects explanations to scientific knowledge; and
5. learner communicates and justifies explanations.

These essential features cannot be brought about simply by students reading textbooks or watching or listening, respectively, to teachers' demonstrations and lectures.

Content information generated by scientists about the natural world has been archived for the last one hundred years according to the structure of the specific disciplines (e.g., biology, chemistry, physics, earth/space science). These products of science appear in textbooks and encyclopedias. But these products are *not* science. Rather, science is a way of thinking, a culturally derived method for systematically and efficiently exercising genetically-based curiosity of human beings (Spector & Strong, 2001). Science in schools is, however, rarely based on student curiosities and interests, even though they are central to the actual practice of scientists.

Technology is a human activity designed to find solutions to human problems. It is often called the designed world, thus differentiating it from the natural world. It uses many of the same procedures as science. It differs, however, in that the final product is always known while in science the final product is but a better understanding of the natural universe and the objects and events that characterize it.

There are hard and soft technologies: hard technology refers to the hardware and instruments developed for use by humans to solve problems. Soft technologies are the systems involved in the development and use of technological devices (Piel, 1981). Technologies ranging from computers to the space shuttle have altered every aspect of our society, from the generation of wealth (power) to health maintenance (Spector, LaPorta, & Simpson, 1995).

Society, of course, is the organization of humans in functional groups and communities in which humans interact with each other and with the world as they experience it.

The interactions among science, technology, and society are complex. Scientifically, literate citizens must understand these complexities and must be able to make data-based, reasoned decisions that affect their personal lives and that of their communities.

MULTIPLE INTERPRETATIONS OF STS

In 1996, a study of reform initiatives in the U.S. indicated that STS had been interpreted by teachers and university professors in many different ways (Spector & Simpson, 1996). Many equated STS to a curriculum organizer. Others equated it to topics or problems to be studied. Still others equated it to particular instructional strategies.

It is helpful to place the interpretations and misconceptions on a continuum: on the left of the continuum people use traditional textbooks, which are organized around the structure of information archived in particular science disciplines. These individuals consider themselves to be teaching STS because there is a paragraph at the end of each chapter identifying specific applications of the scientific principles in that chapter, or to a technology used in modern society. The goal of these teachers is usually defined as covering information in the textbook. The intended outcome is for students to pass a test that allows them to go to the next grade level for whatever "science" is indicated in a given curriculum plan. Moving to the right on the continuum, people use STS as the label for teaching with themes that cut across all the sciences and focus on current issues (locally, regionally, nationally, and internationally). For example, energy, cause and effect, scale, change over time, environmental problems, and other unifying themes are used to address (talk about) concerns as diverse as plate tectonics and the human digestive system.

Moving even further to the right on the continuum are those who consider teaching STS to be a case where one addresses topics comprised of identifiable components of science, technology, and their effects in society as a whole. In other words, here, changing society, even in the smallest way, is enough to be classified as teaching STS. It could be, for example, as simple as talking about cautions in homes while canning fruit during a unit on microorganisms and disease, or discussion of the use of moving walkways to facilitate passage in airports. This approach often uses existing technologies as the means to interest students in learning basic principles of science inherent in the technology (e.g., physics principles inherent in a toy).

Further to the right on the continuum, certain educators insist there must be a problematic issue, something for which there is no single solution, if teaching is to be labeled STS. Their approach vis-à-vis STS requires risk assessment, cost/benefit analysis, environmental impact analysis, tradeoffs, decision-making, and learners taking action toward mitigating a problem.

In this approach, the needs of individuals and diverse groups with vested interests are considered in decision-making. The interaction of moral and ethical values people derive from ways of knowing other than science, such as religion, philosophy, or aesthetics, become part of the data used in the decision-making process (Spector, 1986). The scientific enterprise is portrayed as a dynamic human endeavor; a part of society in which changes in science and technology affect decisions people make. Furthermore, it is believed that decisions people make also affect scientific and technological developments and the future of our planet.

On the right hand end of the continuum, people interpret STS as a synonym for constructivist epistemology (humans make sense of new data by adding, deleting, or rearranging information in their own unique idiosyncratic cognitive frameworks), learning theory, and/or teaching/learning approaches (Vygotsky, 1978). The intended outcome for students is to learn how to learn, so they are capable and inclined to make reasoned decisions in our science- and technology-driven society. Learners are taught to become scientifically and technologically literate through systematically inquiring into STS events, which are multifaceted issues that challenge society and the future of the planet. Many disciplines are integrated. The people functioning at the right hand end of the continuum use STS as an organizer for the entire curriculum. They assume that information from the individual science disciplines does not provide a meaningful organizer for the school science program. Their rationale is that people make meaning from objects and events in context, on a need to know basis, and words used to describe an idea obtain meaning from the context in which they are used (Spector & Glass, 1991).

HISTORY

Science has been an integral part of the school curriculum throughout the history of education in the United States. Basically, science has been a collection of courses in high school that reflect the major disciplines of science; that is, astronomy, biology (botany and zoology), chemistry, geology (physical geography, earth/space science), physics, and physiology. Although science has enjoyed the status as a core "subject" in the secondary school curriculum, along with language arts, mathematics, social studies, and foreign languages, it has never been considered as basic as language arts and mathematics, presumably because of the special skills characterizing these two curricular areas (reading, writing, speaking, quantification, and measuring) that are generally conceived as requisites for science study.

Unfortunately, high school science is invariably associated with preparation for college. And, the science courses prior to high school are thought to be preparatory for the next science course for the next academic year. Traditionally, and historically, most courses were developed around basic concepts, organized according to the way scientists structure the archived information in disciplines. In more recent years, however, they have been organized according to those concepts perceived as being important in state frameworks or those recognized as basic by various professional groups. In fact, though, the major determiner of science content actually taught in schools has been the information found in standard science textbooks, where there has been found to be less than a ten percent variation among those available for a given grade level (Harms & Yager, 1981).

Paul Hurd (1991) established that there had been as many as forty "national" reform efforts in the U.S. between 1776 and 1960. Even so, in school science over our 200-plus year history, there have been few significant changes in terms of content included in the collapse of some "subjects" into biology, chemistry, physics, and earth science. The focus of a vast majority of the early and ongoing national reform efforts for science in the U.S. centered on science content and class experiences that were more practical and useful in the lives of students. In the 1960s, however, the United States government invested millions of dollars in an effort to move in a different direction, and this was directly in response to the Soviet Union's launching of the first human-made satellite, Sputnik, and the ensuing space race. This major event focused reform on developing more scientists who would enable the U.S. to compete successfully in the space race.

Although science and technology originated and evolved from two different academic disciplines and emerged from different needs and different parts of the population, following World War II society came to see them as one unit, married partners jointly impacting their lives and those of their offspring (Krantzberg, 1984). In contrast to society's view, however, the intended outcome of school science for the next two decades, the 1960s and 1970s, was for students to learn/know the structure of the four science disciplines. In that regard, technology was excluded, and applications to daily life were omitted.

With funding from the National Science Foundation, scientists attempted to create "teacher proof" curricula consisting of the big ideas. Teachers, in turn, accepted the latter focus as the state of current knowledge. They also had to scramble to stay up-to-date on the latest findings from diverse science research initiatives. These "national curriculum projects" became known as the alphabet curricula because of acronyms used for their names.

Zacharias (1954), the architect of the Physical Science Study Committee (PSSC) course of the late 1950s, proclaimed that the goal of science teaching reform was to prepare textbooks and other materials to cast science in the way it was "known to scientists." Thus, science teachers came to believe that they were prohibited from teaching about the applications of science findings. Put another way, they believed that they were supposed to stick to the "basic" concepts of science and not deal with "applied science." Furthermore, most teachers found the newer "reform-driven" textbooks of the 60s and 70s to be radical departures since they focused on the big ideas with which scientists were involved. Neither the teachers nor their students found the pure science outline to be important to their daily lives and thus tended to be uninterested in any of the changes. Learning science remained a passive process of focusing on student acquisition of information that research scientists produced.

Concurrently, academic institutions continued to promote a reductionist, mechanistic approach to learning. The learning experiences were generally organized around basic science, technology, engineering, mathematics, social science, and education each residing in different departments, schools, and colleges. Technology studies were often housed in colleges of engineering. The basic sciences were usually found in colleges of arts and sciences. Education studies were commonly found in colleges of education. From each discipline evolved its own specialized culture, including language and operating norms. Academic institutions normally did not prepare learners to make connections among the varied disciplines nor to think in ways necessary to use such information for living, citizenship, and careers. In the end, most citizens were not scientifically and technologically literate and could not make political and personal reasoned decisions essential to living in a highly developed democracy.

During this period (1960–1980), many science educators came to believe that in our society, driven by fast-changing science and technology, teaching abstract science for the elite while using the structure of the traditional disciplines, without any real-world contexts, and isolated from technology, was inappropriate for general students. The students were disinterested, what they learned was often without real understanding, and they could not use what they were taught. Such situations were thought to be no longer acceptable. Numerous grassroots efforts to change school science began springing up in different parts of the U.S. in which teachers (in K–12 schools and in universities, often in the colleges of engineering) began focusing attention on what they, themselves, perceived was needed in the way of teaching of science. Many of these initiatives were described in the *Search for Excellence in Science Education* series published by NSTA (1982).

In 1979 the National Science Foundation funded *Project Synthesis,* a study to ascertain the condition of school science education and to recommend the next steps that would lead to better learning. The results of this research project suggested that

> . . . Education reform should produce informed citizens prepared to deal responsibly with science related societal issues. Science education must instill in students a sense of responsibility and appreciation of the potential science possesses for solving or alleviating societal problems and a sense of custodianship to protect and preserve the natural world with which science concerns itself. (Harms & Yager, 1981, p. np)

The goals framing *Project Synthesis* were as follows:

1. science for preparing for further science study;

2.   science for meeting personal needs;
3.   science for resolving current societal issues; and
4.   science for assisting with career choices.

This synthesis effort spoke to the fact that our democracy depends on a scientific and technologically literate citizenry able to make reasoned decisions in the voting booths as well as in their personal lives.

In 1982, at a National Academy of Science Forum, there were blatant calls for reform of science and mathematics education. This call for reform nationally was accompanied by a nationwide media blitz. Numerous pronouncements by scientists and mathematicians declared there was a "crisis" in science and mathematics in the United States. The National Science Board indicated that if a foreign nation had done to our schools what we had done, it would have been considered a declaration of war (*A Nation at Risk*, 1983). This set the stage for the development of more initiatives throughout the country, and from this emerged the Science/Technology/ Society (STS) movement. STS was called the current megatrend in science education (Roy, 1984). Others have described it as a paradigm shift for the field of science education (Hart & Robottom, 1990; Spector,1993).

Because of the multiple grass roots initiatives, there is no clear-cut lineage for STS as a reform. There are parallels, however, with intersections and overlaps among the initiatives. That said, the philosophical base for all the reform initiatives of the past two and a half decades appear to be consistent with the paradigm shift in society from the dominant, reductionist paradigm to a holistic paradigm. This societal shift has been documented for at least 30 years and is summarized in Table 1.

This societal paradigm shift set the context for the support of major initiatives explicating the paradigm shift in science education. During the 1980s, STS became the focus of two year-books for NSTA (Bybee, 1985; Bybee, Carlson, & McCormack, 1984) and one for the Association for the Education of Teachers of Science (James, 1986). There were also several major NSF grants awarded to foster STS approaches to school science and related curriculum fields. Two of the largest grants were awarded to the Pennsylvania State University (Penn State), which established one of the first STS programs in a major U.S. university.

Rustum Roy of Penn State was the Principal Investigator of a major NSF grant in 1985, a project called *Science through STS*. The effort involved surveying all STS initiatives, kindergarten through college, throughout the United States as well as other nations. Materials were collected, a newsletter was initiated, and new instructional materials were developed. It was from these initiatives that the National Association of Science/Technology/Society (NASTS), now known as the International Association of Science Technology Society (IASTS), was launched.

TABLE 1. The Shift from a Dominant Reductionist Paradigm to a Holistic Paradigm (Spector, 1993)

Dominant Reductionist Paradigm	Holistic Paradigm
There is one objective reality independent of a person that can become known to an individual.	Reality is constructed by individuals within their own minds. Therefore, there are multiple realities.
Truth is correspondent to the objective reality.	Truth is what a group working in a field, at a given time, agrees to call reality. It is socially constructed.
The whole is equal to the sum of its parts.	The whole is greater than the sum of its parts.
Parts are discreet, each having their own identity.	Pieces are altered when they interact to become part of the whole.
Cause and effect are linear and immediate.	Cause and effect relationships involve multiple factors, are complex, and may be difficult to distinguish.
Hierarchies provide the prevailing model organizing information, people, and things.	Networks dominate the organization of information, people, and things.
One can know the world by analyzing isolated smaller and smaller pieces.	One can know the world by examining the whole.
Science, using this reductionist approach, is the legitimate way of knowing.	Science is one of several, equally valid ways of knowing.
	The wholeness of the person, the union of the physical, spiritual, intellectual, and emotional aspects of the individual is acknowledged.
	Process is a product.

Nearly every textbook publisher has added STS materials to its science texts as a result of state mandates and local curriculum development efforts. However, most of these additions do little more than identify more content for teachers to use in their classrooms. They make the problem of science simply something teachers and students must review.

Industrial and private foundations have provided support for specific STS projects. These efforts, though, have tended to treat STS as an "add-on" to an already full curriculum. Countering the above efforts, NSTA has initiated many efforts over the years to define STS as a reform associated primarily with instruction, its effect on students, and the needed changes in teachers as opposed to preparing new instructional materials.

STS as a term was first suggested by John Ziman in his book *Teaching and Learning About Science and Society* (1980). Therein, Ziman identified several courses, titles, and special projects that had many common features dealing with science in a societal context. Most provided a new kind of curriculum organizer designed to make traditional concepts and processes found in typical science and social studies programs more appropriate and relevant to the lives of students. Many appreciated the fact that the traditional perception of science as being little more than accumulative understandings of experts which students only needed to parrot back was a dismal failure.

The 1980s resulted in a great deal of interest and experimentation with STS in U.S. secondary schools. But, it also became controversial, with some proclaiming that STS stood for "Stop Teaching Science." STS leaders were quick to add the following to the latter phrase: "in the same old ways!"

STS reform efforts and the conflicts surrounding them led many to better define STS and influenced the development of national standards. The National Science Foundation provided nine million dollars, supported four years of debate, and arrived at the consensus that characterize the *National Science Education Standards* (1996). The *NSES* enlarged the definition of science *content* and identified eight facets of content, namely:

1. unifying concepts and processes in science;
2. science as inquiry;
3. physical science;
4. life science;
5. earth and space science;
6. science and technology;
7. science in personal and social perspectives; and
8. history and nature of science.

The *NSES* also included visions of reform for teaching, professional development, assessment, programs, and systems. Each of the chapters in the report concluded with a summary of where changes were needed. The teaching standards appear first, because of the importance of how teachers teach; in second was professional development, i.e., how teachers continue to learn; in third place was assessment, i.e., collecting evidence that learning had occurred in all four goal areas; in fourth was content. The standards were constructed in ways that the four goals for teaching science could be realized. These include producing students who:

- experience a richness and excitement of knowing about and understanding the natural world;
- use appropriate scientific processes and principles in making personal decisions;
- engage intelligently in public discourse and debate about matters of scientific and technological concerns; and

- increase economic productivity through the use of knowledge, understanding, and skills of the scientifically literate person in their careers.

The last three goals are almost identical to the ones central to *Project Synthesis* that were proposed fifteen years earlier. The major difference is the omission of a *NSES* goal highlighting the need for science as part of the students' ongoing academic preparation. *Project Synthesis* researchers found that it was the only goal most teachers used to justify what they were doing (in excess of 90% of the time) "because it was expected by the next grade level or academic level" (middle/high school/college) (Harms & Yager, 1981). In place of "academic preparation," the first *NSES* goal, science for experiencing the richness and excitement of knowing about and understanding the natural world is now considered a primary goal.

Still, the fact is, science classroom textbooks remain the primary guides for what is taught on a daily basis. The most widely used textbooks all reflect the content specified by the seventeen states with textbook adoption rules, and such texts focus on what students are to learn each day—which is alien to what science is and how it is operationalized. The aforementioned *NSES* goal highlights the fact that inquiry in science is integral to the overall endeavor, which has been hailed as the major reform ingredient for science education. Again, it cannot be contained in a textbook. Certainly inquiry is central to STS efforts and to the *NSES* visions.

The first section of the *NSES* lists nine changes needed in teaching. These nine also define STS teaching. They are:

1. understanding and responding to individual student's interests, strengths, experiences, and needs;
2. selecting and adapting curriculum;
3. focusing on student understanding and use of scientific knowledge, ideas, and inquiry processes;
4. guiding students in active and extended scientific inquiries;
5. providing opportunities for scientific discussion and debate among students;
6. continuously assessing student understanding (and involving students in the process);
7. sharing responsibility for learning with students;
8. supporting a classroom community with cooperation, shared responsibility, and respect; and
9. working with other teachers to enhance the science program.

The official NSTA STS position paper defined STS in a similar manner and was unanimously approved in 1990. The ten features of STS which define it follow:

1. student identification of problems with local interest and impact;
2. the use of local resources (human and material) to locate information which can be used in problem resolution;
3. the active involvement of students in seeking information that can be applied to solve real-life problems;
4. the extension of learning beyond the class period, the classroom, the school;
5. a focus on the impact of science and technology on individual students;
6. a view that science content is more than concepts which exist for students to master on tests;
7. an emphasis upon process skills which students can use in their own problem resolution;
8. an emphasis upon career awareness, especially careers related to science and technology;
9. opportunities for students to experience citizenship roles as they attempt to resolve societal issues they have identified; and
10. some autonomy in the learning process as individual issues are identified and used as the reasons for study (NSTA, 2006).

As previously mentioned, professional development is the second key component of *NSES*. Again, this is a set of visions for helping teachers move to STS teaching. What follows are the fourteen *NSES* foundational tenets vis-à-vis the professional development of science teachers:

1. inquiry into teaching and learning;
2. learning science through investigation and inquiry;
3. integration of science and teaching knowledge;
4. integration of theory and practice in school settings;
5. collegial and collaborative learning;
6. long-term coherent plans;
7. a variety of continuing professional development activities;
8. mix of internal and external expertise;
9. staff developers as facilitators, consultants, and planners;
10. teachers as intellectual, reflective practitioners;
11. teachers as producers of knowledge about teaching;
12. teachers as leaders;
13. teachers as a member of collegial professional communities; and
14. teachers as source and facilitators of change.

The third facet of the standards deals with assessment. The seven visions for changing assessment strategies include:

1. assessing what is most highly valued;

2.   assessing rich, well-structured knowledge;
3.   assessing scientific understanding and reasoning;
4.   assessing to learn what students do understand;
5.   assessing achievement and opportunities to learn;
6.   students engaged in ongoing assessments of their work and that of others; and
7.   teachers involved in the development of external assessments.

The science content is where most of the four-year debate in developing the *NSES* occurred. It was complicated by a consideration of content in all eight facets, including the collapsing of chemistry and physics into physical science, the inclusion of technology, a focus on the history and philosophy of science, and science for meeting personal and societal challenges (sometimes called *the* STS content).

Many in the STS community are committed to the recommendations made by *NSES* in regard to what should be emphasized in science teaching and learning. In fact, many have suggested dropping "STS" as a title because the *NSES* represents the conditions that characterize STS initiatives in the U.S. It has been argued that using *NSES* eliminates the negativity that the term STS seems to create among traditional science teachers and educators who are most comfortable thinking in terms of discipline categories and the major concepts comprising each.

BARRIERS TO STS IMPLEMENTATION (OR THE RIGHT END OF THE CONTINUUM)

Opponents to the introduction of technology and society into a science course were convinced that basic science concepts would be diluted and/or omitted. A major argument/criticism posited by such individuals is that it would take too much time to include such new dimensions (STS) into K–12 science courses, especially in high schools where college preparation tends to be the major emphasis of concern. Many opponents also proclaimed that social science is not "science." This mirrors earlier arguments when it was suggested that technology and engineering should be removed from science education and placed in "shop" courses, largely for non-college bound students. One of the key opponents to STS efforts was Bill Aldridge, Executive Director of the National Science Teachers Association (NSTA). He was a critic of the Iowa efforts, which were part of the NSF funding to NSTA for its *Scope, Sequence, and Coordination* (SS&C) project.

Many of the barriers to implementation of the STS paradigm apparent in the 1980s continue to exist today, even though the commonly agreed-upon documents guiding science education at the national level are consistent with the STS paradigm. School and university programs remain organized around the structure of the individual disciplines, with little or no connection made among the disciplines. Teachers in schools are still caught in the tradition of the "way things have always been done." For example, existing courses remain constructed on the assumptions that learning can be transmitted from teachers to students directly, and students repeating what teachers and textbooks state is learning. The lack of a clear definition for measuring student achievement beyond what is defined in the "No Child Left Behind Act" is another barrier to attaining the visions of the *NSES* (all of which were outlined in the previous section).

Change itself continues to be the greatest barrier (Spector, Burkett, & Stephen, 2002). Barker (2004) points out that when a paradigm shift occurs, everyone goes back to zero. This is highly threatening to those who have been successful within the old paradigm. It constitutes the erosion of a person's very foundation, thus stimulating serious resistance. Even in schools where teachers had opportunities to study STS reform in the 1980s, when a teacher moved to another school or retired, the new teachers hired did not receive staff development and thus were not prepared to keep the reform moving forward.

Retaining one's professional turf in higher education is a major barrier to implementing STS courses in universities and colleges. Faculty often do not want to give up the captive audiences they have in current courses to allow STS courses to be implemented.

Higher education faculty's need for tenure and promotion has also served as a barrier to the progress of STS. Academics often perceive a need to develop a new area of specialization in which to publish. This enables them to claim recognition as a leader in that field, a status often sought by tenure-promotion committees. Thus, we see things that have long been part of STS education being renamed and presented as "something new," ignoring the fact that the idea has existed in the enterprise for at least three decades. The latter has a tendency to contribute to confusion and murkiness over exactly what is and isn't STS-related. Even worse is the common practice of distorting or denigrating what has come before in order to make this "new" idea/approach seem important. For example, as this chapter has clearly stated, the use of social issues to teach science has been around for at least thirty years. Yet, the concept of using social issues for science teaching and learning has recently been touted by some science education faculty as something "new" and beyond STS, and it's being "sold" under the label of "introduction of socio-scientific issues." Concurrently, debate and role play are being introduced as "new" instructional techniques for science even though they have been used in STS teaching since its beginning.

Project-based, problem-based, place-based, and object-based instruction, conceptual change, service learning, civic engagement, and other strategies have all been features of the STS movement since its inception, yet some higher education faculty write about and teach these ideas as though each is a new and distinct entity separate from the STS reform movement. This is in contrast to identifying those ideas that have been extracted from the STS movement and recycled. All of this makes it extremely difficult for preservice and inservice teacher learners to see the connections that comprise the big picture of science teaching consistent with the holistic paradigm of STS reform, especially as envisioned in the *NSES*. As a result, many science teachers do not understand the holistic nature of reform. As a result, they waste time arguing or defending a particular strategy and have difficulty making meaningful decisions that enable their own teaching approach to be coherent.

It is also true that teachers are not informed by current educational literature of the foundational work of the STS movement. Authors frequently do not cite references that are more than three years old because manuscript referees often dismiss or devalue older citings. This leads to the omission of STS literature citings that present the full context and connections needed by learners to make sense of holistic reform. It further contributes to a view of current science education as a collection of distinct and often competing approaches to reform. Such confusion is a barrier to furthering STS reform.

RESEARCH BASE

Significant funding to document and undertake inquiries into the processes of STS development and implementation as they were occurring has been absent. In general, people involved with implementation of STS innovations were so overwhelmed dealing with issues of change and how to make change happen that they did not usually document the process. A major problem with this is that when we do not identify the lessons learned during the development and implementation phases, we cannot develop theories and test the theories to attain a spiral of knowledge building. Instead, we are destined to keep recycling ideas and theories that have been previously developed, and in some cases, assign new names to these recycled ideas (e.g., problem-based learning, conceptual change, socio-scientific issues, service learning, and civic engagement.)

Additionally, state and federal funding agencies provided no funds to conduct research on the implementation of the STS movement (or any other "education" project). Curriculum development with little attention to instructional concerns or the degree to which students learned was (and is) counterproductive. Finally, in the 1990s, the National Science Foundation began to fund some studies relevant to STS teaching, but many have not yet been published. Thus one finds few serious studies of the impact of STS initiatives, and then only in centers that have been operating over several decades.

IOWA EFFORTS

The University of Iowa and its graduates have been the primary source of research assessing the impact of STS in the United States. The history of STS research begins with the University of Iowa Laboratory School in the early 1960s. Faculty from social studies and science conceived a course called *Science and Culture*, which met graduation requirements in science or in social studies. The course was in operation until the laboratory school closed in 1972. The research indicated that students were able to attain and to retain many skills and competencies defined as science literacy (Cossman, 1967) using the STS approach. Such skills and competencies were *not* developed as a result of study in standard social studies or science courses.

Following the 1960 efforts with *Science and Culture,* Yager served as one of the architects of *Project Synthesis* in 1980. As the result of his previous work and the introduction of the term STS as one of the four thrusts of *Project Synthesis*, several major professional development initiatives for science teachers were funded in Iowa. Both *Iowa Chautauqua* and *Iowa SS&C* were funded by NSF, with leadership and coordination provided by NSTA. The Iowa efforts closely followed the STS definitions and served as a model for efforts in other states, while also identifying the ties to the national reforms.

Some of the Iowa work with STS has resulted in significant research reports from sites across Iowa and across the U.S. with support from the United States Department of Education's National Diffusion Network. It also became the point of criticism as evidenced by a report by Roth (1989) who attacked STS as reform and criticized the Iowa professional development efforts and research tied to schools. Martha Lutz (1992), a staff member with *Iowa Chautauqua*, analyzed Roth's assertion and the Iowa initiative. In doing so, Lutz (1992) examined the congruency of STS and the emerging constructivism paradigm. She contended that Roth's work (1989) had set up a straw man to illustrate the antagonism between STS and constructivism. Roth (1989) suggested that the two are mutually exclusive. Lutz found that Roth's grounds were untenable: addressing current issues is *not* automatically mutually exclusive of constructivism. Relevant contexts for learning can certainly be developed using constructivist perspectives. One could argue very persuasively that the most likely cause of conceptual change is when current issues are under investigation, and students learn when they perceive a need to know.

Roth (1989) made unsupported assumptions about what an STS unit on photosynthesis might be like. On the basis of her imagined hypothetical scenario, she condemned STS teaching and declared that it is both different from and inferior to conceptual change. This is an objectionable use of a hypothetical scenario. The end, which is a glorification of conceptual change, does not justify the means. Instead, it is a misleading condemnation of STS teaching.

One valuable outcome of Roth's (1989) emphatically favorable analysis of constructivism is that it is applicable to STS, in spite of her erroneous assertions that the two are antagonistic. Once that single false premise is recognized and removed, all her arguments in favor of constructivism also weigh in favor of the STS teaching strategy as advocated by Yager (1991).

Roth's description of how she taught photosynthesis to her own fifth-grade students matches exactly the general pattern for an STS teaching unit. Her assertion that this teaching method produces students who are able to "make predictions and observations, to change and develop explanations, and to apply ideas in a meaningful time frame" (Roth, 1989, p. 16) is an excellent testimonial to the benefits of STS teaching.

Yager's work in Iowa provides rich research evidence for the success of STS teaching. His work with the NSTA *What Research Says* series illustrates the power of STS instruction (Yager, 1982; Yager, 1993; Yager & Harms, 1981). Yager also edited a volume entitled *Science/Technology/Society as Reform in Science Education* (Yager, 1996). The book is comprised of twenty-nine chapters, including one dealing with the history of STS. These research efforts began in 1983 with funding of the NSTA *Chautauqua Project*, which involved over 5000 Iowa teachers between the years 1982 and 1997.

The efforts in Iowa terminated with twenty schools attempting to move completely to an STS focus in science grades 6 through 10 as part of the NSTA *Scope, Sequence, and Coordination (SS&C)* project. Unfortunately, the multi-million dollar project ended in 1997 when NSF terminated the funding. This took place just as the 20 schools in Iowa began to tackle the 10th through 12th grades high school curricula which were (and still are) traditionally established as discipline bound entities: biology, chemistry, physics, and in some states, earth science.

In Iowa, the assessment efforts focused on six domains vis-à-vis the importance of STS efforts in K–12 settings (Yager & McCormack, 1989). The six domains were:

1. Concept domain (mastering basic content constructs);
2. Process domain (learning the skills scientists use in "sciencing");
3. Application and connection domain (using concepts and processes in new situations);
4. Creativity domain (improving in quantity and quality of questions, possible explanations, and predicted consequences);

5.   Attitude domain (developing more positive feelings concerning the usefulness of science, science study, science teachers, and science careers); and

6.   World View domain (understanding and using the nature and history of science as important ingredients for science instructional programs).

A look at gender effects, concerns for low- and high-ability students, and successes with other underrepresented groups in science provided additional information concerning the power of STS. Although many of the extensive results come from Iowa where STS has been a focus for over twenty years, supporting research is now beginning to appear from other sources, especially in settings where the *Chautauqua* professional development model is in use.

What We Know About Student Achievement in the Six Domains

Based on data available from comparison of STS-focused science programs with textbook-centered programs in ninth-grade science classes in Muscatine, Iowa, Myers (1992) concluded that science taught with an STS focus was as effective in stimulating student learning of science concepts as traditional teaching. Further, he found that the STS approach to teaching science worked equally well for all grade levels in stimulating learning of science concepts. It also worked as effectively for students for long periods of time as it did for shorter periods of time. The student scores on standardized tests were not found to be different from students who were taught with traditional methods. STS was found to work as well for males as for females and work for higher-achieving students as well as for lower achieving students. Students of teachers utilizing STS strategies for the first time in their science classrooms were found to learn as many science concepts as did students in traditionally taught classrooms.

In a rigorously-controlled experiment involving fifteen experienced STS teachers, Mackinnu (1991) studied differences in concept mastery for students in textbook-bound sections versus those in STS sections where the content focus (unit organizer) was the same. The same pre- and post-tests were given to students in both treatments for each of the fifteen teachers. Mackinnu (1991) found that there were no significant differences between any of the sections taught by the teachers on the pretest measures regarding concept mastery. Since a variety of content areas and grade levels were involved, the experiment can be viewed as separate replications of the same experiment.

Mackinnu (1991) also found that when using the science process skills in an STS context, students had experiences that were more meaningful, relevant, and developmentally appropriate. This type of investigation exceeded the traditional process found in typical classrooms. Mackinnu (1991) also reported that the STS framework provided a meaningful context that students used to build their own knowledge base while resulting in challenges that had students using basic and integrated processes of science. Students reflected more about the consequences of procedural decisions while continuing to develop higher-order thinking skills. They were also provided more opportunities for transfer of processes to new and novel situations.

McComas (1993) also reported that students involved in STS classrooms made significant gains in the use of process skills. Essential to these gains was the positive affective responses of students and a relevant real life context. Students enjoyed the science in which they were involved. The new context which STS demanded was central to these results. Students directed their learning and placed it in situations that were meaningful, relevant, and developmentally appropriate for them.

As students experience the process skills found and practiced in science, they see these processes as integrating one to another and not as isolated skills teachers and curriculum materials often purport them to be. Basic and complex skills intertwine with each other throughout student investigations. Students also find the skills become assimilated into a framework that facilitates a way of knowing. As they experience the process skills in science in authentic contexts, the skills become part of a repertoire of knowledge for them. With repeated experiences, students can demonstrate the transfer of skills to situations that are novel and new. In that respect, process skills offer a "connectedness" that promote a way of knowing.

STS and its utilization of the process skills in science succeed where reforms in the past have failed. STS instruction takes the processes of science and provides a mechanism for their meaningful integration with specific science concepts. As students participate they develop a "way of knowing" and a "desire to know." This is truly unique in the world of reforms. Further, it represents ways that teachers and schools move toward realizing the first major goal for science education reform (NRC, 1996, p. 13).

Most studies show that an STS orientation results in significant changes regarding student attitudes, and this holds true for those classrooms and teachers first testing out STS approaches. Furthermore, these attitudes become resoundingly more positive the more experience one has with STS instruction. An analysis of student attitudes with respect to STS instruction used a meta-analytical approach to summarize three quasi-experimental studies individually and collectively. These studies show effect sizes revealing that, on average, a student in an STS class will likely have final student attitudes approximately two standard deviations more positive than those in traditional textbook classes (McComas, 1993).

The earliest descriptive studies of the effect of STS on student attitudes were tantalizing, because they seemed to show that students in STS classes had more positive attitudes after instruction than they did before such instruction. Such findings are in contrast to most studies which indicate that attitudes tend to worsen the longer students study science in schools (NAEP, 1978; Yager & Yager, 1985). At the same time, these attitude studies regarding STS were frustrating, because the nature of a pre-test–post-test only investigation does not permit a firm link between the mode of instruction and apparent results.

The proponents of STS as an instructional organizer have suggested a number of goals for such instruction within the affective domain. Each of the studies in Iowa illustrates clearly that there were no differences between the control and experimental groups before instruction but significant differences between the two groups of students after instruction with the STS section—that is, those who experienced STS instruction held more favorable attitudes toward science. The effect size calculations for both the individual studies and for all of the investigations taken together strongly confirms that STS instruction produces positive student attitudes toward science, science teachers, and science classes.

Creativity is also enhanced in STS classrooms. Penick (1986), for example, reported on the advantage of STS in improving creativity skills. Through their own questions, students create clear mental images of objects, phenomena, and level of their own understanding. Questions further serve to delineate problems, potential solutions, and other points of view. Questions are often a way of playing with ideas. A close relationship exists between play, creativity, and developing strategies for problem identification and resolution (Iverson, 1983). Such playing with ideas occurs when restraints on time, materials, and tasks are reduced, and generated ideas are treated with respect. And, like most play, self-initiated action is the most satisfying to the learner.

Students with creativity, curiosity, and questions often desire to communicate (Risi, 1982). When one discovers, does, or invents something, a natural first response is to let others in on the excitement. This, "Hey, Mom! Look at me!" syndrome is a feature of both creativity and of science. Without communication of ideas, science would not exist as we know it. Chaudhari (1986) noted that, "Students' questions indicate their curiosity in action, their mind hunger" (p. 31). Students must have a classroom climate conducive to their development of questions if they are to communicate effectively and to formulate and follow-up on questions. The teacher plays a key role in creating that environment where creativity is valued, encouraged, modeled, and rewarded. This environment is well exemplified by STS classrooms.

A variety of studies have examined creativity as a result of STS instruction. Myers (1988), Yager and Ajam (1991), and Yager and Ajeyalemi (1991) used the Torrance Tests of Creative Thinking. In all cases the investigators found that students scored significantly higher after experiencing STS classes than after learning in a more traditional classroom. In one study, Mackinnu (1991), using fifteen creativity indicators, found that STS students scored significantly higher on every item than did students from more text-oriented classrooms.

These results are what one would expect in light of the fact that the STS classroom encourages student ideas, initiative, and communication with other students. These results are significant in the sense that all teachers want students who can raise questions, suggest causes, and predict consequences. Yet, while all STS teachers are overtly seeking these outcomes, more typical teachers only hope for them as a by-product of didactic instruction.

In addition to all these studies having similar findings, there is a common thread that runs through all the STS classes that produce such significant results. This thread is a stimulating classroom climate where student questions and ideas are valued, their initiatives encouraged, and where evaluation is based on a wide variety of criteria. This classroom climate, an essential element for both creativity and STS teaching, is made possible only by the teacher.

Varrella (1997) reported on the advantage of STS in terms of students applying and connecting their learning to their own lives and to new situations. His specific results regarding Iowa teachers who are involved with moves to STS teaching indicate that the Iowa Teacher Leaders have the following features:

1. they emphasize instruction which is hands-on and activity based ;
2. they ask more open-ended questions and seldom if ever lecture, and use appropriate wait time between questions and answers;
3. they create an atmosphere where students are comfortable speaking up and sharing ideas, challenges, and solutions to problems and events experienced through their study of science;
4. they use texts for references rather than as curriculum directives;
5. they use raw data rather than artificial data from contrived or predetermined sources (e.g., validation experiments);
6. they engage students mentally and physically in the learning event, and have the expectation that students will ask questions, work cooperatively and individually, and allow the students latitude to modify and extend their ideas;

7.   they commit to partnerships in the learning experience between themselves and their students—typified by an atmosphere in which students' opinions are valued and constantly sought out by the teacher;

8.   they assess more often, consistently use pre-assessments as planning and learning tools, and clearly link assessment to the subject(s) i.e., performance assessments and the results of problem solving/inquiry strategies are frequently used;

9.   they are well versed in science content and in pedagogy and possess a highly refined set of content specific pedagogical practices. This allows for remarkable teacher flexibility and fluidity as instructional adjustments are made to address emerging needs, appropriate tangents, and important student ideas about their learning experience;

10.   they define their programs of study from a perspective which is personal and relevant to their students;

11.   they teach science from an integrated perspective, melding the areas of physical, life, and earth/space science into studies which are conceptually based and inquiry oriented; and finally

12.   they collaborate with their peers within their own schools as well as with colleagues in other schools and universities.

In science programs using an STS-constructivist approach, science is no longer a search for *the* truth. Rather, it becomes more like the science that scientists do: active, drawing on a variety of disciplines, and involving interactions within the social (and political) context. The broader goal for the student is the personal negotiation of a more accurate and refined understanding of science and its relationship to and impact on technology and society through classroom experiences. Through this process the learner can resolve discrepancies between what he or she knows and what seems to work in the new (problem) situation. The search process is necessary to work out a resolution to the problem (Andre, 1986) and will stimulate personal scrutiny of previously held beliefs and interpretations. If the alternatives considered by the learner provide a more effective resolution of the problem situation, then that individual will more likely incorporate it into his or her personal schema.

The learning partnership between the teacher and student which grows out of studies in the application domain is truly an exciting and dynamic thing. The effective STS-constructivist teacher is the learning coordinator, facilitating and stimulating opportunities for learning, advocating a real-world frame-of-reference, and encouraging eventual cognitive restructuring in the mind of each student. The student must be involved firsthand with the trial and error process, accept his or her personal stake in the classroom learning environment, and individually work toward cognitive re-equilibration as his or her preconceptions and misconceptions are challenged. As each student works through these mental building and resulting processes, the learning that eventually results is more meaningful and enduring.

Kellerman and Liu (1996) have written about the effects of STS instruction on student understanding of the nature and history of science. It is the sixth domain used in the *Iowa Chautauqua* and *SS&C* projects as well as one of the eight facets of content advocated in the *NSES*. The key appears to be teacher understanding of the nature of science and having the willingness to allow disagreement and dissension to occur. In an STS classroom it appears that this occurs. For example, the group of boys who chose not to follow the majority in explaining the demise of the dinosaurs was willing to "take the heat," again a behavior that is a part of science. Once science teachers can get past the notion that dissent is bad, good science can become a part of the science classroom. Such a view of classroom science seems central to a STS classroom.

WHAT RESEARCH SAYS ABOUT THE ADVANTAGES OF STS

It is important that research is available for use in teacher education programs and for professional development efforts designed to improve teaching (Salish, 1997). Unfortunately, most of the research does not use the National Science Education Standards (*NSES*) goals nor the eight facets of science content that the Standards identify. The latter include:

1. Unifying concepts and processes in science;
2. Science as inquiry;
3. Physical science;
4. Life science;
5. Earth and space science;
6. Science and technology;
7. Science in personal and social perspectives; and
8. History and nature of science (NRC, 1996, p. 6).

In a very real sense this broader view of science captures the essence of STS; and Technology, of course, is the connector.

Yager and McCormack (1989) have offered a model for STS for science teachers. Figure 1 delineates shows their six domains for science teaching which indicate the content areas that STS demands. Science concepts and process skills are in the center of the figure. These are the domains that teachers can use to define their K–12 science courses, while also providing an illustration of STS. Unfortunately, these are too often the only foci in-

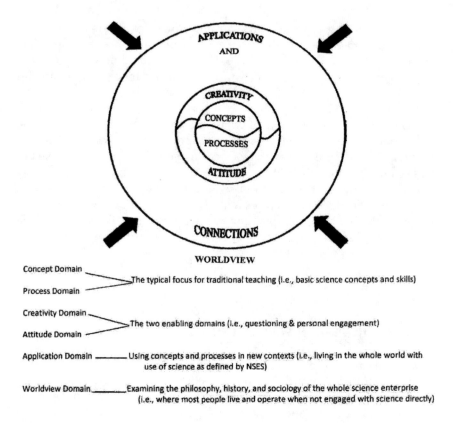

Concept Domain ___
               The typical focus for traditional teaching (i.e., basic science concepts and skills)
Process Domain ___

Creativity Domain ___
               The two enabling domains (i.e., questioning & personal engagement)
Attitude Domain ___

Application Domain ___ Using concepts and processes in new contexts (i.e., living in the whole world with
                     use of science as defined by NSES)

Worldview Domain ___ Examining the philosophy, history, and sociology of the whole science enterprise
                     (i.e., where most people live and operate when not engaged with science directly)

FIGURE 1. Display of the Interactions of Six Domains for Teaching and Assessing Science Learning.

cluded in most state standards. Significantly, Figure One also indicates that there are two enabling domains—attitude and creativity. These domains contribute to making sense of the objects and events in the natural universe and encouraging curiosity to question further. These are central to STS efforts to reform science education. The Enabling Domains in the model can be conceived as acting like a cell membrane controlling all that enters and exits the nucleus. Scientists act in the concept/process arena.

The application and connection domain (beyond the enabling domains) is where most people are. STS aims to deal with students where they operate themselves. This helps them to see the need to know about the explanations of the natural universe and the skills that can be used to know them. This focus is a unique feature for the human mind. The application domain is too often ignored in traditional teaching. It is, however, central to the STS classroom/curriculum. The sixth domain is the worldview domain—defined to include philosophy, history, and sociology. These professions deal with and analyze what scientists and technologists do and how scientists and technologists operate in the world.

In 1996, Yager edited a book entitled: *Science/Technology/Society as Reform in Science Education*. The book contains 29 chapters organized into five parts:

1. STS as Reform Movement in Science Education;
2. What an STS Approach Can Accomplish;
3. What the STS Approach Demands;
4. STS Initiatives Outside the United States; and
5. Supporting the STS Reform.

The volume includes a summary of the research results in the eight domains. These include the following:

1. Mastery of Basic Concepts (Myers, 1996);
2. Process Skills Enhancement (Wilson & Livingston, 1996);
3. The Affective Domain and STS Instruction (McComas, 1996);
4. Creativity and the Value of Questions in STS (Penick, 1996);
5. The Application Domain in an STS-Constructivist Setting (Varrella, 1996);
6. STS: A Crossroads for Science Teacher Preparation and Development (Brunkhorst & Andrews, 1996);
7. Identification of Science Concepts are Essential for STS Classrooms (Lutz, 1996); and
8. Rejoining Technology and Science (Zuga, 1996)

Among some of the many generalities arising from various chapters in Yager's SUNY monograph include the following:

1. Many research reports using typical pre- and post-tests do not result in significant differences with respect to gains in concept mastery (This may be explained by the nature of the tests used which too often focus on student mastery of textbook definitions and other factual information.);
2. STS generally produces students who are more capable of engaging in the process of science (e.g., observations, measurement, classification, predicting);
3. STS results in the formation of more positive attitudes about science and technology;
4. STS treats creativity as an indicator of thinking, questioning, locating and evaluating evidence concerning understanding gained through personal use;

5. Results in the application domain provide important evidence that students can *use* the information and process skills gleaned from their STS experiences in new contexts. This provides important evidence for real understanding of the concepts by students; and

6. STS results in superior student understanding and use of the nature and history of science information. Many of these same outcomes resulting from STS efforts have been reported quite recently (Yager & Ackey, 2010).

Pre-service and in-service science teacher perceptions (beliefs) of how science, technology, and society influence one another were discussed in several studies over the past 25 years within different research contexts around the world. These include the following:

1. USA (Bradford, Rubba, & Harkness,1995);
2. Canada (Aikenhead, 1987);
3. Israel (Nahum, Ben-Chaim, Azaiza, Herskovitz, & Zoller, 2009);
4. Egypt (Mansour, 2008);
5. Korea (Lee & Erdogan, 2007);
6. Turkey (Yalvac, Tekkaya, Cakiroglu, & Kahyaoglu, 2007);
7. Germany (Schallies, Wellensiek, & Lembens, 2002);
8. United Kingdom (Botton & Brown 1998); and
9. Brunei (Tairab, 2001).

A vast majority of the studies consistently reported that: science teachers remain wedded to following a traditional view of science exemplified by textbooks adopted and state curriculum outlines (Aikenhead, 2006; Davis, 2003; Jenkins, 1992, 2002; McGinnis & Simmons, 1999; Wiess, 1997). Aikenhead's 2006 study documents "salient influences" (the culture of school science) on teachers' values, assumptions, beliefs, ideologies, self-identities, self-images, and loyalties to traditional school science (p. 64). Others have reported that science teachers are often confused over differences and similarities between science and technology (e.g., Haidar, 2002; Haidar & Balfakik, 1999; Tairab, 2001). Many have found the greatest problem associated with shifts toward STS teaching and learning to be the failure of most science teachers to have experience studying and learning STS themselves (Lutz, 1996; Salish, 1997; Soldat, 2009; Varrella, 1996). Science teachers are teaching whatever they feel important without concern for reform ideas (Lee & Witz, 2009). Many challenges regarding the implementation of the STS reform, including insufficient knowledge of the social ramifications of science, the lack of awareness among science teachers about STS, limited resources for implementing STS, the inflexibility of the science curriculum, and unfavorable school and community cultures, all contribute to a host of other problems. These problems continue unabated even as schools around the world experience success in using STS (Akcay & Yager, in press; Gayford, 2002; Lee, Abd-El-Khalick, & Choi, 2006; Levinson, 2004; McGinnis & Simmons, 1999).

The results of the 24 years of STS' efforts arising from *Iowa Chautauqua* and *SS&C* have resulted in both projects being validated by the now defunct National Diffusion Network of the U.S. Department of Education. Both required research evidence that STS efforts undertaken did result in more and better student learning. The final reports from both of the projects provide evidence of the successes with STS instruction (Yager, Blunck, & Ajam, 1990; Yager, Liu, & Varrella, 1993).

A major research report in 1999 summarized the results of the *SS&C* efforts (Yager & Weld, 1999). The results of the *Iowa SS&C* project clearly provide evidence for the success of STS in Iowa. The results include four general areas of success. They are:

1. STS teachers are more confident to teach science and they better understand the nature of science and technology than do control teachers;
2. STS teachers can use teaching strategies that reflect a constructivist view of learning, and conduct action research projects related to effective teaching;
3. Students achieve significantly in five of the six assessment domains better in STS courses than they do in traditional textbook-oriented courses; and
4. Historically disenfranchised groups of learners, such as low ability students and females, are especially well served by using STS approaches.

Former Association for Supervision and Curriculum Development President Arthur Combs (1998) has observed that "truly effective change in so complex an institution [as schools] can only be accomplished by effecting change in people—especially through teachers, those men and women in closest contact with students" (p. 39). The Iowa STS project is a model strategy for science education reform internationally, because it starts and ends with the universal players in education, i.e., teachers and their students.

OTHER MAJOR RESEARCH REGARDING STS

There are many other research efforts not identified in this chapter. The work of Roy at Penn State in engineering is certainly significant in terms of the NSF support that resulted in the formation of an international society and an important on-going publication, the *Bulletin of Science-Technology-Society*. The engaging work by Piel and Truxal (1975) at Stony Brook and the NSF-supported textbook the *Man-Made World* is another example of the involvement of engineers with STS. Recently two other STS initiatives for the production of materials for secondary students were accomplished in colleges of engineering: *Material-World Modules* (Northwestern University) and *Integrated Mathematics, Science, and Technology* (IMaST) (Illinois State University).

Other major efforts such as those by Aikenhead in Canada are significant in terms of how STS efforts help students understand the nature and history of science. His *Views on Science-Technology-Society* (VOSTS) research instrument (1992) is significant and illustrates what does not occur in most science classrooms regarding student understanding of science and its history. Possibly most significantly, Aikenhead's reports illustrate significant limitations to teaching science in traditional ways.

Hungerford's work in the STS arena at Southern Illinois University-Carbondale is another example of work focused on curriculum concerns; especially those related to environmental issues (Hungerford, 1992). Pedersen and Totten's work (Pedersen & Totten, 1992, 2001; Totten & Pedersen, 1993; Totten & Pedersen 1996), which focused on exploring the impact of STS curricula on students' attitudes and perceptions toward taking action also have contributed to understanding the greater impact of STS. Such efforts are important and internationally significant. They also indicate the diversity in STS reform efforts.

Dennis Cheek (2006) recently reviewed all the major STS efforts. He noted the differences in foci while contending that STS efforts have grown beyond controversy with the research results being used in the U.S. to finalize the *National Science Education Standards* (even though without reference per se to STS). The results of efforts to gain consensus, the evaluation of several trial versions, and the follow-up support for research have resulted in many STS enthusiasts wondering if Ziman's term "STS" has continued value as we consider the specific visions for reform contained in the *NSES*. It may be more important to know what we mean when we use the term. Instead of fighting about the term (a short cut for experts), maybe we need to go back to its meaning for realizing the four goals for the reform of science education, namely:

1. experience with the whole science sequence beginning with a question/issue;
2. science for making personal decisions;
3. science for dealing with societal issues; and
4. science for career awareness (NRC, p. 13).

This use of all the visions in the *NSES* may be more important than trying to capture all with the term STS and its 30 year history in U.S. science education.

It is unfortunate that more research is not available. However, it is important that what is available be used in teacher education programs as well as for professional development efforts to improve teaching. Surprisingly, many professional development programs focus only on conceptual understanding and do little to make classrooms more student-centered.

THE FUTURE OF STS

NSTA views STS as the teaching and learning of science in the context of human experience. It provides an appropriate science education context for all learners. There are indicators that although many research reports using typical pre- and post-tests provide no significant difference in concept mastery, that students experiencing STS have a richer understanding of the concepts, as evidenced in the application domain, and a stronger ability to use process skills in new contexts. All students improve in terms of creativity skills, more positive attitudes toward science, and the ability to use science concepts and processes in their daily living and in responsible personal decision-making.

There are no concepts and/or processes unique to STS; instead STS provides a setting and a reason for considering and using basic science and technology concepts and processes. STS means determining and experiencing ways that these basic ideas and skills can affect the lives of students and be used in society. STS means focusing on real-world problems that have science and technology components, instead of starting with basic concepts and process skills used by science professionals with the promise they will be useful to the learners in the future. STS teaching should aid students in investigating, analyzing, and applying concepts and processes to real situations. A good program will have built-in opportunities for the students to extend beyond the classroom to their local communities. These activities should be appropriate for the age of the students and be learner-centered. STS should empower students as future citizens who realize they have the power to make changes in society and the responsibility to do so.

STS teaching and learning are increasingly important as we all work for the resolution of the social problems of our day. STS is a way of promoting real science in all K–16 settings. In that respect, it is an educational endeavor in which:

1. *learners* engage in scientifically oriented questions;
2. *learners* give priority to evidence in responding to questions;
3. *learners* formulate explanations from evidence;
4. *learners* connect explanations to scientific knowledge; and
5. *learners* communicate and justify explanations (NRC, 2000, p. 29).

In a real sense, STS reforms exemplify activities and actions that characterize the scientific enterprise itself.

REFERENCES

Akcay, H., & Yager, R. E. (In press). Accomplishing the visions for teacher education programs advocated in the National Science Education Standards. *Journal of Science Teacher Education.*

Aikenhead, G. S. (1987). High school graduates' beliefs about science–technology–society III. Characteristics and limitations of scientific knowledge. *Science Education, 71*(4), 459–487.

Aikenhead, G. S. (2006). *Science education for everyday life: Evidence-based practice.* New York: Teachers College Press.

Aikenhead, G. S., & Ryan, A. G. (1992). Views on science-technology-society. *Science Education, 76*(5), 477–491.

Andre, T. (1986). Problem Solving in Education. In G. D. Phye & T. Andre (Eds), *Cognitive classroom learning* (pp. 169–204). Orlando, FL: Academic Press Inc.

Barker, J. (2004). *The new business of paradigms* (video). Star Thrower Distribution, Inc., St. Paul, MN.

Botton, C., & Brown, C. (1998). The reliability of some VOSTS items when used with preservice secondary science teachers in England. *Journal of Research in Science Teaching, 35*(1): 53–71.

Bradford, C. S., Rubba, P. A., & Harkness, W. L. (1995). Views about science-technology-society interactions held by college students in general education physics and STS courses. *Science Education, 79*(4), 355–373.

Brunkhorst, H. K., & Andrews, D. M. (1996). STS: A crossroads for science teacher preparation and development. In R. E. Yager (Ed.), *Science/technology/society as reform in science education* (pp. 205–218). Albany: State University of New York Press.

Bybee, R. W. (1985). *NSTA yearbook: Science/technology/society.* Washington, D.C.: National Science Teachers Association.

Bybee, R. W., Carlson, J. S., & McCormack, A. J. (Eds.). (1984). *NSTA yearbook: Redesigning science and technology education.* Washington, D.C.: National Science Teachers Association.

Chaudhari, U.S. (1986). Questioning and creative thinking: A research perspective. *The Journal of Creative Behavior, 20*(1), 30–33.

Cheek, D. W. (2006). Reflections on the success of the STS movement within K–12 education in the United States over the past two decades. Paper Presented at the 21st International Association of Science Technology and Society Conference, Baltimore, MD.

Combs, A. W. (1988). New assumptions for educational reform. *Educational Leadership, 45*(5), 38–40.

Cossman, G. W. (1967). *The effects of a course in science and designed for secondary school students.* Unpublished Doctoral Dissertation. Iowa City: University of Iowa, Science Education Center.

Davis, K.S. (2003). 'Change is hard': What science teachers are telling us about reform and teacher learning of innovative practices. *Science Education, 87*(1), 3–30.

Gayford, C. (2002). Controversial environmental issues: A case study for the professional development of science teachers. *International Journal of Science Education, 24*(11), 1191–1200.

Haidar, A. H. (2002). Professors' views on the influence of Arab society on science and technology. *Journal of Science Education and Technology, 9*(4), 257–273.

Haidar, A. H., & Balfakih, N. M. (1999). United Arab Emirates science students' views about the epistemology of science. (ERIC Document No., ED444843).

Harms, N., & Kahl, S. (1980). *Project synthesis final report.* Boulder CO: University of Colorado.

Harms, N., & Yager, R.E. (Eds.). (1981). *What research says to the science teacher, (Vol. 3).* Washington, D.C.: National Science Teachers Association.

Hart, E. P., & Robottom, I. M. (1990). The science-technology-society movement in science education: A critique of the reform process. *Journal of Research in Science Teaching, 27*(6), 575–588.

Hurd, P. DeH. (1991). Why we must transform science education. *Educational Leadership, 49*(2), 33–35.

Iverson, B. K. (1983). Play, creativity, and schools today. *Phi Delta Kappan,* 63, 693–694.

James, R. K. (Ed.). (1986). *1985 AETS yearbook—Science, technology and society: Resources for science educators.* Columbus, Ohio: SMEAC Information Reference Center and Association for the Education of Teachers in Science.

Jenkins, E. W. (1992). School science education: Toward a reconstruction. *Journal of Curriculum Studies, 24*(3), 229–246.

Jenkins, E. W. (Ed.) (2002). Linking school science education with action. In W. M. Roth, & J. Desautels (Ed.), *Science education as/for sociopolitical action* (pp. 17–34). New York, Lang.

Kellerman, L. R., & Liu, C. T. (1996). Enhancing student and teacher understanding. In R. E. Yager (Ed.) *Science/technology/society as reform in science education* (pp. 139–148). Albany: State University of New York Press.

Krantzberg, M. (1984). The wedding of science and technology: A very modern marriage. *Technology & science* (pp. 27–37). Davidson, N.C.: Davidson College.

Lee, H., Abd-El-Khalick, F., & Choi, K. (2006). Korean science teachers' perceptions of the introduction of socioscientific issues into the science curriculum. *Canadian Journal of Science, Mathematics, and Technology Education, 6*(2), 97–117.

Lee, H., & Witz, K. G. (2009). Science teachers' inspiration for teaching socio-scientific issues: Disconnection with reform efforts. *International Journal of Science Education, 31*(7), 931–960.

Lee, M., & Erdogan, I. (2007). The effect of science-technology-society teaching on students' attitudes toward science and certain aspects of creativity. *International Journal of Science Education, 29*(11), 1605–1634.

Levinson, R. (2004). Teaching bioethics in science: Crossing a bridge too far? *Canadian Journal of Science, Mathematics, and Technology Education, 4*(3), 353–369.

Lutz, M. (1992). Carpe diem: Acid rain. *Scope, Sequence, and Coordination Iowa News, 3*(2), 10.

Lutz, M. (1996). The identification of science concepts in STS teaching that are really essential. In R. E. Yager (Ed.), *Science/technology/society as reform in science education* (pp. 219–226). Albany: State University of New York Press.

Mackinnu, N. (1991). *Comparison of learning outcomes between classes taught with a science-technology-society (STS) approach and a textbook oriented approach.* Unpublished Doctoral Dissertation. Iowa City: University of Iowa, Science Education Center.

Mansour, N. (2008). The experiences and personal religious beliefs of Egyptian science teachers as a framework for understanding the shaping and reshaping of their beliefs and practices about science-technology-society (STS). *International Journal of Science Education, 30*(12), 1605–1634.

McComas, W. F. (1993). STS education and the affective domain. In R.. E. Yager (Ed.), *What research says to the science teacher, Volume 7: The science, technology and society movement* (pp. 161–168). National Science Teachers Association: Washington, DC.

McComas, W. F. (1996). The affective domain and STS instruction. In R. E. Yager (Ed.), *Science/technology/society as reform in science education* (pp. 70–83). Albany: State University of New York Press.

McGinnis, J.R., & Simmons, P. (1999). Teachers' perspectives of teaching science–technology—Society in local cultures: A sociocultural analysis. *Science Education, 83*(2), 179–211.

Myers, L. (1996). Mastery of basic concepts. In R. E. Yager (Ed.), *Science/technology/society as reform in science education* (pp. 53–58). Albany: State University of New York Press.

Myers, L. H. (1988). *Analysis of student outcomes in ninth grade physical science taught with a science-technology-society focus versus one taught with a textbook orientation.* Unpublished Doctoral Dissertation, Iowa City: The University of Iowa, Science Education Center.

Myers, L. H. (1992). STS and science concepts. In R. E. Yager (Ed.), *The status of science-technology-society reform efforts around the world: ICASE yearbook 1992* (pp. 76–80). Hong Kong: International Council of Associations for Science Education.

Nahum, T. L., Ben-Chaim, D., Azaiza, I., Herskovitz, O., & Zoller, U. (2009). Does STS-oriented science education promote 10th grade students' decision-making capabilities? *International Journal of Science Education,* First published on: 04 August 2009 (iFirst). http://dx.doi.org/10.1080/09500690903042533.

National Assessment of Educational Progress (1978). *The third assessment of science (1976–77).* Denver, CO: Author.

National Commission of Excellence in Education. (1983). *A nation at risk: The imperative for educational reform.* A report to the Nation and the Secretary of Education United States Department of Education by The National Commission on Excellence in Education, April. *http://www.ed.gov/pubs/NatAtRisk/index.html.*

National Research Council. (1996). *National science education standards.* Washington, DC: National Academy Press.

National Research Council. (2000). *Inquiry and the national science education standards: A guide for teaching and learning.* Washington, DC: National Academy Press.

National Science Teachers Association. (1982). *Search for excellence in science education.* Reston, VA: NSTA Press.

National Science Teachers Association. (2006). *Science/technology/society: Providing appropriate science for all. NSTA position statement.* NSTA Handbook. Arlington, VA: Author.

Pedersen, J. E., & Totten, S. (1992). Status of middle schools in the state of Arkansas: Survey of superintendents' and principals' perceptions. *Current Issues in Middle Level Education, 1*(2), 39–64.

Pedersen J. E., & Totten S. (2001). Beliefs of science teachers towards the teaching of science/technological/social issues: Are we addressing national standards? *Bulletin of Science, Technology & Society, 21*(5), 376–393.

Penick, J. E. (1996). Creativity and the value of questions in STS. In R. E. Yager (Ed.), *Science/technology/society as reform in science education* (pp. 84–94). Albany, NY: State University of New York Press.

Piel, E. J., & Truxal, J. G. (1975). *Technology, handle with care.* New York: McGraw-Hill.

Piel, E. J. (1981). Interaction of science, technology, and society in secondary schools. In N. C. Harms, & Robert E. Yager (Eds.), *What research says to the science teacher, Vol. 3* (pp. 94–112). Washington, D.C.: National Science Teachers Association.

Risi, M. (1982). *Macroscole: A holistic approach to science teaching. A discussion paper, D-82/2.* Ottawa, ON. Science Council of Canada.

Roth, K. J. (1989). Science education: It's not enough to 'do' or 'relate'. *American Educator, 13*(4), 16–22, 46–48.

Roy, R. (1984). *S-S/T/S Project: Teaching science via science, technology, and society material in the pre-college years.* University Park: The Pennsylvania State University.

Salish I Research Project (1997). *Secondary science mathematics teacher preparation programs: Influences on new teachers and their students.* (Final report). Washington D.C.: U.S. Department of Education and Office of Educational Research and Improvement.

Schallies, M., Wellensiek, A., & Lembens, A. (2002). The development of mature capabilities for understanding and valuing in technology through school project work: Individual and structural preconditions. *International Journal of Technology and Design Education, 12*(1), 41–58.

Simpson, G. G. (1963). Biology and the nature of science. *Science, 139*(3550), 81–88.

Soldat, C. (2009). *Investigating the impact of a preservice program on beliefs about science teaching and learning.* Unpublished Doctoral Dissertation. Iowa City: University of Iowa, Science Education Center.

Spector, B. S. (1986). Inservice science teacher preparation in S/T/S: Perspectives and program. In R. K. James (Ed.), *Science, technology and society: Resources for science educators: 1985 AETS yearbook* (pp. 65–91). Columbus, OH: ERIC Clearinghouse for Science, Mathematics and Environmental Education.

Spector, B. S. (1993). Order out of chaos. *School Science and Mathematics, 93*(1), 9–19.

Spector, B. S., & Glass, M. (1991). What's in a label: The vocabulary of interpretive research. In J. Gallagher (Ed.), *Interpretive research in science education (Monograph #4)* (pp. 19–42). Cincinnati, OH: National Association of Research in Science Teaching.

Spector, B. S., & Simpson, P. R. (1996). How is STS implemented in K–12 schools? *Teachers Clearinghouse for Science and Society Education,* (Spring), 15–18.

Spector, B. S., & Strong, P. (2001). The culture of traditional preservice elementary science methods students compared to the culture of science: A dilemma for teacher educators. *Journal of Elementary Science Education, 13*(1), 1–20.

Tairab, H. H. (2001). How do pre-service and in-service science teachers' view the nature of science and technology? *Research in Science and Technological Education, 19*(3), 235–250.

Totten, S., & Pedersen, J. E. (1993). Taking action at the local level: The study of social issues in the middle school. *Inquiry in Social Studies: Curriculum, Research, and Instruction, 29*(1), 19–33.

Totten, S., & Pedersen, J.E., (1996). Social studies student's perceptions and knowledge of social issues: A national study. *Inquiry in Social Studies, 32*(1), 22–46.

Varrella, G. F. (1996). Using what has been learned: The application domain in an STS-Constructivist setting. In R. E. Yager (Ed.), *Science/technology/society as reform in science education*. Albany: State University of New York Press. pp. 95–108.

Varrella, G. F. (1997). *The relationship of science teachers' beliefs and practices.* Unpublished Doctoral Dissertation. Iowa City: The University of Iowa, Science Education Center.

Vygotsky, L. S. (1978). *Mind and society: The development of higher mental processes.* Cambridge, M.A.: Harvard University Press.

Weiss, I. R. (1997). The status of science and mathematics teaching in the United States: Comparing teacher views and classroom practice to national standards. *NISE Brief, 1*(3), 1–8.

Wilson, J., & Livingston, S. (1996). Process skills enhancement in the STS classroom. In R. E. Yager (Ed.), *Science/technology/society as reform in science education* (pp. 59–69). Albany: State University of New York Press.

Yager, R. E. (Ed.). (1982). *What research says to the science teacher (Volume 4).* Washington, DC: National Science Teachers Association.

Yager, R. E. (Ed.). (1993). *What research says to the science teacher (Volume 7).* Washington, DC: National Science Teachers Association.

Yager, R. E. (1991). The constructivist learning model: Toward real reform in science education. *The Science Teacher, 58*(6), 52–57.

Yager, R. E. (Ed.) (1996). *Science/technology/society as reform in science education.* Albany: State University of New York Press.

Yager, R. E., & Ajam, M. (1991). Creativity and the value of questions in STS. In R. E. Yager (Ed.) *Science/technology/society as reform in science education* (pp. 84–94). Albany: State University of New York Press.

Yager, R. E., & Ajeyalemi, D. (1991). Creativity and the value of questions in STS. In R. E. Yager (Ed.). *Science/technology/society as reform in science education* (pp. 84–94). Albany: State University of New York Press.

Yager, R. E., & Akcay, H. (2010). The advantages of an inquiry approach for science instruction in middle grades. *School Science and Mathematics, 110*(1), 5–8.

Yager, R. E., Blunck, S. M., & Ajam, M. (Eds.). (1990). *The Iowa assessment package for evaluation in five domains of science education (2nd ed.).* Iowa City: The University of Iowa, Science Education Center.

Yager, R. E., Liu, C., & Varrella, G. F. (1993). *The Iowa Scope, Sequence, and Coordination (SS&C) project assessment report 1990–93.* Iowa City, IA: University of Iowa, Science Education Center.

Yager, R. E., & McCormack, A. J. (1989). Assessing teaching/learning successes in multiple domains of science and science education. *Science Education, 73*(1), 45–48.

Yager, R. E., & Weld, J. D. (1999). Scope, sequence, and coordination: The Iowa project, a national reform effort in the USA. *International Journal of Science Education, 21*(2), 169–194.

Yager, R. E., & Yager, S. O. (1985). Changes in perceptions of science for third, seventh, and eleventh grade students. *Journal of Research in Science Teaching, 22*(4), 347–358.

Yalvac, B., Tekkaya, C., Cakiroglu, J., & Kahyaoglu, E. (2007). Turkish pre-service science teachers' views on science-technology-society issues. *International Journal of Science Education, 29*(3), 331–348.

Ziman, J. (1980). *Teaching and learning about science and society.* New York: Cambridge University Press.

Zuga, K. F. (1996). STS promotes the rejoining of technology and science. In R. E. Yager (Ed.), *Science/technology/society as reform in science education* (pp. 227–240). Albany: State University of New York Press.

CHAPTER 15

BEANE'S INTEGRATIVE CURRICULAR PROGRAM

Jon Pedersen

INTRODUCTION

For the past 30 years, James A. Beane has worked tirelessly to develop and implement a curriculum for use in middle schools that is germane to the needs and interests of young adolescents (10 to 15 year olds). In doing so, he has developed an integrated curriculum that is age appropriate and that has, at its core, the dual focus of (a) the concerns early adolescents and (b) major social issues at play in the larger world (Beane, 1990). Although the concept of an integrated curriculum is not new, Beane's conception is unique in that it places a heavy emphasis on the concept of a democratic education and one that is truly applicable to the unique needs (social, emotional, cognitive, and physical) of young adolescents. The heart of his conception of such a curriculum is captured in his definition of what he deems a "general education": "General education ought to be of the kind based upon personal and social concerns" (Beane, 1990, p. 36).

Teaching and Studying Social Issues: Major Programs and Approaches, pages 313–339

INTEGRATED CURRICULUM

What needs to be understood at the outset is that the basic framework for Beane's curricular approach is that of an integrated curriculum. This aspect of his work follows in the footsteps of some notable curriculum theorists, including but not limited to John Dewey (1915/1900); William Kilpatrick (1918); Thomas Hopkins (1937), Paul Dressel (1958), and Gordon Vars (1965, 1996, & 2000).

The concept of the integrated curriculum dates back to the beginning of the 20th century when John Dewey (1915/1900) proposed the idea of the relationship of school to the student's own life and interests.

Following Dewey's lead, pedagogical progressives adopted a humanitarian disposition by making education more responsive to the needs of children and integrating the school more closely with the community (Gloer, 2007). Building off the idea of Dewey and other progressives of the time period, William Kilpatrick developed the instructional approach known as the *Project Method*. According to Kilpatrick (1918) The Project Method "... [is] concerned that children get a goodly stock of ideas to serve as stimuli for conduct. In the school procedure here advocated children are living together in the pursuit of a rich variety of purposes, some individually sought, many conjointly...[where] the teacher's success—if we believe in democracy—will consist in gradually eliminating himself or herself from the success of the procedure." (http://www.tcrecord.org). Simply put, the project method was a complete unit of purposeful experience (Hosic, 1918) that centered children's studies on central themes or ideas.

By the 1930s, integrated approaches such as the Project Method (which were child-centered) were adopted by 80 percent of the schools in the United States (ASCD, 2002). While Kilpatrick believed that students should be engaged in purposeful learning around central ideas, Hopkins (1937) argued that integration is more than merely coalescing subject matter areas around common themes. Hopkins believed that integrating the curriculum involved integrating the individual—with the individual as the central theme not the subject itself. The fully integrated person for Hopkins is one whose personal development incorporates the physical, social, mental, emotional, and spiritual aspects of the human organism into a functioning whole (Hopkins, 1937).

Others continued to build on these concepts and further developed and promoted the ideas central to integrated curriculum. For example, in the late 1950s, Dressel (1958) argued that "integrated curriculum," goes beyond connecting the subject matter with the understanding of the world:

> ...the integrative curriculum, the planned learning experiences not only provide the learners with a unified view of commonly held knowledge (by learning the models, systems, and structures of the culture) but also motivate and

develop learners' power to perceive new relationships and thus to create new models, systems, and structures. (pp. 3–25)

The progressive approaches of the 1930s and 1940s began to lose favor in the 1950s and it was at this time that education saw the emphasis turn to rigid, discipline-based approaches. Progressive approaches lost favor in the 1940s and 1950s as conservative political groups (e.g., the American Legion) and conservative educators began attacking the very nature of the progressive movement (Riley & Stern, 2004). These attacks claimed that progressive educators were promoting anti-Americanism and indoctrinating students too socialism and communism (Riley, 2006). During the latter part of the 1950s a heavy emphasis on math and sciences began emerge, and this also contributed to the downfall of the Progressive Movement. The new emphasis on science and math was largely attributed to the Sputnik crisis and the launch of the Space Age.

It was not until the late 1980s and early 1990s that the concept of the integrated curriculum resurfaced. This was due to, at least in part, to the growing support for the application of knowledge, the emergence of the idea that knowledge is not universal, and the continued involvement of educators who believed in progressive educational reforms (Beane, 1996).

It is worth noting that in the mid-1960s, Gordon Vars' research showed that the learning of students who participated in programs that were the forerunners of today's integrated curriculum was equal to or better than those students who participated in regular or separate-subject programs. Utilizing this research, the work of progressives, and, Lounsbury and Vars (1978) delineated, in their book *A Curriculum for the Middle School Years*, a call for the curriculum to be developed around the needs of the learner, the expectations of society, and the disciplines of knowledge.

Lounsbury (1992) continued to focus on curriculum that engaged students in making sense of their own lived experiences, and related it to democratic teaching. Lounsbury saw the need to engage students at the middle level in a study of the disciplines that made a

> [c]ommitment to democracy, a commitment to life in all its manifestations [and] the involvement of pupils actively in it. And, in my judgment, the one way we could improve education quickest, fastest and cheapest is simply to involve kids more in helping to decide what it is you're going to study and how you go about learning it. (Lounsbury, 2005, as cited in Gloer, 2007, p. 85)

In the 1990s, as the middle grades movement across the nation burgeoned, ever-increasing attention was focused on the role of integrated studies within the middle grades curriculum. A key work at the time was Chris Stevenson and Judy Carr's book, *Integrated Studies in the Middle Grades:*

Dancing Through Walls (1993). Therein, Stevenson and Carr (1993) assert that:

> If learners and teachers in the middle grades are to realize their fullest po-
> tential, we must remove lots of "walls"—the mental barriers that derive from
> a textbook-workbook-recitation-test orientation to instruction; the submis-
> sion to vague pressures to "cover" one curriculum or another; the isolation of
> colleague in different disciplines; incongruities between child-development
> theory and prevalent instructional practices. (p. 2)

They go on to provide make a case for integrated studies as well as describe goals for such programs at the middle level. More specifically, Stevenson and Carr (1993) state,

> Our overall goals for integrated study in the middle grades were based not
> only on an understanding of expectations associated with various subject mat-
> ters but also on our understanding of the kids themselves, their observations
> about the world they inhabit, and our expectations of qualities and compe-
> tencies that today's youth needs now and for the future...Inherent in these
> goals are what we recognize as clear implications for innovation in the form
> of an integrated approach toward curriculum. (p. 12)

The four goals outlined by Stevenson and Carr (1993) are:

1.   Students will grow more confident.
2.   Students will work together cooperatively.
3.   Students will develop social-ethical consciousness.
4.   Students will think, think and think.

Stevenson and Carr (1993) describe integrated studies as deviating from the "familiar organization" of traditional junior high/middle schools where the focus or organizational structure "descended to the middle level from high school and college, and...not in any way grounded in what is known about the cognitive and personal development of young adolescents" (p. 11). Thirteen of the fifteen chapters in the book are written by middle level teachers in which they describe the integrated approaches that they developed and implemented at their schools. This attempt to move beyond the theoretical to the practical as it relates to integrated studies became a powerful tool for educators, not though as a template or a recipe: "...in doing this kind of curriculum there never can be [a recipe]. But there are stories...that tell us it is possible that it can be done" (Beane, 1993, p. ix).

Following in the footsteps of Dewey, (1915/1900); Kilpatrick, (1918); Vars, (1965; 1996; 2000), and Lounsbury (1992), Beane (1993) favored an integrated approach to curriculum development versus a fragmented ap-proach to the curriculum found in most schools. He conceptualized an in-tegrated curriculum as the study of themes that are interwoven with eclectic subject matter, theories, ideas, and concepts germane to the focus of study that, ideally, would, as Samuel Totten, Professor of Curriculum and Instruction at the University of Arkansas, Fayetteville (2009) puts it:

> merge in a gestalt of understanding. The latter approximates the way in which ideas, concepts, and theories from various disciplines impact real issues and problems in society and students' personal lives. It is also the way scholars approach problems and issues; that is, bringing to bear the best thought available in various disciplines in order to gain a deeper understanding of a particular issue or problem. Of course, the same process is used when scholars and others attempt to ameliorate a problem, solve a crisis, or create new solution to an old problem. (personal correspondence)

For Beane (1977), an integrated curriculum is one that "teach[es] around themes, or "organizing centers" that students can identify with, such as 'The Environment,' 'Life in School,' or more traditional areas like 'Myths and Legends'" (pp. 13–14). However, leaving integrated curriculum defined only as themes does not do justice to the true nature of how Beane describes integrated curriculum. It must go beyond themes and be "...organized around problems and issues, that are of personal and social significance in the real world" without regard to subject area lines (Beane, 1996, p. 6). Integration, for Beane, is not the simplistic study of any theme, but should focus on rich, provocative themes, not the artificial boundaries set up by the four "big" content areas (math, science, social studies, and English) and should provide the opportunity for students to search for answers to questions, using their own knowledge, that are important to them (Beane, 1991b).

Themes become much more than a tool around which to organize curriculum. This approach, according to Beane, is "...not simply an organizational device requiring cosmetic changes or realignments in lesson plans across various subject areas. Rather, it is a way of thinking about what schools are for, about the sources of curriculum, and about the uses of knowledge" (Beane, 1995, p.1). Ultimately, Beane (1991b) proposes a seamless integration of subject matter into a study of themes that are *of personal and societal relevance to young adolescents.* It is the emphasis on personal *and* societal relevance organized around a central theme within the extant curriculum that distinguishes his curricular approach from both earlier and numerous other integrated approaches (Beane, 1991b, 1996). Integrated curriculum should be a way for students to make sense of experiences in life and understand how they can participate in a democratic society Beane (1997).

Interestingly, and tellingly, Beane created his curricular approach not only to replace the "smorgasbord" approach to the courses of study found in most schools across the nation, but to ameliorate the problematic nature of "interdisciplinary units" so popular in the current middle level movement. More often than not, the interdisciplinary units used in most middle schools are created in such a way that they provide students with a simplistic, elementary and watered down study of some topic or issue that is of minimal interest or relevance to middle school students. Instead of helping middle school students understand how strands of vastly different information come together to impact an issue related to their lives and the world in which they reside, the typical interdisciplinary unit simply results in students learning a chunk of this (e.g., math or history) or a chunk of that (e.g., science or literature) with little to no attempt to truly deepen a student's understanding of that which he/she is studying.

"GENERAL EDUCATION"

Beane aptly asks the question, "What should the middle school curriculum be?" (Beane, 1991b, p. 10). He argues that, "We have many powerful opportunities to engage students' knowledge and skill in the search for self and social meaning" (Beane, 1991b, p. 11). Beane sees the opportunities for schools—specifically middle schools in this case—to provide for students the opportunities to engage in issue-centered curriculum where the students are able to "...expand their critical creative and reflective thinking skills..." (1991b, p. 11). Unlike most who might consider the term "general education" to be a reference to "the basics of education" (e.g., "A, B, Cs," or the four core areas of math, science, English and social studies), in Beane's (1993) nomenclature, "general education" refers to an education that focuses on the "common needs, problems, interests, and concerns of young people and the society" (p. 35).

In the book that delineates his specific curricular approach, *A Middle School Curriculum: From Rhetoric to Reality,* Beane (1993) notes that his concept of "general education" is comprised of three general components:

1. curriculum themes (derived from the intersection of personal and social concerns of young adolescents);
2. skills needed to fully explore the themes; and
3. persistent concepts.

(Each of these will be addressed in more depth below.) Finally, and again, the Beane approach is driven by a focus on the "emerging concerns of early adolescents and the social world of which they are and will be a part of" (Beane, 1993, p. 36).

Recognizing the fact that young adolescents are asking a host of critical questions regarding their very being (e.g., Who am I?; What can I be?; What should I be?; and What should I do?), Beane suggests that such questions can be used to help frame and develop the issues to be studied in the curriculum, which, in turn, will help to make the curriculum relevant for young adolescents. Among the many issues that Beane suggests as solid possibilities for study are as follows:

1. Understanding and dealing with the physical, intellectual, and socio-emotional changes that occur during this particular stage, including the facts about those changes, how they fit within lifespan development, and their implications for personal and social living.
2. Developing a sense of personal identity, including a clear self-concept, positive self-esteem, and the ways in which self-perceptions are formed and how they influence attitudes and behaviors in social interactions.
3. Exploring questions of values, morals, and ethics in immediate and distant social relationships, and with regard to the form and function of social institutions.
4. Finding a place and securing some level of status in the peer group as well as understanding how the peer group forms and operates.
5. Developing a personally acceptable balance between independence from adult authority figures and continuing dependence on them for various kinds of security.
6. Dealing with the dizzying array of commercial interests that are aimed at early adolescents including those related to fashion, music, leisure activities and the like.
7. Negotiating the maze of multiple expectations in the home, the school the peer group, and other settings of everyday life.
8. Developing commitments to people and causes in order to form a sense of self worth, affirmation, achievement, and efficacy (Beane, 1993, p. 37).

The above listing is in no way exhaustive. Neither is it Beane's intention or expectation that such issues would be articulated by students or teachers in this exact manner. Rather, the issues are delineated for students and teachers to reflect on as they develop their own curriculum. The list constitutes an ideal vis-à-vis an "evolving collage of life experiences" (Beane, 1990, p. 38) that any solid middle level program should seriously consider when developing its own middle level curriculum around the personal issues and concerns of young adolescents.

As important as personal issues are to the curriculum approach, social issues also play a key and critical part. As Beane (1993) notes, "early adolescents do not live in isolation within that stage of development or apart from larger realities in the world" (p. 38). Indeed, they are inextricably linked by fate to the common good of our society and the world around us (Beane, 1993).

The multitude of social issues facing the youth of today are as varied as the individuals that the issues impact. Beane (1993) suggests that some of the scores, if not hundreds, of issues that might be examined in any study of social issues at the middle level are as follows:

1. Interdependence among peoples in multiple layers from the immediate network of relationships to the global level.
2. The diversity of culture of those layers, formed by race, ethnicity, gender, geographic region, and other factors.
3. Problems in the environment that range from diminishing resources to disposal of waste that come together in the question of whether we can sustain a livable planet.
4. Political processes and structures, including their contradictions that have simultaneously liberated and oppressed particular groups of people.
5. Economic problems ranging from securing personal economic security to increasing commercialization of interests to the issue of inequitable distribution of wealth and related power.
6. The place of technology as it enters into various aspects of life, and moral issues it presents.
7. The increasing incidence of self-destructive behaviors including substance abuse, crime, adolescent pregnancies, participation in street gangs, and attempted and actual suicides (Beane, 1993, p. 59).

It is at the intersection of both social and personal concerns that Beane sees curriculum themes evolving (Bean, 1993, p. 61). Moving out from the intersection of personal concerns and social issues, Beane (1993) provides examples of possible themes that middle school students and their teachers can tackle:

1. Transitions (understanding personal changes and living in a changing world);
2. Identities (developing a personal identity and cultural diversity);
3. Interdependence (finding a place in the group and global interdependence);
4. Wellness (personal fitness and environmental protection);
5. Social structures (social status and class systems);
6. Independence (dealing with adults and human rights);
7. Conflict resolution (peer conflict/gangs and global conflict);
8. Commercialism (commercial pressures and effects of media);
9. Justice (questioning authority and laws and social customs);
10. Caring (personal friendships and social welfare); and
11. Institutions (living in the school and social institutions) (p. 1).

Significantly, the emphasis of these themes is to connect the "lived experiences" of the young adolescent directly to the curriculum being studied.

As for the skills needed by young adolescents to explore the curriculum themes in depth, Beane (1993) suggests, for example, the following:

1. Reflective thinking, both crucial and creative, about the meanings and consequences of ideas and behaviors;
2. Identifying and judging the morality in problem situations; that is critical ethics;
3. Problem solving, including problem finding and analysis;
4. Identifying and clarifying personal beliefs and standards upon which decisions and behaviors are based; that is valuing;
5. Describing and evaluating personal aspirations, interests, and other characteristics; that is, [a focus on] self-concept and self esteem;
6. Acting upon problem situations both individually and collectively; that is social action skills;
7. Searching for completeness and meaning in such areas as cultural diversity. (p. 60)

While this is far from an exhaustive list, it highlights those skills that Beane believes young adolescents should consider making use of in exploring the themes.

Cognizant of the fact that some middle level educators may look askance at such a list and, indeed, possibly question whether any but the most talented middle level student might be capable of such skills, Beane (1993) has the following to say:

> Some middle school educators may well argue that many early adolescents do not have these skills and would need to learn them first before undertaking the broad curriculum themes I have proposed. However, this reasoning takes us right back into the isolation of skills from meaningful contexts in which they might have applied. And because isolated skill teaching is so ineffective, this reasoning also promises to continue the situation in too many middle schools where the application level is never reached. A more accurate line of reasoning is that early adolescents may not have these skills for precisely the reason that they have been taught in isolated parts of the program where they are removed from functional application. (p. 63)

The final component of the Beane approach includes persistent and critical concepts that must be part and parcel of the "general education" curriculum of any middle school. As noted earlier, young adolescents and the schools in which they study do not exist in isolation; indeed, they are all part of a larger society. Due to this fact, Beane (1993) believes that schools are thus "charged with maintaining and extending the enduring ideas upon which [our] society is based—a democratic tradition" (p. 64). Democracy, thus, becomes one of the critical concepts that Beane believes must be woven throughout the tapestry of each and every middle school curriculum.

Beane argues, persuasively, that previous discussions about democracy have focused primarily on school structures and [we would argue, to a lesser extent] on learning processes. Beane strongly believes that this is a sorely limited view and application of democracy. Beane (1993) goes on to say,

> If the idea of democracy is to really permeate the curriculum, then there are other concerns that must be raised as well. For example, the planned curriculum cannot stand on the grounds of "selective content;" that is, subject matter that includes the views and contributions of some people and not others. To be defensible in a democratic society, the curriculum must include possibilities for all views to be heard and for the presence of all people to be recognized. Too often the present curriculum in middle schools reflects the histories and concerns of white, middle class, and mostly male persons. Absent from the typical subject matter are the lives and contributions of "other" persons and in some cases they are altogether invisible. Moreover, as we have seen, the push for "academic" careers reflects the aspirations of only some people and misrepresents the barriers that prevent others from entering those careers, as well as devaluing other kinds of work. Rather than extend this status quo, the middle schools have a moral obligation, rooted in democracy, to open it up for critical examination and broader understanding. (p. 65)

The second concept that Beane delineates as key to the middle school curriculum is "human dignity and the related ideas of freedom, equality, caring, justice and peace." (p. 66) Beane (1993) argues that it is within these concepts that we find "personal and social efficacy that is now only hinted at in the commercially-packaged, contrived collections of self-esteem and human relations activities" (p. 67). Beane continues:

> The formation of subject matter and the ideas it involves are the result of human struggles and human efforts to make meanings out of their experiences...[and] subject matter is not an abstract, random, or sterile occurrence. Thus, in exploring the broad theses of the curriculum, we must constantly seek human meanings in terms of both the immediate and extended lives of early adolescents. In this way, subject matter may come to life and offer a compelling sense of worth to young people. (p. 67)

Beane is suggesting that young adolescents must be given the opportunity to make sense of their own lives and understand their lives through the lenses of others' experiences.

The final and third concept that Beane sees as enduring and closely related to the first two is that of "cultural diversity." Simply put, young adolescents must have the opportunity to come to an understanding and an appreciation of other cultures as a result of an exploration of the values and products of diverse cultures (Beane, 1993). For Beane (1993), it is the exploration of the intersection of the aforementioned themes and concepts that will lead to an improved "quality of life for early adolescents now and in the future" (p 68). To sum up:

> The centerpiece of the curriculum would consist of thematic units whose organizing centers are drawn from the intersecting concerns of early adolescents and issues in the larger world. Within the units, opportunities would be planned to develop and apply the various skills I have described, including those usually emphasized in middle schools and those that are often called "desirable" but are typically found only on the periphery of the curriculum. Similarly, such concepts as democracy, human dignity, and cultural diversity would persistently be brought to life in the content of units and processes used to carry them out (Beane, 1993, p. 45).

THE "HUMANISTIC SCHOOL" VERSUS THE "CUSTODIAL SCHOOL"

Beane believes that if a curriculum is going to truly be democratic and focus on the personal interests/needs of young adolescents and key social issues of the time then it can and only will be done in what he deems a "humanistic school." More specifically, according to Beane (1980), a humanistic school is "characterized by democratic procedures, student participation in decision making, personalness, respect, fairness, self-discipline, interaction, and flexibility" (p. 85). In contrast, Hoy (2009) defines a custodial school as one that:

> ...provides a highly controlled setting concerned primarily with the maintenance of order. Students are stereotyped in terms of their appearance, behavior, and parents' social status. Teachers do not attempt to understand student misbehavior; in fact, they view misbehavior as bad and believe that irresponsible and undisciplined persons should be controlled through punitive sanctions. Watchful mistrust and autocratic control are the critical aspects of a custodial perspective. (http://www.waynekhoy.com/pupil_ control.html)

The humanistic and democratic climate found in a well-structured humanistic school places a premium on "collaborative student-teacher planning, cooperative learning, thematic units that emphasize personal and social meanings, student self-evaluation, multicultural content, community service projects, and activities that involve making, creating and doing" (Beane, 1991a, p. 27). The primary focus is not simply about students (people) feeling better or good about themselves, but, more significantly, helping them come to believe that they can effect change and make a difference in the world (Beane, 1991).

As for Beane's (2002) emphasis on the democratic nature of the curriculum, he has two main ideas in mind: (1) an emphasis on content that allows students to explore what it means to live in a democratic state—the value of such as well as the responsibilities of living in a democracy; and (2) the need to provide ample opportunity for students to experience, first-hand, a democratic way of life (p. 26).

In regard to the first point, Beane suggests the need to avail students with opportunities to ask, explore and answer a wide array of questions such as: "What questions or concerns do you have about yourself?" and "What questions or concerns do you have about the world?" Going further, Beane (2002) delineates what he perceives as being the five components of a democratic curriculum:

1. It would bring young people together in situations in which they would experience the democratic way of life.
2. It would connect self-interest and the common good.
3. It would be created collaboratively.
4. It would address significant issues and accommodate multiple sources of knowledge.
5. It would involve students in activities that people in democracy engage in to understand themselves, one another and the world around them. (p. 26)

Ultimately, Beane (2002) suggests that the democratic core curriculum involves not only "common knowledge but also the values and processes of the democratic way of life" (p. 27). Beane (2002) continues, stating that concerns "about self and concerns about the larger world" are key questions that "help students see how their fates are tied to the fates of others and how self-interest and the common good might be integrated" (p. 27). The key, then, according to Beane (1998), is for the curriculum to challenge our youth to "imagine a better world and to try out ways of making it so" (p. 10).

STRENGTHS OF THE BEANE CURRICULAR PROGRAM

A major strength of Beane's curricular program is that it is developmentally appropriate. More specifically, its focus is comprised of three critical strands germane to the minds and lives of young adolescents:

1. cognitively, it provides for movement from the concrete to abstract thinking;

2. it focuses on the personal and relevant concerns of young adolescents (e.g., personal and group relationships; one's current and future place in society; how one can deepen friendships, appreciate and honor diversity, and avoid or remedy conflict) and themes tied to social issues of major concern and relevance to young adolescents (e.g., fairness, justice, difference(s)); and

3. a curriculum that is not only challenging cognitively (minds-on, and constructivist-oriented) but one in which they can wrestle with ideas in a concrete manner (hands-on). Combined, the minds-on, hands-on approach constitutes a curriculum that is truly and thoroughly engaging for young adolescents.

Another strength of the Beane curricular program is that while it provides an overview as to what such a curricular program looks like in action (concrete ideas how to interweave ideas/concepts/information in order to address key themes), it is not prescriptive in regard to content (though, handily, it does provide specific ideas for potential themes ideal for use with young adolescents). Ultimately, the Beane approach is adaptable to virtually any curricular content set by an individual school, school district, or state education department. The key for educators involved in developing a Beane-like curriculum is to use the backgrounds, lives, interests, and concerns of their particular students *and* the issues that impact their particular lives within their community, state, and nation as a means for co-constructing or creating the themes and selecting the content for addressing the themes. Unlike any other curricular program available, Beane's approach complements the middle level ideal in that it is designed specifically to meet the various social, emotional, cognitive and physical needs of young adolescents.

A significant caveat is that the Beane program has the *potential* for accomplishing all of the latter. As Samuel Totten (2009), professor of curriculum and instruction at the University of Arkansas, Fayetteville has noted, "Any curricular program, of course, can be watered-down to such an extent that it is all but useless if developed and/or implemented in a mindless, mechanical, and perfunctory manner. Thus, the actual curriculum planned and implemented by teachers must be true to the Beane model" (personal correspondence).

COMPLEXITIES, DIFFICULTIES AND PROBLEMATIC ASPECTS THAT MAY BE CONFRONTED WHEN IMPLEMENTING BEANE'S CURRICULAR APPROACH

All major curricular and instructional change in schools is bound to be both labor- and time-intensive, especially if it is done with care and attention to detail. The latter, though, is bound to be intensified when changing from a traditional approach to something that is likely to be considered radically different (as the Beane curriculum is). Concomitantly, any program perceived to be radical is likely to be met with controversy and resistance.

A mere listing of some of the many details that need to be attended to when making a major curricular change such as the Beane curriculum suggests that the undertaking is not a little daunting:

- initial informational meetings at the school site (involving the administrators, teachers, and students); within the district (involving teachers, site administrators, districts administrators, and school board members); and within the community (involving all of the latter, plus the parents of students and other interested community members);
- the development and implementation of surveys/questionnaires soliciting student, teacher and parent input in regard to their questions, concerns, suggestions vis-à-vis the proposed curricular change;
- the establishment of a steering committee meeting (comprised, ideally, of representatives for the study body, faculty, administration, parents, and other community members);
- meetings at both the site and administrative levels (the latter of which would include the school board) to discuss the change(s) and to make decisions for doing so (e.g., establishing goals, objectives, a timeline; addressing financial issues; planning and carrying out staff development; developing the curriculum (which would have to take into consideration alignment with state and district mandates, and more than likely, the standardized testing used in the district); implementing the curriculum; making decisions regarding ongoing summative evaluations of the development and implementation of the curricular program, which would address the quality of the curriculum itself and the efficacy of the staff development program);
- carrying out the ongoing evaluation of the curriculum in order to address its strengths, weaknesses, gaps, et al; and,
- revising the curriculum (as all curricular programs must be organic if they are not to become ossified and outdated).

In light of the conservative nature of schools and the way their mission has been perceived traditionally in the United States, it is no surprise that any major change/innovation frequently faces controversy at one level or another. Controversy may, and often does, arise for different reasons, including but not limited to the following:

- Anything that does not correspond to what has typified the traditional curriculum (which has been in place close to 100 years) is often looked askance at, and that is true—and not a little ironic—despite the fact that schools often come in for severe criticism at the hands of its critics;
- A program such as Beane's—in which discrete courses in discrete disciplines (e.g., English, social studies, mathematics, science) are looked at in a drastically different way—is often perceived as "radical," and thus suspect since it goes against the grain of the "given," "expected," and/or the "tried and true."
- The overwhelming effort and time required to move from a traditional curriculum of discrete courses to one that is integrated is likely to meet resistance from certain factions within a faculty.
- Those who have developed and/or tout changes that are perceived as radical are often targeted as "radicals," "mavericks," and/or "suspect," and thus maligned as a result of ad hominem attacks that generate further controversy;
- Numerous individuals (possibly the teachers, themselves, parents, administrators, and/or school board members) may raise objections to Beane's curricular program due to their questioning the ability of teachers to adequately handle/teach such a different curriculum;
- Many may question whether the new curriculum provides students with a solid foundation and understanding of the information found in the extant curriculum (which is often perceived as not only absolutely necessary for future success but sacrosanct);
- Many teachers, parents, students, administrators and school board members may fear that radically altering the middle level curriculum by implementing Beane's curriculum program may result in teachers (even those most adept at teaching) not covering all of the information and skills "needed" in order for students to be well-prepared to do well to meet the challenges at the next level of schooling, be it junior high or high school; and
- A curricular program that is perceived as out of the ordinary—such as Beane's—often results in complaints that it will put students "at risk" when it comes to succeeding on standardized tests (e.g., a state or district's testing program—end of instruction tests (EOI's), annual yearly progress reports (AYP's) or such college and university entrance tests as the ACT and SAT).

Because it is labor- and time-intensive and likely to be controversial, a move to the Beane curricular program is also likely to face immense resistance from teachers, site and district administrators, school board members, and the parents of students, among others. Teachers, for example, may resist the change due to the fact that they are either: comfortable and/or satisfied with the curriculum they teach; nervous about their ability to teach such a new curriculum; dubious about the value and efficacy of the new curricular program developed by Beane; and/or doubtful that any amount of staff development will ever prepare them to change from their current mode of teaching to something so radically different. Parents may resist the change due to many, if not all, of the aforementioned concerns raised by the teachers. Furthermore, parents may favor tradition over change; worry about whether the Beane approach would truly prepare their children for the next grade level, if not college; be concerned about the inchoate-like appearance of Beane's program; and/or simply be against the Beane approach because it clashes with their perception of what a school education should look like. And, administrators may side with their teachers, parents and board members who have all of the latter concerns, and/or other concerns such as: the monetary costs of implementing the program (e.g., for staff development, curriculum development, possibly new resources for use by the students and teachers); potential political "costs" (e.g., possibly angering certain parents and/or certain board members); and the time-consuming nature of the change (e.g., including obtaining waivers from the state department of education, additional board meetings, and additional meetings with individual parents and/or groups of parents). Both controversy and resistance to a curricular program can, and often does, result in either a total rejection of the proposed program or a watered-down version of the original.

DRAWBACKS/WEAKNESSES OF
FROM RHETORIC TO REALITY

Although *A Middle School Curriculum: From Rhetoric to Reality* (which is, as previously noted, the major publication in which Beane delineates his plans for an integrated curriculum that meets the personal and social needs of young adolescents) was updated and revised once (1993), it is in dire need of major revision once again. While the book clearly delineates the theory, goals and main ideas behind Beane's curricular program, it is bereft of an adequate discussion of a host of critical issues, including but not limited to the following: what, exactly, needs to be done to win over critics who are skeptical about the Beane curriculum; the best way of implementing the program (e.g., one theme at a time? the entire school curriculum in one fell swoop?); the type and amount of staff development needed in order to thoroughly prepare teachers to develop strong themes and to teach such a radically different curriculum; the impact of such a curriculum on district and state testing; and the impact of such a curriculum on those students who shall eventually attend junior highs and high schools with a traditional curriculum. Another problem is that the current edition of the book does not provide solid examples or discussions of the following: how and where such a curriculum has actually been developed and implemented; the type of adjustments schools and educators have had to make during the course of implementing the new curriculum and teaching strategies; how teachers new to the school are prepared to teach such a curriculum; and the impact of the curriculum on student achievement. By not addressing such concerns, readers (teachers, administrators, school board members, parents, and students in college of education) are left with more questions than answers in regard to if and how such a major change can be undertaken—and not only undertaken, but undertaken successfully. Finally, and this is critical, it would behoove Beane to include a solid discussion of the research base (with complete citations) that exists in regard to the efficacy of *his* curricular program.

Fortunately, Beane and others have written numerous articles addressing some (but certainly not all) of the many concerns raised herein. That said, it would be of great assistance to students in education programs, professors of education, public and private school faculty, school and district administrators, and others to have much of this key information under one cover or available at one website.

RESEARCH BASE VIS-À-VIS AN INTEGRATED CURRICULUM APPROACH

Plain and simple there is a lack—dare we say a dearth—of empirical-based research on integrated curriculum, let alone Beane's specific curricular approach. Although some research has been conducted into the efficacy of an integrated curriculum approach most of the research reported is opinion-based articles or articles that lack a solid methodological approach. These articles do little to promote integrated curricula or Beane's approach. While Beane's curricular approach is certainly different from the typical integrated approach, there are numerous similarities. Thus, it is worth citing some of the research on the efficacy of an integrated curriculum approach.

Purportedly based on a review of the research, Lipson (1993) asserts that when an integrative curriculum is well developed and implemented carefully, there are numerous "positive effects," including:

1. an integrated knowledge base leads to faster retrieval of information;

2. multiple perspectives lead to a more integrated knowledge base;
3. an integrated curriculum encourages depth and breadth in learn-ing;
4. an integrated curriculum promotes positive attitudes in students;
5. an integrated curriculum provides for more quality time for cur-riculum exploration (n.p.).

That said, the research available on integrated curriculum approaches falls into one of three categories:

1. the impact of the curriculum on student attitudes vis-à-vis how and what they are learning;
2. the impact of such a curriculum in regard to what students actually learn, retain and can use; and
3. the implementation of integrated curricular programs.

Much of the available research, however, is weakened by its small "n," its lack of rigor in applying research methods, and/or weak analysis. Further-more, some of what is referred to by some educators as "research" is not research at all. In fact, it is little more than the "self-reporting" of teachers, the latter of whom express their opinions, insights, and beliefs in regard to what they believe they *may have* accomplished in the classroom. Put another way, the latter is not based or predicated on empirical or action research, but simply the teacher's opinions (and possibly, hopes and desires).

In *What Research Says to the Middle Level Practitioner,* Vars (1997) provides some insights into the research on integrative curriculum and instruction. In his review of the literature, Vars (1997) indicates that the lack of com-mon terminology and the varied research designs and methods over the past 60 years complicates any overall analysis regarding the efficacy of in-tegrative curriculum. There are, in his words, "...a lack of consistency in the implementation" of integrated curriculum, which adds an additional complication when examining research related to integrated curriculum (Vars, 1997, p. 181). Based on these limitations, Vars (1997) indicates, "stu-dents in any kind of combined curriculum [in this case Vars included many different types of combined curriculum, including block scheduling] do as well and often better than students in conventional departmentalized programs" (p. 181).

For other aspects of the integrated curriculum (e.g., student motivation, higher order thinking, interpersonal skill enhancement, improving atti-tudes, et al.), there is limited data. Results would indicate students enjoy the classes more but most comparison studies have found few significant differences between integrated and non-integrated curriculum (Vars, 1997, p. 182). Vars (1997) contends this is due to the "didactic nature of the teaching methods [of teachers] even when curriculum is purported to be integrated and student centered" (p. 182). According to Vars (1997), "few studies have attempted to distinguish among the effects of correlated, fused and student centered core approaches. Although most studies found few significant differences, a few in-depth case studies show positive outcomes of curriculum integration when carefully planned and integrated (p. 182).

Czerniak, Weber, Sandmann, and Ahern (1999) found similar results in their analysis of integrated curriculum. They state that few empirical studies exist to support integrated curriculum and the lack of research may be due to the lack of a common conception and definition of integrative curriculum. As described by Vars (1997) and others, Czerniak et. al. (1999) agree that most of the literature found on integrative curriculum are testimonials. They found that there are a few studies that exist that show positive effects of integrative curriculum (Czerniak, et. al., 1999).

Biondo, Raphael, and Gavelek (2000) also indicate that the number of rigorous (empirical) studies vis-à-vis the efficacy of integrated approaches is relatively small. In this regard they report:

- Surprisingly, in a recent review of literature on integrated literacy instruction, we found that... although integrative practices are widely endorsed, there is little research to guide teachers in making thoughtful decisions about what to integrate with what, why, when, how, and for whom.
- In describing integrated literacy instruction, Shanahan (1997) writes, "[G]iven the long history and nearly universal acceptance of the idea of integration, there have been few empirical investigations of its effects. I have been able to identify no study, in any field with any age level, that has clearly demonstrated more coherent or deeper understandings, or better applicability of learning as a result of integration" (p. 15). McGowan, Erickson, and Neufeld (1996) concur, although their focus was specifically on studies integrating social studies and literature.
- The number of convincing arguments for social studies instruction based on literacy sources far outweighs the amount of published research documenting the extent to which literature-based teaching promotes the knowledge, skills, and values that constitute civic competence. Evidence seems limited, inconclusive, and concentrated on how trade books enhance students' knowledge acquisition.
- In our investigations, we found minimal research that discussed areas such as the challenges and potential benefits of integrated instruction or what integrated language arts or inter-disciplinary curricula

look like in classrooms and how such learning environments affect students across grade and ability levels.

- Empirical studies in which disciplines are brought together to contribute to a common inquiry are rare, as are studies in which disciplinary boundaries are broken down in pursuit of a common problem (n.p.)
- In a similar but different vein, researchers at the Northwest Regional Educational Laboratory reported (1994) that:

  [e]ven those research reports that document the effect of an integrated curriculum, when compared with a more traditional, subject-bound curriculum, have involved small numbers of students. It is very difficult to determine all of the variables that come into play when looking at students.

- Achievement. For these reasons, the findings emerging from these studies should be regarded as provisional rather than definite conclusions based on research. It is necessary to keep in mind that a multitude of factors come into play when one considers the success or failure of a program, a class, a school year or a unit. Despite these difficulties, the data reported support the implementation of an integrated curriculum in both elementary and secondary schools (Northwest Regional Educational Laboratory, 1994, n.p.).

Anfara and Andrews (2003), in *Research and Resources in Support of This We Believe*, a companion to *This we Believe: Successful Schools for Young Adolescents* (NMLA, 2003), provides "summaries" of research on programmatic components described in *This we Believe: Successful Schools for Young Adolescents*. Within this volume there is one section that examines the research on curriculum that is "challenging, relevant, and integrative." When referring to integrative curriculum Anfara provides two studies as a basis for supporting integrative curriculum" Nesin's (2000) work, which showed no significant differences for reading achievement, ability to access and process information and mixed results for classroom attitude scales (some in favor of the curriculum integration team and some in favor of the other two teams) and Beane's work, which is a resource on curriculum integration (1997). This again, surprisingly hammers home the point that very little empirical data exists to support integrative curriculum and/or Beane's work.

Over and above the works cited above, there are other large scale and small scale studies that have been conducted over the years that examine various effects of the integration of two or more subjects are as follows: science and math (Friend, 1984); history and language arts (Brophy, 1990); science and a literature-based curriculum (Bristor, 1994; Levitan, 1991, cited in Northwest Regional Educational Laboratory, 1994, n.d.); reading and health (Meckler, 1992); visual arts, math, and reading (Willett, 1992, cited in Northwest Regional Educational Laboratory, 1994, n.d.); and literature, literacy and science (Morrow, Pressley, Smith, & Smith, M., 1997).

There is a clear message here for all those (teachers, administrators, teacher educators and researchers) who tout the value of an integrated curriculum: there is a critical need for the development of strong research base that provides clear evidence, if such exists, of the value of an integrated curriculum in relation to student learning and student attitudes toward learning. To ignore this message is to the peril of those who are supportive of such an approach and to the peril of possibly ever seeing such a curricular approach become the norm versus the anomaly it remains to this day.

Numerous school faculty have also undertaken action research projects vis-à-vis their efforts at curriculum integration. One of the more impressive efforts undertaken thus far is that of the William Diamond Middle School (2006–2007). In carrying out their action research project, the faculty has, seemingly, carefully crafted—and documented—their process. In doing so, they have basically adhered to the educational philosophy and curricular goals set out in the National Middle School Association's "Middle Level Curriculum: A Work in Progress." To develop its curriculum, the administration and faculty established a School Site Council, and organized teams to handle different tasks during the development, implementation, and evaluation of the impact of the curriculum, along with the concomitant action research project. Since the research is still under way, there are no findings to report at this time.

RESEARCH BASE REGARDING THE BEANE'S INTEGRATIVE CURRICULAR PROGRAM

As previously mentioned, numerous schools (though still a minuscule number compared to the great number of schools in the U.S.) have implemented Beane's curricular program. As also previously mentioned, while numerous studies have been conducted into the efficacy of the implementation of an "integrated curriculum," few focus exclusively on the Beane program. As a result of the latter, any attempt to make a definitive statement regarding the efficacy of the Beane approach is impossible. Solid empirical studies are needed before any sort of definitive statement can legitimately be made regarding Beane's approach. In the end, it does little good to focus solely on the many studies on the impact of an integrated curriculum, for Beane's approach is, as delineated above, quite unique in that it focuses, *specifically and strongly*, on both personal and social issues, while many other integrated approaches do not—or, when they do, only in passing or, serendipitously, when a specific teacher uses an integrated model and decides to focus on a personal and/or social issue.

Even the vast majority of Beane's own work is dedicated more to theory than research, and much of the research by others is an analysis of his theoretical construct(s) versus empirical or qualitative studies of its impact on student learning. Still, that which is available is hopeful. In an article in 2001, Beane and Vars commented as follows vis-à-vis the research base on the integrative curriculum approach (not just Beane's program, but various approaches within the integrative field):

- It is still too early to obtain reliable data on how students in integrative programs fare on state proficiency tests. However, recent analyses of studies (Arhar, 1997; National Association for Core Curriculum, 2000; Vars, 1996, 1997) point to the same general conclusion: Almost without exception, students in any type of interdisciplinary or integrative curriculum do as well as, and often better than, students in a conventional departmentalized program. These results hold whether the combined curriculum is taught by one teacher in a self-contained or block-time class or by an interdisciplinary team.
- For the most part, these results were obtained using standardized achievement tests designed for a conventional separate-subjects program. Most standardized tests are *normed*—scores of individual students are compared with the mean or average of whatever group is considered "normal." In contrast, current state tests may have arbitrary cut-off scores that all students must meet in order to "pass" or to be considered "competent." In other words, the rules of the assessment game have been changed radically. Furthermore, the quality of many statewide assessment measures has been widely criticized, raising serious questions about the morality of using them to determine a student's grade promotion or high school graduation.
- It will probably be many years before quandaries vis-à-vis the assessment of student performance are solved. In the meantime, educators considering curriculum integration need to proceed carefully and take full advantage of the research and experience related to this potentially powerful way of designing and carrying out education (Vars, 1993; Beane, 1997). It also is important to keep all stakeholders—students, teachers, families, and the general public—informed and involved in continuing efforts to provide every student with meaningful learning experiences (n.p.)

A program that Beane frequently highlights and touts in his writing is "The Humanitas Program," an interdisciplinary, thematic, team-based approach to high school humanities in Los Angeles. In an article entitled "Integrated Curriculum" by the Northwest Regional Educational Laboratory (1994), it is reported that "The Humanitas Program" had been

- ...compared to six other schools which are more traditional in their approach. Performance-based assessments; surveys of teachers, students, and administrators; classroom observations; teacher and student interviews; analysis of assignments and examinations; analysis of portfolios; records of student attendance; records of discipline incidents; and records of college-oriented behavior and standardized tests were all considered in this research, making it one of the most thorough explorations of curriculum integration (Aschbacher 1991).
- The findings show that the Humanitas program had a statistically significant effect on writing and content knowledge, even after students had been enrolled for only one year. The largest gains were shown in conceptual understanding. The control groups of students made no gains in conceptual under-standing during the same time frame.
- Students in the Humanitas program stayed in school longer, worked harder (by objective measures and their own report), and liked school better. The expectations were higher in this interdisciplinary program, and the students were involved in more complex discussions that required them to make connections between content areas and the real world. These same expectations held true for the students' written work, as students were often asked to write an essay that included a discussion of the beliefs of more than one culture and the way those beliefs are influenced by cultural factors and values. The students were to include perspectives from art history, literature, and social institutions and make links to their own lives (Northwest Regional Educational Laboratory, 1994, n. p.)

Since Beane's curricular approach is being implemented in an ever-increasing number of schools across the U.S. and research is being conducted in many, if not most, of those schools, it is quite possible that in the near future a strong research base will be available in regard to its efficacy.

CONCLUSION

Beane's work, which follows in the footsteps of such curriculum specialists as Kilpatrick, Thomas L. Hopkins, and Vars, among others, marks—at the least—yet another step forward in emphasizing the value of assisting students to address critical social issues in a sophisticated and rigorous manner. Concomitantly, Beane's work has also produced (and continues to produce) efforts in schools across the nation to put his theory into practice.

Such efforts, *if they are carefully analyzed and evaluated vis-à-vis their efficacy,* could possibly influence the future state of education in the United States. As Samuel Totten (2008) has asserted:

> This is a real possibility for it is obvious that the current paradigm of education, largely influenced by the "industrial approach" of the 20th century, is not only archaic but doomed, sooner than later, to an ignominious end. Indeed, once the citizens of the U.S., and their representatives in government, recognize its obsolescence, there will be a ground swell for radical change that will result in something vastly different from what we've seen and experienced in education over the past 100 plus years. In that regard, Beane has developed a powerful paradigm—one of among many now being developed by researchers and practitioners who are awake to the abject failings and failure of the current system. (personal Correspondence)

Continuing, Totten (2008) argues that

> Beane's model has a better than even chance of eventually being perceived by the masses and powers that be for what it is—cutting edge, forward thinking, and a program that, if implemented with great care, can and will result in authentic, powerful and important learning, which is in direct contrast with much of the (in Alfred North Whitehead's words) "inert" information now passed off as "educative" in our nation's schools" (personal correspondence. 2008).

Indeed, it seems those who end up developing alternative schools, magnet schools, and entirely new educational enterprises that are truly dedicated to implementing curricular programs ideal for meeting the cognitive, social and emotional needs of our nation's children, young adolescents and teenagers will gravitate, at least in part, to Beane's curricular program.

REFERENCES

Anfara, V., & Andrews G. P. (2003). *Research and resources in support of this we believe.* Westerville, OH: The National Middle School Association.

Arhar, J. M. (1997). The effects of interdisciplinary teaming on students and teachers. In J. L. Irvin (Ed.), *What current research says to the middle level practitioner* (pp. 49–56). Columbus, OH: National Middle School Association.

Aschbacher, P. (1991). Humanitas: A thematic curriculum. *Educational Leadership, 49*(2), 16–19.

Association for Supervision and Curriculum Development (2002). *Overview of Curriculum Integration.* Alexandria, VA: Author.

Beane, J. A. (1977). *Curriculum integration: Designing the core of democratic education.* New York: Teachers College Press.

Beane, J. A. (1980). Synthesis of research on self-concept. *Educational Leadership,* *38*(1), 84–89.

Beane, J. A. (1990). *A middle school curriculum: From rhetoric to reality.* Columbus, OH: National Middle School Association.

Beane, J. A. (1991a). Sorting out the self-esteem controversy. *Educational Leadership,* *49*(9), 25–30.

Beane, J. A. (1991b). The middle school: The natural home of integrated curriculum. *Educational Leadership, 49*(2), 9–13.

Beane, J. A. (1993). *A middle school curriculum: From rhetoric to reality.* Columbus, OH, National Middle School Association.

Beane, J. A. (1993). Forward, . In C. Stevenson & J. Carr (Eds.), *Integrated studies in the middle grades: dancing through walls* (pp. vii–x). New York: Teachers College Press.

Beane, J. A. (1995). Curriculum integration and the disciplines of knowledge. *Phi Delta Kappan, 76*(8), 616–622.

Beane, J.A. (1996). On the shoulders of giants! The case for curriculum integration. *Middle School Journal, 28*(1), 6–11.

Beane, J. A. (1997). *Curriculum integration: Designing the core of a democratic education.* New York: Teachers College Press.

Beane, J. A. (1998). Reclaiming a democratic purpose for education. *Educational Leadership, 56*(2), 8–11.

Beane, J. A. (2002). Beyond self-interest: A democratic core curriculum. *Educational Leadership, 59*(7), 25–28.

Biondo, S. M.; Raphael, T. E., & Gavelek, J. R. (2000). Mapping the possibilities of integrated literacy instruction. *Reading Online.* (Retrieved at www.readingonline.org/research/biondo/biondo.html)

Bristor, V. J. (1994). Combining reading and writing with science to enhance content area achievement and attitudes. *Reading Horizons, 35*(1), 31–43.

Brophy, J. (1990). *Mary Lake: A case study of fifth grade social studies (american history) teaching. elementary subjects center. Series number 26.* East Lansing, MI: Michigan State University Institute for Research on Teaching, (ED 334 111).

Czerniak, C. M., Weber, W.B, Sandmann, A., & Adhern, J. (1999). A literature review of science and mathematics integration. *School Science and Mathematics, 99*(8), 421–430.

Dewey, J. (1900/1915). *The school and society* (revised edition). Chicago, IL: University of Chicago Press.

Dressel, P. (1958). The meaning and significance of integration. In B. N. Henry (Ed.), *The Integration of Educational Experiences* (pp. 3–25). Chicago, IL: University of Chicago Press.

Friend, H. (1984). *The effect of science and mathematics integration on selected seventh grade students: Attitudes toward and achievement in science.* New York: New York City Board of Education.

Gloer, S. R. (2007). *The contribution of John Lounsbury to the development of the middle school movement in American education: An oral history.* Unpublished Doctoral Dissertation, Waco: Baylor University.

Hopkins, L. T. (1937). *Integration, its meaning and application.* New York: Appleton Century.

Hosic, J. F. (1918). Outline of the problem–project method. *The English Journal,* 7(9), 599–603.

Hoy, W. K. (2009). Conceptualization of pupil control ideology. (Retrieved at http://www.waynekhoy.com/pupil_control.html).

Kilpatrick, W. (1918). The project method. *Teachers College Record, 19*(4), 319–335.

Levitan, C. (1991). The effects of enriching science by changing language arts from a literature base to a science literature base on below average 6th grade readers. *Journal of High School Science Research, 2*(2), 20–25.

Lipson, M., Valencia, S., Wilxson, K., & Peters, C. (1993). Integration and thematic teaching: Integration to improve teaching and learning. *Language Arts, 70*(4), 252–264.

Lounsbury, J. H. (1992). *Connecting the curriculum through interdisciplinary instruction.* Columbus, OH: The National Middle School Association.

Lounsbury, J. H., & Vars, G. F. (1978). *A curriculum for the middle school years.* New York: Harper & Row.

Meckler, T. (1992). Reading improvement using the health curriculum. Paper presented at the Annual Meeting of the American Educational Research Association, San Francisco, CA.

McGowan, T. M., Erickson, L., & Neufeld, J. A. (1996). With reason and rhetoric: Building the case for the literature-social studies connection. *Social Education, 60*(4), 203–207.

Morrow, L.M., Pressley, M., Smith, J.K., & Smith, M. (1997). The effect of a literature-based program integrated into literacy and science instruction with children from diverse backgrounds. *Reading Research Quarterly, 32*(1), 54–76.

National Middle Level Association (2003). *This we believe: Successful schools for young adolescents.* Westerville, OH: Author.

Nesin, G. (2000). *Young adolescents achievement and attitudes in various curriculum designs.* Unpublished Dissertation, Athens: The University of Georgia.

Northwest Regional Educational Laboratory (1994). Integrated curriculum. (Retrieved at www.nwrel.org/scpd/sirs/8/c016.html).

Riley, K. (2006). The triumph of Americanism: The American Legion vs. Harold Rugg. In K. Riley (Ed.), *Social reconstruction: People, politics, perspectives* (pp. 111–126). Charlotte, NC: Information Age Publishers.

Riley, K., & Stern, B. S. (2004). A bootlegged curriculum: The American Legion Versus Harold Rugg. *International Journal of Social Education, 18*(2), 62–72.

Shanahan, T. (1997). Reading-writing relationships, thematic units, inquiry learning...In pursuit of effective integrated literacy instruction. *The Reading Teacher,* 51(1), 12–19.

Stevenson, C., & Carr, J. F. (Eds.). (1993). *Integrated studies in the middle grades: Dancing through walls.* New York: Teachers College Press.

Totten, S. (2008). Personal Correspondence with Dr. Jon Pedersen. December 10th.

Totten, S. (2009). Personal Correspondence with Dr. Jon Pedersen, February 26th.

Vars, G. F. (1965). *A bibliography of research on the effectiveness of block-time programs.* Ithaca, NY: Junior High School Project, Cornell University.

Vars, G. F. (1993). *Interdisciplinary teaching: Why & how.* Columbus, OH: National Middle School Association.

Vars, G. F. (1996). Effects of interdisciplinary curriculum and instruction, pp. 147–164. In P. S. Hlebowitsh & W. G. Wraga (Eds.) *Annual review of research for school leaders.* Reston, VA: National Association of Secondary School Principals.

Vars, G. F. (1997). Effects of integrative curriculum and instruction. In J. L. Irvin (Ed.), *What current research says to the middle level practitioner* (pp. 179–186). Columbus, OH: National Middle School Association.

Vars, G. F. (2000). Lessons from the eight-year study for high school methods, guidance, assessment, and the change process. *Voices from the Field, 2*(2), 4–11.

Willett, L. (1992). The efficacy of using the visual arts to teach math and reading concepts. Paper presented at the Annual Meeting of the American Educational Research Association, San Francisco, CA.

CHAPTER 16

GENOCIDE EDUCATION

Samuel Totten

INTRODUCTION

In 1945, as World War II came to an end, newspapers and newsreels carried stark and shocking photographs of what Allied soldiers confronted as they liberated one Nazi death camp and concentration center after another. The emaciated bodies of the survivors, the bulldozers creating huge mounds of the dead, and the gas chambers and crematoria (some with bodies still in them) shocked the world. In large part, it was the horror over the Holocaust that moved the international community to support and ratify the United Nations Convention on the Prevention and Punishment of the Crime of Genocide (UNCG). The international community believed that with the passage of the UNCG and the world's commitment to fight against genocide that such a crime would become a thing of the past. Unfortunately, that was not to be the case. Far from it. Since 1945 there have been close to a dozen genocides perpetrated in such far-flung places as Bangladesh, Cambodia, Guatemala, Iraq, Rwanda, Srebrenica (in the former Yugoslavia), and Darfur, Sudan.

In the aftermath of the Holocaust, scholars across the globe slowly but surely began an examination of its many aspects. In the mid-1970s a small group of educators at the secondary level began to teach about the Holo-

Teaching and Studying Social Issues: Major Programs and Approaches, pages 341–368
Copyright © 2011 by Information Age Publishing
341

caust. It was not until the mid- to late-1980s, though, that pioneering educators, at both the university and secondary levels, began to focus attention on educating their students about genocides other than the Holocaust.

Due to the complexity of single genocidal events (e.g., the genocide of specific Native American groups in the U.S. and Canada, the Ottoman Turk genocide of the Armenians, the Holocaust, the Cambodian genocide, the 1994 Rwandan genocide), as well as a host of related issues (e.g., the prevention of genocide, the intervention of genocide, post-genocide societies), instructors at both the secondary and university levels must carefully carve out that aspect of genocide they think is most worthy of teaching and learning about, and then develop their units of study accordingly. Even those individuals who have an entire semester to teach a course on genocide need to delimit what they teach for it is virtually impossible to address every significant issue germane to a single genocide in such an amount of time, let alone everything that demands consideration in a comparative study of two or more genocides or a study of the history of genocide through the ages.

Currently, the study of specific genocidal acts other than the Holocaust is extremely limited in U.S.-based educational institutions, both secondary schools (clear evidence of this is provided later in this chapter in a discussion about those states that recommend or mandate teaching about genocide) and colleges/universities. Undoubtedly, there are numerous reasons for this. University professors and secondary level teachers alike are impacted by the following issues/problems: the field of genocide studies is still relatively new, and thus individual courses on genocide are not commonly considered a regular part of the curriculum; relatively few instructors (professors and teachers) feel equipped to tackle such subject matter with confidence; and, in some cases there is simply a lack of interest or care on the teachers' part to tackle such subject matter. Among other key issues faced by secondary level teachers are the following: most teachers have not been prepared by their college/university teacher education programs to teach about genocide; there is scant coverage of the topic of genocide in most textbooks (and that is a serious limitation since adopted textbooks frequently drive the curriculum at the secondary level of schooling); many teachers are expected to teach an already over-packed curriculum, which is, more often than not, driven by standard tests, *and* to adhere closely to state guidelines; and, last but not least, the subject matter is extremely complex, emotionally taxing, and, in certain cases, controversial—and it's a simple but profound fact that many teachers and school districts are averse to courting controversy.

EVOLUTION OF THE FIELD OF GENOCIDE STUDIES

The term "genocide" was initially coined in 1944 by a Polish émigré, Raphael Lemkin, who had fled to the United States from Nazi-dominated

Europe. Lemkin, a jurist, who later taught at Duke University and Yale University Law Schools, was also the individual largely responsible for the establishment of the United Nations Convention on the Prevention and Punishment of the Crime of Genocide (UNCG). Indeed, he led a remarkable one-man campaign to lobby one government after another to support the establishment of the UNCG.

Despite the hopes raised by the ratification of the UNCG, throughout the Cold War neither the United Nations nor individual countries addressed genocide head-on in order to prevent it. Granted, there were cases where individual nation's quelled genocidal actions (India in East Pakistan/Bangladesh, and Vietnam in Cambodia/Kampuchea), but they didn't do so for the express purpose of halting the genocides but rather due to national interests (e.g., for reasons of *realpolitik*).

Beginning in the late 1970s and early 1980s, several scholars, individually, began, conducting studies into the causes of genocide. Among them were Leo Kuper (University of California, Los Angeles), Israel W. Charny (Tel Aviv University), Irving Louis Horowitz (Rutgers University), and Helen Fein (an independent scholar). (For a detailed discussion of the work of these individuals as well as others, see Samuel Totten's and Steven Jacobs' [2002] *Pioneers of Genocide Studies*.) Their work, which was largely theoretical and historical, established the foundation of what was to become the field of genocide studies.

In 1982, Israel W. Charny, a psychology professor at Tel Aviv University, organized and hosted the first international conference on genocide. In various ways, the conference was a watershed event: first, it allowed for scholars in vastly different fields (history, psychology, political science, philosophy, theology) to meet and share ideas, discuss and debate issues, and appreciate how their work was complemented by others in different fields. This single conference was one of the primary catalysts vis-à-vis the genesis of the field of genocide studies.

As the field of genocide studies slowly began to attract new scholars, the 1980s and 1990s saw the establishment of various genocide centers around the world (e.g., in Jerusalem, Israel; New York City; Montreal, Quebec; and Sydney, New South Wales, Australia). Such centers variously published and disseminated newsletters, conducted research and issued reports, undertook publication projects, established archives, and offered courses on different facets of genocide.

Despite all of the aforementioned activity, as late as the 1980s there remained a dearth of books on genocide theory, individual cases of genocide, and research on genocide. That began to drastically change in the early- to mid-1990s, during which a host of books by scholars in diverse disciplines (international law, sociology, history, psychology, political science) began to appear on a wide array of genocide-related issues. By the late 1990s there was a plethora of works on all aspects of genocide, crimes against humanity, war crimes and ethnic cleansing. Part and parcel of this acceleration was the fact that genocides began to be perpetrated one after another in the late 1980s (e.g., the Iraqi government's gassing of the Kurds residing in northern Iraq) and the early to mid-1990s (e.g., the 1994 genocide in Rwanda, the atrocities perpetrated during the ongoing crisis in the former Yugoslavia, the Serb-perpetrated genocide of some 8,000 Muslim boys and men in Srebrenica in 1995). Additionally, there was the UN's establishment of the International Criminal Tribunal for the Former Yugoslavia and the International Criminal Tribunal for Rwanda in the early 1990s. All of this activity drew the attention of many more scholars to the field. Throughout this period and into the early 2000s, the field continued to expand, attracting hundreds of new scholars and the establishment of more genocide centers across the globe, including, for example, in Argentina, Denmark, England, France, and Holland. In early 2000, the international community also saw the establishment of the Hague-based International Criminal Court (ICC), which is now responsible for carrying out investigations into suspected and actual cases of genocide and then prosecuting those responsible for such crimes.

EVOLUTION OF GENOCIDE EDUCATION

Understandably, just as the field of genocide studies is a relatively new field so is genocide education. Early educative efforts vis-à-vis human rights concerns (the mid-1970s through the mid-1990s) generally took one of two forms: human rights education (e.g., theoretical issues germane to human rights, the UN Declaration of Human Rights, human rights violations and where they occurred, and information about efforts to halt human rights violations) or Holocaust education. In certain cases, individual educators addressed both of the latter concerns, but it was more common for educators to focus on one to the exclusion of the other. Seemingly, the very possibility of teaching about other genocides and related issues was not even considered an option by a vast majority of teachers. Put another way, genocide theory, genocidal events other than the Holocaust, the causes and triggers of genocide, ways to prevent genocide, and the intervention of genocide virtually constituted "the null curriculum" (Eisner, 1979, p. 83).

For the most part, and not surprisingly, those scholars who were conducting research into various facets of genocide were the first ones to teach about genocide and genocidal events other than the Holocaust. All such efforts, beginning in the early 1980s, were at the university level by such luminaries as Israel Charny, a psychologist at Tel Aviv University; Leo Kuper, a political scientist at the University of California, Los Angeles; Richard Hovannisian, a historian at the University of California, Los Angeles; Ervin Staub, a psychologist at the University of Massachusetts at Amherst; R. J. Rummel, a political scientist, at the University of Hawaii; Colin Tatz, a historian at the Macquaire University in New South Wales, Australia; and Roger Smith, a political scientist at the College of William and Mary, among others.

In the early- to mid-1980s, a minute number of individual teachers at the high school level delved into teaching about genocide, but more as an ancillary to their units of study on the Holocaust than self-contained units. That began to change, at least somewhat, in the mid- to late-1980s when states such as New York, Connecticut, and California introduced state guidelines for teaching about a combination of topics and issues germane to the deprivation of human rights, the Holocaust, and a small number of other genocides (the latter of which generally were generally comprised of two or more of the following cases: the Ottoman Turk-perpetrated of the Armenian genocide, the Soviet man-made famine in Ukraine, and/or the Khmer Rouge-perpetrated genocide in Cambodia). In most cases, the study of these subjects were "recommended" versus mandated, with New York being the notable exception. A key problem with a curricular topic being "recommended" versus mandated is that if teachers have little to no desire to teach the recommended topics/materials, they may be inclined not to do so—or to do so in a perfunctory manner. Put another way, by "recommending" that teachers teach about genocide, state departments of education basically hope and count on teachers taking it upon themselves to act upon the recommendation. In that regard, recommendations hold little to no weight; and thus, if a teacher chooses to ignore the recommendation the students are not introduced to and taught about the historical events, ideas, concepts, et al. And when teachers are confronted with overwhelmingly-packed curriculums, large classes of students, hundreds of papers to correct, and standardized tests that dictate the exact focus of curriculum (and, which, more often than not, constitute a stranglehold hold on teacher creativity, freedom of choice, and professional decision-making), teachers are not likely to add anything to their already heavy loads and busy lives.

Be that as it may, beginning in the mid 1990s and continuing through today (early 2010), there's been a plethora of activity to incorporate the study of genocide into the extant curriculum of secondary schools, colleges and universities. No doubt that is largely due to five main reasons:

1. the increased focus on genocide by scholars and the concomitant production of monographs, books, and articles;
2. the perpetration of a shocking number of genocides in the 1990s and early 2000s;

3.   the ever-increasing attention by the media (radio, televentions, and internet), documentarians, and Hollywood (feature films on the 1994 Rwandan genocide and Darfur) generated huge amounts of interest in genocide amongst the general public;

4.   the growing number of genocide institutes which, in part, are dedicated to helping educators teach about genocide; and

5.   more and more states and school districts perceiving the value and need to teach about the issue of human rights, and particularly genocide.

But a key question that must be asked is: Was, and is, all of this activity positive? Pedagogically sound? Worth the students' time and effort? Following the lead of New York, Connecticut, and California, a host of states began to either recommend *or* mandate the teaching of the Holocaust in their public schools, and then, gradually, add recommendations or mandates vis-à-vis the teaching of three to five other genocides. Such genocides rarely varied from (and, for the most part, still don't) the following: the Armenian genocide, the Soviet manmade famine in Ukraine, the Cambodian genocide, and, today, the Rwandan genocide. (As of late, more teachers are, on their own, touching on the current crisis in Darfur, Sudan. Ample evidence of this is found on the internet, where teachers share their lessons and discuss their efforts.) While many of the recommendations and mandates were undertaken with the best of intentions, more often than not the latter, as well as teacher guides and resource materials on genocide, seem to have been hastily cobbled together (Totten & Parsons, 1991, pp. 28–48). As for the teacher guides and resource materials, many of the initial editions contained factual errors and questionable assertions/assumptions; and, in many cases, subsequent editions often suffer from the same problems (Totten & Parsons, 1991, pp. 28–48). Concomitantly, in the vast majority of cases, those states issuing recommendations or mandates neither offered staff development programs to help teachers learn the new and complex content nor how to go about teaching it in the most effective manner. As a result, it is safe to say that, for all intents and purposes, education about genocide is still at an incipient stage at the secondary level of schooling.

The upshot is that very few states or school districts have incorporated genocide into their extant curricular programs in a way *that truly helps students gain a solid understanding of the phenomenon of genocide (e.g., how genocide differs from massacres, crimes against humanity, and war crimes; the various factors that contribute to genocide; the antecedents to individual cases of genocide)*, let alone the tools to undertake comparative studies. In fact, more often than not, instruction about "other genocides" (which is how genocides other than the Holocaust are actually referred to by many educators) constitute more of an "add-on" than anything else. In reality, the latter constitutes, for lack of a better term, a hit and miss approach. That is, if teachers have the interest, the knowledge, the time, and ready access to information/materials then they may address one or more of the other genocides. If they are bereft in one or more of the aforementioned areas, then they are much less likely to tackle the subject in their classrooms.

That said, there is a better than even chance that this situation may change for the better in the near future, and that is true for three basic reasons: First, more master degree programs in Holocaust and genocide are likely to be established in colleges and universities around the nation. In the field of genocide education, Richard Stockton's Masters in Holocaust and Genocide Studies (MAHG) is perceived as a model of sorts, and its influence has already been seen, for example, in California, where a Holocaust and genocide studies program has been developed at California State University at Chico (CSUC). While CSUC does not yet offer a Masters Degree in Holocaust Genocide Studies as Richard Stockton does, it is in the process of exploring the possibility of establishing an on-line masters degree program in education with an option in curriculum and instruction and an emphasis in Holocaust and Genocide Education. The planners report that:

> This innovative degree is the first completely online degree offered in Holocaust and genocide education anywhere in the world. While our primary goal is to train teachers in the State of California to teach Holocaust and Genocide units, as mandated in state law and in the State Social Science and History framework, we are also offering our courses for anyone, anytime, anywhere to help train teachers to both teach and prepare curriculum in the area of Holocaust and genocide studies (accessed from website at: http://www.csuchico.edu).

Second, as an ever-increasing number of scholars and teacher educators have moved from solely focusing on Holocaust studies to Holocaust and genocide, they have begun to establish centers of Holocaust *and* genocide study centers (e.g., The State of California Center for Excellence on the Study of the Holocaust, and Genocide, Human Rights, and Tolerance, California State University, Chico; The Center for Holocaust and Genocide Studies at the University of Minnesota; The University of South Florida Libraries and Holocaust and Genocide Center; Holocaust and Genocide Center at Westchester University of Pennsylvania). While some have been established as a result of legislation by their state governments, others were founded by interested individuals or groups of individuals. Such centers not only provide the means for conducting research into various facets of genocide, but, as mentioned above, often provide assistance to secondary level teachers who are interested in teaching about genocide.

Tellingly, a number of Holocaust centers around the U.S. have begun to change their names to reflect a broader mission. Ever so slowly, the focus of work of some of these centers have begun to expand in a way that reflects the new name of their centers—that is, moving from an exclusive focus on the Holocaust to one that encompasses a wide array of genocides. Over time, such centers will not only likely provide individual teachers with key resources for teaching about genocide but will assist school districts and entire states to update their curricular programs that deal with human rights issues and genocide.

Third, STAND: Students Taking Action Now Darfur, whose initial focus was to rally support for an intervention to help protect the black Africans of Darfur from the genocidal assaults carried out against them by the Government of Sudan troops and the *Janjaweed* (Arab militia) (2003–present), now focuses its efforts on organizing and educating students, teachers, and communities about genocidal situations across the globe. As part and parcel of that effort, STAND's Leadership Team recruits, trains, organizes and mobilizes students around the world by providing materials, educational information, online resources, policy expertise, and a network of concerned and active peers, all of whom have the ability to influence, at least to a certain extent, what is addressed and examined within their schools' regular and/ or extracurricular curriculum.

Student members of STAND at the secondary level have influenced their teachers to become more proactive in teaching at least about Darfur, and often the 1994 genocide in Rwanda as well. Perhaps, focusing on the latter two genocides will spawn increased interest amongst such teachers to consider the possibility of teaching about other aspects and cases of genocide. Only time will tell.

RESEARCH BASE

While there is a small but growing research base vis-à-vis Holocaust education, a research base vis-à-vis the teaching of other genocides is minimal (see Riley & Totten, 2002; Totten & Riley, 2005). The latter is true for numerous reasons, including but not limited to the following: genocide studies and education about genocide are relatively new endeavors; educational researchers are still more inclined to conduct such research on Holocaust education; and there are very few pedagogical specialists whose area of research is genocide.

That said, based on the history of teaching about the Holocaust in the United States, it is safe to say that there is a better than even chance that if the interest in teaching about genocide continues to increase over the next several years then research into various facets of genocide education will eventually be conducted (and/or come into its own). If past efforts to conduct research into the efficacy of Holocaust education are a good indicator of the future course of research into genocide education then it seems that Ph.D. students in education may well take the lead. They, in turn, are likely to be followed by teacher educators at the university level (especially those interested in teaching about social issues, human rights, the Holocaust, and genocide).

RESOURCES

Resources for teaching about genocide may be roughly divided into six categories:

1. curricula and pedagogical approaches and strategies for teaching about genocide;
2. books, chapters, and essays about particular genocides, theories of genocide, issues of prevention and intervention, et al., that are ideal for use in the classroom;
3. primary documents;
4. oral histories of specific genocides;
5. films about specific genocides; and
6. fiction.

In 1992, Joyce Freedman-Apsel and Helen Fein published *Teaching About Genocide: A Guidebook for College and University Teachers: Critical Essays, Syllabi and Assignments* (Ottawa: Human Rights Internet, 1992). It was the first book to be comprised of essays and syllabi on teaching about the Holocaust *and* genocide. It is comprised of two parts: Part I. Assumptions and Issues ("The Uniqueness and Universality of the Holocaust" by Michael Berenbaum; "Teaching About Genocide in an Age of Genocides" by Helen Fein; "Presuppositions and Issues About Genocide" by Frank Chalk; and "Moral Education and Teaching" by Mary Johnson); Part II is entitled Course Syllabi and Assignments and includes syllabi by professors of anthropology, history, history/sociology, literature, political science, psychology, and sociology. Some of the syllabi reflect a sophisticated understanding and approach to teaching about genocide (e.g., particularly those by such individuals as Hilda Kuper of the University of California, Los Angeles [UCLA]; Richard Hovannisian of UCLA; Frank Chalk and Curt Jonassohn of Concordia University; Roger Smith of College of William and Mary; Ervin Staub of the University of Massachusetts, Amherst, and Leo Kuper of UCLA), while others do not. Some of the other contributors seem to have little understanding as to what constitutes genocide, and thus their syllabi include highly questionable readings (including pieces on HIV/AIDS, for example). While the booklet's primary audience is university professors, high school teachers are likely to find it instructive in a variety of ways.

A decade later, in 2002, Apsel and Fein updated their book and retitled it *Teaching About Genocide: An Interdisciplinary Guidebook with Syllabi for College and University Teachers* (Washington, D.C.: American Sociological Association, 2002). This version of the book includes two short essays: "Reflections on Studying Genocide for Three Decades" by Helen Fein, and "Teaching About Genocide" by Joyce Apsel. The rest of the book is comprised of a section entitled "Course Syllabi and Other Teaching Resources (Study Questions, Topic Reports, Research, Exams, Bibliography)," and includes syllabi under the following headings: Armenian Genocide; Holocaust; Genocide and Holocaust; Genocide; and Genocide, Human Rights and International Affairs. The last two headings include the greatest number of syllabi. Among the many disciplines represented in the latter sections are: political science, sociology, history, anthropology, sociology, psychology, international affairs and law, philosophy, and theatre and drama. Again, some syllabi are much more sophisticated than others. None though are as weak as the weakest ones found in the first volume.

In 1992, Jack Nusan Porter also edited a volume entitled *The Sociology of Genocide/The Holocaust: A Curriculum Guide* (Washington, D.C,: American Sociological Association Teaching Resources Center). The booklet is comprised of the following: Part I. Special Section on Holocaust & Genocide ("The Uniqueness and Universality of the Holocaust" by Michael Berenbaum; "The 'Not-so-Gay' Genocide of the Nazi Era" by Jack Nusan Porter; and "Non-Jewish Victims in the Concentration Camps" by Konnilyn Feign); Part II. The Teaching of the Holocaust & Genocide ("The Problematic Character of Teaching the Holocaust" by Alan Rosenberg with Alexander Bardosh; "Introducing Genocide into the University Curriculum" by Frank Chalk; and "Teaching About Genocide" by Vicki J. Schlene; SPECIAL SECTION: which is comprised of the entire special issue ("Teaching About Genocide") of *Social Education*, the official journal of the National Council for the Social Studies co-edited by Samuel Totten and William S. Parsons; and Part III: The Syllabi. The latter is comprised of fifteen syllabi on the Holocaust and one on the larger issue of genocide. By overloading the third part with syllabi on the Holocaust, Porter virtually defeated the ostensible purpose of his compilation, and certainly, with the exception the Chalk essay and the special section borrowed from Totten and Parsons, sorely misnamed his booklet.

In 1999, Porter and Steve Hoffman edited and compiled a book entitled *The Sociology of the Holocaust and Genocide: A Teaching and Learning Guide* (Washington, D.C.: American Sociological Association). While it includes many of the same articles found in Porter's earlier edition (including, for example, the essays by Berenbaum, Bardosh, and Chalk), in many ways it is vastly different and substantially stronger. The volume is comprised of five parts: Part I. Special Section on the Sociology of Genocide and the Holocaust (which is comprised of ten essays, all of which solely address various issues about the Holocaust); Part II. The Teaching of the Holocaust and Genocide (which includes two essays on teaching about the Holocaust, one about teaching genocide, and a two-page chronology of genocide); Part III. A special issue ("Teaching About Genocide") of *Social Education* that was guest edited by Samuel Totten and William S. Parsons; Part IV. The Syllabi (which is divided into two sections: Sociology Courses on the Holocaust and Genocide" and "Other Disciplinary and Multi-Disciplinary Courses on the Holocaust and Genocide"); and Part V. Resource Centers and Resource People. While this volume still contains more syllabi on the Holocaust than other genocides, the number is certainly more balanced than it was in Porter's first volume. In the newer volume there are ten syllabi on the Holocaust and seven on genocide. Many of the syllabi, though, are weakened by readings not entirely germane to the Holocaust or other genocides. Educators would be wise to consult (and/or use) the Apsel and Fein's booklets over those by Porter.

In 1992, Samuel Totten and William Parsons served as the guest editors of the previously mentioned special issue on genocide for the National Council for the Social Studies' (NCSS) *Social Education*. The special issue constituted the first time in NCSS' nearly 70-year history that a special issue was dedicated to the broad topic of genocide (versus, for example, the Holocaust). Totten and Parsons included a broad range of articles on various facets of genocide by some of the most noted scholars in the incipient field of genocide studies. Among some of the many pieces in the special issue were the following: "Teaching and Learning About Genocide: Questions of Content, Rationale, and Methodology" by Parsons and Totten; "Genocide: An Historical Overview" by Frank Chalk and Curt Jonassohn; "Burundi: A Case of 'Selective Genocide'" by Rene Lemarchand; "Australia's Genocide: 'They Soon Forget Their Offspring'" by Colin Tatz; "The Armenian Genocide: Context and Legacy" by Rouben Adalian; "The Racial Context of the Holocaust" by Sybil Milton; "The Forgotten Holocaust of the Gypsies" by Gabrielle Trynauer; "The Nature of the Genocide in Cambodia (Kampuchea)" by Ben Kiernan; "Through the Looking Glass: Press Responses to Genocide" by Deborah E. Lipstadt; "When Denial Becomes Routine" by Leo Kuper; and "Genocide: Intervention and Prevention" by Israel W. Charny.

In 1994, Samuel Totten edited a special issue of the *Internet on the Holocaust and Genocide* (a newsletter issued by the Institute on the Holocaust and Genocide in Jerusalem, Israel) whose title was "Educating About Genocide" (Triple Issue, 51/52/53). The special issue was sorely uneven in its coverage of issues germane to genocide versus those relating solely to the

Holocaust. While it contained thirteen articles on the Holocaust, it only included six on others aspects of genocide. The latter included the following: "Educating About Genocide: Progress Is Being Made, But Much Still Needs to Be Done" by Samuel Totten; "Selected Bibliography" compiled by Samuel Totten; "Themes in Genocide Education in North American Colleges" by Helen Fein; "Holocaust and Genocide Education in Australia" by Colin Tatz; "American University Education Relating to Indigenous Peoples and Genocide Issues" by Robert K. Hitchcock; and "Genocide in World History Textbooks" by Dan B. Fleming. At a minimum, it would have been much more useful and valuable to have included articles on the following issues: the efforts of institutes/centers of genocide to promote genocide education; the strategies used by professors to teach about genocide, and whether they differed or not from those used to teach about the Holocaust; and the most valuable texts for teaching about genocide.

A decade later, in 2004, Totten edited a book entitled *Teaching About Genocide: Issues, Approaches and Resources* (Greenwich, CT: Information Age Publishing). It is comprised of a wide array of essays by some of the most noted genocide scholars across the globe: "Educating About Genocide, Yes: But What Kind of Education?" by Carol Rittner; "Issues of Rationale: Teaching About Genocide" by Samuel Totten; "The History of Genocide: An Overview" by Paul R. Bartrop and Samuel Totten; "Wrestling with the Definition of Genocide: A Critical Task" by Samuel Totten; "Defining Genocide: Issues and Resolutions" by Henry R. Huttenbach; "'Case Studies' of Genocide Perpetrated in the Twentieth Century" ("The Armenian Genocide" by Richard G. Hovannisian; "The Soviet Manmade Famine in Ukraine" by James Mace; "The Holocaust" by Michael Berenbaum; "The Indonesian Genocide of 1965–1966" by Robert Cribb; "The Bangladesh Genocide" by Rounaq Jahan; "The Burundi Genocide" by René Lemarchand; "The Cambodian Genocide" by Craig Etcheson; "The 1988 Anfal Operations in Iraqi Kurdistan" by Michel Leezenberg; "Genocide in Bosnia" by Eric Markusen; and "The Rwanda Genocide" by René Lemarchand); "Instructional Strategies and Learning Activities: Teaching About Genocide" by Samuel Totten; "Conducting a Comparative Study of Genocide: Rationale and Methodology" by Henry R. Huttenbach; "Human Rights, Genocide, and Social Responsibility" by William R. Fernekes and Samuel Totten; and "The Intervention and Prevention of Genocide: Where There is the Political Will, There is a Way" by Samuel Totten. It concludes with a lengthy and detailed annotated bibliography of key works germane to all facets of genocide, including teaching about genocide.

In 2005, Joyce Apsel edited a book for educators at both the secondary and college/university levels entitled *Darfur: Genocide Before Our Eyes* (New York: Institute for Genocide Studies). A valuable resource, it is comprised of the following pieces: "Teaching About Darfur through the Perspectives of Genocide and Human Rights" by Joyce Apsel; "Evolution of Conflict and Genocide in Sudan: A Historic Survey" by Jerry Fowler; "Darfur: Genocide Before Our Eyes" by Eric Reeves; "Twelve Ways to Deny a Genocide" by Gregory H. Stanton; "Investigating Allegations of Genocide in Darfur: The U.S. Atrocities Documentation Team and the UN Commission of Inquiry" by Eric Markusen and Samuel Totten; and "The Human Impact of War in Darfur" by Jennifer Leaning. It was the first book on the Darfur crisis to be published expressly for use by educators. While extremely short, it provides a solid overview of the early years of the Darfur crisis, and some solid suggestions for teaching about the crisis.

BOOKS/CHAPTERS/ESSAYS ON GENOCIDE THEORY, CASES OF GENOCIDE, AND RELATED ISSUES

Compared to just over 22 years ago (1988), there is a panoply of outstanding and useful materials available today for teaching about a broad array of issues germane to genocide. In fact, there are so many books, chapters, essays, films, and other materials available today on such a wide range of topics (e.g., individual cases of genocide, comparative genocide, issues of prevention and intervention, the reaction of the international community to threats and instances of genocide, genocide early warning systems, UN peacekeeping missions, post-genocide issues, et al.) that it is impossible to do justice to everything available in a chapter of this nature.

A resource that provides a sense of the burgeoning publications in the field is a series entitled *Genocide: A Critical Bibliographic Review* (which is now comprised of seven separate volumes). Each volume is comprised of a series of critical essays on a particular issue/subject and each essay is accompanied by an annotated bibliography of key works germane to the focus of each essay. The seven volumes in the series have addressed a host of critical issues, including but not limited to the following: various genocides (those committed throughout the history of the world, the Ottoman Turks' genocide of the Armenians, the Soviet manmade famine in Ukraine, the Holocaust, the Khmer Rouge perpetrated genocide of Cambodians, the Iraqi gassing of Kurds in northern Iraq in 1988, the 1994 Rwandan genocide, genocide in the former Yugoslavia, the Darfur genocide); first-person accounts of genocide; art and films about genocide; the prevention and intervention of genocide; the plight and fate of females during genocidal periods; and genocide and ethnocide of indigenous peoples.

Another excellent source for ascertaining the burgeoning number of works in the field are the host of major annotated bibliographies that have been published on various topics. Among the latter are annotated bibliographies on the Ottoman Turk genocide of the Armenians, the plight and fate of the Gypsies during the Holocaust, first-person accounts of genocide, and the prevention and intervention of genocide.

Two encyclopedias on genocide have also been published: *Encyclopedia of Genocide* edited by Israel W. Charny, Rouben Adalian, Steve Jacobs, Eric Markusen, and Samuel Totten (Santa Barbara, CA: ABC Clio Press, 1999), and *Encyclopedia of Crimes Against Humanity and Genocide* edited by Dinah Shelton, Howard Adelman, Frank Chalk, Alexandre Kiss, and William Schabas (New York: Macmillan, 2005). The latter work is the stronger of the two in that it includes a wider array of topics and entries.

In 2008, Greenwood Publishers published *Dictionary of Genocide* by Samuel Totten and Paul Bartrop. The dictionary includes over 1,000 detailed entries on a broad array of issues/topics. It is an excellent resource for faculty and students in upper secondary schools and at the college and university levels. Each entry is almost encyclopedic-like in its coverage of information (key personages, terminology, historical events, agreements, documents, etc.).

Two compilations specifically designed for use by professors and teachers that include key works that address a wide-range of genocide-related issues are: *Genocide: A Comprehensive Introduction* by Adam Jones (New York: Routledge, 2006), and *The Genocide Reader* compiled and edited by Samuel Totten and Paul Bartrop (New York: Routledge, 2009). These books address issues related to genocide theory, definitional concerns, key genocidal events, and the latter also includes numerous primary documents. Both are ideal for use with high level secondary level students and those matriculating at the college and university levels.

FIRST-PERSON ACCOUNTS

Over the past 30 years or so, a great quantity of first person accounts (oral histories and interviews) have been collected by researchers, scholarly institutes, and survivor groups. The greatest number available deal with the Holocaust, with those on the Armenian genocide coming in a far second. Hundreds of accounts have also been collected (many but not all in English) on the following genocides: the Khmer Rouge genocide of the Cambodian people between 1975 and 1979, the 1994 Rwandan genocide of the Tutsis and moderate Hutus by extremist Hutus, and the Soviet man-made famine in Ukraine. A much smaller number exist on the 1971 Bangladesh genocide, and the genocide of Muslim boys and men in Srebrenica in 1995. Even fewer exist on the Indonesian genocide of the East Timorese (1975-1990s), the genocide of the Mayans in Guatemala in the 1980s and early 1990s, and the genocide of the black Africans in Darfur (2003–present). (For a more detailed discussion of first-person accounts of genocide, see

Samuel Totten's "Diaries" in Dinah *Encyclopedia of Crimes Against Humanity and Genocide.* New York: Macmillan, 2004, and Totten's *First Person Accounts of Genocidal Acts Committed in the Twentieth Century.* Westport, CT: Greenwood Publishers, 1991.)

STATE MANDATES TO TEACH ABOUT GENOCIDE

The following states include the topic of genocide (other than the Holocaust) in their legislation regarding the teaching of the Holocaust and genocide in their states' schools. (Note: The vast majority of the facts about each state were gleaned from the United States Holocaust Memorial Museum's Website in a section entitled "State Profiles on Holocaust Education: Beyond Our Walls." Since the actual page numbers from the original state documents are not included on the website, page numbers are not included herein for quoted material.)

States That Have Passed Legislation That Specifically Addresses Genocide Education

California: In 1985, the California State Assembly passed Assembly Bill 1273 which states that "...The State Department of Education shall develop a model curriculum for use by school districts maintaining grades 7 to 12, inclusive, to be incorporated into existing history or social studies courses offered by these districts relating to the issue of genocide."

The 1985 History-Social Science Framework and Content Standards for California Public Schools, which was revised in 2001, "provides the guidelines for teaching" about the Armenian genocide, the Holocaust, the Cambodian genocide, and other human rights atrocities. (Note: Subsequently, "model curriculum standards" were developed and issued by the California State Department of Education.)

Two subsequent bills were passed (2002 and 2004, respectively) that addressed new initiatives, one dealing with the creation of a taskforce and one dealing with the aforementioned development of a center for excellence for the study of human rights, the Holocaust, genocide, and tolerance. The law now requires the center to work cooperatively with designated California State University campuses, as specified, to offer training, curricular materials, and resources, for teachers so as to help them effectively instruct on the Holocaust, genocide, human rights, and tolerance.

Worthy of note is the fact that in April 2009, California Senator Mark Wyland (R-Carlsbad) submitted and had a bill (Senate Bill 234) approved by the Senate Committee on Education that would require that the California Curriculum Commission to consider and vote on whether or not to include oral histories about genocides as a requirement for high school graduation. Speaking of the rationale behind his bill, Wyland said: "There is nothing more powerful in the academic world than hearing personal stories and real-life testimonies that engage students in areas which they have not previously been engaged. The use of oral histories in the teachings of horrific historical events like genocide makes these realities of our world more than just statistics on a page."

> **Illinois**: An Illinois state legislature bill (Public Act 094-0478—"Holocaust and Genocide Study") was enacted in 2005 that mandated the following: "Every public elementary school and high school shall include in its curricula a unit of instruction studying the events of the Nazi atrocities of 1933 to 1945.... To reinforce that lesson, such curriculum shall include an additional unit of instruction studying other acts of genocide across the globe. This unit, shall include, but not be limited to, the Armenian genocide, the Famine-Genocide in Ukraine, and more recent atrocities in Cambodia, Bosnia, Rwanda and Sudan....Each school board shall itself determine the minimum amount of instructional time which shall qualify as a unit of instruction satisfying the requirement of this section."

This legislation provides a great amount of leeway in regard to how schools can go about addressing genocide. This, of course, is in sync with the concept of "local control," but it also opens itself up to the possibility of school boards purposely limiting and minimizing instruction about such concerns.

> **Massachusetts**: In 1998, the Massachusetts state legislature approved Chapter 276 of the Acts of 1998 which required "the board of education [to] formulate recommendations on curricular material on genocide and human rights issues, and guidelines for the teaching of such material. Said material and guidelines may include, but shall not be limited to, the period of the transatlantic slave trade and the middle passage, the great hunger period in Ireland, the Armenian genocide, the holocaust (sic), and the Mussolini fascist regime and other recognized human rights violations and genocides."

The use of "other recognized human rights violations and genocides" can be viewed both as a positive and a negative. In the positive sense, it allows interested and committed teachers to incorporate a whole host of relevant issues into the extant curriculum, but by leaving it so wide open it also means that what is taught is likely to be uneven amongst and between grade levels. Indeed, the situation ostensibly allows for a better than even chance that those who are not conversant with more recent cases of genocide (e.g., the 1975–1979 Cambodian genocide, the Guatemalan genocide of the Mayans, the 1988 Iraqi gassing of Kurds in northern Iraq, the 1994 Rwandan genocide, the 1995 genocide in Srebrenica, the Darfur crisis of the early 2000s in Sudan) will not address them at all.

Pennsylvania: In 1996, a House Bill 297 ("Regarding Public, Private, and Parochial School Education of Human Rights Violations, including Acts of Genocide, The Holocaust, Slavery, and the Mass Starvation in Ireland from 1845") was passed that stated in part: "A resolution was passed by the House which encourages the Department of Education to teach about the Holocaust and other genocides...").

The author's (Totten's) earlier comments concerning the wording of Massachusetts' legislation is applicable to that of Pennsylvania's as well. That said, while the Pennsylvania legislation includes the wording "acts of genocide," it is curious—if not, telling—that its History/Social Studies Academic Standards specifically and solely mention "Nazi concentration camps," "Mao," and "land tensions with Native Americans" but no other specific acts of genocide (or, for that matter, no other names of other perpetrators). Oddly, the authors of the legislation euphemistically describe the treatment of the Native Americans by the U.S. government and its citizens as "land tensions with Native Americans."

The standards also include the issue of genocide under the heading of "Domestic Instability (political unrest, natural and man-made disasters, genocide)" but nothing specific is spelled out.

There are, of course, plenty of other places where genocide could be addressed, but, for whatever reason, the authors chose not to list such instances.

New Jersey: In 1994, the New Jersey legislature passed legislation (A-2780 and S-2006) entitled "An Act Mandating Holocaust Education in Schools." In part, it stated that "2. a. Every board of education shall include instruction on the Holocaust and genocides in an appropriate place in the curriculum of all elementary and secondary school pupils. b. The instruction shall enable pupils to identify and analyze applicable theories concerning human nature and behavior; to understand that genocide is a consequence of prejudice and discrimination and to understand that issues of moral dilemma and conscience have a profound impact on life."

Within its History/Social Studies Standards, Standard 6.2 World History reads as follows: "By the end of grade 12, students will (sic) [have studied?]: D. The Era of the Great Wars (1914–1945): International rivalries leading to WWI; Russian revolutions and aftermath; effects of war and colonialism east and west; search for peace; world depression; rise of fascism; conflicts and imperialism leading to WWII. 2. Demonstrate understanding of the background and global consequences of actions leading to WWII, including Great Depression; rise of totalitarian governments in the Soviet Union,

Germany, and China; Growth of Nazism and the background of European anti-Semitism resulting in the Holocaust and its impact on Jewish culture and European society; Other twentieth century genocides, including Turkey/Armenia, Soviet forced collectivization in the Ukraine, and Japan's occupations in China and Korea; Global economic conflicts."

New Jersey's standards need to be updated, and when they are it would be wise for the authors to recommend, and include by name, some of the more recent acts of genocide, such as: the 1975–1979 Cambodian genocide, the Guatemalan genocide of the Mayans, the Iraqi gassing of Kurds in northern Iraq in 1988, the 1994 Rwandan genocide, the 1995 genocide in Srebrenica, and the Darfur crisis of the early 2000s in Sudan. To not do so would leave such events open to becoming, in Elliot Eisner's (1979) words, part of the "null curriculum" (p. 83).

On a related note, it is important to highlight the fact that pursuant to Public Law 1991, c. 193, The New Jersey Commission on Holocaust Education was created. In 1995–1996, the New Jersey Commission on Holocaust Education developed and distributed a Holocaust curriculum to New Jersey schools. In subsequent years, it also developed and distributed information to schools and teachers in New Jersey about the following: "The Forced Famine in the Ukraine 1932–1933"; "The Right to Live—The American Indian"; "The Killings in Cambodia"; and major human rights violations and/or genocides in Rwanda, Serb and Kosovo.

> **New York**: Senate Bill 7765 (1994), "An Act to Amend the Education Law, In Relation to Instruction On Subjects Of Human Rights Violations, Genocide, Slavery, And the Holocaust," reads, in part, as follows: "The regents shall determine the subjects to be included in such courses of instruction on patriotism (and) citizenship and human rights issues, with particular attention to the study of the inhumanity of genocide, slavery and the Holocaust and in the history, meaning, significance and effect of the provisions of the Constitution of the United States."

It is worth noting that New York was the first state to produce and disseminate an extremely detailed set of readings and related exercises on a wide array of genocide-related issues for use in secondary schools. More specifically, the 1985 publication, comprising three booklets, addressed various human rights issues, the Holocaust, the Armenian genocide, and the Cambodian genocide. With the assistance of genocide specialists, the latter should be revised, updated, and reissued.

> **Rhode Island**: In February 2000, House Bill 7397, "Genocide and Human Rights Education," was passed by the Rhode Island Legislature. It is largely a carbon copy of the bill passed in Massachusetts (see above): "The department of elementary and secondary education shall...develop curricular material on genocide and human rights issues and guidelines. Such guidelines shall

include but not be limited to: the period of transatlantic slave trades and the middle passage; the great hunger period in Ireland; the Armenian Genocide; the Holocaust; and the Mussolini Fascist Regime and other recognized human rights violations."

It is rather sad that the Rhode Island legislators and state department of education personnel did not take the time, thought, and care to develop their own approach to genocide education, which could have, with some effort, resulted in a more comprehensive bill than that passed by their neighbor Massachusetts.

Washington: In 1992, Washington's Senate and House passed a bill (SHB2212), "An Act Relating to the Study of the Holocaust," which included, in part, the following wording: "Every public high school is encouraged to include in its curriculum instruction on the events of the period in modern world history known as the Holocaust, during which six million Jews and millions of non-Jews were exterminated. The instruction may also include other examples from both ancient and modern history where subcultures or large human populations have been eradicated by the acts of humankind. The studying of this material is a reaffirmation of the commitment of free peoples never again to permit such occurrences."

The wording of Washington's Social Studies/History Standards, implemented in 2000 (and updated in 2008), provides a better sense as to what the students of Washington state are introduced to vis-à-vis the issue of genocide: "The student understands and applies knowledge of historical thinking, chronology, eras, turning points, major ideas, individuals, and themes of local…United States, and world history in order to evaluate how history shapes the present and future.

Component 4.3: Understands that there are multiple perspectives and interpretations of historical events.

Grade 5: U.S.—Encounter, Colonization, and Devastation. Analyzes the multiple perspectives and interpretations of historical events in U.S. history.

Examples: Examines different accounts of the colonization era, including colonists' perspective of settlement and indigenous people's perspective of genocide.

Grades 9–10: World—International Conflicts (1870–Present), and Causes of Conflict. Analyzes and interprets historical materials from a variety of perspectives in world history (1450–present).

Examples: Distinguishes between conflicting views of the causes of Rwandan genocide….Distinguishes between conflicting views of the causes of the Holocaust.

Component 4.4: Uses history to understand the present and plan for the future.

Grades 9 and 10: World - Emergence and development of new nations (1900–Present). Analyzes how an understanding of world history can help us prevent problems today.

Example: Examines how study of the Holocaust has led to efforts to prevent genocide across the world.

Geography: Component 3.1: Understands the physical characteristics, cultural characteristics and location of places and regions.

Grade 12. Human Rights. Applies geographic tools, including computer-based mapping systems, to acquire, process, and report information.

Example: Examines the causes of mass killings and genocide in Bosnia using historical and current maps.

Social Studies Skills—The student understands and applies reasoning skills to conduct research, deliberate, form, and evaluate positions through the processes of reading, writing, and communicating.

Component 5.3: Deliberates public issues.

Grade 12: Globalization and the Economy. Evaluates how the discussion and the proposed alternative resolutions changed or solidified one's own position on public issues.

Examples: Evaluates how classroom discussions and possible alternative resolutions have changed or solidified one's own position on whether the events in Darfur should be classified as a genocide.

Up through today (early 2010), the state of Washington has one of the most detailed and well thought out approaches to incorporating the issue of genocide into their curricular programs. While it's not perfect and does not constitute *the ideal,* it does provide a sense as to how schools and teachers can incorporate the issue of genocide into the extant curriculum in various and significant ways.

ACADEMIC STANDARDS/BENCHMARKS

While the following states do not have legislation mandating or recommending Holocaust or genocide education, their history/social studies academic standards and benchmarks allude to and/or actually include a focus on teaching about genocide:

- **Minnesota**: Benchmark 2: Students will understand and analyze impact of the Holocaust and other examples of genocide in the 20th century.
- **Mississippi**: b. Analyze how various regional and global geographic patterns have influenced historical events (e.g., unification of Italy and Germany, decline of the Ottoman and Austrian Empires, impe-

rialism as a precursor to WWI, growth of Germany/WWII, U.S.S.R/ Cold War, SE Asia, Middle East, etc.). e. Examine the global consequences of various world conflicts of the 19th and 20th centuries (e.g., Napoleonic Wars, Revolutions, WWI, WWII, Cold War, Gulf War, etc.).

- **New Hampshire**: SS:WH:8:1.3: Explore the use and abuse of power that results in mass murder and genocide, e.g., Carthage by Rome, the conquest of Aztecs, or the Holocaust. (Themes: A: Conflict and Cooperation, F: Global Transformation, I: Patterns of Social and Political Interaction)
- **Ohio**: Grade 9—Analyze the results of political, economic, and social oppression and the violation of human rights including: a. The exploitation of indigenous peoples; b. The Holocaust and other acts of genocide, including those that have occurred in Armenia, Rwanda, Bosnia and Iraq.

As one can readily ascertain, the inclusion of genocide issues into state standards/benchmarks varies greatly between states. In some cases, the inclusion of genocide is more inferred than actual, hard fact. And, in fact, in most cases the inclusion of the topic is extremely limited. Neither situation is satisfactory.

EFFORTS TO ESTABLISH TASK FORCE/COMMISSION AND/ OR A CENTER OF HOLOCAUST AND GENOCIDE EDUCATION

Some states are so committed to providing their students with solid opportunities to study about the Holocaust and genocide that they have established task forces, commissions, and/or centers focusing on Holocaust and genocide education. Such states are as follows:

- **Maryland**: In 2005, Maryland legislators passed Senate Bill 440 that established a Task Force to Implement Holocaust, Genocide, Human Rights, and Tolerance Education in the state. The task force must advise the University System of Maryland (USM) on the establishment of a pilot program that creates a Center for Excellence on the Study of the Holocaust, Genocide, Human Rights, and Tolerance. The bill terminated on September 30, 2008.
- **Texas**: In 2009, the Texas legislature passed SB 482 which set the stage for establishing a Texas Holocaust and Genocide Commission "whose duties will include providing advice and assistance to public and private primary and secondary schools and institutions of higher education in Texas regarding implementation of Holocaust and genocide courses of study and awareness programs."

As for Texas' History/Social Studies Standards, they already include the following vis-à-vis the issue of genocide: (18) Citizenship. The student understands the historical development of significant legal and political concepts, including ideas about rights, republicanism, constitutionalism, and democracy. The student is expected to: C) Identify examples of political, economic, and social oppression and violations of human rights throughout history, including slavery, the Holocaust, other examples of genocide, and politically motivated mass murders in Cambodia, China, and the Soviet Union.

Other states interested in strengthening their efforts in teaching about the Holocaust and genocide should seriously consider establishing a task force, commission, and/or center focusing on Holocaust and genocide education.

DEVELOPMENT OF A TEACHER'S MANUAL

In 2009, the Virginia Legislature passed HB 2409 which mandates that the State Superintendent of Public Instruction select and distribute a teacher's manual that emphasizes the causes and ramifications of the Holocaust and genocide to all school divisions. Local school divisions must provide grade-appropriate portions of the manual to each history and literature teacher.

The manual was developed to complement Virginia's History and Social Studies Standards, which already include the following in relation to teaching about genocide:

United States History II—1877 to present: Standard USII.6a—The student will demonstrate knowledge of the major causes and effects of American involvement in World War II.

Essential Understandings: The rise of fascism threatened peace in Europe and Asia. Essential Questions: How did the rise of fascism affect world events following World War I?

Essential Knowledge: Causes of World War II—Rise of Fascism—Fascism is a political philosophy in which total power is given to a dictator and individual freedoms are denied.

Essential Understandings: The Holocaust is an example of prejudice and discrimination taken to the extreme.

Essential Questions. What was the Holocaust?

Essential Knowledge: The Holocaust—Anti-Semitism—Aryan supremacy—Systematic attempt to rid Europe of all Jews. World History and Geography: 1500 A.D. to the present.

Standard WHII.10c—Examining events related to the rise, aggression, and human costs of dictatorial regimes in the Soviet Union, Germany, Italy, and

Japan, and identifying their major leaders, i.e., Joseph Stalin, Adolf Hitler, Benito Mussolini, Hirohito, and Hideki Tojo.

Standard WHII.11b—Examining the Holocaust and other examples of genocide in the twentieth century (see p. 48).

Standard WHII.11c—Explaining the terms of the peace, the war crimes trials, the division of Europe, plans to rebuild Germany and Japan, and the creation of international cooperative organizations.

Hopefully, the manual to be developed will be more comprehensive than the current standards are in addressing various genocide, particularly those perpetrated since the establishment of the UN Convention on the Prevention and Punishment of the Crimes of Genocide (1948).

To some, and possibly many, the aforementioned examples of legislation, state standards/benchmarks, development of state commissions and/ or centers, and creation of various types of materials may seem impressive when it comes to educating about genocide, but are they, really? Are they, when one realizes that genocide has become a regular fact of life and death in our world? Are they, when well over twenty states focus attention on teaching about the Holocaust education but not contemporary genocides? Are they, when one realizes that high school is the last time many students will have the chance to be formally introduced to the concept of, and facts about, genocide?

Over and above the latter concerns, there is the question as to just how much attention and detail are actually focused on genocide in the states' curricular frameworks and standards. In fact, with only a few major exceptions (e.g., California, Illinois, New York, and Washington), the answer is not all that positive. In most cases, the inclusion of "genocide" in the frameworks constitutes little more than "a mention"; indeed, almost an afterthought. In some cases, the term/concept of genocide and/or certain genocides seem to be inserted in the frameworks/standards for the sake of appearance—and little more than that. Upon a close examination of the frameworks/standards, the Holocaust is frequently allocated 95 to 99 percent of the attention, while "other genocides" are limited to a mere fraction of space. The result is that the issue of "other genocides" constitutes a classic case of marginalization within the extant curriculum.

As for the few secondary level curricula and teacher guides on genocide (most of which have been developed by either state department of education personnel and/or personnel with state Holocaust and genocide commissions), they largely suffer from the same weaknesses as those found in Holocaust curricula (an overly simple, if not simplistic, discussion of complex issues; a presentation of "whats," "wheres", and "hows" of the genocide but a limited discussion, if that, of the "whys" (e.g., the antecedents and causes); historical inaccuracies; and questionable suggestions vis-à-vis instructional strategies and learning activities. The latter is as true for curricula designed by state departments of education and state Holocaust and genocide commissions as it is individual teachers.

In light of this situation, those teachers who are passionate about teaching about genocide and are willing to put in the time and effort to teach about it in a pedagogically sound and historically accurate manner should bypass such curricula and design their own units of study, *but only after* consulting the United States Holocaust Memorial Museum's (USHMM) *Guidelines for Teaching About the Holocaust.* Co-developed by Samuel Totten, William S. Parsons (co-founder of Facing History and Ourselves, former Director of Education at the USHMM, and currently the USHMM's Chief of Staff) and Sybil Milton (a noted historian and a former Senior Historian at the USHMM), the *Guidelines* provide a set of over-arching suggestions that are highly useful in developing curricula about genocide (with the exception, obviously, of those guidelines that are solely germane to the Holocaust. Even those, though, can, with some thought, be used for issues of genocide other than the Holocaust). The guidelines address a host of key historical and pedagogical issues that are often ignored by curriculum developers but need to be addressed if a curriculum program, unit of study, and lessons on genocide are going to be as strong as they possibly can be.

In light of the lack of a research base, it is impossible to address either the strengths or weaknesses of the implementation of individual courses at the secondary level of schooling. In regard to the university level, it is safe to say that courses taught by experts (e.g., those who have a long and strong record of research and publications in the field—particularly on the special topic under examination) are generally more accurate, more comprehensive, more rigorous, and more thought-provoking than the courses taught by non-experts. This generalization is based, in part, on the examination of the curricula that have been published thus far by both Freedman-Apsel and Fein (1992), Porter (1992), Porter and Hoffman (1999), Apsel and Fein (2002), and those available on-line. Those individuals who are not experts (e.g., individuals who are drawn to the topic out of sheer interest or concern but have not conducted research and/or published on the topic) generally develop curricula that consists of questionable readings (e.g., not totally germane to genocide), general versus scholarly readings, and learning activities that are bereft of rigor.

RECOMMENDATIONS

The following recommendations are offered in full awareness of the fact that various groups ardently desire to see "their" topics/issues addressed in schools *and* that battles are constantly being fought over what is and is not being addressed in the school curriculum (e.g., back to basics versus a progressive curricular program, evolution versus creationism, hard facts versus a "candy-coated" (patriotic) take on events):

- Educators interested in human rights education and/or Holocaust education need to consider the value of teaching "their" topic while skipping the broader issue of genocide (e.g., the pervasiveness of genocide in the latter half of the 20th century and beginning of the 21st century, various genocidal acts, and issues of prevention and intervention). *To neglect to do so contributes to the "null curriculum* (see Totten & Samuel, 2001).
- Each state department of education that recommends or mandates the teaching of the Holocaust should seriously consider broadening such mandates/recommendations to include "issues of genocide" and "other genocides."
- State departments of education all across the U.S. need to include the teaching of genocide (over and above the Holocaust) within their frameworks/benchmarks. A good starting point would be for state department of education personnel to examine how the state of Washington has incorporated genocide-related issues into their frameworks.
- Those state departments of education that have developed curricula, curriculum guidelines, and teacher guides on teaching the Holocaust should revise them in order to broaden their focus so that they are more inclusive of other genocides. *Focusing solely on the Holocaust may leave students with the notion that genocide is a thing of the past, when, in fact, it is anything but that.*
- Curriculum developers, state department of education officials, and individual teachers need to design pedagogically sound ways of incorporating genocide into the extant curriculum (e.g., integrating the topic throughout the study of world history, U.S. history, government, etc. via mini-lessons, special units of study within the larger lesson, etc., and through the use of "post-holing," independent student projects, extension projects, etc.).
- State departments of education should form teams of outstanding teachers (those who are known to be both content and pedagogical experts), experts in genocide studies, and experts in curriculum development to (1) update their state standards/benchmarks so that they include the incorporation of genocide throughout the school curriculum, and (2) design new, up-to-date, historically accurate, developmentally appropriate, highly readable and pedagogically sound curricula, curriculum outlines and/or teacher guides on genocide (including the Holocaust). By combining the expertise of the various

professionals, the resulting curriculum will more likely be factually and conceptually correct as well as pedagogically sound.

- Once a curriculum has been developed by a battery of experts and practitioners, it should be field-tested in the type of classrooms in which it will ultimately be used. After an instructor and his/her class have actually used a section of the curriculum, they should be asked to critique it, and the curriculum developers should take these critiques and revise the curriculum accordingly. This process should be repeated several times until a curriculum is ready for use in a classroom. Only in this way will curriculum developers gain a sense of the efficacy of the curriculum they've developed.
- Teachers must receive thorough, engaging, and highly practical staff development on both the content as well the teaching strategies that are known to engage students and lead to in-depth learning. The history of curriculum is fraught with examples of one curriculum program after another meeting a quick death due to the fact that the individuals who were supposed to teach the curriculum were either not conversant or comfortable with the new information and concepts, or did not know how to effectively teach the material.
- Finally, it imperative that genocide scholars, teacher educators, and teachers begin to conduct research into the efficacy of genocide education (e.g., effectiveness in regard to increasing student knowledge, raising student awareness of genocide-related issues, becoming more sensitive to the threat of and causes of genocide around the globe). Without such research, teaching about genocide is not likely to be as effective as it could or should be.

CONCLUSION

Without a strong constituency it is probable that lessons, units, and courses on genocide both at the university and secondary levels of schooling will remain "add-ons," the purview of a small core of dedicated and interested instructors, and thus peripheral to subjects that are perceived as "critical" to a student's success in the world and/or those courses that have a louder and/or more powerful constituency. With a strong constituency, there is hope that the teaching of genocide will come into its own.

It is the hope of this author that those curriculum developers, state department of education officials, and individual teachers who care about the issue of human rights will not simply bend and capitulate to those with the louder voices and cave in by focusing solely on teaching that which is "popular" or "the already accepted"(as many have done in focusing attention on the Holocaust and not other genocides). In other words, it is my hope that such individuals will address the "null curriculum," and in doing "speak" so to the fact that simply teaching about the Holocaust as a historical event that took place 50 or 60 years ago (as important as that is) and not relating it to the present and future lives of our students verges on the unconscionable. Indeed, at a minimum, educators must, I believe, avail their students of the fact that genocide is not a thing of the past but a very real horror that continues to engulf the lives of millions in its horrific maw.

It is also my hope that all curriculum developers and teachers will move beyond simply presenting the horrors of such events, which sometimes results in providing students with something that verges on vicarious thrills, and engage students in deep thought—or, in other words, with a learning situation in which they are encouraged, prodded, and assisted to weigh complex issues fraught with moral issues and conundrums. In doing so, teachers need to guide students in addressing the complex causes of genocide (none of which are singular and none of which are givens), the many and varied ramifications of genocide, the complexities in preventing genocide, *and* what needs to be done to apply pressure on both genocidal regimes not to commit such atrocities and the international community to not stand idly by, as it has done time and again, as such atrocities are perpetrated.

REFERENCES

Apsel, J., & Fein, H. (Eds.) (2002). *Teaching about genocide: An interdisciplinary guidebook with syllabi for college and university teachers* (2nd ed.). Washington, D.C.: American Sociological Association (for the Institute for the Study of Genocide).

Armenian National Committee of America (Western Region) (April 13, 2007). ANCA-WR announces support for California genocide/holocaust bill. Press Release. www.anca.org/press_releases

Eisner, E. (1979). *The educational imagination: On the design and evaluation of school programs.* New York: Macmillan.

Feinberg, S. (2009). Personal correspondence with the author. September 8.

Freedman-Apsel, J., & Fein, H. (Eds.). (1992). *Teaching about genocide: A guidebook for college and university teachers—Critical essays, syllabi and assignments.* Ottawa, Ontario: Human Rights Internet on Behalf of the Institute for the Study of Genocide (New York City).

Parsons, W. S., & Totten, S. (Eds.). (1991). Teaching and learning about genocide: Questions of content, rationale, and methodology. *Social Education, 55*(2), 146–150.

Porter, J. (Ed.). (1992). *The sociology of genocide/the Holocaust: A curriculum guide.* Washington, D.C.: American Sociological Association.

Porter, J., & Hoffman, S. (Eds.). (1999). *The sociology of the holocaust and genocide: A teaching and learning guide.* Washington, D.C.: American Sociological Association.

Riley, K., & Totten, S. (2002). Understanding matters. Authentic pedagogy and the holocaust. *Theory and Research in Social Education, 30*(4), 541–562.

Totten, S. (Ed.) (1994). Educating about genocide. Special Triple Issue of *Internet on the Holocaust and Genocide, 51/52/53,* 1-30.

Totten, S. (1991). Educating about genocide: Curricula and inservice training. In I. W. Charny (Ed.), *Genocide: A critical bibliographic review.* London: Mansell Publishing Limited, pp. 194-225.

Totten, S. (1991). *First-person accounts of genocide in the twentieth century: An annotated bibliography.* Westport, CT: Greenwood Publishers.

Totten, S. (Ed.) (2004). *Teaching about genocide: Issues, approaches, resources.* Greenwich, CT: Information Age Publishers.

Totten, S., & Jacobs, S. (2002). *Pioneers of genocide studies.* New Brunswick, NJ: Transaction Publishers.

Totten, S., & Parsons, W .S. (Eds.) (1991). Special issue (Teaching about genocide) of *Social Education* (the official journal of the National Council for the Social Studies), *55*(2).

Totten, S., & Parsons, W. S. (1991). State developed teacher guides and curricula on genocide and/or the Holocaust: A succinct review and critique. *Inquiry in Social Studies: Curriculum, Research, and Instruction: North Carolina Journal of Social Studies, 28*(1):27–47.

Totten, S., & Riley, K. (2005). Authentic pedagogy and the Holocaust: A critical review of state sponsored Holocaust curricula. *Theory and Research in Social Education, 33*(1), 120–141.

Tottel, S, & Samuel. (2001). Addressing the "Null Curriculum:" Teaching about genocides other than the Holocaust. *Social Education, 65*(5), 309–313.

United States Holocaust Memorial Museum (1994). *Guidelines for teaching about the Holocaust.* Washington, D.C.: Author.

United States Holocaust Memorial Museum (2009). State profiles on Holocaust education: Beyond our walls. Accessed at: http://www.ushmm.org/

BIOGRAPHIES

EDITORS

Samuel Totten is Professor of Curriculum and Instruction at the University of Arkansas at Fayetteville. Totten holds a BA and MA in English from California State Universities, and a doctorate in Curriculum and Instruction from Teachers College, Columbia University.

Prior to entering academia, he taught English and social studies in Australia, Israel, California, New Jersey, and Washington, D.C. He also served as a principal of a K–8 school in northern California.

Over the past 25 years, Totten's main research and publishing efforts have focused on the teaching of social issues, human rights education, Holocaust education, genocide education, the prevention and intervention of genocide, and the history of the genocides in Rwandan and Darfur.

His articles and essays have appeared in such journals as *The NWP Quarterly*, *Journal of Supervision and Curriculum Development*, *Educational Leadership*, *Theory and Research in Social Education*, *Social Education*, *Research in Middle Level Education*, *British Journal of Holocaust Education*, *Journal of Genocide Research*, and *Genocide Studies and Prevention: An International Journal*.

Teaching and Studying Social Issues: Major Programs and Approaches, pages 369–377
Copyright © 2011 by Information Age Publishing

Since 2003, Totten has served as the managing editor of a series of volumes entitled *Genocide: A Critical Bibliographic Review* . In 2005, Totten was named one of the inaugural chief co-editors of *Genocide Studies and Prevention: An International Journal,* which is the official journal of the International Association of Genocide Scholars (IAGS).

Among the books Totten's edited and co-edited on genocide are: *First-Person Accounts of Genocidal Acts Committed in the Twentieth Century* (Westport, CT: Greenwood Press, 1991); *Genocide in the Twentieth Century: Critical Essays and Eyewitness Accounts* (co-edited with William S. Parsons and Israel W. Charny; New York: Garland Publishers, Inc., 1995); *Century of Genocide* (co-edited with William S. Parsons and Israel W. Charny; New York: Routledge, 2004);*Teaching About Genocide: Issues, Approaches, Resources* (Greenwich, CT: Information Age Publishers, 2005); and *Genocide in Darfur: The Investigation and Findings of The Darfur Atrocities Documentation Team* (with Eric Markusen; New York: Routledge, 2006); *Dictionary of Genocide* (with Paul Bartrop; Wesport, CT: Greenwood Publishers, 2008); and the third edition of *Century of Genocide* (with William Parsons; New York Routledge, 2009).

In July and August of 2004, Totten served as one of 24 investigators on the U.S. State Department's Darfur Atrocities Documentation Project whose express purpose was to conduct interviews with refugees from Darfur in order to ascertain whether genocide had been perpetrated or not in Darfur. Based upon the data collected by the team of investigators, U.S. Secretary of State Colin Powell declared on September 9, 2004, that genocide had been perpetrated in Darfur, Sudan, by Government of Sudan troops and the *Janjaweed.*

Totten served as a Fulbright Scholar in Rwanda—Centre for Conflict Management, National University of Rwanda—from January through July 2008.

Jon E. Pedersen is a professor of science education and Director of Science Education for the Center for Mathematics, Science and Computer Education at the University of Nebraska-Lincoln. Pedersen received his B.S. in Agriculture (Biochemistry and Nutrition, 1982), M.Ed. in Administration, Curriculum & Instruction (Science Education, 1988), and Ph.D. in Administration, Curriculum & Instruction (Science Education, 1990) from the University of Nebraska-Lincoln. He began his teaching career as a secondary school science teacher and taught high school chemistry and physics.

Pedersen is very active in several national organizations including: the National Association for Research in Science Teaching, the National Science Teachers Association, and the Association for the Education of Teachers of Science, for which he currently serves as president. He is the author of over ninety publications on science teaching and the incorporation of social issues into the extant curriculum. He has also published six books and two teacher manuals.

During his tenure in higher education at the University of Arkansas, in Fayetteville, East Carolina University in Greenville, North Carolina, The University of Oklahoma, and The University of Nebraska-Lincoln, Pedersen has been primary investigator and co-primary investigator of numerous grants and grant-supported projects related to science curriculum development, science inservice education, middle level education and international education totaling well over $9 million. Over the years Pedersen has also worked in more than a dozen countries around the world.

AUTHORS

Michelle Bauml is a Logan Wilson Graduate Fellow and a doctoral student in Curriculum Studies at The University of Texas at Austin.

Allan R. Brandhorst has been Professor of Education at Valparaiso University since 1992. Previously he served as Associate Professor of Education at both the University of North Carolina-Chapel Hill and the University of South Carolina-Columbia.

Over the past two years Professor Brandhorst served as Director of the Valparaiso University Overseas Studies Program in Cambridge, England where he taught a sociology course addressing English perspectives on the United States and Americans.

He has worked for the U.S. Peace Corps as a Volunteer geography teacher in Ethiopia (1964-1966); for the United Nations as a teacher of political science in the Marshall Islands (1967–1969); and as an educational consultant to the Lafoole College of Education, Somali National University, Mogadishu, Somalia (1983–1984).

He has published widely in the area of social education, and has been a frequent presenter at National Council for the Social Studies Conventions. In the 1990s he served as NCSS/NCATE Folio Review Coordinator for Social Studies Teacher Education Program Accreditation.

Ronald W. Evans is Professor in the School of Teacher Education, San Diego State University. He is author of *This Happened in America: Harold Rugg and the Censure of Social Studies* (Charlotte, NC: Information Age Publishing, 2007), *The Social Studies Wars* (New York: Teachers College Press, 2004) and the *Handbook on Teaching Social Issues* (Washington, D.C.: National Council for the Social Studies, 1996, and Information Age Publishing, 2007) and numerous articles and book chapters.

Thomas D. Fallace is an Assistant Professor of education at the University of Mary Washington in Fredericksburg, VA. He is author of *The Emergence of Holocaust Education in American Schools* (PalgraveMacmillan, 2008). Besides Holocaust education, Fallace has also authored articles on the origins of the social studies, history teacher education, and the philosophy of John Dewey for journals such as *Teachers College Record, Review of Educational Research, Curriculum Inquiry, Theory and Research in Social Education, Educational Theory,* and *the Journal of the History of the Behavioral Sciences.*

William R. Fernekes (Ed. D., Rutgers University) is social studies supervisor at Hunterdon Central Regional HS in Flemington NJ, a comprehensive suburban high school enrolling approximately 3,200 students. He supervises 30 full-time social studies faculty and oversees the social studies program, which received the NCSS Programs of Excellence award in 1997.

He has published widely on the topics of social studies curriculum design, issues-based instruction, human rights education, and Holocaust and genocide studies. He serves as a consultant to the NJ Commission on Holocaust Education, is a member of the Archives Committee of the National Council for the Social Studies, and has authored two books: *Children's Rights: A Reference Handbook* (with Beverly Edmonds, ABC-CLIO, 1995) and *The Oryx Holocaust Sourcebook* (Greenwood Press, 2002). He is currently writing a biography of former U.S. Senator from NJ, Clifford P. Case II, and working with and serving as co-editor, with Dr. Valerie Pang and Dr. Jack L. Nelson, of the forthcoming Bulletin of the National Council for the Social Studies, *Natural Disasters and Human Rights* (expected publication in 2010). He resides in Flemington, NJ with his wife Sheila, a visual artist and jewelry designer.

Sherry L. Field is the Catherine Mae Parker Centennial Professor of Education and serves as Associate Dean for Teacher Education, Student Affairs, and Administration at The University of Texas at Austin. Her research interests include history of social studies education and elementary social studies curriculum and teaching.

Dr. Field has served as the editor of *Social Studies and the Young Learner,* Chair of Executive Board of the College and University Faculty Assembly (CUFA) of the National Council for the Social Studies, President of the Society for the Study of Curriculum History, Chair of the Research in Social Studies Special Interest Group for AERA, and Chair of the Lawrence E. Metcalf Distinguished Dissertation Award Committee for the National Council for the Social Studies.

Emma K. Humphries is a second year doctoral student and Alumni Fellow in the School of Teaching and Learning at the University of Florida.

Chris McGrew is a doctoral student in Curriculum and Instruction at Purdue University and is the Graduate Research Associate with the James F. Ackerman Center for Democratic Citizenship. His research focus is on experiential education for in-service teachers in social studies. He has been an instructor in an economics methods course for future teachers in the School of Management for the past twelve years. He is a former Social Studies Supervisor for the Indiana Department of Education.

He co-authored an article in the *National Social Science Association Journal* that focuses on public choice and social issues entitled, "Somewhere Out There…:An Experiential Learning Model for Teachers."

He recently served on the National Council for the Social Studies Standards revision Task Force and is also serving as President of the Indiana Council for the Social Studies and President Elect of Global Indiana: A Consortium for International Exchange.

Merry Merryfield is Professor of Social Studies and Global Education at The Ohio State University. Her research has examined how teachers in diverse African, Asian and North American nations teach about world cultures, citizenship and global issues. Since she began teaching web-based courses in 1997, she has been intrigued with the potential for a global classroom of teachers across the planet and cross-cultural experiential learning online.

Jeff Passe is Professor and Chair of the Department of Secondary Education at Towson University. He has served as President of the National Council for the Social Studies, Chair of College and University Faculty Assembly (CUFA), and Chair of the AERA Research in Social Studies Education Special Interest Group. A long-time member of the NCSS Social Issues community, he was co-author (with Ron Evans) of "Discussion Leadership" in *The Handbook on Teaching Social Issues*. He also authored a chapter devoted to the work of Lawrence Metcalf in *Addressing Social issues in the Classroom and Beyond: The Pedagogical Efforts of Pioneers in the Field* edited by Samuel Totten and Jon E. Pedersen. Passe is the author of five books, including *When Students Choose Content* and *Elementary School Curriculum*.

Mark A. Previte is an assistant professor of secondary education at the University of Pittsburgh at Johnstown. He is president-elect of the Pennsylvania Council for the Social Studies and the program chair for the National Council for the Social Studies (NCSS) Issues Centered Education Community. He is a co-editor of the two volume publication *The NCSS Presidential Addresses: Perspectives on the Social Studies 1936–2000*. He is currently working on two publications: a chapter for an NCSS Bulletin on teaching about natural disasters through issues centered education and an article on the status of issues centered education in teacher education. His research interests include the foundations of the social studies and issues centered education.

Karen L. Riley is Distinguished Research Professor and Distinguished Teaching Professor at Auburn University Montgomery (AUM). She is also a two-time recipient of the Wiesman Distinguished Researcher Award from the AUM School of Education. Her research areas include curriculum history, the history and politics of education, and social studies education. She is the author of *Schools Behind Barbed Wire*, a history of the family internment camp, its schools and its children, at Crystal City, Texas, during World War II. Other scholarly pursuits include her book series entitled "Studies in the History of Education," (Information Age Publishing), and an edited book, *Social Reconstruction: People, Politics, Perspectives* as well as numerous articles.

Mindy Spearman, an assistant professor in Teacher Education at Clemson University in South Carolina, teaches graduate and undergraduate courses in social studies education, elementary curriculum, multiculturalism, and the historical foundations of education. Influenced by her work as an archaeologist, Dr. Spearman's current research investigates the ways in which teachers can use artifacts to further children's cultural-historical understandings. She is particularly interested in the intersections of sustainability education with art, artifacts, and social justice. Dr. Spearman has been researching preservice teachers' conceptions of environmental education for young learners and the ways in which elementary students connect artifacts and sustainability through reclaimed object art explorations. She is currently working on environmental education curricula for young learners connected to gardening, natural habitats and sustainable living practices.

Barbara S. Spector, a Fellow of the American Association for the Advancement of Science, is Professor of Science Education at the University of South Florida and Director of the *Informal Science Institutions Environmental Education Graduate Certificate Program*. She developed three major centers at USF, two of which targeted social issues in science: The Science/Technology/ Society Center and the Center for Ocean Sciences Education Excellence-Florida. She also developed the Science/Technology/Society Program initially targeting teachers and later involving learners from various colleges on campus. She has received 61 grants totaling more than $7.5 million, and authored 511 publications, presentations, and media. She has served on advisory boards and steering committees for the National Science Foundation and NASA, was Director of Education for the National Sea Grant and the Marine Technology Society.

Barbara Slater Stern is a professor of curriculum and social studies education at James Madison University. She is editor of *Curriculum and Teaching Dialogue* and of the forthcoming *The New Social Studies: People, Projects and Perspectives*.

Felisa Tibbitts is Executive Director of Human Rights Education Associates and Adjunct Faculty at the Harvard Graduate School of Education and the United Nations' University for Peace in San Jose, Costa Rica. She has written numerous articles and book chapters related to human rights education, which have appeared in such publications as *Social Education, Encyclopedia of Peace Education, International Review of Education,* and *European Journal of Education,* and has served as the guest editor for special issues on human rights education for the *Journal of Social Science Education* and *Intercultural Education.* In addition to her scholarly activities, she is actively involved in curriculum development, trainings and research related to human rights education programming.

Phillip J. VanFossen is the James F. Ackerman Professor of Social Studies Education and Director of the Ackerman Center for Democratic Citizenship in the College of Education at Purdue University where he teaches courses in elementary and secondary social studies education. He is also the Associate Director of the Purdue University Center for Economic Education (and holds a courtesy appointment in the Krannert School of Management at Purdue) where he teaches introductory economics courses for the Department of Economics. He is the program author for the high school economics text *Economics Alive! The Power to Choose* (Teachers Curriculum Institute, 2009)

A former middle and high school social studies teacher, VanFossen is Chair of the Advisory Board of *EconEdLink*, the National Council on Economic Education's on-line resource site. He has published articles in *Theory and Research in Social Education, Social Education, The International Journal of Social Education, The International Journal of Educational Media, The Senior Economist, The Southern Social Studies Journal* and *Economics for Kids*, and has twice been a guest editor for *Social Studies and the Young Learner.* VanFossen serves on the editorial boards of three journals (including *Theory and Research in Social Education*) and was the economics advisor for the Harcourt textbook series *Horizons.* In 2009, he was awarded Miami University's "Profound Impact Award' given to an alumni who is "making a difference in their communities and their profession."

His research interests include how social studies teachers use the Internet and digital media in their teaching, and in 2001 he co-authored *Using Internet Primary Sources to Teach Critical Thinking in Government, Economics and World Issues* (Greenwood Press). In 2008, he co-edited *The Electronic Repub-*

lic?: The Impact of Technology on Citizenship Education (Purdue University Press). This has led him to explore the potential of virtual worlds (e.g., MMORPGs such as *World of Warcraft*) for economic and citizenship education. VanFossen also has an interest in the intersection between civic education and economic education and has conducted more than two dozen workshops and inservice training seminars and given numerous invited lectures on curriculum development and teacher training in economic education in six eastern European and Baltic countries and Indonesia . In 2006, he was elected to the Executive Board of the National Council for the Social Studies' College and University Faculty Assembly.

Mary Lee Webeck is Director of Education at the Holocaust Museum Houston. Her research interests include preservice and inservice teacher education, the literature and art of the Holocaust, and social justice issues.

Robert Yager has been on the faculty at the University of Iowa for 50 years as a professor of science education. He received his M.S. and Ph.D. in plant physiology from the University of Iowa, and was initially employed to create a new Center for Science Education—initially situated in a laboratory school. Yager has been extremely active professionally, having served on boards, committees, and as president of seven national organizations including the National Association for Research in Science Teaching, the Association of Science Teacher Education and the National Science Teachers Association (NSTA). He has headed one of the largest graduate programs in science education and has chaired 130 Ph.D. dissertations. His publications total over 600. He has directed over 100 National Science Foundation (NSF) projects for teachers and directed the Salish Project which funded science teacher educator research projects involving ten diverse universities active in preparing new science teachers. He currently works on the NSF-supported Investigating the Meaningfulness of Preservice Programs Across the Continuum of Teaching (IMPPACT) research effort studying the effectiveness of science teacher education programs. He also heads the NSTA Exemplary Science Programs which has resulted in seven monographs describing, and evaluating, science programs that illustrate the visions elaborated in the National Science Education Standards. These visions enlarge those which frame the National Science Education Standards (NSES) by using social issues to indicate real student learning of science, technology, and society. Use of social issues in science has been central to all Yager has done and accomplished since the beginning of his teaching career in Iowa in 1950.

Elizabeth Yeager Washington is Professor and Coordinator of Social Studies Education at the University of Florida and a Senior Fellow of the Florida

Joint Center for Citizenship. She was editor of *Theory and Research in Social Education* from 2001–2007. Her research interests include civic education, the teaching and learning of history, and wise practice in the teaching of social studies. In addition to two books, she has published articles in *Theory and Research in Social Education, Journal of Teacher Education, Social Education, Urban Education, Canadian Journal of Education, The Social Studies,* and *Social Studies Research and Practice.*

Jack Zevin is Professor of Secondary Education at Queens College of the City University of New York. He has been an active lifelong member of NCSS throughout his career, at which he has made well over one hundred presentations since 1969 and is still active. His research career has focused mainly on studying the process of political socialization, how students and youth acquire their sense of identity in the political sphere, their attitudes toward politics, and the way in which change occurs with maturation and educational intervention. He has published on a wide range of topics including students' attitudes toward politics, curriculum inquiry, and instructional methodology. Much of this work has evolved from a long-standing interest in how students see their world, and their local communities.

With Dr. David Gerwin of Queens College, Zevin co-authored *Teaching American History as Mystery* (Heinemann, 2003), and co-authored a new edition of his methods book, *Social Studies for the 21st Century* (Routledge/Erlbaum, 2008). Most recently Zevin has co-authored, with Dr. Michael Krasner (Department of Political Science), "A Curriculum for 9/11" (Social Studies School Services, 2009), which is based on research from first-hand interviews with the World Trade Center United Families Group.

As co-director of The Taft Institute for Government, with Michael Krasner, Jack has pursued research and development on simulation games dealing with political topics such as voting rights, city council, and mock election games, along with research into teacher and student attitudes toward exercising their right to vote.

INDEX

Teaching and Studying Social Issues: Major Programs and Approaches, pages 379–384
Copyright © 2011 by Information Age Publishing
379